ASIAN HISTORICAL DICTIONARIES
Edited by Jon Woronoff

Vietnam, Laos,
And Cambodia

Historical Dictionary

of

VIETNAM

by
WILLIAM J. DUIKER

Asian Historical Dictionaries, No. 1

The Scarecrow Press, Inc.
Metuchen, N.J. & London
1989

Frontispiece: This map of Vietnam, Laos, and Cambodia is reprinted by permission from <u>Vietnam Since The Fall of Saigon</u>, rev., 2nd ed., by William J. Duiker (Athens, OH: Ohio University Press, 1985).

British Library Cataloguing-in-Publication data available

Library of Congress Cataloging-in-Publication Data

Duiker, William J., 1932–
    Historical dictionary of Vietnam.

    (Asian historical dictionaries ; no. 1)
    Bibliography: p.
    1. Vietnam--History--Dictionaries.   I. Title.
II. Series.
DS556.25.D85   1989   959.7'003'21   88-29721
ISBN 0-8108-2164-8

To the memory of

my mother

CONTENTS

EDITOR'S FOREWORD

This is the first volume in the new series of Asian Historical Dictionaries. And it would be hard to pick a more appropriate country for it to cover. Vietnam is one of the places Americans know--or think they know--best; it is also undoubtedly one of the places they know worst. Too much of this "knowledge" has been focused on the period of the Vietnam War and the events related to it. Too little attention has been devoted to the long history preceding that or the equally dramatic era that followed. Fortunately, this book breaks that restricted mold.

One purpose of this volume, like all others in the series, is to provide an introduction to newcomers who want a broad survey of the country. This is done through the entries and chronology as well as a bibliography which points them toward more specialized works. But, as is perfectly evident, even specialists will find a wealth of information in a very handy form. The "dictionary" should thus accompany readers as they deepen their understanding of what remains a dimly perceived yet crucial country.

William J. Duiker is an excellent guide. He studied East Asia at Georgetown University and then put his education to practical use with the Department of State, serving in Saigon among other posts. Since 1967, he has been teaching East Asian history at Pennsylvania State University. Dr. Duiker has written numerous articles and monographs on Vietnam as well as several books: The Communist Road to Power in Vietnam, Vietnam Since the Fall of Siagon and Vietnam: Nation in Revolution. This latest effort is clearly built on a very strong foundation.

Jon Woronoff
Series Editor

PREFACE

The writing of a historical dictionary, I have discovered, is an intimidating project. The author very quickly becomes aware of the bewildering variety of information, much of which is inevitably outside his particular area of expertise, that should be included in the volume. On the other hand, he is persistently reminded by his editor that financial considerations limit the number and length of individual entries. Only the most important items can be included, and individual entries themselves must likewise be limited to the most important facts. What finally appears is the result of a series of compromises that are not likely to satisfy many readers, not to mention the author himself.

In attempting to pack the most important information about Vietnam into a manageable amount of space, I have adhered to the following general guidelines set by the series editor. Recent events and individuals receive priority treatment over those from the remote past. Primary emphasis is placed on history and politics. Items dealing with economic, social, and cultural issues follow in that order. To save space and facilitate effective use of this volume, I have made liberal use of the technique of cross-listing. For those in need of more detailed information, I have also included a fairly extensive bibliography at the end of the volume. The bibliography is divided into separate topics and time periods for the reader's convenience.

One of the distinctive problems faced by the author of any historical dictionary of Vietnam is that of language. Although modern Vietnamese--known in the Vietnamese language as quoc ngu, or "national language"--is written in the roman alphabet, the alphabetical order of words in a Vietnamese-language dictionary does not entirely follow Western usage. For example, there are two forms of the letter "D." One "D" or "d" is pronounced as "dz." The other written as "Đ" or "đ", is pronounced like a hard "d" in English. In a Vietnamese dictionary, these two letters are listed separately, but in Western-language works, both letters are written the same. Because most readers of this book will be English speakers, I have adopted the alphabetical order used in the West. Words beginning with "D" or "Đ" are included together according to Western usage.

A second problem that all authors of works dealing with Vietnam must face is the question of whether to include diacritical marks.

Because spoken Vietnamese, like several other Asian languages, is a tonal language, these diacritical marks are essential to meaning. However, they are too expensive to reproduce in a volume published in the United States and may be a distraction to many readers who do not speak or read Vietnamese. I have therefore omitted these marks.

Another problem familiar to Vietnam specialists is the question of proper names. Like the Chinese, the Vietnamese place their proper name first, while given names follow. Since the colonial period, however, it has been common to refer to individuals by the last word appearing in their name. President Ngo Dinh Diem, for example, was commonly known as President Diem, although his family name was Ngo. Ho Chi Minh, on the other hand, was known as President Ho, probably because the name "Ho Chi Minh" was a pseudonym that he had adopted from the Chinese. I have attempted to conform with current usage as much as possible. Names are listed in this dictionary according to the family name, but when individuals are referred to in the text, the last name is frequently used. It is an awkward compromise, but it is not up to a foreigner to solve the problem.

Still another issue is that of the geographical divisions of Vietnam. In addition to the separate villages, districts, and provinces into which the state of Vietnam is divided, the Vietnamese often refer to their country in terms of three separate regions: the North (known in Vietnamese as Bac Bo or Bac Ky), the Center (Trung Bo or Trung Ky), and the South (Nam Bo or Nam Ky). These divisions correspond roughly with the colonial divisions adopted by the French for the protectorates of Tonkin and Annam and the colony of Cochin China. While these regions are often not subject to precise definition, they are often referred to by the Vietnamese, and I have used the terms (in their English form) in the text.

I am grateful to Ohio University Press and Westview Press for permission to reproduce maps that appeared earlier in their publications. It would be fruitless for me to attempt to express my gratitude to all those who in one way or another have contributed to this volume. The author of a historial dictionary, more than most writers, is dependent upon the entire community of scholars and other specialists who have added to our knowledge of the civilization in which we share a common interest. I am uncomfortably aware that I have undoubtedly made a number of errors of fact, as well as of omission and commission, in making my selections for this volume. I am consoled by the hope that colleagues will point out these errors so that they can be corrected in a future edition. In a very real sense, this has been a learning experience, and I trust that the learning will not cease with the publication of this volume.

William J. Duiker
The Pennsylvania State University

ABBREVIATIONS

AFIMA	Association pour la Formation Intellectuelle et Morale des Annamites
ARVN	Army of the Republic of Vietnam
COSVN	Central Office of South Vietnam
DMZ	Demilitarized Zone
DRV	Democratic Republic of Vietnam
FULRO	United Front for the Liberation of Oppressed Peoples
ICC	International Control Commission
ICP	Indochinese Communist Party
NLFSVN	National Liberation Front for South Vietnam
NVA	North Vietnamese Army (People's Army of Vietnam)
PAI	Parti Annamite de l'Indépendance
PAVN	People's Army of Vietnam
PLAF	People's Liberation Armed Forces
PRG	Provisional Revolutionary Government
PRP	People's Revolutionary Party
RVN	Republic of Vietnam
SRV	Socialist Republic of Vietnam
VCP	Vietnamese Communist Party
VNA	Vietnamese National Army
VNQDD	Vietnam Quoc Dan Dang (Vietnamese Nationalist Party)
VWP	Vietnamese Workers' Party

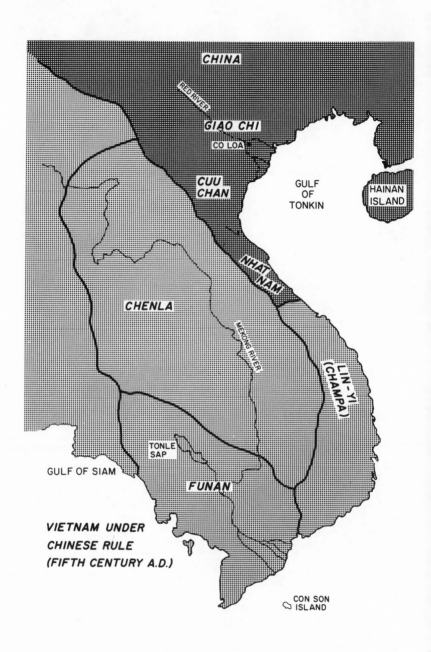

VIETNAM UNDER
CHINESE RULE
(FIFTH CENTURY A.D.)

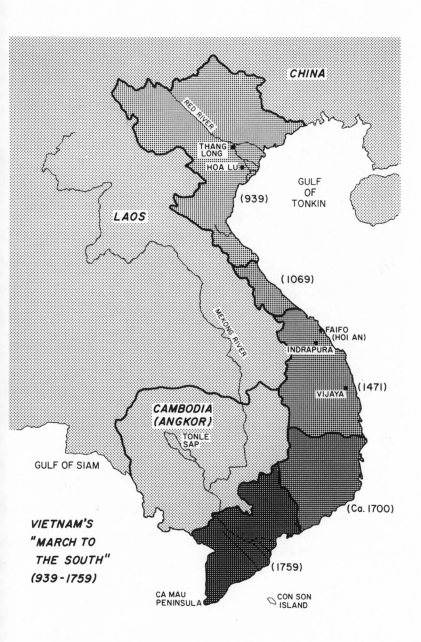

CHINA

RED RIVER

THANG
LONG
HOA LU

(939)

GULF
OF
TONKIN

LAOS

(1069)

MEKONG RIVER

FAIFO
(HOI AN)
INDRAPURA

(1471)

VIJAYA

CAMBODIA
(ANGKOR)

TONLE
SAP

GULF OF SIAM

(Ca. 1700)

VIETNAM'S
"MARCH TO
THE SOUTH"
(939-1759)

(1759)

CA MAU
PENINSULA

CON SON
ISLAND

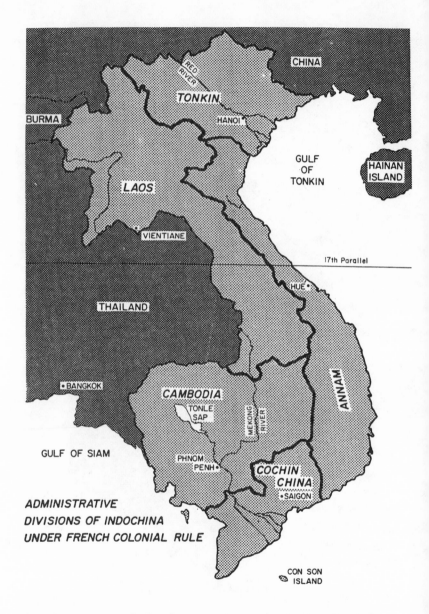

Reprinted by permission from The Communist Road to Power in Vietnam, by William J. Duiker (Boulder, CO: Westview Press, 1982).

INTRODUCTION

For most Americans, Vietnam is identified almost exclusively with
the recent Vietnam War. Before the war, few were aware of its
existence. To those who were, Vietnam was a small and unimpor-
tant country in a faraway part of French Indochina, located in a region of the world in which the United States had little or no political, economic, or security interest.

During the Vietnam War, the situation was dramatically reversed.
At the height of the conflict in the middle and late 1960s, Vietnam
was a constant topic of conversation among the American people,
while the U.S. government informed them that faraway Vietnam was
crucial to the survival of the United States.

Today, Vietnam has once again receded into the background of
the consciousness of most Americans. While political tensions in the
area have aroused the concern of policy-makers in Washington, D.C.,
the country is once again rarely in the public eye. To most Americans, the most important issue in U.S.-Vietnam relations is the return of the remains of U.S. soldiers killed in action during the
Vietnam War.

In fact, the truth probably lies somewhere between the two
extremes. While Vietnam is not the first in a line of dominoes vital
to the defense of the Free World--as it was portrayed by several
U.S. administrations during the 1950s and 1960--it is one of the
most powerful and potentially influential nations in Asia. With a
population of 62 million, it is the 12th largest nation in the world.
Its army is currently the fourth largest throughout the globe.
Whatever its present political and economic difficulties, it is indispu-
tably one of the most dynamic societies in mainland Southest Asia.

The importance of Vietnam for the destiny of the region is not
a product of the twentieth century. The fact is, the Vietnamese
nation has been a vital force in Southeast Asia for centuries. One
of the earliest identifiable people to settle in the region, the Vietnamese had created a distinct and separate culture well before the
end of the first millennium B.C.

1

Today Vietnam stretches more than 1,000 miles north to south from the Chinese border to the Ca Mau Peninsula on the Gulf of Thailand. Its total area is 329,566 square kilometers (127,246 square miles). For much of its length, the western border is formed by the watershed of the Truong Son (Annamite Mountains). On the east is the South China Sea. The country is shaped like a gigantic letter "S," with the most populated areas at the two extremities of the country--the Red River Delta in the North and the Mekong River Delta in the South. In between is a narrow strip of coastland that in some areas stretches only about 50 kilometers (30 miles) from the South China Sea to the border of Laos on the west.

Vietnam did not always occupy such a prominent position on the Southeast Asian mainland. At the dawn of Vietnamese civilization in the first millenium B.C., the territory inhabited by the Vietnamese people was limited to the region of the Red River Delta in what is today known as North Vietnam. In the second century B.C., the small Vietnamese state was absorbed by the Han Dynasty in China. During over 1,000 years of Chinese rule, the Vietnamese were introduced to Chinese political and social institutions, Chinese architecture, art, and literature, and even the Chinese written language. The imprint of the Chinese period left its mark on Vietnamese society, an indelible stamp that was clearly visible well into the present century. But the Vietnamese people were able to retain their sense of separate destiny and, during a period of political instability in China, restored their national independence in A.D. 939.

During the next several hundred years, the Vietnamese state expanded southward along the central coast from its original homeland in the Red River Valley. By 1700 the entire eastern coast of the peninsula of mainland Southeast Asia had come under Vietnamese rule. Internally, the Vietnamese Empire developed in power and sophistication and had clearly become one of the most dominant states in the region.

Expansion, however, brought problems. In the relatively empty lands of the Mekong Delta to the south, Vietnamese settlers developed a "frontier mentality" which frequently came in conflict with the centralizing tendencies of the imperial court in the North. Growing tension ultimately led to civil war, and a division of the country into two separate regions divided roughly at the seventeenth parallel, a poignant reminder of a similar conflict that would divide the nation three years later.

It was in these weakened conditions that Vietnam first encountered a new challenge, the most serious to its ultimate survival since the period of Chinese rule. Western adventurers first arrived in Southeast Asia in the early sixteenth century. During the next two hundred years merchants and missionaries from several European countries travelled to Asia in search of trade and converts. The Vietnamese court eventually grew distrustful of the motives of these barbarians from the West, and attempted to limit European influence inside Vietnamese territory. The French, however, were particularly persistent and in the mid-nineteenth century, under severe pressure from missionary and commercial interests, the government of Emperor Napoleon III launched a naval attack on Vietnam which resulted in the transformation of the southern provinces of the empire into a new French colony of Cochin China. Twenty years later, the French advance into Southeast Asia was completed with the establishment of a protectorate over the remainder of the country. By the 1890s, Vietnam was joined with its two neighbors to the west, Cambodia and Laos, into an Indochinese Union dominated by the French.

The imposition of French colonial rule brought about the end of traditional society in Vietnam. Over the next half a century, the Vietnamese people were introduced to Western political institutions, Western technology, and the Western way of life. Defenders of colonialism sometimes maintain that the experience was ultimately beneficial to the subject peoples since it introduced them to modern ways and prepared them to compete in the modern world. In the case of Vietnam, however, the case is not very convincing. Although the French built roads, railroads, and an extensive irrigation system in the Mekong River Delta, they did not encourage the development of a local industrial and commercial sector, preferring to maintain their colonial territory as a source of cheap labor, raw materials, and a market for the export of manufactured goods from France. Some historians of the colonial period maintain that for most Vietnamese, the standard of living may have actually declined under French rule.

Whatever the truth of such assertions, there is no doubt that colonialism represented an affront to Vietnamese pride and its sense of national identity. Within a few years, opposition to colonial rule began to grow, not only in the countryside, where impoverished peasants sporadically protested against high taxes, official corruption, and the growing concentration of land into the hands of a small absentee landlord class, but also in the cities, where educated youths began to form nationalist parties to struggle for the restoration of national independence.

By the late 1930s, there were two major types of anticolonialist organizations in Vietnam--a mixed group of non-communist nationalist parties mutually divided over tactics and the ultimate nature of the future Vietnamese state, and a small Indochinese Communist Party (ICP) led by the revolutionary figure Ho Chi Minh. Although the communists were severely persecuted by the French colonial regime, in Ho Chi Minh they possessed a leader of unusual capacity, and by the late 1930s, the Party had become the most effective organization opposed to French rule in Vietnam.

As was the case throughout South and Southeast Asia, it was

World War II which created the conditions for the final destruction of colonialism in Indochina. Under the cover of the Japanese occupation of all of Indochina in 1941, the ICP began to prepare for a nationwide popular insurrection against French rule, to be launched at the end of the war. Keystone of the Party's strategy was the creation of a broad united front called the Vietminh (League for the Independence of Vietnam), which united patriotic Vietnamese of all social classes and political persuasions in a common struggle to restore independence.

The uprising, popularly known as the "August Revolution," broke out at the end of August 1945, shortly after the surrender of Japanese forces throughout the Pacific region. At first it succeeded, and in early September Ho Chi Minh declared the formation of an independent Democratic Republic of Vietnam (DRV), with its capital in Hanoi, located in the heart of the Red River Delta. But returning French military forces quickly gained control over the Colony of Cochin China in the South, and the Vietnamese nation was divided once again. After abortive efforts between French and Vietnamese representatives to reach a negotiated settlement, war broke out in December 1946.

For the next eight years, all of Indochina was wracked by a bitter conflict between the French and guerrilla forces led by the ICP. At first, it possessed the character of a purely anticolonial struggle for national liberation, but by 1950, with the rise to power of the Chinese Communists in mainland China and growing anticommunist sentiment in the United States, it entered the vortex of the Cold War. The United States agreed to provide military and economic assistance to the French (and to the puppet government under ex-Emperor Bao Dai that the French had created in 1949), while the People's Republic of China (PRC) gave aid and diplomatic recognition to the Vietminh.

By 1954, the French had wearied of the war, and at the Geneva Conference held in the spring and early summer, the long Franco-Vietminh conflict came to an end. All three countries of French Indochina were granted their formal independence. Vietnam itself was divided into two separate "regroupment zones," with the communists in control of the North, and the non-communist Bao Dai government in the South. According to arrangements agreed upon at Geneva, representatives of the two zones were to consult jointly to prepare for national elections and the reunification of the entire country in the summer of 1956.

The elections never took place. In the South, a new government under the anti-communist politician Ngo Dinh Diem refused to hold consultations with representatives of the DRV in the North and, with assistance from the United States, attempted to build a viable state (called the Republic of Vietnam, or RVN) which would prevent the further expansion of communism into mainland Southeast Asia.

Communist leaders in the DRV protested, but were temporarily un-
prepared to contest the decision, and turned to the consolidation of
their power and the building of socialist society in the North. For
the third time in three centuries, the Vietnamese nation was divided.

Communist strategy was based on the conviction that the regime
of Ngo Dinh Diem, based in the city of Saigon, was inherently unstable and could eventually be overthrown by a popular uprising
led by forces loyal to the Party. In that expectation they were
partly correct. Ngo Dinh Diem's autocratic tendencies and the
failure of his government to reduce the inequity in landholding in
South Vietnam aroused a growing chorus of protest and resistance
throughout the country. In 1959, Party leaders in Hanoi decided
to provide full backing to a movement to overthrow Diem and reunify
the country under their authority. The Second Indochina War was
about to begin.

By 1961, the battle lines were clearly drawn. In Hanoi, communist
leaders attempted to provide coherence and firm party leadership to
the struggle in the South by creating the so-called People's Liberation
Armed Forces (popularly known in the West as the Viet Cong) and
a new united front organization known as the National Front for the
Liberation of South Vietnam (NLFSVN, or NLF). To the new
Kennedy Administration in Washington, D.C., these developments
represented clear evidence that the Hanoi regime was prepared to
use force to destroy the Republic of Vietnam and unite the country
under communist rule. Although Kennedy had serious reservations
about the quality of leadership provided by Ngo Dinh Diem, he felt
the United States had no choice and provided full backing to Diem's
effort to defeat the communist-led insurgency.

The effort by the Kennedy Administration to prevent the further
erosion of the situation in South Vietnam was undermined by Diem's
own weaknesses. Popular discontent against the Saigon regime
steadily mounted during the early 1960s and in November 1963 U.S.
policymakers, with some misgivings, gave their approval to a coup
d'état launched by anti-Diem military officers which overthrew the
Diem regime and placed a military junta in power in Saigon. Two
weeks later, Kennedy was assassinated in Dallas.

From that point on, the situation in Vietnam began increasingly
to take on the character of a Greek tragedy, with Fate manipulating
the actions of the main actors. In Hanoi, Party leaders decided to
escalate the level of the struggle by infiltrating units of the
North Vietnamese Army (real name, People's Army of Vietnam, or
PAVN) into the South. The action made their allies in Beijing and
Moscow nervous, but Hanoi was convinced by past experience in
China and Korea (and in Laos, where the United States had recently
accepted the formation of a coalition government including the
communists) that Washington would eventually give in and withdraw
its support for the Saigon regime.

Hanoi had miscalculated. In Washington, Kennedy's successor Lyndon Johnson was determined not to lose in Vietnam, and when the faction-ridden regime in Saigon continued to deteriorate, leading to intelligence predictions that the communists could seize power within six months, he approved the launching of sustained air strikes against the North (Operation "Rolling Thunder") and the dispatch of U.S. combat troops into the South. The stage for a full-scale military confrontation was set.

The period from 1965 to 1968 represents the height of the Vietnam War. By the end of that period the Johnson Administration had introduced over 500,000 U.S. troops into South Vietnam in order to carry on "search and destroy" missions and break the back of the insurgency. Strategists in Hanoi were convinced that the war could only be won if high casualty figures led to a decline in public support for the war in the United States, and decided to match the U.S. escalation on the battlefield. The decision was a gamble, for the North Vietnamese could not hope to match American firepower.

By late 1967 two factors were clear. On the battlefield, the sheer weight of U.S. arms and troops (backed by the growing size and strength of the Army of the Republic of Vietnam, or ARVN) was beginning to turn the tide against the forces of the revolution. On the other hand, the political side of the war was as yet unresolved. The Saigon regime remained weak, despite the emergence of a strong figure in President Nguyen Van Thieu, while protests against the war were growing steadily in the United States and throughout the globe.

In February 1968, Hanoi launched the famous "Tet Offensive" in towns and villages throughout South Vietnam. The ultimate objective was to force the collapse of the Saigon regime and bring about the withdrawal of U.S. forces from the RVN, but a strong secondary goal was to influence public opinion in the United States. Essentially, Hanoi failed in the first and succeeded in the second. Saigon survived, although in weakened condition, but public protests against the war heightened in the United States, leading the Johnson Administration to open talks on a negotiated settlement of the war. When Richard Nixon took office in January 1969, peace talks in Paris were underway.

Nixon came into office with a self-proclaimed strategy to end the war. In a program called "Vietnamization," U.S. combat forces would be gradually withdrawn from Vietnam, while ARVN would be strengthened to the point where it could cope with the revolutionary forces (whose numbers had been decimated by the Tet Offensive) on its own. Faced with declining possibilities for total victory, Hanoi might agree to a compromise settlement in Paris.

For its part, the Hanoi regime remained hopeful that public protests might yet force the United States out of the war. But when a second offensive launched in March 1972 (the Easter Offensive)

failed to achieve a substantial victory, Party leaders decided to
accept a negotiated settlement. The Paris Agreement, finally signed
on January 22, 1973, called for the final withdrawal of U.S. military
forces from Vietnam. The DRV and its counterpart in the South,
the Provisional Revolutionary Government (PRG), agreed to accept
the continued authority of the Saigon regime under President Nguyen
Van Thieu, but the agreement called for the formation of a National
Council for Reconciliation and Concord to achieve a political
settlement between the contending parties in the South and arrange
for new national elections. There was no mention of the North
Vietnamese forces stationed in the South, estimated at over 150,000
men.

To the American people, the Paris Agreement brought the Vietnam War to an end. To the Vietnamese, it continued for two more
years. Like its predecessor at Geneva, the Paris Agreement quickly
broke down in discord, and in late 1974 Hanoi strategists approved
a plan calling for a major military offensive in the South early the
following year. The original plan called for a two-stage campaign,
with the final push to total victory taking place during the dry
season in early 1976. But military resistance from the Saigon regime,
weakened by declining levels of U.S. military aid, unexpectedly
collapsed throughout the central and northern provinces, and
Hanoi decided to push for total victory in April. Saigon was finally
occupied by North Vietnamese forces on the 30th, bringing the
Second Indochina War to an end.

For Party leaders in Hanoi, the postwar era opened a potential
vista of peace throughout the region, national reunification, and the
successful march of the entire country (now renamed the Socialist
Republic of Vietnam, or SRV) to an advanced socialist society. The
reality has been far different. In foreign affairs, Hanoi's plan to establish a "special relationship" with new revolutionary regimes in neighboring Laos and Cambodia ran aground when the latter (now renamed
Democratic Kampuchea) refused to accept the relationship, which it described as disguised domination by the Vietnamese. In December
1978, the Vietnamese lost patience and launched an invasion which
placed a new pro-Vietnamese regime in power in Phnom Penh. But
Hanoi's effort to solidify its own influence in the changing lands of
old French Indochina aroused the anger of China, which wished to
assert its own historic role in the region. As a deterrence against
a Chinese attack, the SRV had signed a Treaty of Friendship and
Cooperation with the Soviet Union. China, however, viewed the
treaty as an additional provocation and, labelling Hanoi "Moscow's
puppet in Southeast Asia," launched a short punitive invasion of the
SRV in February 1979.

Chinese troops met with fierce resistance from Vietnamese defenders and withdrew shortly after, but Beijing's hostility to Vietnam
has not diminished. During the 1980s, Chinese strategy has focussed
on supporting guerrilla forces under the command of the deposed

Pol Pot regime in Kampuchea while attempting to isolate the SRV
on the international scene. In their effort to drive the Vietnamese
out of Kampuchea they have been joined by the non-communist
states of the ASEAN (Association of the Southeast Asian Nations)
alliance, as well as the quiet support of the United States. The
Vietnamese have managed to maintain their position, but at a high
cost in military expenditures and international support.

Hanoi's problems in foreign affairs have compounded its existing
difficulties inside the country. Political reunification was achieved
with the formation of a united Socialist Republic of Vietnam in early
July 1976. But the efforts of Party leaders to move rapidly toward
socialist transformation in the South encountered strong passive resistance from the local population, whose attitudes had been shaped
not only by two decades of a U.S. presence but by different experiences during the traditional period and under the French.

To make matters worse, the Vietnamese economy, far from
advancing rapidly toward socialist industrialization, virtually
collapsed in the years after the end of the Vietnam War. Bad
weather, war damage, lack of capital, and managerial inexperience
all contributed to the problem, but certainly a key factor was the
regime's decision to move quickly toward socialism in the South.
By 1979, the economy was in a shambles, and political unrest appeared to reach dangerous levels.

In the 1980s, Party leaders attempted to address the problem
by relaxing controls on private economic activities in order to promote a heightened level of economic growth. But conservative
elements within the veteran leadership remained suspicious of capitalist activities and determined to push for an early transition to full
socialist ownership throughout the country. Rent by disagreements
over policy at the highest level, the regime uneasily straddled the
fundamental question of centralized planning or local initiative while
the national economy continued to stagnate.

In July 1986 General Secretary Le Duan died after a long illness.
Le Duan had for years adopted a policy of compromise as a means
of avoiding a bitter split within the Party. His death brought the
simmering dispute between ideologues and innovative elements within
the leadership to a head. His immediate replacement as General
Secretary was Truong Chinh, another Party veteran and reputed
leader of the conservative faction. But in December, the Sixth
National Congress of the Party (now renamed the Vietnamese Communist Party, or VCP) forced Chinh's resignation and elected
Nguyen Van Linh, a leading member of the reformist faction, to
the top position in the Party.

In the brief time since his ascension to power, Nguyen Van Linh
has attempted to accelerate the trend toward innovative methods and
local initiative in the Vietnamese economy. The key words of the

regime, in a manner reminiscent of trends in the USSR, are "modernization" (canh tan) and "openness" (cong khai). But the habits of Leninist orthodoxy, Party leadership, and centralized planning are deeply rooted in the Vietnamese Communist Party, and it will take all of Linh's ability to resolve the complex problems of the Vietnamese revolution and achieve the goals of economic prosperity, national security, and true national unity of the Vietnamese people.

THE DICTIONARY

AGRICULTURE. Vietnam has traditionally been an agrarian society. Until quite recently, approximately 90 percent of the entire population were peasants living off the land. Most peasants were rice farmers, living in the two rich river deltas, the Red River in the North and the Mekong River in the South. The cultivation of wet rice emerged several thousand years ago in Southeast Asia, and many archeologists believe that the Vietnamese were among the first peoples to achieve the domestication of agriculture. Throughout the traditional period, rice was the staple crop for the Vietnamese, and the primary basis for the wealth and prosperity of the state.

Under French rule, agriculture became diversified, and a number of tropical cash crops such as coffee, tea, and natural rubber made their appearance. Most were grown in large plantations owned by European interests in the Central Highlands and adjacent areas. The production of rice and other food crops increased, but much of the increase was exported, to the profit of a new class of wealthy absentee landlords.

After the departure of the French, agricultural growth was seriously hindered by the outbreak of the Vietnam War. In both North and South, rice production stagnated, forcing both governments to import food in order to provide subsistence. With reunification in 1975, the Hanoi regime attempted to increase agricultural production through a combination of improved irrigation, mechanization, the increased use of fertilizers, and collectivization. The results have been disappointing. Grain production stagnated in the years following the war, and has achieved only modest increases in the 1980s. Today government policy is emphasizing agriculture over industry, promoting export crops, and granting incentives to farmers in an effort to increase the production of grain. (See Collectivization of Agriculture)

AGROVILLES (ap tru mat). Program adopted by the regime of Ngo Dinh Diem in 1959 to regroup Vietnamese peasants into large rural settlements in the South Vietnamese countryside. The program was motivated by both economic and security concerns. Eighty agrovilles were planned for implementation by 1963, with each unit containing about 400 families moved from less secure

11

areas into the new centers. Smaller centers consisting of
about 100 families were planned as clusters around larger units.
Put into operation in the last half of 1959, the program was
marked by corruption, government insensitivity, and lack of
adequate funding, and soon aroused widespread criticism. The
program was abandoned in 1961 and soon replaced by a new one
calling for the construction of so-called strategic hamlets (ap
chien luoc). (See Land Reform; Ngo Dinh Diem; Strategic
Hamlets)

ALONG BAY AGREEMENT (See Ha Long Bay Agreement).

AN DUONG VUONG (King An Duong). Founder of the early Vietnamese kingdom of Au Lac and the first historical figure in
Vietnamese history. In the mid-third century B.C., An Duong
(real name Thuc Phan) became the ruler of a kingdom called Nam
Cuong based in South China. In 258 B.C., Thuc Phan defeated
the kingdom of Van Lang, whose base of power was in the Red
River Delta, and declared himself King An Duong (An Duong
Vuong) of a new state of Au Lac. For nearly half a century
he ruled through the local aristocratic class, the Lac Lords,
until his state was overthrown in 207 B.C. by Trieu Da, who set
up a new state of Nan Yüeh(Nam Viet), with its capital at Canton
in South China.
    While there are many legends connected with the life and
reign of An Duong Vuong (including the story that he came to
power with the assistance of a golden tortoise that gave him a
magic crossbow in order to defeat his enemies), he is considered
the first truly historical figure in Vietnamese history. (See
Au Lac; Lac Lords; Nam Viet; Trieu Da)

AN NAM (See Annam).

AN NAM CHI LUOC (Annals of Vietnam). An early history of
Vietnam. (See Le Tac)

ANNAM. An administrative term for Vietnam. The term was first
applied in the seventh century, when the T'ang Dynasty integrated several provinces of occupied Vietnam into the single
protectorate of Annam. The term, meaning "pacified South"
in Chinese, was insulting to patriotic Vietnamese, and was
dropped after the restoration of independence in A.D. 939. But
after the French conquest of Vietnam in the late nineteenth
century, the French adopted the term to describe one of the
two protectorates of Vietnam--along with the colony of Cochin
China and the protectorates of Laos and Cambodia--which formed
the Indochinese Union.
    The protectorate of Annam was located along the central coast
of Vietnam, and included all the provinces from the lower edge
of the Red River Delta to the southern boundary of the Central
Highlands in the South. Although technically left under the

the control of the Vietnamese emperor and his imperial bureaucracy, in practice Annam was ruled by the emperor's French
adviser, titled the resident superieur, leaving the emperor
with solely honorific functions. In 1949 the protectorate of
Annam, along with the protectorate of Tonkin and the colony
of Cochin China, was absorbed into a single associated state
of Vietnam. (See Associated State of Vietnam; Bao Dai)

ANNAMESE COMMUNIST PARTY (An Nam Cong San Dang). Short-
lived communist party formed in 1929. It is sometimes referred
to as Annamese Communism (An Nam Cong San). (See Indochinese
Communist Party; revolutionary Youth League of Vietnam)

ANNAMESE INDEPENDENCE PARTY (Parti Annamite de l'Indépendance,
or PAI). Short-lived political party organized by Vietnamese
patriots living in France in the 1920s. The primary founder of
the party was Nguyen The Truyen, a North Vietnamese who
went to Paris shortly after World War I and soon became involved
in expatriate activities. The PAI issued a public appeal for the
formation of a commission to study conditions in Indochina, but
the French ignored the suggestion and the party disintegrated
after the return of Nguyen The Truyen to Vietnam in 1929.
(See Nguyen The Truyen)

AP BAC, BATTLE OF. Battle between forces of the People's Liberation Armed Forces (PLAF, popularly known as the "Viet Cong")
and the Saigon regime in late December 1962. A village in My
Tho province, Ap Bac was attacked by revolutionary forces that
inflicted a serious defeat of government troops before retiring.
In communist histories of the war, it marked the beginning of a
new stage of battalion-level operations in the struggle in South
Vietnam. (See People's Liberation Armed Forces)

ARCHEOLOGY. Because of the Vietnam War, archeology is still at
a relatively primitive stage of development in Vietnam. During
the war, archeologists in North Vietnam discovered a number of
important Neolithic and Bronze Age sites in the northern provinces,
but because of a lack of funds and isolation from colleagues
abroad, little was done to exploit such finds and interpret their
meaning.
  Since the end of the Vietnam War in 1975, interest in the
importance of Vietnam as the site of important finds from the
prehistorical period has quickened. At the University of Hanoi,
several doctoral degrees in archeology have been awarded, and
plans are now being made for further research. Of particular
importance is the finding of remains of Gigantopithecus and Homo
Erectus in limestone karsts in Ha Long Bay. (See Bronze Age;
Dong Son Culture; Hoa Binh Culture; Mount Do; Neolithic Era)

ARGENLIEU, THIERRY D' (See d'Argenlieu, Thierry).

ARMED FORCES (See Army of the Republic of Vietnam; People's
Army of Vietnam; People's Liberation Armed Forces; Vietnamese
National Army).

ARMED PROPAGANDA BRIGADE (Doi Viet Nam Tuyen Truyen Giai
Phong Quan). Revolutionary unit created by the Indochinese
Communist Party in December 1944. The Armed Propaganda Brigade was established at the suggestion of Ho Chi Minh, leader
of the Indochinese Communist Party (ICP), as a means of moving
gradually from political to armed tactics in the struggle against
the French colonial regime. Its task was to combine agitation
and propaganda activities among the local population with military attacks on French and Japanese military installations and
units in the Viet Bac.

The first brigade, created near the border town of Cao Bang
on December 22, 1944, was composed of a platoon of 34 lightly-
armed revolutionary troops under the command of party leader
Vo Nguyen Giap. The following May, the Brigade was merged
with Chu Van Tan's Army for National Salvation in a new Vietnamese Liberation Army (Viet Nam Giai Phong Quan).

ARMY OF NATIONAL SALVATION (Cuu Quoc Quan). Revolutionary
military organization set up by communist party militant Chu
Van Tan in the early 1940s. The army originated in the Bac Son
Uprising in the autumn of 1940, when local leaders of the Indochinese Communist Party (ICP) launched an insurrection against
the French administration at the time of the brief Japanese invasion across the Sino-Vietnamese border in September. After the
defeat of the rebel forces, Chu Van Tan led one section of the
remnants into the mountains near the border and organized them
into guerrilla units which created a small liberated zone at Bac
Son-Vo Nhai in the border region. In early 1945, the army
was merged with the Armed Propaganda Brigades created in
December 1944 into a single organization--the Vietnamese Liberation Army under the command of Vo Nguyen Giap. (See Armed
Propaganda Brigade; Bac Son Revolt; Chu Van Tan; Vietnamese
Liberation Army; Vo Nguyen Giap)

ARMY OF THE REPUBLIC OF VIETNAM (ARVN). Army of the
Republic of Vietnam, established after the Geneva Conference
of 1954. It was the successor of the Vietnamese National Army,
created as a combat auxiliary force by the French during the
Franco-Vietminh war After Geneva the Vietnamese National Army
was reorganized with assistance from the United States, which
created a 342-man Military Assistance Advisor Group (MAAG)
to provide training for the inexperienced Vietnamese. During
the late 1950s the growth of the Vietnamese army, targeted at
a force level of 150,000 men by U.S. planners, was hampered
by a controversy over its proper role in combatting the communist-
led insurgency movements.

During the Vietnam War, ARVN grew substantially in size

to nearly one million men (including territorial defense forces) and, along with combat forces from the United States, bore the brunt of fighting against the revolutionary forces in South Vietnam. The role of ARVN was concentrated on the pacification effort and suppressing the activities of the revolutionary forces at the local level (the People's Liberation Armed Forces), while U.S. combat forces engaged primarily in "search and destroy" missions against the regular units of the People's Army of Vietnam (PAVN). Some outside observers were critical of this strategy, concluding that the United States was bearing the brunt of the conflict in South Vietnam. In actuality, casualties suffered by ARVN were considerably higher than those suffered by U.S. military units in South Vietnam.

After the departure of U.S. combat forces as a result of the Paris Agreement of January 1973, ARVN was given full responsibility for defending the Republic of Vietnam against external and internal attack. Poorly equipped by the United States as a result of cutbacks ordered by Congress, and poorly led as the result of strategical errors by President Nguyen Van Thieu and several military commanders, ARVN was no match for the well-trained and well-equipped North Vietnamese regular forces and collapsed rapidly in the face of the "Ho Chi Minh" offensive launched by the latter in the spring of 1975. (See Ho Chi Minh Campaign; People's Army of Vietnam; People's Liberation Armed Forces; Republic of Vietnam: Vietnamese National Army)

ASSOCIATED STATE OF VIETNAM. Semi-independent state established within the French Union in 1949. The Associated State of Vietnam came into being as the result of negotiations between ex-emperor Bao Dai and representatives of the French government in 1947 and 1948. The agreement was finalized by the so-called Elysée Accords signed on March 8, 1949. According to the agreement, the new state, along with similar states in Cambodia and Laos, had most of the attributes of an independent state. In some key areas, however, independence was limited by membership in the French Union. In practice, major decisions related to foreign affairs and the conduct of the Franco-Vietminh War continued to be made by the French. The Associated State of Vietnam did not receive broad support from nationalist elements inside the country, but it was formally recognized in February 1950 by the United States and several of its allies.

The Associated State came to an end as the result of the Geneva Agreement, which divided Vietnam temporarily into two separate regroupment zones in the North and the South. Many members of the Associated State joined the new government of the Republic of Vietnam, which was set up after 1954 in Saigon. (See Bao Dai; Bao Dai solution; Elysée Accords; Geneva Agreement)

ASSOCIATION OF LIKE MINDS (Tam Tam Xa). Radical political party organized among Vietnamese exiles in South China in 1923.

Founded by several Vietnamese patriots such as Ho Tung Mao,
Le Hong Phong, and Pham Hong Thai, it was originally connected
with Phan Boi Chau's Vietnamese Restoration Society (Viet Nam
Quang Phuc Hoi), established in Canton in 1912. Leaders of the
Association broke away from Chau's organization in 1923, appar-
ently convinced that it was insufficiently activist.

The program of the Association of Like Minds was relatively
simple. Believing, like the French revolutionary Auguste Blan-
qui, that disputes over ideology were divisive, the party's
leaders concentrated on uniting all resistance elements through
a program of assassination and propaganda for a general uprising to overthrow the colonial regime in Vietnam. The future
political system would be determined by a constituent assembly
elected by majority vote.

The Association apparently sponsored an abortive effort by
Pham Hong Thai to assassinate French governor-general Martial
Merlin in Canton, China. When Ho Chi Minh (then known as
Nguyen Ai Quoc) arrived in Canton at the end of 1924, he en-
listed many members of the Association in his Revolutionary
Youth League. (See Ho Chi Minh; Ho Tung Mao; Le Hong
Phong; Pham Hong Thai; Phan Boi Chau; Revolutionary Youth
League; Vietnamese Restoration Society)

AU CO. Wife of Lac Long Quan and mythical co-progenitor of the
Vietnamese Race. (See Lac Long Quan)

AU LAC. Early kingdom in what is now North Vietnam. In the
mid-third century B.C., a Chinese warlord named Thuc Phan
conquered the Bronze Age Civilization of Van Lang, located in
the Red River Valley of North Vietnam. In 258 B.C., Thuc
Phan, who may have been the ruler of a kingdom called Au Viet
in the hilly regions along the Sino-Vietnamese border, then united
the mountain kingdom of Au Viet (also known as Tay Au) with
the remnants of Van Lang into a new state called Au Lac. Thuc
Phan then declared himself An Duong Vuong (King An Duong)
and set up his capital in the lowlands at Co Loa, about twenty
miles north of the present Vietnamese capital of Hanoi. Like
the rulers of Van Lang whom he had overthrown, King An Duong
attempted to rule with the cooperation of the landed aristocratic
class, called the "Lac Lords" in the feudal ruler-vassal relationship. In 207 B.C., the kingdom of Au Lac was defeated by
Trieu Da (in Chinese Chao T'o), who set up a new state called
Nam Viet (Nan Yueh).

While too little is known of the kingdom of Au Lac to attempt
to reach a definitive assessment, it has considerable significance
in Vietnamese history. It may have represented the first unification of the hill peoples (most of whom are not ethnic Vietnamese) and the valley Lac peoples (the ancestors of the modern
Vietnamese) into a single state, the precursor of contemporary
Vietnam. It also may have been the first indication of the
danger represented by the growing force of China in the North,

because some historians speculate that Thuc Phan may have
originally come from the state of Shu, in present-day Sichwan
(Szechuan) province. The term itself is the Vietnamese ver-
sion of the Chinese character Ou, the name of a river in
Chekiang province. (See Hung kings; An Duong Vuong; Van
Lang)

AUGUST REVOLUTION (Cach Mang Thang Tam). Insurrection
launched by Indochinese Communist Party (ICP) in August
1945. The uprising was planned by ICP leader Ho Chi Minh
to take place at the point of Japanese surrender and prior to
the return of the French. Responding to the appeal by the
party and its front organization, the Vietminh Front, at the
Tan Trao Conference in mid-August, military, paramilitary,
and popular forces under ICP direction took advantage of the
political vacuum at the end of the war and seized control of
cities, towns, and villages throughout the country. In the
North, Vietminh authority was virtually complete, and in early
September an independent Republic of Vietnam was proclaimed
in Hanoi. In the Center, Vietminh forces seized the imperial
capital of Hue and forced the abdication of the reigning emperor,
Bao Dai. In Cochin China to the South, Vietminh forces aided
by non-communist nationalist groups seized power in a bloodless
coup and shared authority in a so-called Committee of the South
(Uy Ban Nam Bo), set up in late August.
    The results of the uprising were mixed. Allied occupation
forces began to arrive in October, Nationalist Chinese above the
Sixteenth parallel, and British forces below. In the North, Ho
Chi Minh, provisional president of the new DRV, was able to
conciliate Chinese occupation authorities by offering positions
in his cabinet to members of non-communist parties such as the
VNQDD and the Dong Minh Hoi. But in the South, General
Douglas Gracey, commander of the British expeditionary forces,
released French prisoners and cooperated with them in driving
the Vietminh and their allies out of Saigon. By October, the
South was back under French control.
    The August Revolution was thus not an unqualified success.
Within a year, negotiations to end the split between North and
South broke down with the outbreak of the Franco-Vietminh War.
But the August Revolution is viewed in Hanoi today as a glorious
first stage in the Vietnamese revolution and, in its combination
of military and political struggle, a possible model for wars
of national liberation in other Third World societies. (See Bao
Dai; committee of the South; Ho-Sainteny Agreement; Vanguard
Youth Movement)

AUSTROASIATIC. A family of languages spoken in mainland Southeast Asia since prehistoric times. It is generally considered to
be a branch, along with Austronesian (spoken in maritime Southeast Asia), of an original Austroasian group of languages spoken
throughout the region. Two of the more prominent modern

languages identified as Austroasiatic are Vietnamese and Mon-Khmer. (See Vietnamese Language)

AUTONOMOUS REPUBLIC OF COCHIN CHINA. Autonomous "free state" within the Indochinese Federation created by the French in March 1946. According to the preliminary Ho-Sainteny Agreement reached between Ho Chi Minh and French representative Jean Sainteny in March 1946, the protectorates of Annam and Tonkin would be recognized by the French as a "free state" within the French Union. In a separate clause, a referendum was to be held in the colony of Cochin China in order to permit the people of that colony to decide whether or not to associate themselves with the new "free state" to the north. Outraged by the possibility that Cochin China might be lost to French rule, colonial elements led by the new High Commissioner Thierry d' Argenlieu established a separate Republic of Cochin China which was firmally recognized by France as a "free republic" in June. Doctor Nguyen Van Thinh was chosen president of the provisional government of the republic, but committed suicide in November at the failure of the new republic to receive recognition either from the Democratic Republic of Vietnam in the North or from the French, who treated it as a tool in their negotiations with Ho Chi Minh.

For two years the autonomous republic lived a shadow existence as a catspaw for French efforts to restore its authority in Indochina. It was formally abolished in March 1949 with the signing of the Elysée Agreements that created a united Associated State of Vietnam. A Territorial Assembly of Cochin China voted for union with the Associated State under Chief of State Bao Dai on April 23rd. (See Dalat Conference; Elysée Agreement; Fontainebleau Conference; Nguyen Van Thinh; d'Argenlieu, Thierry)

- B -

BAC BO (Northern region, also known as Bac Ky). Vietnamese term for the northern provinces of Vietnam. During the period of French colonial rule it was often used by Vietnamese to refer to the provinces contained in the Protectorate of Tonkin. The other regions of Vietnam are Central Vietnam (Trung Bo) and South Vietnam (Nam Bo)

BAC SON CULTURE (Van Hoa Bac Son). Prehistoric civilization of the Neolithic period in what is today North Vietnam. Bac Son sites, so-called because of their proximity to the Sino-Vietnamese border town of Bac Son, date from about 8,000 to 4,000 B.C. A distinctive feature of Bacsonian culture was the use of the so-called Bacsonian axe, with polished edges to facilitate cutting and scraping. While there has been speculation that this technological advance was the result of an immigration of external (perhaps Caucasian) elements into existing Hoa Binh culture into North

Vietnam, Vietnamese archeologists contend that Bac Son
civilization emerged gradually from technological advances taking
place within the existing Hoa Binh civilization in the area.
    Bone fragments indicate that, as in Hoa Binh, the inhabitants
of Bac Son sites were Australoid-Melanesoid in racial composition
and lived primarily in limestone caves, leading some archeologists
to describe Bac Son as a "late Hoabinhian" culture. (See Hoa
Binh Culture; Neolithic Era)

BAC SON UPRISING. Rebellion against French colonial regime in
    the fall of 1940. In September 1940, Japanese troops briefly
    crossed the Sino-Vietnamese border into Vietnam to punctuate
    Tokyo's demand for economic and military privileges in French
    Indochina. In the ensuing confusion, local leaders of the Indo-
    chinese Communist Party (ICP) launched a revolt against French
    authority in the area around the town of Bac Son, an area in-
    habited primarily by minority peoples from the Tai, Nung, and
    Tho nationalities. The French struck back and crushed the
    uprising, but rebel leaders such as Chu Van Tan and Le Quang
    Ba turned to guerrilla warfare. Their units eventually became
    part of the Vietnamese Liberation Army, formed in 1944. (See
    Chu Van Tan; Vietnam Liberation Army; Vo Nguyen Giap)

BACH DANG RIVER, BATTLES OF. Two major military engagements
    fought by Vietnam against Chinese invading forces in the tenth
    and thirteenth centuries A.D. The first was led by Ngo Quyen,
    the Vietnamese rebel leader who won independence for Vietnam
    in 939 after 1,000 years of Chinese occupation. The second was
    directed by Tran Hung Dao, who defeated a Mongol fleet at the
    same spot in 1287. The tactics adopted by the Vietnamese were
    the same in both cases. Stakes were imbedded into the river
    bed at the mouth of the Bach Dang River, which exits into the
    Gulf of Tonkin east of modern-day Hanoi. Then the enemy
    fleet was lured onto the stakes at high tide, sinking the ships
    and leading in both cases to a Vietnamese victory. Some of the
    stakes have survived, and can be seen at the Museum of History
    in Hanoi. (See Ngo Quyen; Tran Hung Dao)

BAO DAI (Reigned 1926-1945). Last Emperor of the Nguyen Dynasty
    in Vietnam and Chief of State of the Associated State of Vietnam
    from 1949 to 1955. Born as Prince Vinh Thuy in 1913, he suc-
    ceeded his father Khai Dinh on the latter's death in 1925, and
    adopted the dynastic title Bao Dai (Protector of Grandeur).
    During his adolescence Bao Dai studied in France while imperial
    duties were handled by a regency council in Hue, the capital of
    the French Protectorate of Annam. In 1932 he returned to Vietnam
    and formally occupied himself with the limited duties assigned by
    the French.
    After the Japanese overthrow of the French colonial regime
    in March 1945, Bao Dai was offered limited Vietnamese indepen-
    dence under Japanese protection. He accepted and named the

historian Tran Trong Kim as prime minister. After the defeat of Japan in August 1945, however, Bao Dai was pressured to announce his abdication by the Vietminh, accepting instead the innocuous position of "Supreme Advisor" to the new Democratic Republic of Vietnam (DRV). For a brief period, he cooperated with the new government and its president, Ho Chi Minh, but eventually concluded that his position was a mere sinecure and left for exile in Hong Kong. After the outbreak of the Franco-Vietminh War in December 1946, Bao Dai immediately became the focus of efforts by the French and anti-communist elements in Vietnam to persuade him to return as Chief of State of a new Vietnamese government which would provide an alternative to Ho Chi Minh's DRV. Bao Dai attempted to use his bargaining power with the French to achieve the latter's agreement on the creation of a united and independent Vietnam. Eventually he settled for a compromise. In the Elysée Accords, signed in March 1949, he agreed to an autonomous Associated State of Vietnam within the framework of the French Union. In June, he returned to assume the office of Chief of State in the new capital of Saigon.

Bao Dai's compromises, which gave the French control over foreign affairs and the waging of the war against the Vietminh, prevented many Vietnamese patroits from supporting his new government. Moreover, his reputation as a playboy convinced many that he lacked the capacity to lead Vietnam into independence. During its brief four years of existence, the Associated State of Vietnam won only limited recognition at home and abroad as the legitimate representative of the national aspirations of the Vietnamese people.

The Geneva Accords divided Vietnam into two de facto separat states in North and South. In Saigon, supporters of the French and Bao Dai's Associated State of Vietnam administered all of Vietnam south of the seventeenth parallel in preparation for national elections called for by the Political Accords reached at Geneva. For a year, Bao Dai remained as Chief of State, but in 1955 his prime minister, Ngo Dinh Diem, held a referendum to determine who should lead South Vietnam into the future. Bao Dai chose not to contest the referendum and remained in France. In elections widely considered fraudulent, Ngo Dinh Diem won over 90 percent of the vote and in 1956 was elected President of the Government of Vietnam. The defeat ended Bao Dai's long involvement with the history of the Vietnamese people. (See Bao Dai Solution; Elysée Accords; Ha Long Bay Agreement; Khai Dinh; Ngo Dinh Diem)

BAO DAI SOLUTION (Also known as Bao Dai Formula, or Bao Dai Experiment). An effort in the late 1940s by non-communist nationalists, aided by the French, to create a government under ex-Emperor Bao Dai that could present the Vietnamese people with an alternative to the communist-controlled Democratic Republic of Vietnam (DRV). The effort began after the opening of

the Franco-Vietminh War in December 1946, when the French
broke off peace negotiations with the DRV. Throughout the next
two years, French representatives met with ex-Emperor Dao Dai,
then living in exile in Hong Kong, in an effort to persuade him
to return to Vietnam as Chief of State of an Associated State
within the French Union. Agreement was finalized in the so-
called Elysée Accords, signed in March 1949. (See; Halong Bay
Agreements Associated State of Vietnam; Bao Dai; Elysée
Accords)

BEAU, PAUL (1857-1926). Governor-general of Indochina from 1902
until 1908. A lawyer and then a diplomat, Paul Beau was appointed to the governor-generalship in 1902. He was a believer
in a policy of "association" between the colonial regime and the
native population in Indochina, and inaugurated a number of
reforms in the area of education, including the opening of the
University of Hanoi and the establishment of consultative assemblies in the protectorates of Annam and Tonkin. His period in
office was marked by the rise of social unrest which would result in peasant riots in central Vietnam and a rising sense of
anticolonial sentiment among intellectuals, exemplified by the
formation of the Tonkin Free School. (See Tonkin Free School)

BINH XUYEN. River pirates active in the Saigon area after World
War II. Created by Le Van Vien (also known as Bay Vien),
an ex-convict escaped from Poulo Condore, the Binh Xuyen
(named for a small village once used for their headquarters)
preyed on river shipping along the Saigon River during the
1930s and 1940s. After World War II the Binh Xuyen cooperated
briefly with the Vietminh against the French, but changed direction in 1948 after several clashes with Vietminh troops (whose
leader, Nguyen Binh, Le Van Vien had known in Poulo Condore)
in the region surrounding Saigon. Le Van Vien was named an
honorary colonel by Nguyen Van Xuan, president of the Provisional Vietnamese Government in 1948 and the Binh Xuyen were
permitted to run the police and the gambling concession in the
Chinese suburb of Cholon. They were eliminated in 1955 by
Prime Minister Ngo Dinh Diem, who viewed them as a threat to
his efforts to assume control over the South after the Geneva
Conference. (See Le Van Vien; Ngo Dinh Diem; Nguyen Van
Xuan)

BLACK FLAGS (Co Den). Bandit unit operating in the Viet Bac
during the French conquest of North Vietnam in the late nineteenth century. Led by Luu Vinh Phuc (in Chinese, Liu Yung-
fu), a Chinese secret society leader who fled to Vietnam in 1863,
the Black Flags were primarily pirates who made their living
preying on local villagers and merchants in the hills of North
Vietnam in the 1820s. When the French attempted to place
Vietnam under their control in the 1880s, the Black Flags cooperated with Vietnamese imperial forces in resisting a French

takeover of the Red River Delta, and were instrumental in the deaths of Francis Garnier in 1873 and Captain Henri Rivière in 1882. After the establishment of the French Protectorate in 1884, the Black Flags engaged in resistance activities in the mountains until the area was pacified at the end of the nineteenth century. (See Rivière, Captain Henri)

BOAT PEOPLE. Refugees who fled from Vietnam by sea after the end of the Vietnam War. The exodus began in the late spring and summer of 1978 under the impact of a government decree nationalizing industry and commerce and other official measures allegedly discriminating against the ethnic Chinese population residing in Vietnam. By 1982, over a million Vietnamese (an estimated two-thirds of whom were of Chinese extraction) had fled Vietnam to other countries in Southeast Asia. Most traveled in small boats, sometimes with the connivance of local Vietnamese authorities, who accepted bribes to ignore the departures. Some refugees later charged that the Hanoi regime officially permitted departures on payment of a standard fee. Thousands died at sea, from storms, hunger or attacks by pirates.

Of those who arrived in other Southeast Asian countries, most were housed in refugee camps, and many have now been permanently settled in other countries outside the region. The United States accepts several thousand refugees each year through an Orderly Departure Program negotiated with Vietnam. The exodus continues today, although at reduced levels. According to one estimate, over 600,000 boat people had arrived in other countries since the end of the Vietnam War.

BOLLAERT, EMILE. High Commissioner of French Indochina from March 1947 to October 1948. A deputy in the French National Assembly and a member of the Radical Socialist Party, Emile Bollaert was appointed to replace Thierry d'Argenlieu as High Commissioner on March 5, 1947, slightly over two months after the beginning of the Franco-Vietminh War. Bollaert attempted to adopt a relatively conciliatory attitude toward negotiations with Ho Chi Minh's Vietminh while at the same time seeking to create a new government composed of non-communist elements who would cooperate with the French against the communist-dominated Vietminh.

The key to Bollaert's scheme was his ability to persuade ex-Emperor Bao Dai to return to Vietnam as Chief of State of a Vietnamese government closely linked with France. Negotiations were held at Ha Long Bay in the spring of 1948, but when Bao Dai made it clear that he would not come to an agreement without a French commitment on Vietnamese unity and national independence, Bollaert resigned on October 19, 1948. He was replaced two days later by Léon Pignon. (See Bao Dai; Bao Dai Solution; Ha Long Bay Agreement; Pignon, Léon)

BORDER OFFENSIVE OF 1950. First major military offensive launched by Vietminh forces in the Franco-Vietminh War. Reacting to the rise to power of the Communist Party in China, Vietminh leaders in the summer of 1950 planned a major campaign to wipe out French military posts along the Chinese border in order to open up the area for the shipment of military supplies from China. During the fall of 1950, a series of attacks launched by well-armed Vietminh units destroyed French forces in the area and led the French high command to evacuate the entire inland border region and retreat to a single outpost at Mong Cai on the coast.

By choosing not to defend the border region, the French allowed the Vietminh free access to south China and virtually guaranteed their ultimate defeat in the war. (See Carpentier, Marcel)

BREVIE, JULES. Governor-general of French Indochina from 1937 to 1939. A former colonial administrator in French North Africa, and author of a book on Islam, Brevié was appointed to his post in Indochina by the Popular Front Government under Léon Blum. Liberal-minded and well-meaning, Brevié attempted to apply conciliatory measures to an explosive political situation, granting political amnesties to political prisoners, liberalizing press laws, and permitting nationalist political parties to function in a legal or quasi-legal manner. These efforts were undone with the collapse of the Popular Front in France and the coming of war in Europe. (See Popular Front)

BRONZE AGE. Period succeeding the Neolithic Era and the beginning of the Iron Age in human civilization. In Vietnam the bronze age reached its apogee during the so-called Dong Son period, beginning in the seventh century B.C.

Until recently, archeologists had believed that bronze-casting techniques, which resulted in the manufacturing of the famous bronze drums characteristic of the Dong Son culture, had been imported into Vietnam from China, or even from Europe. Recently, however, excavations in Indochina and Thailand have suggested that such techniques developed independently among the indigenous Neolithic cultures in the area. Current evidence indicates that bronze technology first appeared in mainland Southeast Asia as long ago as the mid-third millenium B.C. and reached its peak in the Dong Son culture during the centuries leading up to the beginning of the Christian era. Bronze had many uses for prehistoric man in Vietnam: as a source for the manufacture of such weapons as knives, axes, arrowheads, and spears; in agriculture, in the manufacture of hoes and ploughs; and in the manufacturing of such ritualistic implements as bronze drums.

With the discovery of iron at the end of the Dong Son period, the use of bronze gradually declined, and it was used primarily for the making of household implements. (See Dong Son Culture; Bronze Drums; Phung Nguyen Culture)

BRONZE DRUMS (Trong) (Dong Co). Decorated bronze musical
instruments created by prehistoric Dong Son civilization in
North Vietnam and other areas of East and Southeast Asia.
Many have been found at prehistoric sites in South China,
Thailand, and in the Red River Valley in Vietnam, where over
300 have been unearthed since the first was discovered in 1925.
  The drums are considered to be a sophisticated example of
the art of bronze casting, manufactured from an alloy of copper
and tin. Most have been engraved with human figures or
geometric designs. They were apparently viewed as sacred
objects by rule as musical instruments during official ceremonies
to invoke rain for the harvest and in preparation for battle.
(See Bronze Age; Dong Son Culture)

BUDDHISM. The Buddhist religion entered Vietnam in the first
century A.D., brought by missionaries passing between India,
the original home of the religion, and the Chinese Empire.
During the next several centuries, while Vietnam was under
Chinese rule, Buddhism became the dominant religion in Vietnames
society. When Vietnam restored its independence in the tenth
century, Vietnamese monarchs used monks as advisers, and
declared Buddhism the official religion of the state.
  Under the Le Dynasty (1428-1788), Confucianism gradually
replaced Buddhism as the leading ideology in Vietnam. Buddhism
remained popular among the local population, but Confucian
doctrine became dominant among the ruling scholar gentry class
and the sole subject of study for the civil service examinations
used for entry into the imperial bureaucracy.
  In the twentieth century, Buddhism enjoyed a modest revival
among intellectuals. Under the regime of Ngo Dinh Diem, Buddhist monks in Hue and Saigon vigorously protested alleged
official favoritism to Catholics and the vigorous repression of
revolutionary forces practiced by the Diem regime. The Diem
regime accused the Buddhist hierarchy of falling under communist
influence, but in actuality party leaders in North Vietnam were
suspicious of the "petty bourgeois" mentality of such southern
Buddhist leaders as the monk Thich Tri Quang.
  Since reunification in 1975, the government has officially declared its tolerance of the Buddhist religion, but a number of
monks have been arrested for suspected dissident activities,
and the activities of the church have been severely curtailed.
(See Le Dynasty; Ngo Dinh Diem; Tri Quang)

BUI QUANG CHIEU (1872-1945). Journalist and reformist political
figure in colonial Vietnam. Born in a scholar-gentry family in
Ben Tre Province in the Mekong Delta, Bui Quang Chieu was
educated at the Ecole Coloniale and the National Institute of
Agronomy in Paris. In 1897 he returned to Saigon and became
an agronomical engineer. In 1917, with the encouragement of
Governor-general Albert Sarraut, he published the French-
language newspaper La Tribune Indigène, which became a

mouthpiece for an informal group of reform-minded Vietnamese in Cochin China who called themselves the Constitutionalist Party. Its primary political goal was to increase Vietnamese participation in the political process while maintaining the French presence in Indochina.

In the mid-1920s, Bui Quang Chieu became a prominent spokesman for moderate reformist views through the publication of a new journal entitled La Tribune Indochinoise, which sometimes voiced cautious criticism of French policies. But Chieu was horrified at the violence that erupted with the Yen Bay Revolt and the Nghe Tinh Soviets in 1930, and subsequently became more closely identified with the colonial regime, serving as a Vietnamese member of the Supreme Council for Indochina. The Constitutionalist Party split over the issue of cooperation or resistance to the French and declined as a political force. Bui Quang Chieu was assassinated shortly after the end of World War II, reportedly by order of the Vietminh. (See Constitutionalist Party).

- C -

CA MAU PENINSULA. Southernmost tip of Vietnam on the Gulf of Thailand. Located in An Xuyen Province, the Ca Mau Peninsula is relatively underpopulated and covered with dense mangrove swamps. During the early stages of the Vietnam War, revolutionary forces reportedly built a revolutionary base area in the U Minh Forest, located in the center of the peninsula.

CAM RANH BAY. Site of major U.S. military base during the Vietnam War and the current location of a Soviet naval facility in the Socialist Republic of Vietnam (SRV). Located on the central coast about twenty miles south of the resort city of Nha Trang, Cam Ranh Bay is often described as one of the most ideally located portages in Asia. In 1905, the Russian fleet stopped at Cam Ranh Bay on the way to a major confrontation with Japanese warships off the coast of Korea.

In early 1946, President Ho Chi Minh of the Democratic Republic of Vietnam (DRV) offered the location to the United States as a naval base in return for U.S. support for Vietnamese independence. President Truman did not accept the offer, but twenty years later the Administration of Lyndon Johnson constructed facilities there to accelerate the arrival of U.S. military equipment in South Vietnam. The area has been used by the Soviet Union as a naval base since 1978, when the USSR signed a Treaty of Friendship and Cooperation with Vietnam.

CAN BO. Vietnamese term meaning "cadre" currently used in the Socialist Republic of Vietnam (SRV). A cadre is normally a government official, and may be a member of the Vietnamese Communist Party.

CAN LAO PARTY (Personalist Labor Party). Clandestine political organization during the regime of Ngo Dinh Diem in South Vietnam. Created in 1955 by Diem's brother Ngo Dinh Nhu, the Can Lao (full name Can Lao Nhan Vi Cach Mang Dang, or Revolutionary Personalist Labor Party) represented the inner corps of top officials and influential figures within the Diem regime and South Vietnamese society. The Can Lao did not operate as a normal party, competing for office in elections, but operated behind the scenes to influence policy and protect the interests of the Diem regime. After the overthrow of President Diem in 1963 a number of its members formed a new political organization, the Nhan Xa party, which became active during the regime of Nguyen Van Thieu. (See Ngo Dinh Diem; Ngo Dinh Nhu; Personalism)

CAN VUONG MOVEMENT (Save the King). Anti-French resistance movement in Vietnam in the late nineteenth century. It emerged in July 1885 at the time of the flight from the imperial capital of Hue by Emperor Ham Nghi and his regent Ton That Thuyet. One week later Ham Nghi issued an appeal entitled "Save the King" (Can Vuong) to mobilize popular support in an effort to drive out the French and restore Vietnamese independence.

The movement received support from Vietnamese of various walks of life throughout the country, despite the capture of Ham Nghi in 1888. By the late 1880s a widespread guerrilla movement led by the patriot Phan Dinh Phung was in operation in the central provinces. The movement lacked weapons and a coherent strategy, however, and after the death of Phan Dinh Phung from dysentery in 1896, it collapsed. But it is remembered today as one of the first organized resistance movements against French rule in Vietnam. (See Ham Nghi; Phan Dinh Phung; Ton That Thuyet)

CAO BA QUAT (1809-1854). Rebel and patriot in nineteenth-century Vietnam. Born near Hanoi in 1809, he was talented, but although he became a cu nhan in 1831, he failed to pass the metropolitan examination in Hue. After serving in several minor posts in the bureaucracy, he was dismissed from office for rebellious behavior. He returned to his native village and took part in a local peasant uprising, popularly known as the "locust revolt," in which he was killed. He is still remembered as an outstanding poet and a staunch defender of the poor and oppressed.

CAO DAI. Syncretic religion in twentieth-century South Vietnam. The religion Cao Dai, meaning "High Tower," was founded in 1919 by Ngo Van Chieu, a minor functionary in the French colonial government. The new religion incorporated elements from a number of other major religions and ideologies such as Buddhism, Confucianism, Islam, Taoism, and Christianity, and achieved rapid success among the urban and rural population of Cochin China. It established its headquarters at the city of Tay Ninh, near the Cambodian border, and by World War II had a membership of several hundred thousand.

During the war, Cao Dai leaders cooperated with Japanese occupation forces. In 1945 the Cai Dai movement became entangled in the struggle between the French and the Vietminh Front. Some Cao Dai leaders supported the Vietminh, but the dominant group under Pope Pham Cong Tac offered qualified support to the French in an effort to preserve autonomy in areas under their control. After the Geneva Conference in 1954, Cao Dai leaders unsuccessfully resisted the attempt by Ngo Dinh Diem to consolidate his authority over South Vietnam, and during the Vietnam War they cooperated somewhat reluctantly with the Saigon regime against the revolutionary movement led by the National Liberation Front (NLF).

Since 1975 the Cao Dai Church has been permitted to function, although it has been purged of elements suspected of hostility to the revolution and it no longer possess the autonomy it exerted under the Saigon regime. (See Hao Hao; Ngo Dinh Diem; Socialist Republic of Vietnam)

CARAVELLE GROUP. Faction composed of politicians opposed to Ngo Dinh Diem in South Vietnam. The group originated among a number of moderate political figures who petitioned the Saigon regime to undertake reforms in 1960. Formally known as the "Bloc for Liberty and Progress" (Khoi Tu Do Tien Bo), they were popularly called the "Caravelle Group" because their manifesto was issued at the Caravelle Hotel in downtown Saigon. The petition won approval from a wide spectrum of political, religious and social groups in South Vietnam, but it was not publicized in the local press, and Diem broke up the group in November after an abortive coup against the regime. (See Ngo Dinh Diem)

CARPENTIER, MARCEL. Commander-in-chief of the French Expeditionary Corps during the Franco-Vietminh War. Appointed to the post as a successor of General Valluy in September 1949, Carpentier showed excessive caution in his strategical calculations and was sacked after French forces were exposed to a major defeat in the Border Offensive in the Fall of 1950. He was replaced in December by General Jean de Lattre de Tassigny. (See Border Offensive; de Lattre de Tassigny, Jean)

CATROUX, GEORGES (1877- ?). Governor-general of French Indochina in 1939 and 1940. A career military officer, Catroux had served in a civilian and military capacity in North Africa as well as French Indochina. Appointed governor-general in August 1939 to succeed Jules Brevié, he immediately encountered the rising crisis caused by the spread of Japanese power in China. Pressured by Tokyo to grant military privileges for Japanese troops in French Indochina, he first appealed to the United States for military assistance to resist the Japanese. When President Roosevelt rejected the request on the grounds that all U.S. military equipment in the Pacific was needed to strengthen U.S. forces in the region, Catroux capitulated and agreed to the Japanese demands. For this he was criticized by the new Vichy Government in France and recalled to France. Catroux protested but left Indochina in July. Named to replace him was Admiral Jean Decoux, commander of the French naval fleet in the Pacific. Catroux later held a number of high-ranking posts with the French government. (See Decoux, Jean)

CENTRAL HIGHLANDS (Tay Nguyen). Sparsely populated plateau and hill region north of the Mekong Delta in South Vietnam. It extends roughly from the fifteenth parallel north latitude to a point about fifty miles north of Saigon and comprises a total area of approximately 20,000 square miles. Most of the area consists of mountains ranging from 4,000 to 8,000 feet and is heavily forested. The vast majority of the inhabitants are tribal peoples like the Rhadé and the Jarai who have traditionally supported themselves by slash-and-burn agriculture.

During the Vietnam War the area was frequently the site of heavy fighting between revolutionary forces and U.S. and South Vietnamese troops. War planners in the DRV viewed the area as a strategically vital base area from which to attack lowland regions along the coast and in the Mekong River Delta. The seizure of the Highlands by North Vietnamese forces in early 1975 was a major setback for the Saigon regime and represented the opening stage of the final North Vietnamese seizure of the South. (See Ho Chi Minh Campaign)

CENTRAL OFFICE FOR SOUTH VIETNAM, or COSVN (Trung Uong Cuc Mien Nam). Headquarters unit for communist revolutionary operations during the Franco-Vietminh War and the Vietnam War. The office was first created in 1951 to serve as the command unit for Vietminh operations in the South against the French, replacing the old Committee of the South (Uy Ban Nam Bo) which had been established at the end of World War II. In 1954 the office was abolished and replaced by a Regional Committee for the South (Xu Uy Nam Bo), but was recreated in 1961 as the second Indochina conflict, commonly called the Vietnam War, began.

COSVN was directly subordinated to the Central Committee of the Vietnamese Workers' Party (VWP) in Hanoi, and its top staffers, such as Le Duan, Pham Hung, and Nguyen Chi Thanh, were leading figures in the VWP. COSVN was placed in charge of the Party's overall political and military operations in the South as carried on by the People's Liberation Armed Forces. Below its central headquarters, which was located north of the Parrot's Beak inside Cambodia, were five regional party committees and a sixth for the Saigon-Cholon metropolitan area, as well as party committee and branch offices at the provincial, district, and village level. COSVN was abolished after the takeover of the South in 1975. (See Committee of the South; Le Duan; Nguyen Chi Thanh; People's Liberation Armed Forces)

CHAM. Descendants of the peoples who inhabited the kingdom of
Champa in precolonial Southeast Asia. The Cham are considered
to be of Malay descent and adhere to the Islamic faith. There
are an estimated 50,000 Cham living in Vietnam today. Most
live along the central coast near the port cities of Nha Trang
and Phan Rang and engage in fishing or rice farming. (See
Champa)

CHAMPA. Kingdom located on the central coast of Vietnam during
the traditional era. Originally established under the name of
Lin-yi (in Vietnamese, Lam Ap) in A.D. 192, the Kingdom
of Champa was founded by rebellious elements living in the
southern regions of Vietnam during the period of Chinese rule.
By the fifth century, the state began to fall under the control
of Indian elements penetrating northwards from the Indonesian
archipelago. Later it absorbed Islamic influence from Arabic
traders operating throughout the region of the Indian Ocean
and the South China Sea, and the majority of the population,
a dark-skinned people speaking a Malayo-Polynesian language,
became Muslim. The economy was based primarily on fishing
and commerce.

After the restoration of Vietnamese independence in the tenth
century, Champa and Vietnam (then known as Dai Viet) became
bitter rivals. After several hundred years of intermittent fighting,
the rulers of Champa were forced to move their capital from
Indrapura in Quang Nam Province to Vijaya, further south in
modern-day Binh Dinh Province. In 1471, Vijaya itself was
captured by the Vietnamese. The state of Champa, deprived
of most of its northern territories, became a dependency of Dai
Viet. In the nineteenth century, the state was formally absorbed
by Vietnam.

Today, an estimated 30,000 to 50,000 people of Cham ethnic
stock live in various areas of central Vietnam and Cambodia.
Archeological remains of Cham urban centers and religious
structures are found along the Vietnamese coasts from south of
Hue to Phan Nang along the southern coast. Cham influence is
evident in Vietnam in various ways--from music to architecture,
dancing, and words in the Vietnamese language. (See Cham;
Lin-yi)

CHINH PHU NGAM (Lament of a Soldier's Wife). Famous poem
written in eighteenth-century Vietnam. Written in literary
Chinese by Dang Tran Con, it was translated into chu nom by
the woman poet Doan Thi Diem. (See Doan Thi Diem)

CHOLON (Cho Lon). Commercial "Chinatown" of Ho Chi Minh City
(previously known as Saigon). Cholon (literal translation,
"great market") originally developed as a market city inhabited
primarily by overseas Chinese and adjacent to the citadel, which
was located in what is today downtown Ho Chi Minh City. During
the Vietnam War, the population was estimated at approximately

800,000 and was noted for its restaurants, markets, and gambling establishments. (see Ho Chi Minh City; Overseas Chinese)

CHRISTIANITY. The Christian religion was introduced into Vietnam in the sixteenth century by Catholic missionaries from France, Portugal, and Spain. Eventually the French became the most active through the Paris-based Society of Foreign Missions, founded in 1664. Despite growing efforts to repress missionary activities by the Vietnamese authorities, the Society won many converts to the Church, and by 1700 there were several hundred thousand Vietnamese Christians.

During the eighteenth and early nineteenth centuries, Vietnamese Christians and their priests were severely persecuted. But after the French conquest of Vietnam in the last half of the century, colonial authorities tolerated or even encouraged missionary efforts on the conviction that this would promote the acceptance by the local population of French culture and French rule. The Catholic community, numbered at over two million, became a dominant force in commerce, education, and the professions. After World War II some Catholics supported the Vietminh Front in its struggle against the French, but many distrusted the movement's Marxist orientation and eventually supported the Bao Dai government, formed in 1949. After the Geneva Conference of 1954, over 600,000 Catholics fled to the South to avoid Communist rule.

During the Vietnam War, the Catholic community in the South became a major bulwark of the Saigon regime in its struggle against the insurgency. Relations between Catholics and Buddhists grew tense during the last years of the Diem regime but the problem subsided somewhat under Nguyen Van Thieu.

Reunification has not ended the problem of assimilation for the Catholic community in Vietnam. The constitution of the Socialist Republic of Vietnam promises freedom of religion, but the regime remains suspicious of the loyalty of many Catholics and priests to the revolutionary cause. While the estimated three million Vietnamese Catholics are officially permitted to practice their faith, Church activities have been severely restricted and several Vietnamese priests and nuns have been arrested on the charge of taking part in counter-revolutionary activities. (See Pigneau de Behaine; Gia Long; Rhodes, Alexander of)

CHU NOM (Southern characters). Adaptation of Chinese written characters widely used as written form of Vietnamese language in traditional Vietnam. The origins of Chu Nom (often called simply nom) are obscure. During the long period of Chinese rule, all official communications and many literary works were written in literary Chinese. Chu Nom probably came into use by the late eighth or early ninth century, although the earliest surviving examples date from the late thirteenth century, and was devised to provide a written form for spoken Vietnamese.

Because some Vietnamese words did not have a Chinese counterpart, special characters had to be invented that combined elements providing meaning and phonetic value. The character
"nom" itself combined the Chinese characters for "south" and
"mouth."

Until the late traditional period, nom was scorned by many
bureaucrats and court figures as vulgar. A few such noted
writers as Nguyen Trai and Nguyen Binh Kiem, however, wrote
occasionally in nom, and by the eighteenth century it had become an accepted medium for the writing of Vietnamese verse
novels. The most famous literary work written in nom was
Nguyen Du's Kim Van Kieu (Tale of Kieu). Nguyen Hue,
founder of the short-lived Tay Son Dynasty, prescribed it for
use by the bureaucracy, possibly for patriotic reasons, but
the orthodox Nguyen Dynasty (1802-1945) returned to literary
Chinese. Its use eventually declined under French rule with
the rising popularity of quoc ngu (national language), a modern
transliteration of spoken Vietnamese based on the roman alphabet.
(See Kim Van Kieu; Quoc Ngu)

CHU VAN AN (? -1370). Influential scholar-official during the
Tran Dynasty in fourteenth-century Vietnam. A famous Confucian scholar and writer, Chu Van An was selected by Tran
Anh Tong as tutor for his son, the crown prince who later became Tran Minh Tong under the reign of Tran Minh Tong's
successor Tran Du Tong. Chu Van An appealed to the emperor
to fire several corrupt mandarins in the imperial administration;
when the appeal was refused, Chu Van An followed the classical
practice of Confucian scholar-officials in China and resigned
from office. (See Tran Du Tong)

CHU VAN TAN (1908-   ). Veteran revolutionary leader and ranking
military officer in modern Vietnam. Born in a peasant family
of Nung ethnic background in Thai Nguyen province, Chu Van
Tan attended the Whampoa Academy in Canton and joined the
Indochinese Communist Party in the early 1930s. In 1940 he
took part in the abortive Bac Son revolt along the Chinese border.
When the rebel units were defeated by combined French and
Japanese forces, Chu Van Tan reorganized the remnants of the
rebel bands into the so-called National Salvation Army (Cuu Quoc
Quan) and continued resistance activities in the Viet Bac through-
out the war, becoming deputy commander of the Vietnamese
Liberation Army after its formation in December 1944.

Chu Van Tan rose rapidly in the ranks of the ICP after the
war and became a member of the Central Committee and the newly-
formed Revolutionary Military Committee in 1945. In 1960 he was
named secretary of the regional bureau of the Party and commander-
in-chief of military forces in the Viet Bac. He also held a number
of civilian positions in the government, including that of vice
president of the Standing Committee of the National Assembly.

After the end of the Vietnam War, Chu Van Tan's role declined, possibly because of suspicion of dissent from the regime's China policy. In 1976 he was dropped from the Central Committee, although he retained his government positions until 1979, when he was reportedly confined to house arrest. (See Bac Son Revolt; National Salvation Army; Vietnamese Liberation Army)

CIVIL SERVICE EXAMINATION SYSTEM. Examination procedure for evaluating potential candidates for the imperial bureaucracy in traditional Vietnam. The civil service examinations, patterned after a similar system used in China, were first put into operation by the Ly dynasty in the eleventh century. Unlike its Chinese equivalent, the Vietnamese system tested candidates on their knowledge of Buddhist and Taoist writings as well as those of Confucianism (the so-called "tam giao" or "three doctrines").

At first, only members of the hereditary aristocracy were permitted to sit for the examinations and enter the ranks of officialdom. Eventually, however, the examinations were opened up to all Vietnamese males except for those convicted of crimes or engaged in proscribed occupations, and their contents were restricted exclusively to Confucian subjects. The examinations took place at three levels, the baccalaureate (tu tai), given annually in local centers, the master's (cu nhan), given in regional cities, and the doctorate (tien si), given triennially in the imperial palace in the capital. Graduates at the top levels were placed on a list for possible future entrance into the imperial bureaucracy.

Not all graduates became officials, known commonly as mandarins. Some preferred a life of scholarship, or became teachers at Confucian academies established to train young Vietnamese for the examinations.

In a nation where bureaucracy was the most respected occupation, the civil service examinations were the primary ladder of upward mobility for aspiring young males. It was by no means egalitarian (women were excluded, and only those with sufficient leisure and financial resources were able to undergo the difficult educational process necessary to succeed in the examinations). But they did provide the state with a bureaucracy based on merit and an exposure to Confucian political and moral philosophy by the Vietnamese ruling class.

The civil service examination system was abolished under French rule. (See Confucianism; Education)

CLOCHE FELEE, LA (The Cracked Bell). Short-lived newspaper in colonial Indochina. The weekly periodical was founded by the political reformer Nguyen An Ninh (1900–1943) in 1923. It had no specific ideological point of view but was outspokenly critical of many policies of the French colonial regime and was forced to close its doors two years later, by order of the governor of the colony. The meaning of the term has never been satisfactorily explained, although some have speculated that it referred

to Vietnam's state of dependency, or the author's declaration of
his own lack of talent. (See Journalism; Nguyen An Ninh)

CO LOA THANH (Old Snail City). Ancient capital of Vietnamese
kingdom of Au Lac and major archeological site in modern
Vietnam. In the mid-third century B.C. Thuc Phan, ruler of
the state of Tay Au in the mountainous region of North Vietnam,
conquered the kingdom of Au Lac centered in the northwest
corner of the Red River Delta, near Mount Tan Vien. Thuc Phan,
declaring himself king of the new state, moved the capital to
Ke Chu, a town at the confluence of the Duong and Red Rivers,
about fifteen miles north of the modern capital of Hanoi. On
this site King An Duong built a massive citadel to protect the
new Kingdom from its internal and external enemies. The citadel
was called Co Loa Thanh, or "old snail city" from the fact that
it was composed of a series of three concentric spiralling earth
ramparts to protect the inner citadel. The outer wall was eight
kilometers long and averaged four to five meters in height. The
wall was six to twelve meters thick at the top, wide enough for
chariot traffic, and was protected by a bamboo fence, and a moat
beyond it. Mounds and hills in the surrounding countryside
provided a further natural defense work.
    During the period of Chinese rule, Co Loa ceased to be the
capital of Vietnam, but in A.D. 939, Ngo Quyen, the first ruler
of the independent state, placed his capital here. It was moved
further south to Hoa Lu by the Dinh Dynasty in 968. (See
An Duong Vuong)

CO MAT VIEN (Privy Council). First council of state in Vietnamese
empire. It was set up by Emperor Minh Mang in 1834 on the
pattern of a Chinese institution called the chun-chi-ch'u (Military Plans Department, usually known as the Grand Council)
during the Ch'ing Dynasty. Composed of a few ministers drawn
from such positions as Board presidents, grand secretaries, high
military officials and members of the royal family, the Privy
Council functioned as a confidential advisory board to assist the
emperor in dealing with issues of grand strategy. It was composed of "northern" and "southern" sections which were responsible for issues dealing with the northern and southern provinces
of the empire. In terms of foreign affairs, the northern section
was responsible for China, the southern for relations with other
Southeast Asian countries.
    The Privy Council was abolished in 1897 and replaced by a
Council of Ministers under the presidency of a French résident
superior.

COCHIN CHINA. French colony established in South Vietnam in the
nineteenth century, and composed of six provinces in the area of
the Mekong Delta. In September 1862 the three provinces of
Bien Hoa, Dinh Tuong, and Gia Dinh were ceded to France by
the Nguyen court as a result of the Treaty of Saigon. Five

years later, three additional provinces (An Giang, Ha Tien, and Vinh Long) were seized by the French and annexed to the original territory. French ownership was confirmed by treaty in 1874. The origins of the term Cochin China are in dispute, although some scholars feel that "Cochin" is a corruption of the Chinese term "Giao Chi," meaning "crossed toes" or "intertwined feet."

After World War II, Cochin China was not included in the new "free state" envisaged by the Ho-Sainteny Agreement reached in March 1946. A referendum was scheduled to be held to permit the local population to decide whether to join the two protectorates of Vietnam (Annam and Tonkin) in the "free state" or make a separate arrangement with France. Under the sponsorship of High Commissioner Thierry d' Argenlieu, native elements set up a separate Cochinchinese Republic and requested membership in the French Union. In 1949, Cochin China was joined with Annam and Tonkin in the new Associated State of Vietnam. (See d'Argenlieu, Thierry; Elysée Accords; Giao Chi; Ho-Sainteny Agreement; Republic of Cochin China; Treaty of Saigon)

COLLECTIVIZATION OF AGRICULTURE. For communist leaders in the Democratic Republic of Vietnam (DRV), the socialist transformation of agriculture went through two major stages. The first stage was that of land reform. Beginning in the early 1950s, land belonging to the landlord class in areas controlled by the Vietminh Front was redistributed to the poor. The program continued after the Party's return to Hanoi in 1954 and concluded in the North two years later.

The second stage, that of the collectivization of agriculture, began in 1958, with the creation of small semi-socialist cooperatives (known formally as agricultural producers' cooperatives, (nong nghiep san xuat hop tac xa) throughout the northern countryside. By 1960, over 80 percent of all farm families in the DRV were enrolled in cooperative organizations averaging fewer than one hundred farm families each. During the next several years, the cooperatives increased in size (150 to 200 farm families) and in the level of socialist ownership. The impact of collectivization on food production, however, was disappointing. Throughout the remainder of the war, the DRV was forced to rely on food imports to feed its population.

After reunification in 1975, the Hanoi regime decided to delay the building of collectives in the southern countryside until the late 1970s in an effort to encourage an increase in grain production. The program was launched in the winter of 1977-1978, when peasants in the South were encouraged to join various types of low-level cooperative organizations (most common were so-called production collectives and production solidarity teams). Although the program was classified as voluntary, official press reports conceded that coercion was often involved at the local level and many private farmers resisted joining the new organizations. In the early 1980s the campaign was continued, but at a slower pace of development. In late 1986 the regime asserted that collectivization in the South had been completed "in the main," with most farmers enrolled in organizations at the semi-socialist level. (See Agriculture; Production Collectives; Production Solidarity Groups)

COLONIAL COUNCIL (Conseil Colonial). Administrative council set up by the French in the colony of Cochin China in 1880. Dominated by French colonial elements--although it did have six Vietnam representives chosen from wealthy natives sympathetic to the French colonial regime--its primary function was to institute the colony's budget. Later its Vietnamese representation was increased to ten, elected by a constituency of 22,000 voters.

COMMISSION ON COCHIN-CHINA (Brenier Commission). Commission set up by Emperor Napoleon III in Paris in April 1857 to study the advisability of armed intervention in order to establish and protect French commercial, missionary, and security interests in Vietnam. Not surprisingly, considering the pressure applied by special interest groups representing the missionaries and traders, the Commission concluded that intervention would be justified, when "circumstances were opportune." Napoleon III approved an invasion project in July. (See Genouilly, Admiral Rigault de)

COMMITTEE OF THE SOUTH (Uy Ban Nam Bo). Committee set up by the Indochinese Communist Party (ICP) and non-communist nationalist parties in Saigon at the end of World War II. The Committee was established on August 23, 1945 as nationalist forces siezed power in Saigon shortly after the surrender of Japan, and was designed as a means to achieve the cooperation of various anticolonial groups in seeking Vietnamese independence at the close of the war. At first, the committee was dominated by the Vietminh, the front organization of the ICP. Six of the nine members of the Committee were delegates from the Vietminh, and the ICP leader Tran Van Giau was the chairman. General Douglas Gracey, commander of British expeditionary forces which began to arrive in October, refused to recognize the Committee and after riots and demonstrations broke out in Saigon, assisted the French in driving nationalist forces out of Saigon. The Committee fled from Saigon on September 23rd and attempted to organize resistance in rural areas. Negotiations to find a solution were carried on throughout the remainder of the year, and resulted in a preliminary agreement between Ho Chi Minh and French representative Jean Sainteny in March 1946. (See August Revolution; Ho-Sainteny Agreement; Tran Van Giau)

COMMUNAL LAND (Cong Dien). Land belonging to the commune (village) in traditional Vietnam. The land was managed by

the administration of the commune and periodically distributed
to poor families for their temporary use. Sometimes, however,
the Council of Notables (the leading administrative body at the
village level) would permit commune land to be occupied and
exploited by wealthy elements in the village.

The concept of communal land may have been the normal form
of land ownership in Vietnam prior to the Chinese conquest in
the second century B.C. After the restoration of Vietnamese
independence in the tenth century A.D., as much as one-third
to one-half of all village land was under communal ownership.
The system was frequently abused, however, as wealthy land-
owners often confiscated the land for their own use, a practice
that was sometimes restricted by the imperial government. The
system gradually declined under French colonial rule, when the
Western concept of individual landownership was adopted. (See
Agriculture; Council of Elders; Village)

CON DAO (Con Dao Islands). Group of fourteen Vietnamese islands
located southeast of Vung Tau in the South China Sea. The
hilly islands (the highest attains a height of 577 meters) had
no permanent inhabitants during the precolonial period, but the
British seized the islands in 1702 to prevent occupation by the
French. The British departed after a mutiny by the local garrison and the islands were eventually claimed by Franch as part
of Indochina. The largest island in the group, Con Son (Poulo
Condore) was used by the French, and later by the government
of South Vietnam, as a prison. Today the islands have been
transformed into a national park, and have a total population of
about 1,000 persons.

CONFUCIANISM (Nho Giao). Confucianism has been an important
force in Vietnamese society since the time of the Chinese conquest in the second century B.C. Introduced by Chinese administrators during the early years of Chinese rule, it gradually
developed into the foundation for much of Vietnamese society,
including its political institutions, its world view, its educational
system, its system of ethics, and even its form of family organization.

After the restoration of Vietnamese independence in the tenth
century A.D., Confuciansim shared influence at court with Buddhism and Taoism (the so-called "tam giao," or "three doctrines"),
also introduced from China. But in the late fifteenth century,
Confucian doctrine became dominant at court during the reign
of Emperor Le Thanh Tong (1460-1497). From that point it
permeated the entire educated class of the country through the
civil service examinations, the training ground of the Vietnamese
bureaucracy. Through the scholar-gentry class, Confucian
ethics and social values, emphasizing the virtues of hierarchy,
obedience, filial piety, and human heartedness, gradually permeated village life and the minds of the Vietnamese people.

How much Confucian values affected the lives of the average

Vietnamese is a matter of debate. Throughout the traditional
period, a popular counterculture emphasizing indigenous themes
and ridiculing the pomposity, pedantry, and hypocrisy of Confucian orthodoxy coexisted with official doctrine and won ad-
herents from intellectuals and peasants alike. Still, there is
no doubt that Confucianism remained the dominant ideology at
court and within the bureaucracy and--through the scholar-
gentry class--Confucian ethics and social values undoubtedly
became a major force in village life as well. During the Nguyen
Dynasty in the nineteenth century, the court actively promoted
Confucian orthodoxy as the guiding doctrine of the state.

The French conquest in the late nineteenth century brought
an end to the ideological dominance of Confucianism in Vietnam.
Under colonial rule, Western cultural values rapidly replaced
those of the Sino-Vietnamese heritage. Confucianism was reduced to a ritualistic role at the court in Hue and a residual
half-life among conservative scholar-gentry at the village level.
In the 1950s, President Ngo Dinh Diem attempted to revive
Confucian values through the medium of his philosophy of Personalism in the Republic of Vietnam, but his efforts bore little
fruit, and disappeared with his death in 1963. Still, it would
be erroneous to assume that Confucian values and attitudes have
disappeared in modern Vietnam. Even in contemporary Vietnam,
Confucian attitudes intermingle with official Marxist Leninist doctrine within the bureaucracy, while Party leaders constantly rail
against the feudalistic attitudes still prevalent at the village level.
(See Buddhism; Civil Service Examination System: Le Thanh Tong;
Nguyen Dynasty; Scholar-Gentry Class; Sino-Vietnamese Culture)

CONSTITUTIONALIST PARTY. Informal political organization set
up by moderate reformist elements around Bui Quang Chieu, editor of La Tribune Indigène, in 1917. Key concerns of the Party
were an expansion of representative government, equal pay for
equal work in the colonial bureaucracy, and a greater role for
Vietnamese in the local manufacturing and commerical economy.

During the mid-1920s the Party briefly took an active role
in demanding changes in French colonial policy, but many members were shocked by the violent measures adopted by many
anticolonial elements and during the 1930s played a steadily declining role in Vietnamese politics. (See Bui Quang Chieu;
Nguyen Phan Long)

CONSTITUTIONS OF VIETNAM. Since the end of French colonial
rule in 1954, there have been two de facto independent governments in Vietnam, the Republic of Vietnam (the successor state
of the Associated State of Vietnam set up by the French in 1949),
and the Democratic Republic of Vietnam (DRV) first created in
1945 and renamed the Socialist Republic of Vietnam (SRV) in
1976. The Republic of Vietnam had two constitutions, the first
promulgated by the regime of Ngo Dinh Diem in 1956, and the
second by the regime of Nguyen Van Thieu in 1967. Although

there were substantive differences between the two constitutions, they were both based on a combination of the presidential and the parliamentary models practiced in the West, and both paid lip service to the concept of pluralism without actually putting it into practice.

The Democratic Republic of Vietnam and its successor, the Socialist Republic of Vietnam, have had three constitutions: the first, promulgated shortly after the establishment of the DRV in 1946; the second, approved in 1959, in between the two Indochina wars; and the current one in 1980, five years after reunification. All have been Marxist-Leninist in inspiration, combining elements of the western liberal democratic model with the Leninist concept of a dominant communist party ruling through the dictatorship of the proletariat. As with other communist systems, each constitution was designed to reflect the state of society at a particular stage of its development, from the national democratic stage in 1946 to the beginnings of socialist transformation in 1959 to the effort to complete the socialization process in the 1980s. (See Democratic Republic of Vietnam; Republic of Vietnam; Socialist Republic of Vietnam)

CONTRACT SYSTEM (Khoan San Pham, or Production Contracts). Economic policy recently adopted by the Socialist Republic of Vietnam (SRV) in an effort to promote increased food production. Under the system, farmers enrolled in collective farms have been permitted to lease land from the collective organization in return for a commitment to provide an agreed quota of grain or other crop to the state. Grain production in excess of the quota can be sold on the free market or consumed by the farmer and his family.

The program was adopted during the early 1980s and was patterned on a concept briefly put into effect in the 1950s, but soon abandoned as ideologically counterproductive. It was resurrected on a spontaneous basis by local collective officials after the regime announced plans to grant incentive to increase food production in 1979. It received official approval in 1984 and has become common practice on collective farms throughout Vietnam. (See Collectivization of Agriculture)

CONVENTION OF 1925. Political convention signed between the French colonial government and the regency council of Vietnam after the death of Emperor Khai Dinh in 1925. According to the convention, the regency council for the new emperor, the young Bao Dai, would meet under the presidency of the French résident supérieur in Annam. Virtually all political and judiciary power was placed in the hands of the latter, and only ritual functions were left as the prerogative of the emperor. The convention was abolished on September 1932 on the return of nineteen-year-old Bao Dai from schooling in France. (See Bao Dai; Khai Dinh; Pasquier, Pierre; Protectorate of 1884)

COUNCIL OF ELDERS (Hoi Dong Ky Muc). Village governing body
in traditional Vietnam. Normally composed of leading members of
dominant families or clans in each village, the Council was responsible for making key decisions affecting the village. Most
of the members were members of the scholar-gentry class, and
many had degrees in the civil service examinations. Meetings
of the Council were held in the village community hall (dinh)
and dealt with such issues as taxation, civil affairs, local public
works projects, distribution of village communal land, and administration of the village cult. A village chief (xa truong)
served as administrative officer and liaison between the Council
and higher levels of government.
    The village council survived with some revisions into the
French colonial era but after 1954 was replaced by other institutions in both North and South Vietnam. In the North, elected
People's Councils (Hoi Dong Nhan Dan) were set up at village
and higher levels after the formation of the DRV in 1945. In
the South, the regime of Ngo Dinh Diem replaced the Council
with appointed councils headed by a village chief with strengthened powers and subordinate to the provice chief. (See
Local Government)

COUNCIL OF STATE (Hoi Dong Nha Nuoc). Collective presidency
of the Socialist Republic of Vietnam (SRV). It was established
by the Constitution promulgated in 1980 and replaces the office
of the Presidency which existed under the Constitution of 1959.
The Chairman of the Council serves as the de facto Chief of State
of the SRV. (See Constitution of Vietnam; Democratic Republic
of Vietnam; Ho Chi Minh; Socialist Republic of Vietnam; Truong
Chinh; Vo Chi Cong)

CU NHAN   Degree awarded to graduates of the regional civil service
examinations in traditional Vietnam. The title, "recommended
man," was adopted under the Nguyen Dynasty and replaced the
earlier term huong cong (local tribute) used earlier. It corresponded to the degree of chu-jen in the Chinese system and is
the rough equivalent of a Master's Degree in the Western educational system. Regional exams (thi huong) were given at a
number of sites on the provinces. Successful candidates were
then eligible to enter the administration to compete in metropolitan examinations (thi hoi) given triennially in the capital.
(See Civil Service Examinations)

CUONG DE, PRINCE. Member of the Nguyen royal house who took
an active role in anti-colonial activities in French-ruled Vietnam.
A descendent of Prince Canh, the first son of founding Emperor
Gia Long (1802-1820), Cuong De served as the titular leader of
Phan Boi Chau's Modernization Society (Duy Tan Hoi), established
in 1903. For the next several decades he was active in the re-
sistance movement while residing in Japan. During World War
II he was connected with the pro-Japanese political organization,

the Restoration Society (Quang Phuc Hoi) and was considered
by the Japanese as a possible replacement for Wig Emperor Bao
Dai, but the Japanese eventually granted independence to Vietnam
with Bao Dai as chief of state in March 1945. Cuong De died
in 1957. (See Bao Dai; Gia Long; Modernization Society; Phan
Boi Chau)

CUU CHAN. Ancient administrative term used to refer to the area
of modern-day North Vietnam. First used by King Trieu Da
of Nam Viet to describe the area of modern Thanh Hoa and Nghe
Tinh provinces, it was adopted by the Han Dynasty during the
period of Chinese rule. The origins of the term are obscure,
although technically it means "nine verities."

- D -

DA NANG (Tourane). Fourth largest city in Vietnam. Situated in
a protected naval harbor on the central coast in the province
of Quang Nam, Da Nang was overshadowed in the traditional
period by the nearby seaport of Hoi An (Known to European
merchants as Faifo), a major commercial center during the sixteenth and seventeenth centuries. When the harbor at Hoi An
began to silt up in the nineteenth century, Da Nang, originally
known as Cua Han (mouth of the Han), emerged as the major
seaport along the central coast. In 1857, French and Spanish
fleet occupied the city in an unsuccessful effort to seize the
nearby Vietnamese imperial capital at Hue.
    During the colonial era, Da Nang (renamed by the French
Tourane) became a major commercial center. After the Geneva
Conference, Ngo Dinh Diem renamed the city Da Nang. It had
become the second largest city in the Republic of Vietnam.
During the Vietnam War, it was the site of a major U.S. naval
and airbase. Flooded with refugees at war's end, Da Nang today
has an estimated population of 350,000 people and covers an area
of 79 square kilometers. (See Genouilly, Admiral Charles Rigault
de)

DAI CO VIET (Great Viet). Vietnamese kingdom established by Dinh
Bo Linh in 966. The term means "Great Viet," with the phrase Da
Co combining the Chinese and Vietnamese language terms for
"great." Some historians identify the term "co" with "hawk," a
bird sometimes symbolizing rebellion in Vietnamese mythology. In
1054 during the Ly dynasty, the name was changed to Dai Viet.
(See Dai Viet; Dinh Bo Linh; Dinh Dynasty)

DAI LA (Dai La Thanh). Name of a citadel built by the Chinese on
the site of Hanoi at the end of the ninth century. The area of
Hanoi, located just south of the Red River at the junction of the
Duong and the To Lich Rivers, had been made into the admini-
strative capital of the Protectorate of Annam by the T'ang
Dynasty in China. A citadel, called Tu Thanh (in Chinese,

Tzu-ch'eng) had been built to protect the area from attack.
Later a larger citadel, called La Thanh (in Chinese, Lo ch'eng)
had replaced the original. In 791, La Thanh citadel was repaired
and strengthened by the construction of a large earth wall
nearly 20 miles long and over 20 feet high. The defense works
were strengthened with bamboo hedges, watchtowers, and a
surrounding moat. The name of the walled citadel was Dai La
(in Chinese, Ta lo, or Great Nest). The outer wall was eventually destroyed, but the inner citadel was frequently strengthened and became the main bastion defending the imperial capital
of Hanoi. (See Hanoi; Thang Long)

DAI NAM (Great South). Name applied to the Vietnamese Empire
during the Nguyen Dynasty (1802-1945). The formal name "Viet
Nam" had been adopted by the founding emperor Gia Long in
1802. Under his successor Minh Mang (1820-1840), the term
"Dai Nam" was often used. (See Minh Mang; Nguyen Dynasty;
Viet Nam)

DAI NGU. Term applied to the state of Vietnam under the Ho
Dynasty (1400-1407). (See Dai Viet; Ho Dynasty; Ho Quy Ly)

DAI VIET (Great Viet). Formal name of Vietnamese Empire during
the Ly, Tran, and La Dynasties. The name, meaning "Great
Viet," was first adopted by Ly Thanh Tong in 1054, replacing
the former name Dai Co Viet. In 1802, the Nguyen Dynasty
changed the name of the country to Viet Nam. (See Dai Co
Viet; Ly Thanh Tong; Viet Nam)

DAI VIET PARTY (Dang Dai Viet). Nationalist political party in
twentieth-century Vietnam. Formed shortly before World War
II by patriotic elements among the urban middle class in Tonkin,
the Dai Viet Party sought assistance from the Japanese occupation authorities to obtain independence from French rule, and
took part with other pro-Japanese groups in a so-called United
National Front established in Cochin China after the Japanese
coup d'état against the French administration in March 1945.
The Front was superseded by the Committee of the South (Uy
Ban Nam Bo) in August.
    Plagued with internal factionalism and elitist in its membership,
the party had little success in the postwar period against its
main rival, the Vietminh Front, and was eventually outlawed in
the Democratic Republic of Vietnam (DRV).
    After the division of the country at Geneva in 1954, the Dai
Viet resumed political activities in the Republic of Vietnam. Still
factionalized, it became one of several parties in the northern
provinces during the 1960s. (See Committee for the South;
League for the Independence of Vietnam)

DAI VIET SU KY (Historical Record of Great Viet). Classic history
of the Vietnamese Empire, written in the thirteenth century.
(See Le Van Huu).

DAI VIET SU KY TOAN THU (Complete Book of the Historical Records Vietnam). Famous history of Vietnam written by the fifteenth-century historian Ngo Si Lien. (See Ngo Si Lien)

DALAT (Da Lat). Mountain resort city in South Vietnam. Located in Lam Dong province in the middle of the Central Highlands (Tay Nguyen), the city of Dalat sits at an altitude of approximately 1,500 meters. Because of its relatively cool climate, Dalat became a popular resort for sweltering Europeans during the French colonial era, a practice that continued after the departure of the French, not only for affluent elements in Saigon society but also reportedly for the revolutionary movement, which used the mountains surrounding the city as a rehabilitation center for its own cadres.

During the Vietnam War, Dalat became the site of the first nuclear reactor in Vietnam and a military academy. It was also known as the vegetable garden of Saigon, providing fruit and vegetables to the capital region in considerable quantities as well as for export. Today the city has an estimated population of about 100,000 people.

DALAT CONFERENCE. Conference held between France and the Democratic Republic of Vietnam (DRV) in April and May 1946. The purpose of the conference, held at the resort town of Dalat in the Central Highlands, was to discuss the terms of the Ho-Saintainy Agreement, reached in March, and to prepare for formal negotiations at Fontainebleau in June. Chairman of the DRV delegation was the non-Communist Foreign Minister Nguyen Tuong Tam, and only two members of the Indochinese Communist Party, including the party's military strategist Vo Nguyen Giap, were included in the delegation. The delegates were unable to reach an agreement on outstanding issues and adjourned without a result, but the two sides agreed to try to resolve their differences at the upcoming Fontainebleau Conference in June.

In early August, while negotiations at Fountainebleau were still in session, High Commissioner Thierry d'Argenlieu convened a second conference at Dalat without representatives of the DRV to discuss the formation of the proposed Indochinese Federation. The delegates, from Annam, Cochin China, Laos, and Cambodia agreed on the creation of a Federation under the French Union and denounced the DRV as unrepresentative of the Vietnamese people. (See Ho-Sainteny Agreement; Indochinese Federation)

DAN CHUNG (The People). Newspaper published by the Indochinese Communist Party in the 1930s. Unofficially tolerated by the French colonial regime, it was closed down in August 1939 after the signing of the Nazi-Soviet pact. (See Journalism)

DANG CONG SAN DONG DUONG (See Indochinese Communist Party).

DANG CONG SAN VIET NAM (Vietnamese Communist Party) (1930) (See Indochinese Communist Party).

DAO DUY ANH (1904-1988). Renowned scholar in colonial Vietnam. One of the original founders of the Tan Viet Revolutionary Party in the mid-1920s, Dao Duy Anh became a teacher in Hue and a prominent essayist and scholar in colonial Vietnam. A vigorous advocate of Westernization, he participated in an effort to broaden public knowledge by publishing a series of books on prominent Western writers and thinkers and was the author of several studies on Confucianism and the historical dialectic and of a widely-read book on Vietnamese history, the Outline History of Vietnamese Culture (Viet Nam Van Hoa Su Cuong). (See Literature)

D'ARGENLIEU, THIERRY (1889-1964). High Commissioner of French Indochina from August 1945 to February 1946. A naval officer in his early years, Thierry d'Argenlieu became a Carmelite monk after World War I and rose rapidly to a high position in that order. As World War II approached he resumed his naval career and eventually joined the Free French forces under the overall command of General Charles de Gaulle. Promoted to rear admiral, he served in a number of high positions until named High Commissiioner (the new designation for the term governor-general, used until World War II) of Indochina in August 1945.
     During his term in office, Admiral d'Argenlieu displayed a uncompromising determination to restore full French sovereignty in Indochina. In the spring of 1946, he encouraged separatist sentiment among French residents and pro-French Vietnamese in Cochin China to avoid a referendum as called for by the Ho-Sainteny Agreement. In June he announced the establishment of a separate Republic of Cochin China and two months later sabotaged the negotiations at Fontainbleau by convening his own conference at Dalat. In February 24, 1946, after the opening of the Franco-Vietminh conflict, he was recalled to Paris and replaced by High Commissioner Emile Bollaert. (See Autonomous Republic of Cochin China; Dalat Conference; Fountainbleau Conference)

DE LA GRANDIERE, ADMIRAL PIERRE (1807-1876). Naval officer and Governor of Cochin China from 1863 to 1868. A career naval officer, he was appointed governor of the newly-acquired provinces in Cochin China in 1863. Lacking firm instructions from the French government in Paris, de la Grandière on his own initiative extended French influence in the area. In 1863 he compelled the King of Cambodia to accept a French protectorate over his country. In June 1867, on a slim pretext French forces seized the remaining three provinces of Cochin China (Chau Doc, Soc Trang, and Vinh Long) from the Vietnamese. The seizure was ratified by the second Treaty of Saigon, signed in March 1874. (See Phan Thanh Gian; Treaty of Saigon; Tu Duc)

DE LATTRE DE TASSIGNY, JEAN (? -1952). Commander-in-chief of French forces and High Commissioner of French Indochina

from December 1950 until December 1951. A renowned com-
mander in the French Army during World War II, General de
Lattre de Tassigny was appointed High Commissioner and
Commander-in-chief of the French Expeditionary Corps in
Indochina in December 1950 after the disastrous defeat of French
units in the campaign along the Chinese border in the autumn.
A man of enormous presence and self-esteem, de Lattre immediately charged the French effort in Indochina with a new
dynamism. His decision to rush reinforcements to Vinh Yen in
January blunted a major Vietminh offensive on the fringes of
the Red River Delta and eventually forced General Vo Nguyen
Giap, the primary Vietminh strategist, to abandon his efforts
to seize Hanoi during the early spring. General de Lattre
then ordered the construction of a string of pillboxes (the
famous "de Lattre" line) to protect the delta from further infiltration and attack.

Whether de Lattre could have turned the tide in Vietnam is
open to dispute. While his energy and self-confidence heartened
French personnel in Indochina, Vietminh military strength continued to increase at the expense of that of the French, leading
to the costly confrontation at Hoa Binh, on the Black River
southwest of Hanoi. On the political front, his unswerving determination to maintain French dominance in Indochina hindered
his effort to achieve the full cooperation of non-communist
nationalist elements in Vietnam. Stricken with cancer, de Lattre
resigned from office in December 1951 and died in France a
few weeks later. He was replaced as Commander-in-chief by his
deputy, General Raoul Salan. A new High Commissioner, Minister
for the Associated States Jean Letourneau, was appointed in
April.

DE THAM (also known as Hoang Hoa Tham) (? -1913). Pirate
leader and patriot in French-ruled Vietnam. Born in a poor
peasant family in Hung Yen Province in the mid-nineteenth
century, De Tham was raised in Yen The, in the rugged mountains north of the Red River Delta, and as a young man joined
the Black Flag bandit organization led by the pirate leader Luu
Vinh Phuc. When the French established their protectorates
in Annam and Tonkin in the 1880s, De Tham became a bandit
leader of some renown, with a reputation as a Vietnamese Robin
Hood, stealing from the rich to help the poor.

After vainly attempting to suppress his movement, the
French made a truce with De Tham in 1893, but the latter began
to cooperate with anticolonial elements and allegedly took part
in a plot to poison the Hanoi military garrison planned by Phan
Boi Chau. The French resumed their efforts to capture him, and
he was assassinated by an agent of the French in 1913. (See
Black Flags; Phan Boi Chau)

DECOUX, JEAN. Governor-general of French Indochina from 1940
to 1945. Admiral Jean Decoux, commander of the French Pacific

Fleet, was selected by the Vichy Government to replace Georges Catroux as governor-general in July 1940. On arrival, he was faced with an ultimatum from Tokyo demanding free passage through Indochina for Japanese troops and the use of local airports. On order of Vichy, he agreed and a Franco-Japanese Treaty to that effect was signed on August 30, 1940.

For the next years, Decoux followed the Vichy policy of cooperating with the Japanese in the hope of preserving French Indochina after the end of the war. But many officials and military officers in his administration joined the Free French movement and plotted the overthrow of the Japanese occupation regime. On March 9, 1945, Japan presented Decoux with an ultimatum demanding that all French military units be placed under Japanese command. A few hours later, no reply having been received, Admiral Decoux and most French personnel were placed in internment camps. Released at the end of the war, he returned to France and was tried and exonerated of the charge of collaboration. (See Catroux, Georges)

DEMILITARIZED ZONE (DMZ). Cease-fire zone established at the Geneva Conference on Indochina in 1954. When conferees agreed on a partition of Vietnam between Vietminh supporters in the North and supporters of the French and Bao Dai's Associated State of Vietnam in the South, the line of partition was ultimately established at the seventeenth parallel, placing approximately half the population and territory in each zone. The demilitarized zone was established at the Ben Hai River to prevent clashes between the two sides prior to a political settlement called for by the Accords. Supervision of the cease-fire agreement was vested in an International Control Commission composed of representatives of Canada, India, and Poland.

When the Vietnam War resumed in the early 1960s, the DMZ did not become directly involved in the fighting, although U.S. officials suspected that infiltration of troops from the DRV took place through the zone. The bulk of troop movement, however, undoubtedly took place along the so-called Ho Chi Minh Trail, a series of mountain trails across the border in Laos. (See Geneva Conference; Ho Chi Minh Trail; International Control Commission)

DEMOCRATIC REPUBLIC OF VIETNAM (Viet Nam Dan Chu Cong Hoa). Government established under the leadership of the Indochinese Communist Party after the August Revolution in 1945. The government was officially established on September 2, 1945 when Ho Chi Minh, president of the provisional government established in mid-August by the League for the Independence of Vietnam (Vietminh Front), read a declaration of independence for the new republic in its capital of Hanoi. The Democratic Republic of Vietnam (DRV) replaced the French colonial regime and was the first independent government of Vietnam since the French conquest in the late nineteenth century.

At the time of its creation, the DRV was intended to serve a government for all of Vietnam. In actuality, its authority did not effectively extend below the sixteenth parallel, where French armed forces were able to restore colonial rule until the Geneva Conference in 1954. The Geneva Agreement divided Vietnam into two separate regroupment zones which in the course of time became de facto independent states--the DRV north of the Demilitarized Zone at the seventeenth parallel, and the Republic of Vietnam (Viet Nam Cong Hoa) to the south. The DRV consisted of an area totalling 158,750 square miles (61,294 square kilometers) and an estimated population of 15,903,000 (1960 census).

According to the first constitution, promulgated in 1946, the DRV was a parliamentary republic, with supreme authority vested in a unicameral National Assembly elected by the citizens over the age of 18 years. Executive power was lodged in a President, assisted by a Government Council consisting of a Prime Minister and other appointed ministerial officials. Below the central level, the DRV was divided into provinces (tinh), districts (huyen), and villages. At each level, governmental power was exercised by a legislative assembly, the People's Council (Hoi Dong Nhan Dan), elected by the local population, and an executive organ elected from the members of the Council, the Administrative Committee (Uy Ban Hanh Chinh).

As in all Marxist-Leninist societies, the Communist Party (known from 1951 to 1976 as the Vietnamese Workers' Party, or VWP) was the ruling party in the state. Two smaller parties, the Socialist Party (representing progressive intellectuals) and the Democratic Party (representing the national bourgeoisie) were permitted to exist, however, under the guidance of the VWP.

On July 2, 1976, the DRV was formally replaced with a new Socialist Republic of Vietnam (SRV) uniting the two zones established at the Geneva Conference into a single unitary republic under the aegis of the Vietnamese Communist Party (the new name for the Vietnamese Workers' Party). (See August Revolution; Ho Chi Minh; Socialist Republic of Vietnam; Vietnamese Communist Party; Vietnamese Workers' Party)

DIEN BIEN PHU, BATTLE OF. Major battle fought between French and Vietminh military forces in the spring of 1954. Dien Bien Phu, a district capital near the Laotian border in the northwestern corner of Vietnam, had originally been set up by the Nguyen Dynasty in 1841 to consolidate the borderland and prevent bandit forays into the Red River Delta. The region around the town was inhabited primarily by tribal peoples of Tay ethnic stock.

In November 1953 Dien Bien Phu was occupied by French military forces in an effort by General Henri Navarre to prevent Vietminh units from crossing from North Vietnam into Laos to threaten the royal capital of Luang Prabang. Early in 1954,

Vietminh strategists decided to attack the French garrison to strengthen their bargaining position at the upcoming Geneva Conference. The town was placed under siege in March and, after a brief attempt to overrun the French military post by frontal attack, General Vo Nguyen Giap decided on a protracted approach involving massive artillery attacks from the surrounding mountains and the construction of trenches to enable Vietminh troops to approach the fort without coming under direct French fire.

The French High Command attempted to supply its beleaguered garrison by air, but bad weather and intense Vietminh artillery fire prevented the arrival of reinforcements and provisions in sufficient numbers and on May 6th, the day before the Geneva Conference began to discuss the Indochina issue, the post and the surrounding town were overrun. Virtually the entire French garrison of 15,000 were killed or taken prisoner, while Vietminh losses were estimated at more than 25,000.

Whether the loss of Dien Bien Phu was a major military debacle for the French is a matter of dispute. But there is no doubt that it represented a severe blow to French morale and contributed to the signing of the Geneva Accords in July. (See Navarre, Henri; Vo Nguyen Giap)

DINH BO LINH (reigned 965-979). Founder of the Dinh dynasty and significant figure in the restoration of Vietnamese independence in the tenth century. Dinh Bo Linh was born in 923 at the town of Hoa Lu, at the southern edge of the Red River Delta, the bastard son of a provincial governor under the Ngo Dynasty. Growing up in a local village he became a local military commander, and on the death of the last Ngo king in 963, seized power and founded the new kingdom of Dai Co Viet (Great Viet), with its capital in his home region at Hoa Lu, far from the traditional center of Chinese power in the heart of the Red River Delta. To consolidate his legitimacy, he married a member of the Ngo family.

At first, Dinh Bo Linh had been careful to avoid antagonizing the Southern Han Empire in Quangzhou, but in 966 he adopted the title of Emperor (Hoang De), thus declaring his independence from Chinese rule. Seven years later, however, he pacified the new Sung Dynasty by sending a tribute mission to demonstrate his fealty to the Chinese Emperor, who subsequently recognized the Vietnamese ruler as An Nam Quoc Vuong (King of Annam).

Dinh Bo Linh energetically reformed the administration and the armed forces to strengthen the foundation of the new Vietnamese state. But in 979 an assassin killed both Dinh Bo Linh and his eldest son Dinh Lien in their sleep. During the period of anarchy that followed, power was seized by Le Hoan, a general in Dinh Bo Linh's army and the founder of the next dynasty, called the Early Le state. (See Dinh Dynasty; Le Hoan; Early Le)

DINH DYNASTY (Nha Dinh) (968-980). Short-lived Vietnamese
imperial dynasty established by Dinh Bo Linh in A.D. 966.
Dinh Bo Linh, a native of Hoa Lu at the southern edge of the
Red River Delta, seized power after the death of the last ruler
of the Ngo Dynasty in 963. Declaring himself emperor of the
new state of Dai Co Viet in 966, he moved the Vietnamese capital from Co Loa, in the heart of the Red River Delta, to Hoa Lu.
In a decade of power, Dinh Bo Linh attempted to lay the foundations of a stable and independent Vietnam with its own national
traditions. He had three sons, Lien (the eldest) Toan, a child,
and Hang Lang, an infant. In 978, for unexplained reasons,
Bo Linh designated Hang Lang his heir apparent. Shortly after,
the eldest son Lien had the infant killed. Only a few weeks later an
assassin killed both Dinh Bo Linh and Lien, leaving the throne
to Toan, the sole surviving male member of the family. In the
confusion that followed, the Sung Empire in China prepared to
invade, and Le Hoan, a general in Dinh Bo Linh's army and
rumored to be a lover of the queen, seized power and declared
the creation of a new Le Dynasty. (See Dinh Bo Linh, Le Hoan)

DINH TIEN HOANG (See Dinh Bo Linh).

DO SAT VIEN (Censorate). The censorate in traditional Vietnam.
Modelled on the Chinese administrative body of the same name,
the censorate was responsible for evaluating the functioning of
the system and the officials within it. It was composed of
two chief censors and six branches (luc khoa) headed by senior
supervisors. The Censorate was considered to be an independent body which reported directly to the emperor.

DOAN THI DIEM (1705-1746). Noted poet in eighteenth century
Vietnam. One of several well-known women writers in Le
Dynasty Vietnam, Doan Thi Diem was born in Bac Ninh Province
in 1705. She became a teacher in Ha Dong province, but is best
known for having translated the famous poem Chinh Phu Ngam
(Lament of a Soldier's Wife) from literary Chinese into Nom. The
work is noteworthy for pointing out the suffering and misery
rather than the glory of a war. It was the first Vietnamese
poem to focus on the impact of war on a soldier's wife. (See
Literature)

DON DIEN. Agricultural settlements established by the Vietnamese
empire to pacify areas recently conquered and bring them under cultivation. The system was apparently first used during the early
years of the Le Dynasty (1428-1788) to boost production by bringing virgin lands under cultivation through incentives to private
farmers, landed aristocrats, and mandarins. Later it was actively
utilized by the Nguyen court in the eighteenth century to settle
population in uninhabited frontier areas of the South, and particularly in the fertile Mekong Delta.
    At first the settlements were composed of soldiers under the

direct command of military officers. Later the authorities began
to rely increasingly on volunteers, or even on prisoners, who
were established in several colonies (lao trai) and given their
freedom once their obligations had been met. Settlers often
initially received their supplies from the state and were given
tax incentives to persuade them to remain on the land. Once
the area had been brought under cultivation the settlement was
given official recognition as a village or a hamlet.

In recent years, the government of the Socialist Republic of
Vietnam has utilized similar settlements, called New Economic
Zones, to bring new lands under cultivation. (See March to
the South; New Economic Zones)

DONG A DONG MINH HOI (East Asian Alliance). Multi-national
revolutionary organization established by Vietnamese patriot Phan
Boi Chau. The movement was set up in Japan in 1908 and included members from China, Korea, the Philippines, and India,
as well as Vietnam. It was suppressed by Japanese authorities
in 1909. (See Phan Boi Chau)

DONG DU (Study in the East). Movement organized by Vietnamese
patriot Phan Boi Chau in early twentieth century. In 1905 Phan
Boi Chau decided to set up an exile headquarters in Japan in
order to promote resistance activities in French-occupied Vietnam. A key component of this effort was to train young Vietnamese patriots in Western knowledge in preparation for the
building of a modern Vietnamese nation. In the Dong Du movement, Phan Bo Chau encouraged Vietnamese youth to come to
Japan to study and prepare for a national insurrection. The
movement came to an end when Phan Boi Chau's exile organization was evicted from Japan in 1908. (See Phan Boi Chau)

DONG DUONG TAP CHI (Indochinese Review). First periodical published entirely in quoc ngu in North Vietnam. Founded by the
reformist Francophile Nguyen Van Vinh in 1913, the review
attempted to popularize Western ideas, customs, and literature
among its readers. After 1919, it ceased to play a major role
in the Vietnamese reform movement and became a pedagogical
journal. (See Nguyen Van Vinh)

DONG KHANH (Reigned 1885-1889). Emperor of Vietnam under the
French Protectorate. Born in 1865, he was a nephew of Nguyen
Emperor Tu Duc (1847-1883) and an elder brother of Emperor
Ham Nghi, who was raised to the throne in 1885. When the latter
fled the imperial palace to launch a movement of anti-French
resistance in July, Dong Khanh replaced his brother as Emperor.
A docile ruler, Dong Khanh was dominated by the French, who
extended their authority under his reign. He died suddenly in
1889 and was succeeded by Thanh Thai, a son of Emperor Duc
Duc. (See Ham Nghi; Indochinese Union; Thanh Thai; Treaty
of Protectorate; Tu Duc)

DONG KINH NGHIA THUC (Tonkin Free School). School founded by patriotic intellectuals in early twentieth-century Vietnam. Modelled after Fukuzawa Yukich's Keio University in Japan, the school was established in 1906 by the scholar and patriot Luong Van Can. Privately financed, it aimed at introducing Western ideas into Vietnamese society, and included among its instructors and contributors such figures as Duong Ba Trac and Phan Chu Trinh and promoted the use of quoc ngu as the national language. It placed strong emphasis on modern subjects such as geography, mathematics, and science.

The organization tended to follow a reformist rather than a revolutionary orientation, although advocates of the latter were involved in the school's activities. The French were suspicious of the intentions of the school's founders and forced it to close after a few months. A number of the leaders were imprisoned and, sent to Poulo Condere. (See Phan Chu Thinh; Quoc Ngu)

DONG MINH HOI (Viet Nam Cach Menh Dong Minh Hoi). (See Vietnamese Revolutionary League)

DONG SON CULTURE (Van Hoa Dong Son). Bronze age civilization which flourished in the Red River Delta area in what is now North Vietnam during the first millenium B.C. Called Dong Son from the location of the first site, found in the village of Dong Son in Thanh Hoa province in 1925, Dong Son culture is now considered the zenith of Bronze Age civilization in prehistoric Vietnam.

It was characterized by the manufacture of richly decorated bronze drums, used as musical instruments and for ritualistic purposes. Similar drums have been found elsewhere in mainland Southeast Asia and in China, and it was previously believed that the technique of bronze-casting had been imported into Vietnam from China, or from the West. Many archeologists are now convinced that the technology may have developed in mainland Southeast Asia, and spread from there to other societies in Asia.

According to present evidence, Dong Son civilization arose during the seventeenth century B.C. and historians believe that it coexisted with the rise of the kingdom of Van Lang in the Red River Valley. Dong Son civilization came to an end with the coming of the Iron Age and the Chinese conquest of Vietnam in the end of the second century B.C. (See Bronze Age; Bronze Drums; Van Lang)

DOUMER, PAUL. One of primary architects of French Indochina in the late nineteenth century. A member of the Radical Party and an ex-Minister of Finance, he was appointed governor-general of the new Indochinese Union in 1897. Doumer played a major role in fleshing out the concept of the Union by providing it with a stable source of revenue in the state monopolies on salt, alcohol, and opium, and setting up central administrative offices in key areas such as agriculture, civil affairs, post and telegraph and public works. Resigning from the governor-generalship in 1902, he later became President of France and was assassinated in 1930. (See Indochinese Union)

DUC DUC (reigned 1883). Emperor of Vietnam in 1883. (See Tu Duc)

DUONG DINH NGHE. Rebel leader who restored Vietnamese independence from Chinese rule in the early tenth century A.D. At that time, Chinese rule over its occupied territory of Vietnam had been weakened because of the collapse of the T'ang Dynasty in 907. In the unstable conditions, a revolt against Chinese rule was launched by Khuc Thua Du, a local governor of the province of Giao. Chinese rule was temporarily restored when Khuc Thua Du's government was defeated by a military force launched by the Southern Han Dynasty, located in present-day Quangzhou (Canton). But rebellion continued under Duong Dinh Nghe, one of Khuc Thua Du's generals. Dinh Nghe seized the administrative capital of Dai La (present-day Hanoi) and ruled in the Red River Delta for several years. He was assassinated in 937, but his family played a major role in the restoration of Vietnamese independence in succeeding years. (See Ngo Quyen)

DUONG VAN MINH ("Big Minh"). General in the Army of the Republic of Vietnam and a leading force in the coup d'état that overthrew President Ngo Dinh Diem in November 1963. Educated in France, Duong Van Minh joined the French army and rose to the rank of commander of the Saigon-Cholon garrison at the end of the Franco-Vietminh War. He supported Ngo Dinh Diem against the Binh Xuyen in 1954 and became one of the leading figures in the Army of the Republic of Vietnam. Eventually, however, Diem became suspicious of Minh's loyalty and removed him from command. In 1963 he became a leading member of the group of Vietnamese generals who overthrew the Diem regime and president of the Military Revolutionary Council set up in 1970. Genial and plain-spoken in manner, a southerner by family background and a Buddhist, Big Minh was popular with the local population and well liked by most American officials, but his political capacities were limited and in January 1964 he was briefly detained in a coup led by Colonel Nguyen Khanh, and left for exile.

Big Minh was suggested as a candidate for president in the elections of 1966 and 1971 but he declined. In the spring of 1975 he briefly accepted the presidency of the Republic of Vietnam in an unsuccessful effort to obtain conciliatory terms from Hanoi. He remained in Saigon after the communist takeover and was placed in detention. (See Ho Chi Minh Campaign; Ngo Dinh Diem; Nguyen Van Thieu; Tran Van Don)

DUPRE, ADMIRAL JULES-MARIE (1813-1881). Governor of French Cochin China from 1871 to 1874. A career naval officer, Admiral Dupré was appointed governor of Cochin China in 1871. A

supporter of French colonial expansion in Asia, Dupré sent
Francis Garnier to Hanoi in 1873 to rescue the French merchant-
adventurer Jean Dupuis and extend French influence into North
Vietnam. Disavowed by the French government in Paris, Dupré
resigned in December 1873. The French withdrew from North
Vietnam, but were granted a loose protectorate over the Viet-
namese Empire in a treaty signed in 1874. (See Garnier, Francis
Treaty of 1874; Tu Duc)

DUPUIS, JEAN. French merchant-adventurer in mid-nineteenth
century Vietnam. (See Dupré, Admiral Jules-Marie; Garnier,
Francis)

DUY TAN (reigned 1907-1916). Emperor of Vietnam under the
French protectorate. Duy Tan, a son of Emperor Thanh Thai
(1889-1907) replaced his father on the throne at the age of
eight when the latter was deposed by the French and sent in
exile to the island of Réunion. Patriotic in inclination, he complained frequently about his lack of authority and in May 1916
he fled the imperial palace in support of a revolt led by Tran
Cao Van. Apprehended two days later, he was deposed and sent
in exile to the island of Reunion. He served as a commandant in
the French army during World War II and was reportedly considered as a possible replacement for Emperor Bao Dai during
the government of General Charles De Gaulle in 1945. (See
Khai Dinh; Thanh Thai)

DUY TAN HOI (See Modernization Society).

- E -

EARLY LE DYNASTY (Nha Tien Le) (980-1009). Dynasty founded
by Le Hoan in late tenth century A.D. Le Hoan, a general in
the army of Dinh Bo Linh, founding emperor of the Dinh Dynasty, seized power after the latter's assassination in 979.
Emperor Le Hoan, (reign title Le Dai Hanh) defeated a Chinese
invasion, then agreed to a tributary relationship with the Sung
Empire in return for Chinese recognition of Vietnamese independence. Later he fought a successful conflict with neighboring Champa and extended the Vietnamese border to the south.
Internally, the dynasty strengthened the institutions of the state
and revived the economy after several years of internal and external conflict. Buddhism was at the height of its popularity
and became virtually a state religion.
After Le Hoan's death in 1005, his tyrannical son Le Long
Dinh seized the throne after a brief succession crisis. On his
death in 1009, Le Cong Uan, a mandarin at court, usurped the
throne and declared the founding of the Ly Dynasty. (See Le
Hoan; Ly Thai To)

EARLY LY DYNASTY (<u>Nha Tien Ly</u>) (A.D. 544-545). Short-lived
dynasty founded by Ly Bi, a rebel against Chinese rule, in
A.D. 544. Ly Bi was defeated by a Chinese army in 545 and
died shortly after. Resistance to the restoration of Chinese
rule continued for several years, however, as his followers
retreated into the mountains. (See Ly Bi)

EASTER OFFENSIVE. Major military offensive launched by North
Vietnamese forces in South Vietnam in late March 1972. Unlike
the Tet Offensive four years earlier, the Easter Offensive took
place primarily in rural areas rather than in the major cities.
The attack took place in three sectors, in northernmost Quang
Tri province, in the Central Highlands, and along the Cambodian border in Binh Long province.

The offensive was most successful in the North, overrunning the
provincial capital and causing panic among South Vietnamese
divisions defending the area. According to some sources, only
the intervention of U.S. air power prevented a total collapse
of Saigon's defensive position in the area. Elsewhere, South
Vietnamese units generally were able to hold their positions.

Hanoi's motives in launching the offensive have been widely
debated. Party leaders may have hoped that a major triumph
on the battlefield would lead to a collapse of the Saigon regime.
At a minimum, they undoubtedly hoped to demonstrate the failure of the U.S. strategy of "Vietnamization" during a presidential
election year and force U.S. concessions at the Paris peace talks.
(See Paris Agreement; Tet Offensive; Vietnamization)

EDUCATION. Education has traditionally had considerable importance
in Vietnamese society. During the precolonial period, the primary
purpose of education was to train candidates for the imperial
bureaucracy. The educational system was based on the concepts
of the Chinese philosopher Confucius and was composed of
village schools whose purpose it was to train students for the
civil service examinations, the traditional route into the bureaucracy. Emphasis within the system was placed on the need to
inculcate young males with proper moral training and civic virtues.

After the French conquest of Vietnam in the late nineteenth
century, the French introduced Western educational values and
institutions into Vietnam. Emphasis was placed on knowledge of
the arts and sciences, while Confucianism was phased out. As
in the traditional period, however, higher education was for the
few. Most Vietnamese received only a rudimentary education in
village schools, and literacy rates were low.

Major advances in education occurred after the division of
Vietnam into two separate states in 1954. In the South, the
Republic of Vietnam (RVN) adopted the U.S. educational system
based on the development of the individual. In the North, the
Democratic Republic of Vietnam (DRV) introduced a system based
on mass education and the indoctrination of the entire population
in the principles of Marxism-Leninism. After the unification of

the two zones in 1975, the system in use in the North was extended throughout the entire country.

Today the Socialist Republic of Vietnam (SRV) is endeavoring to transform the educational system into a tool to promote the creation of an advanced socialist society. Dual emphasis is placed on technological modernization and ideological purity. (See Civil Service Examination System)

ELYSEE ACCORDS. Compromise agreement signed between French government and ex-emperor Bao Dai of Vietnam in 1949. Signed on March 8, 1949, the accords called for French recognitition of the independence of the so-called Associated State of Vietnam within the French Union. In foreign relations, Vietnamese independence was limited by its membership in the French Union. Internally, Vietnamese autonomy was confirmed except for some limitations in the judicial sphere, and an agreement that Vietnam would give priority to French political and technical advisers. Vietnam would have its own national army, with French forces limited to designated areas, but in practice Vietnamese forces were placed under French command for the duration of the Franco Vietminh war.

Because the Republic of Cochin China was technically not included within the scope of the agreement, the National Assembly in Paris authorized the creation of a territorial assembly of Cochin China to vote union with the Associated State of Vietnam. It did so on April 23rd. The Elysée Accords went formally into effect on June 14th with a ceremony in Saigon, and ratification by the French National Assembly took place on January 29, 1950. Diplomatic recognition by the United States took place a few days later, but considerable doubt existed in the minds of many observers, both within Vietnam and on the world scene, whether Vietnam was yet in control of its own destiny. (See Bao Dai; Bao Dai Solution; Ha Long Bay Agreement)

ENERGY RESOURCES. Lack of sufficient energy resources has been one of the crucial problems hindering economic development in Vietnam. While there are substantial amounts of coal, estimated at 130 million tons northeast of Haiphong along the Tonkin Gulf, and recently-discovered oil fields off the coast near Vung Tau (currently estimated at one billion tons), neither source has been adequately developed to promote the rapid growth of the Vietnamese industrial sector.

Since reunification in 1975, official policy has placed increased emphasis on the development of energy resources as a crucial element in the building of a modern economy. Coal extraction equipment has been modernized, a number of projects to develop hydroelectric power have been initiated, and Soviet assistance has been used to develop the offshore oil reserves in the South China Sea. Results so far have been somewhat disappointing. Coal production is stagnant, and while the oil fields are now producing several hundred thousand tons of crude oil annually,

output is not expected to play a major role in solving the energy
shortage until sometime in the 1990s. In the meantime, lack of
sufficient energy will remain one of the primary obstacles of
rapid industrial growth in Vietnam. (See Five-year Plans; Industry; Socialist Republic of Vietnam)

- F -

FAIFO (Hoi An). Port city in Quang Nam Province, Central Vietnam.
Located at the point where the Thu Bon River meets the coast,
about twenty miles south of present-day Da Nang, the city
first achieved prominence during the seventeenth century when
it was used as a port of entry by Western commercial interests
trading with Le Dynasty Vietnam. First opened by the Portuguese
in the mid-sixteenth century, it later housed merchants from
several other countries, including Holland, China, and Japan. It
declined in the eighteenth century when the Thu Bon River
began to silt up and then was badly damaged during the Tay
Son Rebellion. Eventually it was replaced by Da Nang as the
major port center in Central Vietnam, but a number of old houses
and temples from the traditional period remain standing.
Renamed Hoi An, it eventually became the capital city of Quang
Nam Province when independence was restored in 1954.

FATHERLAND FRONT (Mat Tran To Quoc). Umbrella front organization in the Socialist Republic of Vietnam (SRV). Originally
created in Hanoi in 1955, the Fatherland Front was the successor
to the so-called Lien Viet Front, (League for the Independence
of Vietnam) in 1951. The creation of the new front was apparently
motivated by the peace agreement signed at Geneva in 1954 and
the need for the DRV to focus on new objectives, namely the construction of socialism in North Vietnam and the peaceful reunification of the South with the North. Since that time it has served
as the umbrella organization for the various functional, ethnic,
and religious mass associations that are used by the regime to
mobilize support for its policies.
    The Fatherland Front also served as the main front organiza-
tion for the revolutionary movement in the South until December
1960, when the National Front for the Liberation of South Vietnam, or NLF, was proclaimed at a congress held at a secret
location near the Cambodian border. The NLF was merged with
the Fatherland Front in 1976, when the two zones were reunited
into the Socialist Republic of Vietnam. (See Lien Viet Front;
National Front for the Liberation of South Vietnam)

FESTIVALS. Like most agricultural societies, the majority of Vietnamese holidays are connected with the harvest cycle. Many were
inherited from China during the long period of Chinese rule,
while others emerged after the restoration of independence in the
tenth century A.D.

The most famous holiday in Vietnam is the traditional New Year's Festival (known in Vietnamese as <u>Tet</u>, from the Chinese <u>chieh</u>). The <u>Tet</u> festival marks the beginning of the new year based on the lunar calendar of 355 days each year. The holiday is a period of family festivity and begins when the Kitchen God (Tao Quan) is sent to Heaven to report on family affairs, which hopefully will bring good fortune for the remainder of the year.

Another major holiday in Vietnam is the so-called Mid-Autumn Festival (<u>Tet Trung Thu</u>), also known as the Moon Festival. Also inherited from China, the Mid-Autumn Festival takes place on the fifteenth day of the eighth month, and is marked by the lighting of colored lanterns and the eating of so-called "moon cakes" made specially for the occasion.

One annual ceremony practiced in traditional Vietnam involved the participation of the emperor. Known as the Plowing Ritual (Le Tich Dien), it was initiated by Emperor Le Dai Hanh in the tenth century A.D. on the basis of previous Chinese practice. The emperor plowed a furrow at the beginning of the annual harvest cycle as a symbolic act to guarantee a good harvest. Abolished under the Trinh lords, it was revived during the Nguyen Dynasty.

FIVE-YEAR PLANS. A series of plans adopted by the Democratic Republic of Vietnam and its successor, the Socialist Republic of Vietnam, to promote economic development and socialist transformation. The first plan, adopted in 1960, attempted to consolidate the initial stages of socialist construction and industrialization in the North. After a decade of annual plans at the height of the Vietnam War, the SRV adopted a second plan for the period 1976-1980 to eliminate capitalism in the South and promote socialist industrialization throughout the entire country. Neither goal was achieved, and the third plan (1981-1985) had more mode objectives while still aiming at achieving socialism "in the main" in the southern provinces by 1985. The current plan, adopted in 1986, retains the dual goal of economic development and socialist transformation, but is more tolerant of the small capitalist sector and the concept of incentives, and stresses the promotion of consumer goods and production of goods for export.

Planning is undertaken by the State Planning Commission in Hanoi. In recent years, each five-year plan has been coordinated with similar plans adopted in the Soviet Union and other socialist countries. (See Democratic Republic of Vietnam; Socialist Republic of Vietnam)

FONTAINEBLEAU CONFERENCE. Conference between representatives of France and the Democratic Republic of Vietnam (DRV) at the Palace of Fontainebleau in the summer of 1946. The conference was held to discuss the provisions of the Ho-Sainteny Agreement, reached in March. An earlier conference held at Dalat in the Central Highlands of South Vietnam had failed to resolve differences.

It soon became clear at Fontainebleau that the French government was not prepared to be conciliatory in key issues related
to the Ho-Sainteny Agreement, the formation of a "free state"
of Vietnam, and the holding of a referendum in Cochin China
on the possible association of the colony of Cochin China with
the DRV. When High Commissioner Thierry d'Argenlieu unilat-
erally convened a second conference at Dalat in early August
to create an Indochinese Federation without the participation
of the DRV, the Vietnamese delegation under Pham Van Dong
despaired of an agreement and shortly thereafter left for Hanoi.
President Ho Chi Minh, in France as an observer, remained in
Paris and negotiated a modus vivendi calling for renewal talks
early in 1947. Tensions increased during the fall, however, and
the Franco-Vietminh conflict broke out in December 1946. (See
Dalat Conference; d'Argenlieu, Thierry; Ho-Sainteny Agreement;
Indochinese Federation)

FRANCO-VIETMINH WAR. Extended conflict between the French
colonial regime and the communist-dominated Vietminh Front
after World War II. The war began on December 22, 1946 when
Vietminh forces attacked French installations in the city of Hanoi,
and then withdrew to prepared positions in the mountains surrounding the Red River Delta. During most of the next several
years, Vietminh units under the command of the Indochinese
Communist Party waged a guerrilla struggle against French forces
stationed throughout Indochina. The conflict came to an end
after the French public began to tire of the war and doubt the
possibility of a favorable outcome. A peace treaty was signed
at Geneva on July 21, 1954, calling for a withdrawal of the French
and the temporary division of Vietnam into two separate zones.
(See Geneva Conference; Ho Chi Minh; League for the Independence of Vietnam)

- G -

GARNIER, FRANCIS (1839-1873). Naval officer and adventurer who
promoted French colonial efforts in nineteenth-century Vietnam.
After serving as a young lieutenant in the French navy, Garnier
entered the French administration as Inspector of Indigenous
Affairs in the new colony of Cochin China in the early 1860s.
Ambitious and convinced of France's destiny in Asia, Garnier
organized an expedition to explore the Mekong River basin in
1866. The published results caught the attention of commercial
interests in France.
    In 1873, supported by Governor Jules-Marie Dupré, Garnier
launched a military operation in North Vietnam to secure the
safety of the French merchant Jean Dupuis, who was running
weapons up the Red River into South China. On arrival in
Hanoi, Garnier supported Dupuis' demands for the opening of
the Red River to international commerce and stormed the citadel.

He then attempted to extend French control over neighboring areas between Hanoi and the Tonkin Gulf. He died in battle on December 21, 1873.

In his brief and meteoric career, Garnier earned a reputation as one of the pioneers of French expansion in Asia. Although the French, on orders from Paris, now withdrew from North Vietnam, a treaty was signed in 1874 which opened the Red River to foreign commerce and established an informal French protectorate over the Vietnamese Empire. (See Dupré, Admiral Jean-Marie; Dupuis, Jean; Tu Duc)

GENEVA ACCORDS (See Geneva Conference).

GENEVA CONFERENCE. A major international conference attended by representatives of several nations to seek a settlement of the Franco-Vietminh War in the spring of 1954. An agreement among the Great Powers to meet at Geneva had been reached at the beginning of the year. At first, the sole topic proposed for discussion had been the issue of divided Korea, but at a meeting in Berlin in January, major world leaders had agreed to raise the Indochina conflict for possible settlement.

The conference began to discuss the Indochinese problem on May 7th. Attending were the existing governments in Indochina (the Associated States of Vietnam, Laos, and Cambodia), the People's Republic of China, France, Great Britain, the Soviet Union, and the United States. The U.S. attended with reluctance, in the conviction that any compromise settlement could have dangerous effects on the security of the remainder of Southeast Asia.

The fall of the French garrison at Dien Bien Phu on the eve of the conference cast a pall on the non-communist delegations at the conference. At first, French representatives refused to consider major concessions to the Vietminh, but in June a new government under Prime Minister Pierre Mendes-France came into office on a commitment to bring the war to an end within one month. Mendes-France accepted a partition of Vietnam into two separate regroupment zones (the communists in the North, the non-communists and pro-French elements in the South) divided at the Ben Hai River on the seventeenth parallel. The zones were not to be construed as sovereign entities, however, but solely as administrative areas (to be governed by the DRV in the North and Bao Dai's government in the South) until the holding of reunification elections. The issue of elections was resolved in the so-called Political Protocol, which called for consultations between representatives of the two zones one year after the signing of the Geneva Agreement. These consultations were to result in an agreement to hold national elections throughout the country one year later. The cease-fire and the carrying out of the provisions of the Political Protocol were to be supervised by an International Control Commission composed of representatives of Canada, India, and Poland. The cease-fire agreement was signed by representatives of the DRV and France on

July 21, 1954. The Political Protocol received verbal approval
from seven of the participants. The United States and the Bao
Dai government abstained, with the U.S. representative stating
that the United States would not hold itself responsible for the
Geneva Accords, but would take no steps to disturb them.

The Geneva Conference resulted in a compromise agreement
that in effect presented the Vietminh with half of Vietnam. The
South remained under the control of non-communist elements.
France now abandoned its responsibility for Indochina, and was
replaced in the South by the United States. Hardline elements
on both sides were displeased, with some supporters of the
Vietminh expressing bitterness that their cause had been sold
out by China and the Soviet Union. The United States now
prepared to defend South Vietnam, as well as the independent
states of Laos and Cambodia, from a further advance of communism. The reunification elections never took place as Ngo Dinh
Diem, successor to Bao Dai in South Vietnam refused to hold
consultations with representatives of the DRV. By the end of
the decade, the Vietnam War would resume. (See Bao Dai;
Demilitarized Zone; Dien Bien Phu, Battle of; International Control Commission; Ngo Dinh Diem)

GENOUILLY, ADMIRAL RIGAULT DE. Naval Commander in French
Pacific fleet who directed attack on South Vietnam in 1857-8.
Captain de Genouilly had taken part in a bombardment of Vietnamese ships in Tourane harbor in March 1847. In November
1857, now promoted to Admiral and in charge of the Pacific fleet,
he was instructed by the French government to seize the city
with the aid of Spanish warships. The attack was launched in
August, and at first succeeded. But malarial conditions and local
resistance prevented a projected advance to the imperial capital
of Hue, and de Genouilly abandoned Tourane and moved further
south, where he captured the citadel of Saigon in February 1859.
He returned to Tourane for a second attempt in April, but had
no more success and resigned from his command. He later became
Minister of Marine and Colonies in Paris.

GIA DINH BAO (Journal of Gia Dinh). First newspaper to be printed
in quoc ngu, the romanized transliteration of spoken Vietnamese.
Established in 1865 by the French colonial administration in Saigon,
it played a major role in popularizing quoc ngu in the colony of
Cochin China. One of its editors and primary contributors was
the pro-French collaborator Truong Vinh Ky. (See quoc ngu;
Truong Vinh Ky)

GIA LONG (Nguyen Anh). Founding emperor of the Nguyen Dynasty
(1802-1945) in early nineteenth-century Vietnam. As the last
surviving member of the Nguyen Lords, who had ruled South
Vietnam since the sixteenth century, Gia Long (real name Nguyen
Anh) had launched a campaign which resulted in the overthrow
of the Tay Son Dynasty in 1802. Taking the dynastic name Gia

Long, Nguyen Anh declared himself founding emperor of a new Nguyen Dynasty, which would last until 1945.

Once in power, Gia Long placed his capital at Hue in central Vietnam, and changed the name of the empire from Dai Viet to Viet Nam. He launched a number of administrative reforms and proclaimed a new penal code, known as the Gia Long Code.

In providing a moral and ideological foundation to the empire, he imitated the Confucian orthodoxy of the Ch'ing Dynasty in China, and replaced Chu Nom (the written form of spoken Vietnamese) with Chinese as the official language of the country. The Nguyen Dynasty had come to power with the aid of the French bishop Pigneau de Behaine, who hoped that France would be granted favorable commercial and missionary privileges under the new regime. But Gia Long was suspicious of Western influence, and although he tolerated a measure of missionary activity in Vietnam he refused to permit a substantial French commercial presence.

Gia Long died in 1820 at the age of 59 and was succeeded by his son, Chi Dam, who took the dynastic title of Minh Mang. (See Hue; Nguyen Anh; Nguyen Dynasty; Nguyen Hue; Pigneau de Behaine; Tay Son Rebellion; Viet Nam)

GIA LONG CODE. Penal code adopted by the Nguyen Dynasty in nineteenth-century Vietnam. Patterned after its counterpart used in Ch'ing Dynasty China, it was promulgated in 1815 and replaced the so-called Hong Duc Code adopted by the Le Dynasty in the fifteenth century. Compared with its predecessor, it took less account of local custom and rigidly followed the Chinese model. Its fundamental objective was to maintain the power of the emperor and law and order in the social arena. Penalties were severe and a male-oriented perspective characteristic of the Chinese system replaced the more liberal provisions of the Hong Duc Code.

The Gia Long Code continued in force under the French colonial regime until it was superseded by a new one adopted in 1880. (See Hong Duc Code; Gia Long; Nguyen Dynasty; Women)

GIAO. An administrative region of Vietnam under the rule of the Chinese empire. The province of Giao was established in the third century A.D. and was located in the area of the lower Red River Delta in the vicinity of the present-day capital of Hanoi. At the time, it was the most populous province in occupied Vietnam, with an estimated total population of about 100,000 people.

GIAO CHI. Ancient administration term for the Red River Delta in North Vietnam. The word Giao Chi, which means "intertwined feet" (sometimes translated as "crossed toes"), was first introduced during the reign of Trieu Da in the kingdom of Nam Viet and may have referred to the Chinese view of the sleeping habits of the non-Chinese peoples of the south, who slept in communal

fashion with their feet together and their heads extending
outwards. Under Nam Viet, Giao Chi became one of two provinces into which the region of the Red River Delta was divided
and referred to the lower region of the Red River.

Under Chinese rule, the term was retained as the name of
one of the three provinces into which the Red River Delta was
divided. The others were called Cuu Chan (South of the Delta)
and Nhat Nam, south of the Hoanh Son spur. With the coming
of the first Western adventurers in the sixteenth century, the
term was corrupted by the Portuguese into Cochin, which would
later be used by the French to refer to their colony of Cochin
China in the region of the Mekong River Delta.

GRACEY, DOUGLAS. Commander of British Expeditionary Forces
in Indochina at the close of World War II. General Gracey
sympathized with French plans to restore colonial rule in French
Indochina and assisted French forces in South Vietnam to drive
nationalist forces out of Saigon. (See Committee of the South)

GRAND CONSEIL DES INTERETS ECONOMIQUES ET FINANCIERS
DE L'INDOCHINE (Supreme Council of Economic and Financial
Interest in Indochina). Advisory body set up by French colonial
regime in Indochina. Established by Governor-general Pierre
Pasquier in 1928, the Council possessed limited powers connected
with economic policy and the budget. Its predecessor, the
Conseil Supérieur de l'Indochine, was established in Cochin China
in 1887.

- H -

HA LONG BAY AGREEMENT (also known as Along Bay Agreement).
Accord reached between representatives of the French government and ex-Emperor Bao Dai of Vietnam in June 1948. According to the terms of the agreement, signed aboard a French
cruiser in Ha Long Bay in the Gulf of Tonkin, Bao Dai tentatively
agreed to return to Indochina as soon as France agreed to the
creation of a united Vietnam. The new state would be granted
independence within the French Union, but its foreign relations
would be conducted by France, and its military forces would be
"available for the defense of any part of the French Union."

Bao Dai had signed an earlier declaration with French representatives at Ha Long Bay in December 1947, but many of his
followers had been dissatisfied with the terms of the agreement,
which placed severe restrictions on Vietnamese sovereignty, and
he later denounced it, explaining that he had initialed it as a
private individual. A second round of talks was held at Ha
Long Bay in early June 1948. The French now agreed to recognize the unity and national independence of Vietnam as an
"Associated State" within the French Union. Its independence
would be limited "only by that which its attachment to the French

Union imposes upon itself." Detailed arrangements would be made after the creation of a provisional government in Vietnam.

The agreement did not win unanimous support, either in France or among nationalist elements in Vietnam, but was finally ratified by the signing of the Elysée Accords on March 8, 1949. (See Bao Dai; Bao Dai Solution; Bollaert, Emile; Elysée Accords)

HAIPHONG (Hai Phong). Major seaport located about 70 miles (112 kilometers) southeast of Hanoi in North Vietnam. Located on the Cam River about twelve miles (twenty kilometers) from the Gulf of Tonkin, Haiphong first assumed significance in the late nineteenth century when it was transformed from a small market town into a major seaport for the Red River Delta by the French. It eventually became the second largest city in the Protectorate of Tonkin.

In November 1946, French warships bombarded the native quarter of the city, exacerbating tensions between the French and the Democratic Republic of Vietnam (DRV). War broke out a few weeks later. After the Geneva Conference of 1954, Haiphong became the major seaport of the DRV and a center for cement, shipbuilding, fishing, and machine construction. Today Haiphong is the third largest city in the Socialist Republic of Vietnam (SRV), with a population of 1.3 million people, divided into three urban quarters and seven suburban districts. Like Hanoi and Ho Chi Minh City, it is ruled directly by the central government. (See Haiphong Incident)

HAIPHONG INCIDENT. Armed clashes between military forces of France and the Democratic Republic of Vietnam (DRV) in November 1946. The incident was triggered by a dispute over the control of Vietnamese customs in the port of Haiphong, but was actually a consequence of the rising tension in Franco-Vietnamese relations since the failure of the Fontainbleau Conference in the summer of 1946.

In early November the French government, basing its action on the Ho-Sainteny Agreement of March 1946, announced that it would open a customs house in Haiphong despite a protest by Vietnamese President Ho Chi Minh. Tension rose in the city during the next few days, and when a French patrol boat seized a Chinese junk running contraband in Haiphong harbor, it was fired upon by Vietnamese troops on shore. On the orders of High Commissioner Thierry d'Argenlieu, then in Paris, the French fleet launched a massive bombardment on the native sections of the city on November 23rd, killing an estimated 6,000 persons. Street riots after the incident were suppressed by French troops, but France and the DRV had taken a major step toward war.

HAM NGHI (reigned 1884-1885). Emperor of Vietnam after establishment of French Protectorate in 1884. Brother of Emperor Kien Phuoc, who died after a brief reign in 1884, Ham Nghi rose to the throne at the age of twelve. In July 1845 he fled the capital

of Hue with Regent Ton That Thuyet to launch the Can Vuong
resistance movement against French occupation. In September,
he was replaced on the throne by his brother Dong Khanh.
Captured in November 1888, Ham Nghi was sent to live out his
life in exile in Algeria, and died there in 1947. (See Can Vuong
movement; Ton That Thuyet)

HANOI (Ha Noi). Capital city of the Socialist Republic of Vietnam
(SRV). The city is located at the confluence of the Duong River
and the Red River, about 45 miles inland from the Gulf of Tonkin.
Hanoi is one of the oldest cities of Vietnam, and first became the
capital in the eleventh century A.D. Until the early nineteenth
century, it was called Thang Long (Soaring Dragon). The term
Hanoi (within the river) was adopted from the name of the territorial district surrounding it.

In the late nineteenth century, Hanoi became the headquarters
of French Indochina. It was primarily an administrative rather
than an industrial city, although it did contain a small manufacturing and commercial sector. After the August Revolution
in 1945, Hanoi became the capital of the Democratic Republic of
Vietnam (DRV). Driven from the city after the beginning of the
Franco-Vietminh war the following year, DRV leaders returned
in October 1954 after the Geneva Agreement awarded the DRV
all of Vietnam north of the seventeenth parallel. Since then it
has remained the capital of the DRV and its successor, the SRV,
founded in 1976.

Hanoi today is the second largest city in Vietnam, with a
population of about 830,000 in the inner city, and 2.6 million
in the metropolitan area. Like Ho Chi Minh City and Haiphong,
it is run directly by the central government. Executive power
is exercised by a People's Committee, headed by a Chairman.
The city is divided into four urban precincts and four suburban
districts, comprising slightly over 100 communities. (See August
Revolution; Dai La; Thang Long)

HARKINS, PAUL. General in the U.S. Army and commander of the
U.S. Military Assistance Advisory Group (MAAG) in the Republic
of Vietnam from 1962 until 1964. Harkins was strongly criticized
for remaining optimistic about the situation in South Vietnam
despite rising evidence to the contrary. He was replaced by
General William C. Westmoreland in the summer of 1964. As the
U.S. presence in South Vietnam increased, MAAG was replaced
by a new Military Assistance Command-Vietnam (MAC/V). (See
Westmoreland, William C.)

HARMAND TREATY (1883) (also known as Treaty of Protectorate).
Treaty signed between France and the Vietnamese Empire in
August 1883. The treaty, signed by the French scholar and
diplomat François Harmand a few months after the death of Captain
Rivière near Hanoi, established a French protectorate over Central
and North Vietnam. The southern provinces had already been

ceded to the French as the colony of Cochin China in 1874. The
treaty was signed under duress as French naval forces had
bombarded the entrance to the imperial capital of Hue a few days
previously. The treaty was replaced a year later by a second
Treaty of Protectorate, signed in June 1884. (See Rivière,
Captain Henri; Treaty of Protectorate)

HIEP HOA (reigned 1883). Emperor of Vietnam in the Nguyen
Dynasty. (See Tu Duc)

HO CHI MINH (1890-1969) (also known as Nguyen Ai Quoc). Assumed name of Nguyen Tat Thanh, founder of the Vietnamese
Communist Party and long-time president of the Democratic
Republic of Vietnam (DRV). Born the son of a scholar-official
of humble means in Nghe An province in Central Vietnam, Nguyen
Tat Thanh was educated at the Quoc Hoc (National Academy) in
the imperial capital of Hue. Absorbing the highly patriotic and
anti-colonialist views of his father, he left Vietnam in 1911 as
cook's apprentice on a French ocean liner. After several years
at sea, he settled briefly in London and then at the end of
World War I went to France.

In Paris, Thanh changed his name to Nguyen Ai Quoc (Nguyen
the Patriot), submitted a petition to the Allied leaders meeting
at Versailles demanding Vietnamese independence and in 1920
became a founding member of the French Communist Party. In
1923 he was summoned to Moscow for training as an agent by
the Communist International and in December 1924 travelled to
Canton in South China where he formed the first avowedly
Marxist revolutionary organization in Vietnam, the Revolutionary
Youth League of Vietnam. Charismatic, dedicated, as well as
an effective leader, Nguyen Ai Quoc built up the League into the
most prominent organization opposed to French rule in Indochina
and in 1930 it was transformed under his direction into the Indochinese Communist Party (ICP).

Nguyen Ai Quoc was arrested by British authorities in Hong
Kong in 1931, and after his release in 1933 spent the next several
years in the Soviet Union, allegedly recovering from tuberculosis.
In 1938, however, he left for China, where he spent a short
period at Yan'an, the headquarters of the Chinese Communist
Party. He then settled in South China, where he restored contact with the leadership of the ICP. In 1941, at a plenary session
of the Central Committee at Pac Bo, near the Sino-Vietnamese
border, Nguyen Ai Quoc declared the formation of the so-called
League for the Independence of Vietnam, or Vietminh Front, an
organization formed to seek Vietnamese independence from French
rule and wartime Japanese occupation.

In August 1945, now using the new pseudonym of Ho Chi
Minh (roughly translated as "he who enlightens") Nguyen Ai Quoc
led the ICP and its front organization, the Vietminh, in a successful uprising to seize power in Vietnam at the moment of
Japanese surrender to the Allies. A new Democratic Republic

of Vietnam (DRV), with Ho Chi Minh as president, was proclaimed in Hanoi in September. The French refused to recognize Vietnamese independence, however, and seized control of the southern provinces in the fall of 1945. Negotiations between the DRV and France resulted in a preliminary agreement in March 1946, but further negotiations at Fountainebleau failed, and war broke out in December 1946.

For eight years, Ho Chi Minh led the DRV and its fighting arm, the Vietminh, in a struggle against France and the Associated State of Vietnam, a rival government set up by the French in 1949. The Vietminh were unable to win a clearcut military victory, but their ability to win public support and wage a protracted struggle undermined the French war effort, and at the Geneva Conference in 1954 the DRV agreed to a compromise settlement, dividing Vietnam into two de facto separate states, with the DRV in the North, and supporters of the Associated State of Vietnam in the South. Some of the more militant members of the Party resisted the compromise settlement, but Ho Chi Minh was able to achieve majority compliance by pointing out the danger of U.S. intervention and the possibility of achieving total reunification of the two zones by peaceful or revolutionary means in the near future.

For the remaining fifteen years of his life, Ho Chi Minh remained President of the DRV and leader of the Party. A convinced Marxist-Leninist, he led North Vietnam toward socialism while at the same time seeking to complete unification with the South, now renamed the Republic of Vietnam. Although increasingly fragile in health, he was successful in avoiding factionalism within the Party and maintained the DRV independent in the Sino-Soviet dispute. While the stern policies of his regime undoubtedly alienated many Vietnamese, overall he was revered by the people of North Vietnam, who often referred to him as "Uncle Ho." He died in September 1969 at the age of 79. Since his death, his successors have attempted to use his memory as a symbol for the building of a united socialist nation. A mausoleum containing his embalmed body now stands on a main square in the capital of Hanoi. (See August Revolution; Democratic Republic of Vietnam; Geneva Agreement; Ho-Sainteny Agreement; Indochinese communist party; League for the Independence of Vietnam; Revolutionary Youth League of Vietnam)

HO CHI MINH CAMPAIGN. Military offensive launched by forces of the People's Army of Vietnam (PAVN) in South Vietnam in the spring of 1975. Initially, the 1975 campaign, directed by Senior General Van Tien Dung, was designed to seize territory in the Central Highlands in preparation for a major offensive to seize power in the South the following year. But initial attacks resulted in unexpected success and in April, the Politburo of the Vietnamese Workers' Party (VWP) approved an intensive effort to seize Saigon and topple the Republic of Vietnam before the onset of the rainy season in May.

The offensive, named for ex-President Ho Chi Minh in honor of his lifelong struggle for national reunification, was a spectacular success, and North Vietnamese forces entered Saigon in triumph on April 30, 1975. (See Ho Chi Minh: People's Army of Vietnam; Van Tien Dung; Vietnamese Workers' Party)

HO CHI MINH CITY (Ho Chi Minh Thanh). Current name for the city of Saigon, capital of the Republic of Vietnam until its fall in 1975. The name was changed by leaders of the Democratic Republic of Vietnam in honor of ex-President Ho Chi Minh, who has struggled for national reunification throughout his life.

In terms of population, Ho Chi Minh City is currently the largest city in Vietnam, with a population of approximately four million people (1985 estimate). Like other major cities in the Socialist Republic of Vietnam, Ho Chi Minh City is administered directly by the central government in Hanoi. The Vietnamese Communist Party, the ruling party in the SRV, is represented by a Municipal Party Committee, headed by a Chairman, who is a leading member of the party.

Since the integration of North and South in 1975, Ho Chi Minh City has represented a persistent challenge to the party leadership in Hanoi. Bourgeois attitudes and practices have survived among the population despite vigorous efforts by the regime to stamp them out. Efforts to eliminate capitalism and create a dominant state sector have had little success, and led to a high degree of malaise among local residents, many of whom have little trust in the socialist system. Current policy permits the existence of a small capitalist sector, while planning on socialist transformation by gradual means. The city currently ranks as the leading industrial and commercial center in Vietnam, and the home of much of the nation's technological expertise. (See Saigon)

HO CHI MINH TRAIL. Series of trails used by the Democratic Republic of Vietnam (DRV) to infiltrate men and equipment into South Vietnam during the Vietnam War. The trail was first put into operation in 1959 as the result of a decision by DRV leaders to return to a strategy of revolutionary war in the South. Initially a fairly simple affair leading from the southern provinces of the DRV around the DMZ into South Vietnam, the trail eventuall developed into a complicated network of trails, paths, roads, and waterways extending down the Truong Son mountain range in southern Laos and Cambodia and was popularly known in the West as the Ho Chi Minh Trail. Despite heavy bombing by the U.S. Air Force, during the height of the war in the mid-1960s it serviced the needs of several hundred thousand regular troops of the People's Army of Vietnam (PAVN) operating in the South. (See Dimilitarized Zone [DMZ]; Democratic Republic of Vietnam; People' Army of Vietnam)

HO DYNASTY (Nha Ho) (1400-1407). Short-lived Vietnamese imperial

dynasty that replaced the Tran and was overthrown by China.
(See Ho Quy Ly)

HO QUY LY (Le Quy Ly). Powerful court figure at the end of the
fourteenth century and founder of the shortlived Ho Dynasty
(1400-1407). Ho Quy Ly was born in a family descended from
Chinese immigrants that achieved prominence at court at the end
of the Tran Dynasty (1225-1400). Ho Quy Ly (original name Le
Quy Ly) was a cousin by marriage of Emperor Tran Nghe Tong
(1370-1372), who appointed him to an influential position in the
imperial administration. In the 1380s he served as a high military
officer and commanded Vietnamese armed forces against Champa.

Ho Quy Ly used his position of prominence to advance his
own interests. In 1388 he persuaded Tran Nghe Tong, now serving as royal adviser, to replace the reigning emperor with
Tran Nghe Tong's own son. He later served as regent for the
new Tran Thuan Tong, who was still an adolescent. Ho Quy Ly
forced him to abdicate in 1398 and shortly after assumed power
himself as founder of a new Ho Dynasty. One year later he
turned the throne over to his son, Ho Han Thuong, while re-
taining influence through his position as royal adviser.

Ho Quy Ly had risen to the throne in the classic manner of
the usurper seizing power during the declining years of a
disintegrating dynasty. Yet Ho Quy Ly is remembered in history not solely as a usurper, but also as a progressive who
attempted to resolve some of the pressing problems that has
brought down the powerful Tran dynasty. During his years
in power, he launched a number of reforms in the fields of civil
and military administration, education, and finance. He also
attempted to reduce the power of feudal lords and reduce unrest in the countryside by reforming the tax system and limiting
the amount of arable land that could be held by powerful mandarins and the aristocracy. Land in excess was confiscated by
the state and leased to landless peasants at modest rent.

Ho Quy Ly had the misfortune to rule at a time when the
Ming Dynasty was becoming increasingly powerful and expansion-
ist. To strengthen the nation's defense, Ho Quy Ly initiated a
number of military reforms and increased the size of the armed
forces. In 1397 he moved the capital to Vinh Lac, in Thanh Han
province south of the flat and highly exposed Red River Delta.
The new capital was renamed Tay Do (Western Capital). But
the Ming took advantage of internal resistance to Ho Quy Ly's
reforms and seizure by launching an invasion of Vietnam, renamed
Dai Ngu (Great Ngu), in 1407. The pretext for the attack was
to restore the Tran to power, but China's actual motives were
undoubtedly to restore Chinese authority over Vietnam. Despite
Ho Quy Ly's efforts, the Vietnamese were quickly defeated. Ho
Quy Ly, his son, and other leading members of his administration,
were shipped off to China were Ho Quy Ly, now over 70 years of
age, was forced to serve as a common soldier. Vietnam was returned to Chinese rule. (See Tran Nghe Tong; Tran Dynasty)

HO-SAINTENY AGREEMENT. Preliminary agreement between France and the Democratic Republic of Vietnam (DRV) on March 6, 1946. The agreement was signed by president Ho Chi Minh of the DRV and French representative Jean Sainteny. Negotiations had gotten under way the previous autumn as France and the new Vietnamese republic in Hanoi attempted to resolve their differences over the future of Indochina. According to the agreement, France would agree to recognize the Democratic Republic of Vietnam as a "free state" within the French Union, with its own "army, parliament, and finances." A referendum would be held in Cochin China to determine whether the people in that French colony united to join the new free state or make their own separate arrangement with the French.

In return, Vietnam would agree to permit the restoration of a French economic and cultural presence in the DRV. Chinese occupation forces in North Vietnam would be replaced by a mixed Franco-Vietnamese army under French command. French troops would be permitted to provide protection for French installations in the DRV. (See Autonomous Republic of Cochin China; Dalat Conference; Fontainebleau Conference; Sainteny, Jean)

HO TUNG MAU (1896-1951). Founding member of the Indochinese Communist Party in 1930. Little is known about his early life, although he was probably born in 1896 in Nghe An Province. He became a founding member of the Association of Like Minds (Tam Tam Xa), established in South China in 1924. From there he entered Ho Chi Minh's Revolutionary Youth League and reported also became a member of the Chinese Communist Party. One of Ho's most trusted colleagues and party of the inner circle of the League in the Communist Youth Group, he headed the League after Ho's departure from China until his arrest in December 1928. He escaped from jail in August 1929 and helped to arrange the unity conference in February 1930 that led to the formation of the Indochinese Communist Party. In June 1931 he was arrested by French police in Shanghai and condemned to a life sentence at Lao Bao Prison. Released in 1945, he was reportedly killed in an air attack in 1950 or 1951. (See Association of Like Minds; Indochinese Communist Party; Revolutionary Youth League of Vietnam)

HO XUAN HUONG. Prominent woman writer in eighteenth-century Vietnam. Born in Nghe An province in the mid-eighteenth century, Ho Xuan Huong was raised in Hanoi (then known as Thang Long) and became a noted scholar and popular writer who used irony, wit, and sarcasm to attack the ills of contemporary Vietnamese society. Once herself the concubine of a district magistrate, she reserved her most powerful attacks for the hypocrisy, the corruption, and the double standards practiced at court in the Buddhist temples, and throughout Vietnamese society. Among the best-known and most controversial poets of her time, she wrote in nom, and is considered one of the founders of modern Vietnamese literature. (See Literature)

HOA BINH CULTURE. Prehistoric civilization of the Mesolithic or
early Neolithic period in North Vietnam. Located in limestone
hills near the present-day city of Hoa Binh, the site was discovered in 1927. Later, additional sites were discovered elsewhere in Vietnam, and archeologists today speculate that Hoa
Binh culture was not a homogeneous culture but had existed
possibly as far away as Madagascar and the Mediterranean Sea.

According to present evidence, Hoa Binh civilization emerged
from the late Paleolithic civilization about 11,000 years ago. It
is often called a "pebble culture," characterized by the emergence
of a cave-dwelling society based on the use of chipped stones
made of pebbles found along the banks of streams. The most
frequently found implements are pebbles whose faces have been
chipped on one side only, creating an edge with a simple bevel.

Skull and bone fragments found at the site suggest that the
inhabitants of Hoa Binh were of Australoid-Negroid stock and
lived primarily by hunting and gathering. At later sites, there
is some evidence of the cultivation of plants and pottery making.
(See Bac Son Culture; Neolithic Era)

HOA HAO. Reform Buddhist religious sect in twentieth-century South
Vietnam. Founded by the young mystic Huynh Phu So in 1939,
the Hoa Hao religion is an offshoot of the Buu Son Ky Huong
(Strange Fragrance from the Precious Mountain), a millenarian
sect formed in the Lower Mekong delta by Doan Minh Huyen
(known as the "Buddhist Master of the Western Peace") in the
mid-nineteenth century. It represented a synthesis of reformed
Buddhism, folk religion, and populist social attitudes among
Vietnamese peasants in the frontier region in the delta. The
movement spread rapidly in the 1940s and 1950s among the rural
population in Chau Doc, Bac Lieu, Rach Gia, and Long Xuyen
provinces, for whom it served not only as a religion but a means
of political and social organization.

During World War II, Hoa Hao leaders cooperated with Japan.
After the Japanese surrender, Huynh Phu So flirted briefly with
the Vietminh, but soon came to see them as rivals. After his
assassination by the Vietminh in 1947, the Hoa Hao hierarchy
cooperated reluctantly with the French. But relations with the
French and the various Vietnamese governments that followed were
uneasy, as the Hoa Hao attempted to maintain political autonomy
in Hoa Hao areas in order to maintain their simple way of life.

The Communist seizure of South Vietnam in 1975 brought new
troubles to the Hoa Hao. The new revolutionary regime forced the
Hoa Hao central church organization to disband and arrested
several of the leaders although private worship is permitted.
Communist distrust of the Hoa Hao was probably justified, as
many Hoa Hao have reportedly engaged in resistance activities
against the Hanoi regime. Today there are an estimated one
million Hoa Hao living in Vietnam.

HOA KIEU   (See Overseas Chinese).

HOA LU. Capital of the independent state of Vietnam under the Dinh Dynasty (968-980). Located on the southern edge of the Red River Delta in what is now Ha Nam Ninh Province, Hoa Lu was the birthplace of Dinh Bo Linh, founder of the Dinh Dynasty in the eleventh century. After declaring himself king, Dinh Bo Linh moved the national capital from the ancient city of Co Loa in the heart of the Red River Delta to Hoa Lu, partly for defensive reasons (Hoa Lu was located on a valley surrounded by low mountains and far from China) and partly because it was outside of the area of traditional pro-Chinese sentiment in the province of Giao, to the North. Early in the following century, the Ly dynasty moved the capital back North to Dai La, the site of present-day Hanoi. (See Co Loa; Dinh Bo Linh; Dai La; Thang Long)

HOAN KIEM LAKE (also known as Ho Guom, or Returned Sword Lake). A famous lake in the center of the city of Hanoi. Originally called Luc Thuy (Green Lake), it was once a branch of the Red River which silted over as the river bed shifted. It was renamed Returned Sword (Hoan Kiem) Lake in the fifteenth century because of a legend that Le Loi, the founder of the Le Dynasty, had drawn a sword from the lake, inhabited by a golden tortoise, to achieve his great victory over the Chinese. Later the sword was returned to the water.

During the traditional era, the lake was larger than at present and the site of a number of princely palaces and monuments built during the Ly and Tran Dynasties. The Trinh Lords held naval maneuvers there for entertainment.

There are currently two small islands on the lake. One, connected to the mainland by a wooden bridge, contains Ngoc Son Temple, originally built during the Le Dynasty and restored during the nineteenth century. The other contains Tortoise Tower, a symbol of the city of Hanoi.

HOANG CAO KHAI (1850-1933). Scholar and official in nineteenth-century Vietnam. A native of Ha Tinh Province, he earned his Master's Degree (cu nhan) at an early age and became a mandarin in the imperial bureaucracy. After the establishment of the French Protectorate he joined the colonial administration and served as viceroy of Tonkin from 1888 to 1892. A believer in the French civilizing enterprise, he collaborated with the colonial regime during a long a financially rewarding life. In the 1880s he attempted unsuccessfully to persuade his friend Phan Dinh Phung to abandon the path of resistance to the French. (See Phan Dinh Phung)

HOANG DAO (1906-1948) (real name Nguyen Tuong Long). Prominent novelist in colonial Vietnam. Born Nguyen Tuong Long in 1906 in Quang Nam Province, he was a younger brother of Nguyen Tuong Tam, who wrote under the name of Nhat Linh. After earning a law degree, he became a judicial official in Hanoi and a novelist. Under the pen name of Hoang Dao, he wrote a number of romantic novels during the interwar period, such as Bright Road (Con Duong Sang), The Ten Commandments (Muoi dien tam niem), and Slums and Huts (Bun lay nuoc dong).

Actively interested in politics, Hoang Dao was one of the main theoreticians with the so-called Tu Luc Van Doan (Self-Reliance Literary Group) and a member of the VNQDD. His writings reflected an admiration for Western culture, but at the same time a concern over social conditions in Vietnam and an implicit dislike of the French colonial regime. Hoang Dao died in 1948. (See Literature; Tu Luc Van Doan)

HOANG HOA THAM   (See De Tham).

HOANG NGOC PHACH (1896-1973). Well-known romantic novelist in colonial Vietnam. Educated in the traditional Chinese style, Hoang Ngoc Phach became a teacher at a secondary school in Hanoi. In 1925 his novel entitled To Tam (To Tam) took educated Vietnamese society by storm. Based on the French novel La Dame aux Camélias, To Tam was a story involving the conflict between young love and family duty, with the protagonist eventually dying of a broken heart. The novel evoked a brief rash of suicides among educated young Vietnamese women and inaugurated a flurry of novels in quoc ngu on romantic themes. It was his only novel. (See Literature)

HOANG QUOC VIET (1905- ?). Veteran Communist Party member and labor union official in Vietnam. Born Ha Ba Can in a worker family in 1905, Hoang Quoc Viet became active in revolutionary affairs in the mid-1920s, organizing protest activities in the coal mines of Tonkin. After joining Ho Chi Minh's Revolutionary Youth League in 1928, he left for France and worked as a sailor on a French ship, bringing Marxist materials to French Indochina and serving as a contact between the French Communist Party and the Vietnamese revolutionary movement.

After joining the Indochinese Communist Party (ICP) as a founding member in 1930, he was arrested by the French and sent to Poulo Condore, where he remained until his release in 1936. Thereafter he resumed his revolutionary activities and was elected to the Central Committee in 1941.

After World War II, Hoang Quoc Viet continued as an influential member of the Communist Party and occupied several leading positions in the Democratic Republic of Vietnam. In 1950 he was named chairman of the Vietnamese Confederation of Labor. Ten years later he became chief prosecutor of the People's Supreme Organ of Control and in 1973 was named chairman of the Vietnam Fatherland Front. Whether because of advancing age or suspected disagreement with the Party's current policies, he was dropped from the Central Committee at the Fifth National Congress in 1982.

HOANG VAN HOAN (1905-   ). Leading member of the Vietnamese communist movement who defected to China in 1979. Born in

Nghe An Province in 1905, Hoang Van Hoan joined Ho Chi Minh's Revolutionary Youth League in the late 1920s and became a founding member of the Indochinese Communist Party in 1930. Rising steadily in the ranks of the party, he served as Vietnamese ambassador to the People's Republic of China in the early 1950s, and became a member of the Politburo in 1957.

In 1976 he was dropped from his leading positions in the party, reportedly because of his pro-Chinese views. In 1979 he defected to China while on a trip abroad for medical reasons. He currently lives in Beijing, and is a frequent critic of the current government in Vietnam.

HOANG VAN THU (1906-1943). Leading figure in the Indochinese Communist Party (ICP) before World War II. Born in Lang Son Province of Tho parentage in 1906, Hoang Van Thu went to South China in 1926 to study at a training institute run by Ho Chi Minh's Revolutionary Youth League and became a member of the Indochinese Communist Party in 1930. After setting up the first party chapter in Cao Bang Province, he rose rapidly in the ranks and was named to the Central Committee in 1938 and secretary of Party's regional committee for North Vietnam a year later. He was active in the Viet Bac during the war years until captured by the French in August 1943. He was executed in May 1944 in Hanoi.

HOI AN (See Faifo).

HONG DUC CODE. Penal code adopted by the Le Dynasty during the reign of Le Thanh Tong (1460-1497). The Hong Duc Code, named after the dynastic period relating to the reign of Emperor Le Thanh Tong, was promulgated in 1483. Representing a comprehensive effort to systematize the civil and criminal laws in Vietnamese society, it combined a strong Confucian content, borrowed from China, with Vietnamese practice. For example, it followed Vietnamese custom in granting certain rights to women not followed in Chinese society. Women possessed property rights and shared equally with males in inheritance. Common law marriage were recognized as valid while wives were given the right in certain cases to divorce their husbands.

With respect to the land question, the Hong Duc Code attempted to provide a stronger legal basis for state ownership of the land, and followed the practice of the founder of the Le Dynasty, Le Thai To (1428-1433), in prescribing specific limits on the possession of land depending on the status, profession, or age of the individual.

The Hong Duc Code consisted of 721 articles drawn together in six books. Revised in subsequent years, it remained in force until the Nguyen Dynasty in the nineteenth century. (See Le Thanh Tong; Nguyen Dynasty)

THE HOPES OF YOUTH PARTY (Thanh Nien Cao Vong). Short-lived

political movement in early twentieth-century Vietnam. The inspiration of the group was the progressive Saigon intellectual Nguyen An Ninh (1900-1943), who hoped to spur the French to grant reforms and eventually grant independence to the Vietnamese. Ninh's speeches and writings attracted considerable support among patriotic intellectuals throughout Cochin China, who adopted as a name for their informal group the title of one of Nguyen An Ninh's most famous political speeches. Nguyen An Ninh did not wish to organize a formal political party, which in any event was illegal, and the organization collapsed after his arrest in 1926. It may have inspired the formation of a second party, the Youth Party (Dang Thanh Nien) formed by such radical intellectuals as Tran Huy Lieu, in Saigon in late 1925. (See Nguyen An Ninh; Youth Party)

HUE (Hue). Important city in Central Vietnam and capital of the Vietnamese Empire during the Nguyen Dynasty (1802-1945). Located on the short River of Perfume (Song Huong), Hue (originally known as Phu Xuan) first assumed importance as the capital of the Ngueyn Lords in the eighteenth century. In 1802 Emperor Gia Long, founder of the Nguyen Dynasty, moved the capital there from its existing location at Hanoi, probably in recognition of his desire to unite North and South for the first time since the Early Le Dynasty two hundred years before. It remained the imperial capital until 1945, when Emperor Bao Dai abdicated the throne and accepted the position of Supreme Advisor to the Democratic Republic of Vietnam (DRV).

Hue's imperial past is thoroughly stamped on the physical appearance of the city. The Imperial Palace and its adjacent buildings and gates, surrounded by extensive battlements patterned after the style of the seventeenth-century French architect Vauban, lie within the city on the north side of the river. In the western suburbs, also on the north bank, is the beautiful Thien Mu Pagoda. In the river valley to the southwest are the tombs of several nineteenth-century emperors.

Under the Republic of Vietnam (RVN), Hue became the capital of Thua Thien province and the headquarters of the politically active An Quang Buddhist Association. In 1968 the city was attacked and briefly occupied by North Vietnamese troops during the Tet Offensive. During the ensuing battle for control of the city, many buildings within the Imperial City were damaged. Today Hue is the capital of Binh Tri Thien province. Its population was estimated in 1979 at approximately 165,000. (See Bao Dai; Gia Long; Nguyen Dynasty; Tet Offensive)

HUNG KINGS (Hung Vuong). A series of semi-legendary rulers in prehistoric Vietnam. According to an early history of Vietnam, the Dai Viet Su Luoc, the Hung kings ruled a kingdom called Van Lang which had originally been founded in 2000 B.C. by the legendary hero Lac Lang Quan, the mythical founder of Vietnamese civilization. There were a series of eighteen kings, all blessed with abnormally long lives. The last had a beautiful daughter who was courted by two suitors, Son Tinh (a mountain spirit) and Thuy Tinh (a water spirit). The king awarded his daughter to the former, who had arrived first with sumptuous gifts. Thuy Tinh was angry at his rejection and every year unleashes floods to punish the Vietnamese people.

Although the legend of the Hung kings is clearly apocryphal, it contains elements of interest to historians. In fact, the military adventurer who overthrew the last of the Hung Kings in the third century B.C. united the valley peoples living in the Red River Delta (the Lac Viet) with the upland peoples living in the surrounding area (the Au Viet) in his new kingdom of Au Lac. The story of the water spirit wreaking his vengeance is an interesting explanation by the early Vietnamese for the disastrous floods and typhoons that have so often caused havoc on their land. (See Au Lac; Van Lang; Lac Long Quan)

HUNG VUONG (See Hung Kings).

HUYNH PHU SO (1919-1947). Founder of the messianistic Hoa Hao religious sect in South Vietnam. Born in 1919 in a rich peasant family from the village of Tan Chau in Chau Doc Province, Huynh Phu So led a normal childhood, but after an illness during adolescence went to live with a hermit who instructed him to sorcery, hypnotism, and acupuncture. In 1939 he declared himself to be a holy man and was interned at a psychiatric hospital for observation, where he allegedly converted his doctor.

After his release, Huynh Phu So rapidly gained followers for his new reformist Buddhist religion known as Hoa Hao (peace and plenty). The movement rapidly spread among the rural population in the lower Mekong Delta provinces of Rach Gia, Bac Giang and Bac Lieu. Anti-French in his political orientation, Huynh Phu So cooperated with the Japanese occupation authorities during World War II. In August 1945 he briefly joined forces with the Vietminh against the returning French, but rivalry between the two movements rapidly intensified, and in April 1947 Huynh Phu So was assassinated by the Vietminh. He was succeeded by Tran Van Soai, who rallied with most of his followers to the side of the French. (See Hoa Hao)

HUYNH TAN PHAT (1913-). Leading member of the National Liberation Front (NLF) in South Vietnam and currently an official in the Socialist Republic of Vietnam. Born in 1913 in My Tho, South Vietnam, Huynh Tan Phat was educated in architecture at the University of Hanoi. In the 1940s, while practicing architecture in Saigon, he became active in political activities promoted by the Indochinese Communist Party.

After the Geneva Agreement in 1954, Phat became a leading critic of the regime of Ngo Dinh Diem. Arrested twice and released, he turned to clandestine activities, serving as secretary general of the NLF and in 1969 was named prime minister of the Provisional Revolutionary Government.

After reunification in 1976, he was appointed a vice premier of the new Socialist Republic of Vietnam and chairman of the State Commission for Capital Construction. In 1982 he was named vice chairman of the State Council and was relieved of his other government positions. (See National Liberation Front)

HUYNH THUC KHANG (1876-1947). Anticolonial journalist and scholar in French-occupied Vietnam. Trained in the traditional educational system, Huynh Thuc Khang became involved in political activities in 1908, when he was arrested with Phan Chu Thinh for inciting violence during the peasant revolt in central Vietnam. After release from Puolo Condore he turned to journalism. During the 1920s he was occasionally an outspoken opponent of the French colonial regime and editor of the Hue-based newspaper, Tieng Dan (Voice of the People), published from 1927 to 1943. After World War II he was appointed Minister of the Interior in the Democratic Republic of Vietnam and served a brief term.

HUYNH TINH CUA (Paulus Cua) (? -1907). Prominent Vietnamese linguist and writer in late nineteenth-century Vietnam. A Catholic, Huynh Tinh Cua had Francophile tendencies and became an official in the colonial administration in Cochin China. For the next three decades, he was a prolific writer, helping to popularize quoc ngu, the roman alphabet transliteration of spoken Vietnamese, and contributed frequently to the quoc ngu newspaper, Gia Dinh Bao (Journal of Gia Dinh). (See Gia Dinh Bao; Truong Vinh Ky)

- I -

IA DRANG VALLEY, BATTLE OF. Major battle between U.S. combat troops and units of the People's Army of Vietnam (PAVN) in November 1965. Ia Drang Valley, located beneath Chu Pong Mountain near the Vietnam-Cambodian border in South Vietnam, was near one of the main entry points for infiltrators from North Vietnam into the South. In the fall of 1961 the newly-arrived U.S. First Cavalry Division engaged regular PAVN forces in heavy fighting in the area, resulting in high casualties on both sides. It was the first major engagement between U.S. and North Vietnamese troops in the Vietnam War. (See People's Army of Vietnam)

IMPERIAL ACADEMY (Quoc Tu Giam). Institute set up to train officials and candidates for the bureaucracy in traditional Vietnam. The academy was first established by the Ly Dynasty in 1076 and was located on the precincts of the Temple of Literature (Van Mieu) in the imperial capital of Thang Long (present-day Hanoi). At first it was intended solely as a school for sons of high mandarins and the bureaucracy (the original name, Quoc Te Giam, meant literally "Academy for the children of the state"). Renamed the Institute for National Studies (Quoc Hoc Vien) under the Tran

Dynasty, it began to serve as a training institute for candidates for the civil service exams from throughout Vietnam. In 1433, Le Thai To, founder of the Le Dynasty, opened it to selected commoners recommended by provincial institutes and renamed it the Thai Hoc Duong. After a period of decline in the eighteenth century, it was revived and moved to Hue, the new capital of the Nguyen Dynasty, in 1807. The original site of the academy in Hanoi is now a museum. (See Civil Service Examinations; Confucianism; Education; Temple of Literature)

INDOCHINA. Generic term often applied to territories under French colonial rule in nineteenth- and early twentieth-century Southeast Asia. Originally applied to all of mainland Southest Asia, it eventually referred to the colony of Cochin China and the protectorates of Annam, Tonkin, Laos, and Cambodia, known collectively as French Indochina. (See Indochinese Union)

INDOCHINESE COMMUNIST PARTY (Dong Duong Cong San Dang). Short-lived communist party formed by Vietnamese radicals in June 1929. The party was founded by North Vietnamese members of the regional committee of Ho Chi Minh's Revolutionary Youth League of Vietnam, who had become convinced that the League placed insufficient emphasis on the cause of social revolution in its effort to promote the cause of national independence. The result was an organization composed primarily of urban intellectuals and functionaries rather than peasants and workers.

In May 1929, representatives from North Vietnam led by the regional committee secretary Tran Van Cung withdrew from the First National Congress of the League in Hong Kong and returned to Hanoi, where they founded a new organization, the Indochinese Communist Party (Dong Duong Cong San Dong, or ICP). For several months, the ICP competed with the League, itself now transformed into an organization entitled the Annamese Communist Party (An Nam Cong San Dang). In February 1930, at a meeting chaired by Ho Chi Minh and held in Hong Kong, the two factions were dissolved and, together with remnants of the New Vietnamese Revolutionary Party, (Tan Viet Cach Menh Dang), merged into a new Vietnamese Communist Party (Dang Cong San Viet Nam). In October, the Party was renamed the Indochinese Communist Party (Dang Cong San Dong Duong). (See Ho Chi Minh; Indochinese Communist Party [Dang Cong San Dong Duong]; Revolutionary Youth League of Vietnam)

INDOCHINESE COMMUNIST PARTY, or ICP (Dang Cong San Dong Duong). Communist Party founded by Vietnamese revolutionaries in October 1930. The party had originally been entitled the Vietnamese Communist Party (Dang Cong San Viet Nam) at a founding meeting held in February 1930. But at the first plenary session of the Party Central Committee held in October in Hong Kong, the name was changed to Indochinese Communist Party (Dang Cong San Dong Duong) on the instructions of the Comintern in Moscow.

Soviet strategists believed that the Vietnamese revolutionaries were too weak to defeat the French colonial regime on their own and should link up with radical groups in Laos and Cambodia in a joint party representing all of Indochina.

In fact, the ICP was dominated by ethnic Vietnamese throughout its entire existence, although a few members of Khmer or Lao nationality began to join the Party in the late 1940s. Repressed by the French authorities after the Nghe-Tinh Soviet revolt in 1930-1931, the ICP revived during the Popular Front period (1936-1938) and became the primary political organization opposed to French rule in Vietnam. In 1939, it was again suppressed after the signing of the Nazi-Soviet Non-aggression Treaty.

In 1941, an ICP Central Committee meeting held at Pac Bo declared the formation of the so-called League for the Independence of Vietnam, or Vietminh Front. Although broadly nationalist in its program the Front was under firm ICP control. In August 1945, the Vietminh seized power over most of Vietnam and declared the establishment of a provisional democratic republic, with Ho Chi Minh as president. In the fall, the ICP declared itself abolished in order to strengthen the new government's appeal to moderates, although it continued to operate in secret.

In February 1951, during the Franco-Vietminh war, the ICP changed its name to the Vietnamese Workers' Party (Dang Lao Dong Viet Nam), while independent People's Revolutionary Parties were established in Laos and Cambodia. The change was made to satisfy rising national sensitivity among Lao and Khmer members of the ICP. (See August Revolution; Ho Chi Minh; Nghe Tinh Soviets; Pac Bo Plenum; Revolutionary Youth League of Vietnam; Vietnamese Workers' Party)

INDOCHINESE CONGRESS. Popular movement promoted by Indochinese Communist Party (ICP) and other anticolonial groups in colonial Vietnam in late 1930s. The movement originated with the stated intention of the Popular Front government under Prime Minister Leon Blum in France to send a governmental commission of inquiry to the French colonies to consider reforms. In Indochina, various political parties and groups attempted to solicit popular feeling in preparation for the visit. The ICP itself formed so-called "Committees of Action" (Uy Ban Hanh Dong) in offices, factories, and villages to draw up a list of popular demands for presentation to the inspection team. Concerned over the rising political unrest, the colonial authorities closed down the action committees. In June 1937, the French government cancelled the visit of the Commission of Inquiry. (See Brevié, Jules; Popular Front)

INDOCHINESE FEDERATION (Fédération Indochinoise). A concept announced by the French government of General Charles de Gaulle in March 1945. According to General De Gaulle's plan, the existing Indochinese Union would be replaced with a federation of five quasi-independent states of Indochina (Cochin China,

Annam, Tonkin, Cambodia, and Laos) as part of a new French Union planned for France and its colonies after the end of World War II. The Federation would have a federal government presided over by a governor-general appointed in Paris and a cabinet composed of citizens of both France and the Indochinese countries. Legislative bodies in each nation would vote on taxes, the budget, and other legislation of primarily local concern. Foreign affairs and defense would be handled essentially by the French government in Paris.

The Federation was briefly put in place at the second Dalat Conference, held in August 1946, but events in Indochina impeded any efforts to create a meaningful political and administration structure, and the concept was superseded with the creation of three separate Associated States in Vietnam, Laos, and Cambodia by the Elysée Agreements in March 1949. (See Dalat Conference; d'Argenlieu, Thierry; Elysée Agreements)

INDOCHINESE FEDERATION (Lien Bang Dong Duong). Concept developed by the Indochinese Communist Party (ICP) in the 1930s for the creation of a federation composed of Vietnam, Laos, and Cambodia after the victory of revolutionary forces in those countries. The original idea of the Federation probably came from Moscow, where strategists of global revolution were convinced that social revolutions could not succeed in small states. They therefore advised Vietnamese revolutionary leaders to unite with their counterparts in Laos and Cambodia to seek liberation from French rule. For the next two decades, documents issued by the ICP periodically mentioned the possible future formation on a voluntary basis of a so-called Indochinese Federation between the three countries after the eviction of the French.

In recent years, official spokesmen for the Socialist Republic of Vietnam have maintained that the concept of an Indochinese Federation was expressly abandoned at the Second National Congress of the party in 1951. At that time, the ICP divided into three parties representing the revolutionary movements in each country. At the close of the Vietnam War in 1975, the Hanoi regime did not attempt to resurrect the concept of a federation, but spoke instead of "special relationship" between the three countries created by history and revolutionary experience. Critics have charged that the "special relationship," which now exists among the three countries, is simply the Indochinese Federation under a new name. (See Indochinese Communist Party; Vietnamese Workers' Party)

INDOCHINESE UNION (Union de l'Indochine). Administrative structure for French rule in Indochina. The Union emerged from the Office of the Governor-general which had been set up under the Ministry of Colonies in 1887. At first the powers of the governor-general were limited to coordinating the separate activities of the governor of Cochin China and the resident superiors in Annam, Tonkin, Laos, and Cambodia. Under Governor-general Paul

Doumer (1897-1902), however, the office gained considerable
stature and authority with the establishment of a number of
offices and a centrally-controlled budget and a major factor in
the affairs of the Union. The Indochinese Union was abolished
after World War II with the establishment of separate Associated
States in Vietnam, Laos and Cambodia. (See Doumer, Paul;
Elysée Agreements)

INDRAPURA. Early capital of the state of Champa in Central Vietnam. Located at Dong Duong, near the town of An Hoa in
present-day Quang Nam Province, it was the capital of the Cham
Empire from the ninth century until 982, when it was destroyed
during a Vietnamese invasion led by Le Hoan. A new king of
Champa moved the capital south to Vijaya, in modern Binh Dinh
Province. Indrapura and its surrounding area were integrated
into the Vietnamese Empire during the fifteenth century (See
Champa; March to the South).

The architecture of the Indrapura period, called the Dong
Duong style, reflected both Khmer and Javanese influence and is
considered to represent the zenith of Cham creative art. (See
Champa; Lin-yi; Vijaya)

INDUSTRY. At the time of the French conquest in the mid-nineteenth
century, Vietnam was still an essentially agricultural society, and
industry was at a relatively primitive stage of development. The
stated objective of French rule was to introduce Vietnam to modern
technology, but although the French did take the initial steps to
provide Vietnam with a modern transportation network, on the
whole they did little to create an industrial sector, preferring to
use Vietnam as a source of raw materials and a market for French
manufactured goods.

After the Geneva Conference in 1954, the governments that
replaced the French in the North and South did little to rectify
the situation. In the North, the Democratic Republic of Vietnam
adopted an ambitious program of industrialization with the inauguration of the First Five-year Plan in 1961, but lack of capital
and technology, and the intensification of the war in the South,
derailed plans for economic development. In South Vietnam, economic assistance from the United States and other capitalist
countries led to the emergence of a modest light industrial sector
based primarily on the production of consumer goods, but the
lack of industrial resources and the disruption caused by the war
represented insuperable obstacles to rapid industrialization.

After reunification in 1975, the Hanoi regime embarked on a
major effort to promote socialist industrialization with the Second
Five-year Plan, launched in 1976. But inadequate capital, lack
of energy resources, agricultural failures, and a primitive infrastructure continue to hinder the growth of the industrial sector,
which remains based primarily on light industry. Current policy
emphasizes the growth of agriculture and production of consumer
goods while long-term plans for the development of energy resources

such as coal, oil, and electricity, are in the process of implementation. (See Agriculture; Energy Resources)

INTERNATIONAL CONTROL COMMISSION (ICC). Supervisory commission set up by the Geneva Agreement to oversee the cease-
fire in Indochina in 1954. It was composed of Canada (representing the West), India (representing the neutral countries),
and Poland (representing the socialist camp). The ICC was hampered by the failure of both sides to adhere to the letter of the
Agreement and by the inability of the delegations of the three
countries themselves to agree on the definition of the issues.
By the early 1960s the Geneva Agreement, and the functions
of the ICC itself, had become virtually a dead letter. (See
Demilitarized Zone; Geneva Agreement)

IRON TRIANGLE. Base area used by revolutionary armed forces in
South Vietnam during the Vietnam War. Called "Zone D" by
strategic planners in the Democratic Republic of Vietnam, the Iron
Triangle was a densely forested area about thirty miles north of
Saigon that was heavily fortified by revolutionary forces at the
outset of the war. In January 1967, U.S. combat forces launched
a major assault into the area to destroy enemy emplacements and
destroy the ground cover that made the area ideal for insurgency
operations. The attack, known as Operation Cedar Falls, removed
the potential threat to Saigon but incurred resentment from much
of the local population, which was forcibly evacuated in order to
transform the area into a free-fire zone.

- J -

JARAI (also known as Djarai or Gialai). A non-Vietnamese tribal
people living in the Central Highlands of South Vietnam. Numbering slightly over 150,000, the Jarai are one of the dominant
minority peoples. They are probably of Malayo-Polynesian extraction and speak a Cham language. Their religion is spirit
worship. Administration is at the village level, and most live
in joint family units.
    In precolonial times, the Jarai accepted tributary status to the
Nguyen lords in South Vietnam. After the French conquest, they
were granted autonomy status within French Indochina. During
the Vietnam War, the Jarai opposed assimilation by the Republic
of Vietnam and were an active force in the United Front for the
Liberation of Oppressed Peoples (FULRO) which fought for tribal
autonomy in South Vietnam, but were also distrustful of the Hanoi
supported revolutionary movement.
    Since 1975, the Socialist Republic of Vietnam has attempted
to assimilate the Jarai peoples into Vietnamese society and introduce
them to settled agriculture. There were reports in the early 1980
that Jarai groups were active in a revived FULRO organization
that continues to oppose Vietnamese authority. (See United Front

for the Liberation of Oppressed Peoples; Rhadé; Tribal Minorities)

JOURNALISM. Newspapers and journals in the modern Western sense did not exist in Vietnam until after the French conquest in the mid-nineteenth century. The first journal published in quoc ngu, the roman transliteration of the Vietnamese spoken language, was the Journal of Gia Dinh (Gia Dinh Bao), issued under the auspices of the colonial government. It first appeared in Saigon in 1865. The first privately-published quoc ngu newspaper of note was the News from the Six Provinces (Luc Tinh Tan Van) published in Saigon by the journalist Gilbert Chieu. The first journal in quoc ngu to be published in Tonkin was Nguyen Van Vinh's Indochinese Review (Dong Duong Tap Chi), which opened its doors in 1913. The 1920s and 1930s saw the publication of a number of newspapers and periodicals appearing in Vietnamese, French, or Chinese in all three regions of Vietnam.

Under the colonial regime, strict limitations were placed on the discussion of political subjects. Many, like Pham Quynh's Wind from the South (Nam Phong) were published under official sponsorship and reflected the views of the colonial administration. Those that contravened the restrictions of censorship were quickly closed down. During the period of Popular Front in the late 1930s, however, controls were relaxed and a number of new newspapers appeared, including some published by the Indochinese Communist Party. They were permitted to undertake cautious criticism of government policies until the approach of World War II in 1939.

After the granting of independence in 1954, journalism developed rapidly in both North and South Vietnam, although the governments in both regions imposed strict North and South Vietnam, although the governments in both regions imposed strict censorship on the discussion of subjects of a controversial or political nature. (See Cloche Fêlée, La; Dong Duong Tap Chi; Gia Dinh Bao; Lutte, La; Nam Phong)

- K -

KAO P'IEN. Chinese general who defeated the forces of the Nan Chao kingdom in occupied North Vietnam (then known as the Protectorate of Annam) in the mid-ninth century. After defeating the invading Nan Chao army, Kao remained in Vietnam and earned the respect of the local population for his political and economic policies before his departure in 865. Although Kao P'ien reestablished the authority of the T'ang Empire in China over its dependency in the South, the Dynasty was now in a period of steady decline, resulting in increased degree of autonomy for local administrators in Vietnam.

KHUC THUA DU   (See Ngo Quyen).

KHAI DINH (reigned 1916-1925). Emperor of Vietnam under the
French colonial regime. Born the son of Emperor Dong Khanh in
1884, Khai Dinh replaced Emperor Ham Nghi on the throne when
the latter was sent in exile to the island of Reunion in 1916. He
was a pliant tool of the French and was strongly criticized by
the reformist Phan Chu Trinh for his failure to improve conditions
in Vietnam. He died in November 1925 and was succeeded by
his son, the young Bao Dai. (See Bao Dai; convention of 1925;
Ham Nghi; Phan Chu Trinh)

KHAI HUNG (1898-1940). Pen-name of Tran Khanh Du, well-known
romantic novelist in colonial Vietnam. Born in 1898 in a scholar-
gentry family in Hai Duong Province, Khai Hung attended the
famous Lycée Albert Sarraut in Hanoi. After becoming a writer,
he joined the Tu Luc Van Doan (Self-Reliance Literary Group),
an organization of romantic novelists established by Nhat Linh
to promote the Westernization of Vietnamese literature and society.
Many of his novels contained a biting critique of the emptiness
and hypocrisy of the upper class in colonial Vietnam.
  By the late 1930s, Khai Hung's activities moved from literature
to politics. He joined the pro-Japanese Dai Viet Party during
World War II and was assassinated, reportedly by the Vietminh,
in 1947. (See Literature; Nhat Linh; Tu Luc Van Doan)

KHAI TRI TIEN DUC (Association pour la Formation Intellectuelle et
Morale des Annamites, or AFIMA). Cultural society formed with
official encouragement in colonial Vietnam. Formed by Pham
Quynh, Nguyen Van Vinh and other moderate reformists in 1922,
AFIMA's aim was to promote East-West collaboration and the in-
troduction of Western ideas and literary works into Vietnam. Some
Vietnamese viewed AFIMA and its mouthpiece, Nam Phong journal,
as a tool of the French. (See Literature; Nam Phong; Nguyen
Van Vinh; Pham Quynh)

KHMER KROM. Inhabitants of Khmer (Cambodian) descent living in
South Vietnam. Most are descendants of settlers who had lived
in the lower region of the Mekong River Delta before the Vietnamese
conquest in the seventeenth century. The majority are Theravada
Buddhists and live in villages isolated from the surrounding Viet-
namese community.
  There were an estimated 300,000 Khmer Krom living in South
Vietnam at the end of the Vietnam War. According to reports,
some may have taken part in the Vietnamese invasion of Democratic
Kampuchea in December 1978. An unknown number have resettled
in Kampuchea since the establishment of the People's Republic of
Kampuchea in January 1979.

KIEN PHUC (reigned 1883-1884). Emperor of Vietnam in Nguyen
Dynasty. (See Ham Nghi; Tu Duc)

KLOBUKOWSKI, ANTONI-WLADISLAS (1855-1934). Governor-general

of French Indochina from 1908 until 1911. A career diplomat and a protégé of his predecessor Paul Beau, he first served in Indochina in the early 1880s. After several posts in the diplomatic service, he was appointed governor-general of Indochina at a moment when social unrest had reached a momentary peak in Vietnam with peasant riots in Central Vietnam and rising dissent among intellectuals sparked by the activities and writings of Phan Boi Chau in Japan and the Tonkin Free School in Hanoi. Klobukowski attempted to crack down on the unrest by closing the University of Hanoi and the advisory assembly in Tonkin, both set up by his predecessor Paul Beau. At the same time he attempted to eliminate some of the root causes of the disorder by rectifying abuses in the infamous state monopolies of alcohol, opium and salt--an effort that aroused the ire of many French residents in Indochina and led to his dismissal in 1911. (See Beau, Paul; Tonkin Free School)

KY HOA, BATTLE OF (also known as Chi Hoa). Military battle during which French forces defeated Vietnamese troops in the struggle for control of South Vietnam in February 1861. When the French launched their second attack in the area of Saigon in early 1861, General Nguyen Tri Phuong established a defensive bastion southwest of the city, manned by more than 20,000 Vietnamese troops.

The French attack began in late February. Although the French had fewer than 5,000 troops, General Nguyen Tri Phuong adopted a defensive strategy, and the French were victorious in two days. The French later expanded their advance into neighboring areas in the face of guerrilla resistance led by Truong Dinh. (See Nguyen Tri Phuong; Treaty of Saigon; Truong Dinh)

- L -

LABOR UNIONS. The Vietnamese labor movement emerged during the period of French colonial rule, when progressive intellectuals, many of whom had first become involved in labor activity in France during World War I, began to organize Vietnamese workers in large cities like Hanoi, Haiphong, Saigon, and the industrial city of Vinh. The first labor organization was formed in Saigon in 1920 by Ton Duc Thang, later to become a prominent member of the Indochinese Communist Party.

From the outset, the Communist Party was actively involved in organizing Vietnamese workers, who numbered only about 200,000 before World War II. In 1929, a forerunner of the Indochinese Communist Party formed local "Red Workers' Associations" to mobilize workers to support the revolution. Within a year, about 6,000 workers had become members. Although suppressed during the Nghe-Tinh Revolt, the workers' movement revived during the Popular Front Period in the late 1930s.

In July 1946, a few months after the founding under Communist Party leadership of the Democratic Republic of Vietnam

(DRV), the Vietnamese Confederation of Labor Unions was established in Hanoi. Including virtually all blue collar workers
in the DRV, the Confederation reached a membership of over
400,000 by 1960, and an estimated 3.7 million members in 1983.
As in all Marxist-Leninist systems, the labor movement is under
strict party supervision. The Confederation is a member of the
World Federation of Trade Unions, a global organization most of
whose unions are from countries belonging to the socialist
community of nations.

LAC LONG QUAN (Dragon Lord of Lac). A legendary figure considered the mythical founder of Vietnamese civilization. According
to Vietnamese mythology, Lac Long Quan had his original home
in the sea, but came to the Red River Delta to defeat evil spirits
and bring advanced civilization to the people of the area. Then
he returned to the sea, promising to return if needed. Later
the region of the Delta was conquered by a warlord from the
North. Lac Long Quan returned, drove the invader back to
China, and kidnapped the latter's wife, Au Co, (in some sources,
Au Co was the warlord's daughter) and made her his consort.
Au Co gave birth to 100 sons, one of whom became the first of
the Hung Kings, the rulers of the first Vietnamese kingdom of
Van Lang. Lac Long Quan then returned once again to the sea,
while Au Co and her children became the progenitors of the
Vietnamese race.

The legend of Lac Long Quan, while clearly in the realm of
myth, has strong symbolic significance for the Vietnamese, pointing out the linkage between land and sea that has historically
characterized the Vietnamese nation, and indicating the constant
danger of conquest from China. Later Vietnamese historians
attempted to link the legend of Lac Long Quan with Chinese
tradition, identifying him as an immediate descendant of the
mythical Chinese figure of Shen Nung. (See Hung Kings; Van
Lang)

LAC LORDS. Indigenous landed aristocracy in early Vietnam. This
class of hereditary nobles originally emerged under the Van Lang
dynasty during the first millenium B.C. They apparently coexisted in a feudalistic ruler-vassal relationship with the kings of
Van Lang and had considerable power over the peasants in their
domains, which were located in the region of the Red River Delta.
The peasants were organized in communes (xa), and were required
to provide their local manor lord with grain, handicraft goods,
and conscript labor.

The authority and status of the Lac Lords survived the initial
Chinese conquest of the independent Vietnamese state in the second
century B.C., and many apparently retained their economic and
political power until the Trung Sisters rebellion in A.D. 39-43.
After suppressing the revolt, Chinese General Ma Yuan destroyed
the power of the Lac Lords, killing many and dispossessing others
of their estates. He then replaced the local aristocracy with an

appointed bureaucracy, although some may have survived as local officials. (See Au Lac; Trieu Da; Ma Yuan)

LAC PEOPLE. The original name for the ethnic Vietnamese, living in the Red River Delta in what is today North Vietnam. Most scholars believe that the Lac peoples represent an admixture of Australoid peoples living in the Red River Delta during the Paleolithic and Neolithic periods and Mongoloid migrants who entered the area at a later date. During the first millenium B.C., the Lac formed an advanced Bronze Age civilization which called itself the kingdom of Van Lang. In the third century B.C., the Kingdom of Van Lang was replaced by a new state called Au Lac, composed of the lowland valley peoples (known as Lac Viet) and hill tribes surrounding the Red River Delta (Au Viet).

The Lac peoples were primarily rice farmers who lived in lowland regions surrounding the estuary of the Red River. They were distinguished by their habit of chewing betelnut and lacquering their teeth in black. After the Chinese conquest of the Red River region in the first century B.C., the term "Lac" was gradually replaced by the term "Yueh" (in Vietnamese, Viet), used by the Chinese at that time to describe all the non-Chinese people living in Southeastern China and mainland Southeast Asia. (See Au Lac; Van Lang; Vietnamese People; Yueh)

LAC YUEH (Lac Viet). Term used by Chinese historians during the Han dynasty to describe the Vietnamese peoples living in the region of the Red River Delta. It is sometimes also used to refer to the lowland Lac peoples who were joined with the Au Viet peoples living in the hilly uplands surrounding the Red River Delta into the state of Au Lac in the late third century B.C. (See Au Lac; Lac Peoples; Vietnamese Peoples; Yueh)

LADY TRIEU (Be Trieu, or Trieu Au). Famous woman rebel leader during the period of the Chinese occupation of Vietnam. Trieu Thi Trinh, known in history as Ba Trieu, or Lady Trieu, was born in the prefecture of Cuu Chan, in what is today Thanh Hoa province of North Vietnam, the daughter of a village chief. At that time Cuu Chan was seething with political and social unrest because of unhappiness with Chinese occupation policies and the presence of the aggressive state of Champa to the south. When in A.D. 248 Champa fought Chinese troops near the border of Cuu Chan, the local population, led by Lady Trieu, erupted in revolt. After several months of battle, the rebels were suppressed, and Lady Trieu was killed.

The memory of Lady Trieu and the revolt she inspired became famous in Vietnamese history and legend. Popular belief described her as leading her followers to battle on the back of an elephant. She is today one of the leading figures in the pantheon of Vietnamese heroes struggling against the Chinese invader.

LAM SON UPRISING. Insurrection against Chinese occupation led by Le Loi in 1418-1427. (See Le Loi; Nguyen Trai)

LAND REFORM. Land reform has been a key political issue in Vietnam since the colonial era, when the commercialization of land and the development of export crops changed the economics of landholding in Indochina. The issue was particularly sensitive in South Vietnam, where the draining of the swamps in the Mekong River Delta created a new class of absentee landlords who owned an estimated half of the total irrigable land in Cochin China.

After the departure of the French in 1954, the Vietnamese governments in both the North and the South enacted land reform legislation in an effort to resolve the inequality in landholdings in the countryside. In the Democratic Republic of Vietnam (DRV) a major redistribution of agricultural land took place in 1955 and 1956 which resulted in the transfer of land to more than half the farm families in the country. The program was marred, however, by revolutionary excesses in the form of executions of local landlords who allegedly owed "blood debts" to the people, leading in 1956 to the demotion of a number of leading figures in the Party and the government. Two years later, the DRV introduced a new program to collectivize the countryside.

In South Vietnam, where inequality of landholding was more prevalent, the regime of Ngo Dinh Diem introduced its own land reform program in 1956. But maximum limits on landholding were set quite high, and loopholes enabled many to evade the regulations. By the end of the decade only about ten percent of all eligible peasants had received land through the program. In 1969 the government of President Nguyen Van Thieu enacted a much more comprehensive "land to the tiller" program which essentially abolished the problem of tenancy in the South.

After the fall of Saigon in 1975, the Hanoi regime announced that, because of the relative absence of landlordism in the southern provinces, no new land reform program would be required. Collectivization of land began in the South in 1978 and had not been completed by the beginning of the Fourth Five-year Plan in 1986. (See Collectivization of Agriculture; Democratic Republic of Vietnam; Production Collectives; Production Solidarity Teams; Republic of Vietnam; Socialist Republic of Vietnam)

LATER LE DYNASTY (Nha Hau Le) (1428-1788). Third great dynasty which ruled in Vietnam after the restoration of independence in tenth century, and distinguished from the so-called Early Le, which ruled from 980 to 1009. The Le came to power in 1428, when the rebel leader Le Loi drove out the Chinese occupation regime and established a new dynasty. He himself became emperor under the reign title Le Thai To (1428-1433). For the remainder of the fifteenth century, the Le was blessed with strong rulers and good government. During the reign of the greatest of the Le monarchs, Le Thanh Tong (1460-1497), the Vietnamese Empire (then known as Dai Viet, or Great Viet) developed in wealth and power and expanded its territory at the expense of the neighboring kingdoms of Champa and Laos. Under Le Thanh Tong, the influence of Confucian ideology and institutions gradually replaced that of Buddhism, which had been dominant under the Tran (1225–1400).

After the death of Le Thanh Tong, the competence of Le rulers began to decline and in 1527, the Le Dynasty was overthrown by Mac Dang Dung. Supporters of the Le continued to fight for its restoration, and did succeed in overthrowing the Mac regime in 1592. But the Le monarchs were now mere figureheads, with political power dominated by two great families, the Trinh Lords and the Nguyen Lords. The so-called "restored Le Dynasty" (Nha Le Trung Hung) lasted until 1788, when it was overthrown by the Tay Son Rebellion. (See Le Loi; Le Thanh Tong; Mac Dang Dung; Nguyen Kim; Nguyen Hoang; Nguyen Lords; Trinh Kiem; Trinh Lords)

LE CHIEU TONG (reigned 1516–1524). Ninth emperor of the Later Le Dynasty. (See Le Uy Muc; Mac Dang Dung)

LE DAI HANH (See Le Hoan).

LE DUAN (1908–1986). Leading member of the Vietnamese Communist movement and general secretary of the Party from 1960 until his death in 1986. Le Duan was born in 1908, the son of a rail clerk in Quang Tri province, Central Vietnam. He entered Ho Chi Minh's Revolutionary Youth League in 1928, and became a founding member of the Indochinese Communist Party (ICP) in 1930. Arrested for seditious activities in 1931, he was released five years later and rose rapidly in the ICP, becoming a member of the Central Committee in 1939.

In 1940 Le Duan was rearrested and spent the war years in Poulo Condore prison. Released in 1945, he served briefly under president Ho Chi Minh in Hanoi and then was sent to South Vietnam where he became secretary of the Party's leading bureau in the South, the Central Office for South Vietnam (COSVN). After the Geneva Conference he remained in South Vietnam and became a vocal spokesman within Party councils for a more active effort to seek the overthrow of the Saigon regime.

In 1957, Le Duan was recalled to Hanoi to become a member of the Politburo and de facto general secretary of the Party after the demotion of Truong Chinh. In 1960 his position was formalized and, with Ho Chi Minh ageing and in poor health, Le Duan became the leading figure in the Party. A staunch advocate of the revolutionary effort in the South, he excelled in the art of reconciling rival factions within the Politburo and maintaining an independent Vietnamese posture in the Sino-Soviet dispute.

After 1975, Le Duan led the Party into an intimate relationship with the Soviet Union and a bitter dispute with China. Under his leadership, the Party encountered severe difficulties in

promoting economic growth and the construction of a socialist
society, leading to growing criticism of the "old men" at the top.
Amidst rumors of impending retirement because of poor health,
he died in July 1986 and was replaced by his contemporary and
reputed rival Truong Chinh. (See Indochinese Communist Party;
Truong Chinh; Vietnamese Communist Party)

LE DUC THO (1910-   ) (real name, Phan Dinh Khai). Chief
Vietnamese negotiator at the Paris peace talks and leading figure in the Vietnamese Communist Party. Born in a scholar-gentry
family in Nam Ha province in 1910, he attended the Thang Long
School in Hanoi, where he was reportedly taught by Vo Nguyen
Giap. Entering the Indochinese Communist Party shortly after
its founding in 1930, he was arrested by the French and served
time at Poulo Condore and other prisons in colonial Vietnam.
   During World War II, Le Duc Tho reportedly served in the
liberated zone north of the Red River Delta. After 1945 he
served as Le Duan's deputy in the Party's regional bureau in
South Vietnam and allegedly spent time with the revolutionary
movement in Cambodia. He was summoned to Hanoi after the
Geneva Conference of 1954, where he was named to the Politburo
and headed the Party's Organization Department for twenty years.
He came to public attention in the late 1960s as Hanoi's chief
delegate to the Paris peace talks.
   After the end of the war, Le Duc Tho was a prominent member of the Party's veteran leadership and was often rumored as
a possible successor to Le Duan as general secretary. But at
the Sixth Party Congress in December 1986, he was dropped
from the Politburo and, with Truong Chinh and Pham Van Dong,
named an "adviser" to the Central Committee. (See Indochinese
Communist Party; Paris Agreement; Vietnamese Communist Party)

LE DYNASTY (See Early Le Dynasty; Later Le Dynasty).

LE HIEN TONG (1497-1504). Fifth emperor of the Later Le Dynasty.
(See Le Thanh Tong)

LE HOAN (Le Dai Hanh) (reigned 980-1005). Founder of the short-
lived Early Le Dynasty in eleventh-century Vietnam. Le Hoan,
a native of the province of Ai, along the Ma River south of the
Red River Delta, became commander-in-chief of the armies of
Emperor Dinh Bo Linh, founder of the Dinh Dynasty. On the
death of Dinh Bo Linh in 979, the state fell into chaos as the
new king was a child of five. Le Hoan, who had reportedly been
the queen's lover, seized power in 980 and declared himself king
of a new Le Dynasty, under the reign name Le Dai Hanh.
   Le Hoan's 25-year reign was marked by foreign wars. The
Sung Dynasty in China had hoped to take advantage of the instability in Vietnam by launching an invasion of its ex-dependency,
but Le Hoan defeated the Chinese armies in 981 and obtained official Chinese recognition of Vietnamese independence. He then

turned his attention to the South and waged a successful campaign against the kingdom of Champa, seizing some of its territory and forcing it to move its capital from Indrapura (in
present-day Quang Nam) to Vijaya, farther to the south.

On the domestic scene, the reign of Le Hoan was marked by
efforts to strengthen the fragile structure of the infant Vietnamese state. He relied to a considerable degree on his sons,
several of whom he appointed as governors of key provinces. Le
Hoan died in 1005, leading to fratricidal strife among his heirs. The
victor himself died two years later, leaving an infant son as successor. Through intrigues at court, a mandarin by the name of
Ly Cong Uan was placed on the throne and founded a new Ly
Dynasty. (See Early Le Dynasty; Ly Thai To)

LE HONG PHONG (1902-1942). Prominent member of the Indochinese
Communist Party (ICP) in the 1930s. Born in Nghe An Province
in 1902, he was working at an auto repair shop in Hanoi in 1918
when he was recruited by a member of Phan Boi Chau's Vietnamese Restoration Society to study abroad. In 1924 he joined
the radical Association of Like Minds (Tam Tam Xa) in South
China, and Ho Chi Minh's Revolutionary Youth League a year
later. After studying at the Whampoa Academy, in 1926 he was
sent to the Soviet Union to attend aviation school and served as
a liaison between the Comintern and the League Leadership in
South China.

After the arrest of Ho Chi Minh by British police in Hong
Kong in 1931, Le Hong Phong became the de facto leader of the
ICP and the head of its Overseas Leadership Committee (Ban Chi
Huy Hai Ngoai) set up in South China as the provisional leading
organ of the Party. In the summer of 1935 he attended the
Seventh Congress of the Comintern and returned to Vietnam the
following year to pass on its instructions to the newly-constituted
Central Committee. He was arrested by French authorities in
1940 and sent to Poulo Condore prison, where he died of torture
in 1942. (See Association of Like Minds; Indochinese Communist
Party; Nghe Tinh Revolt)

LE HONG SON (also known as Hong Son) (1899-1933). Leading
revolutionary militant and founding member of the Indochinese
Communist Party in 1930. Born in Nghe An Province in 1899,
Le Hong Son (real name Le Van Phan) reportedly became a revolutionary in his adolescence, when he joined Phan Boi Chau's
Vietnamese Restoration Society. In 1924 he helped to organize
the Association of Like Minds (Tam Tam Xa) in South China. One
year later he became a member of Ho Chi Minh's Revolutionary
Youth League and the Chinese Communist Party (CCP). Jailed
in the late 1920s, he was released in December 1928 and attended
the National Congress of the League, held in Hong Kong the
following May. In 1930 he became a member of the new Indochinese
Communist Party and, according to French sources, its liaison with
the CCP.

In September 1932 Le Hong Son was arrested by French police

in the International Settlement in Shanghai, where he was allegedly attempting to restore liaison activities between the CCP
and communist parties in Southeast Asia. He was convicted in
a French court in Vinh of assassinating two government agents
during the 1920s, and was executed in February 1933. (See
Association of Like Minds; Revolutionary Youth League of Vietnam; Indochinese Communist Party)

LE LOI (Le Thai To) (1385-1433). Founder of the Le Dynasty (1428-
1788) in fifteenth-century Vietnam. Le Loi was born in 1385,
the son of a wealthy landlord in Lam Son village, Thanh Hoa
Province. He was successful in the civil service examinations
and entered the imperial bureaucracy under the brief Ho Dynasty,
which succeeded the Tran in 1400, but resigned after the country
was restored to Chinese rule in 1407.

Returning to his native village, Le Loi began to organize a
resistance movement to overthrow Chinese occupation and restore
Vietnamese independence. Calling himself the Pacification King
(Binh Dinh Vuong), he gathered around himself several hundred
close followers, including the scholar-patriot Nguyen Trai, and
inaugurated a struggle for national liberation.

At first conditions were difficult, but Chinese occupation
policies were harsh, and Vietnamese of many walks of life gathered
to his standard. Le Loi's was by no means the only anti-Chinese
rebel organization in Vietnam, but it gradually became the most
effective movement opposed to Chinese rule. A brief truce was
negotiated in 1423, but war resumed on the death of Chinese
Emperor Yung Lo the following year, and the rebels, from their
base in modern day Nghe Tinh province, gradually seized control
of most of the country south of the Red River Delta. In 1426,
rebel forces won a major battle over the Chinese west of the
modern day capital of Hanoi. Two years later Chinese forces
evacuated Vietnam.

Le Loi had fought in the name of restoring the Tran Dynasty
(1225-1400) to power in order to provide China with a means of
saving face, and for that purpose had kept members of the Tran
family in his entourage. After victory was secured, however,
Le Loi was persuaded to accept the throne, and became founding
emperor Le Thai To of what became known as the "Later Le"
dynasty.

The key problem facing his new imperial administration was to
reduce the size of the great landed estates that had been owned
by nobles and high mandarins under the Tran. To do so, Le
Thai To returned to the concept of the "equal field" system
that had first been put into operation by the early emperors of
the Ly Dynasty (1009-1225) and set established limits on the
amount of land that could be possessed by individuals, depending on their age and status. Le Thai To also initiated a number
of reforms in the area of administration, the civil service, the
military, and the system of justice. He died in 1433 at the age
of 49. (See Later Le Dynasty; Ho Dynasty; Nguyen Trai)

LE MYRE DE VILERS. French governor of Cochin China from 1879
to 1883. Although he had previously been a naval officer, he
was the first civilian governor of Cochin China. In 1882 he dis-
patched Captain Henri Rivière to North Vietnam to extend French
influence into the area, but was reluctant to support Rivière's
belligerent actions and resigned from office when his remon-
strances to Paris were rejected. (See Rivière, Captain Henri)

LE QUY DON (1726-1784?). Historian of the Le Dynasty (1428-1788)
in Vietnam. A native of Son Nam District, Thai Binh Province,
Le Quy Don was born in 1726. His father was a holder of the
doctorate in the civil service examinations, and an official of
the Le Dynasty. Le Quy Don himself passed the metropolitan
examination in 1752 and entered the bureaucracy. As an official Le Quy Don was active as a provincial governor, where he
was known for his firm adherence to the principles of Confucianism. He strongly repressed rebellious elements, but showed
some sympathy for the needs of the common people, attempting
to reduce bureaucratic corruption and inefficiency. He also
served as a diplomat, leading a Vietnamese mission to the Ch'ing
court in China in 1761.
     Le Quy Don is best known as one of the most prominent scholars
and historians of eighteenth-century Vietnam. Among his historical writings were Le Trieu Trong Su (A Comprehensive History of the Le Dynasty) and Phu Bien Tap Luc, a six-volume
collection of geographical, economical, and cultural information
on collections of miscellaneous information on various subjects from
the Tran to the Le Dynasties. His interests were encyclopedic,
and he wrote in both Chinese and Nom on such subjects as science,
morality, philosophy, and agronomy. Le Quy Don is remembered
as one of the towering intellects of late traditional Vietnam. (See
Literature)

LE TAC. Vietnamese scholar and official in thirteenth-century Vietnam. Le Tac, member of a noble family dating back several hundred years, became a well-known scholar during the reign of
Tran Nhan Tong (1279-1293). During the Mongol invasion of the
1280s he collaborated with the invaders and after their defeat settled in China. While there he wrote An Nam Chi Luoc (Annals of
Annam), a twenty-volume history of Vietnam culled from Chinese
historical records and published in 1340. A modern version of
the work was published in South Vietnam in 1961.

LE THAI TO (Le Loi) (reigned 1428-1433). Founding emperor of later
Le Dynasty in fifteenth-century Vietnam. (See Le Loi)

LE THAI TONG (reigned 1433-1442). Second emperor of later Le
Dynasty in fifteenth-century Vietnam. Le Thai Tong ascended
to the throne on the death of his father, Le Thai To, in 1433.
Because he was only eleven years of age at the time of accession,
power rested in the hands of Chief Minister Le Sat. Le Loi's

chief adviser, Nguyen Trai, had already retired from office as
a result of court intrigue. As he reached early maturity, Le
Thai Tong developed a reputation for debauchery. He died under
mysterious circumstances in 1442 while returning from a visit
to Nguyen Trai at the latter's retirement home at Chi Linh mountain, west of present-day Hanoi. (See Le Thai To; Nguyen Trai)

LE THANH TONG (1460-97). Fourth and perhaps greatest emperor
of the later Le Dynasty (1428-1788). Le Thanh Tong ascended
the throne in 1460 at the age of 19. During a reign of 37 years,
he made a significant contribution to the growth and strengthening of the Vietnamese state. First and foremost he was responsible for a number of changes in the government. He reorganized the central administration, formalizing the duties of the six
ministries (Rites, War, Justice, Interior, Public Works, and
Finance) and streamlined the operation of the civil service. He
strengthened the hand of the central bureaucracy over the
provincial and local administration, thus limiting the power of
the landed aristocracy. He ordered a national census, a geographical survey of the entire country, and the writing of a new
national history by the noted historian Ngo Si Lien. He sponsored
the promulgation of a new penal code--the famous Hong Duc code
--which systematized the rules and regulations of the state.
And he infused the entire system with the spirit of Confucianism,
which under his direction now assumed a position of dominance
over Buddhism in the administration and in setting a moral tone
over the population at large.
    Le Thanh Tong also attacked the chronic problem that had
plagued so many of his predecessors--the land question. Inspection of the dike system was promoted, and peasants were encouraged by various means to bring virgin land under cultivation.
And the government attempted to prevent the increasing concentration of land in the hands of wealthy landlords by levelling heavy
penalties for the seizure of commune land.
    In the field of foreign affairs, Le Thanh Tong presided over
a significant strengthening of the armed forces and an expansion
of the territory of the Vietnamese empire at the expense of Champa
Continual clashes along the common border led the Vietnamese
to invade Champa in 1470, resulting in the seizure of the Cham
capital of Vijaya and the virtual collapse of the kingdom of Champa.
The northern segment of the kingdom--corresponding to the
modern province of Quang Nam--was assimilated into the Vietnamese
empire and settled with military colonies (don dien). The remainder was turned into a vassal state. Vietnam also expanded to the
west at the expense of Laos.
    Le Thanh Tong died in 1497 at the age of 56. He was succeeded
by his son, Le Hien Tong, who carried on in the tradition of his
father until his death in 1504. (See Confucianism; Hong Duc
Code; Le Dynasty)

LE UY MUC (1505-1509). Seventh emperor of the Later Le Dynasty.

Le Uy Muc acceded to the throne on the death of Le Tuc Tong
in 1504. He quickly showed himself to be a ruthless ruler,
killing his grandmother and two of his ministers. His unpopularity led to the popular nickname given to him, the "devil king"
(vua quy). He was assassinated by his cousin in 1509, who then
seized the throne under the dynastic title of Le Tuong Duc.
The latter's reign was marked by continued instability at court
and peasant uprisings in the countryside. In 1516 a rebellion
was launched by a pretender to the throne, Tran Cao, who
claimed to be a descendant of the Tran royal family. Le Tuong
Duc, known popularly as "the hog king" (vua lon), was killed
by one of his own lieutenants during the insurrection. He was
succeeded by Le Chieu Tong, who managed to suppress the rebellion, but was then deposed and assassinated by Mac Dang
Dung, an ambitious military official who had become influential
at court. (See Later Le Dynasty; Mac Dang Dung)

LE VAN DUYET (1763-1832). Regional official in South Vietnam
during the nineteenth century. An ex-military commander who
had led Nguyen forces against the Tay Son at Qui Nhon in 1799,
Le Van Duyet rose to prominence at court during the reign of
Emperor Gia Long, founder of the Nguyen Dynasty (1802-1945).
Gia Long appointed him regent of South Vietnam, where he
exercised enormous vice-regal power, including the authority to
conduct foreign relations with Europe and other Southeast Asian
nations.
    Le Van Duyet was relatively sympathetic to the Western
presence in South Vietnam, and protested when Gia Long's
successor Minh Mang (1820-1841) attempted to evict Christian
missionaries. This may have contributed to his strained relations
with the new emperor, and when he died in 1832, he was post-
humously convicted and his grave desecrated, leading his adopted
son, Le Van Khoi, to rebel. (See Gia Long; Le Van Khoi Rebellion; Minh Mang; Nguyen Dynasty)

LE VAN HUU. Renowned historian during the Tran Dynasty in Vietnam. Born in the mid-thirteenth century, Le Van Huu was a
gifted youngster and succeeded in the civil service examination
while still at an early age, and became a member of the prestigious
Han Lam Academy and the National Board of History. In 1272 he
wrote a comprehensive national history of the Vietnamese nation,
entitled the Dai Viet Su Ky (Historical Record of Great Viet).
This dynastic history of Vietnam from the time of Tireu Da in the
third century B.C. to the end of the Ly Dynasty is no longer
extant, but parts have been incorporated into the Dai Viet Su
Ky Toan Thu (Complete Historical Record of Great Viet), written
by the noted historian Nge Si Lien during the fifteenth century
under the Le Dynasty. Dai Viet Su Ky was written in part on
the basis of an earlier work, the Viet Chi (Annals of Viet) written
by Tran Pho, a scholar-official who served under the Tran Dynasty in the mid-thirteenth century. Although Le Van Huu's

work, like much historical writing in imperial Vietnam, had
been officially commissioned by the court, it displays a strong
Confucian bias, although Buddhism remained dominant at court.
A condensed version of the work, written later in China and
available in both Vietnamese and Chinese, is available under the
title of Viet Su Luoc (Outline of Viet History). (See Literature)

LE VAN KHOI REBELLION. Rebellion launched by Le Van Khoi in
South Vietnam in 1833. A Muong by origin, Le Van Khoi was
the adopted son of the regional warlord in South Vietnam, Le Van
Duyet. In 1833, shortly after the latter's death, a major revolt
broke out in the South against efforts by the court in Hue to
curtail its autonomy. Le Van Khoi, leader of the rebellion,
sought help from Western missionaries and the kingdom of Siam,
and proclaimed the son of Prince Canh, first son of Emperor Gai
Long (1802-1820), as the legitimate ruler of Vietnam. Khoi died
in 1834 while his fortress at Diagon was under siege by imperial
troops. The revolt, after spreading briefly throughout the South,
was suppressed the following year. (See Gia Long; Le Van Duyet;
Minh Mang; Nguyen Dynasty)

LE VAN VIEN (Bay Vien) (See Binh Xuyen).

LEAGUE FOR THE INDEPENDENCE OF VIETNAM (Viet Nam Doc Lap
Dong Minh, or Vietminh). Front organization set up by the
Indochinese Communist Party (ICP) during World War II. It was
founded at the suggestion of Ho Chi Minh at the Eighth Plenum
of the ICP Central Committee meeting at Pac Bo in North Vietnam
in May 1941. Popularly called the Vietminh, the League was a
broad front organization under ICP leadership designed to win
broad popular support for national independence and social and
economic reform. Its organization was both vertical and horizontal.
Branch committees were set up at province, district, and village
levels in virtually all areas of Vietnam. At the same time, so-
called "national salvation associations" (cuu quoc hoi), a form of
mass association for such functional groups as workers, peasants,
women, students, writers and artists, and religious organizations,
were also organized under the broad rubric of the League.

In August 1945 guerrilla forces under the leadership of the
ICP launched a nationwide insurrection which seized power in
Vietnam at the surrender of the Japanese. A Democratic Republic
of Vietnam (DRV) was established in Hanoi, with Ho Chi Minh,
the chairman of the ICP, as president. But negotiations with
France failed, and in December 1946, the so-called Franco-Vietminh
war began. At the outset of the conflict, the DRV used the Vietminh Front and its attendant mass associations as the vehicle to
achieve broad mass support in the struggle against the French.
Eventually, however, the Front became openly identified with
the ICP, and in 1951 it was merged into a larger Lien Viet Front
in an effort to win increased support from moderate elements.
The term "Vietminh," however, was still commonly applied to

the movement, and its supporters, and the organization is viewed as a classic case of a communist-front organization in wars of national liberation. (See Ho Chi Minh; Lien Viet Front; National Salvation Association)

LEAGUE FOR THE NATIONAL RESTORATION OF VIETNAM (Viet Nam Phuc Quoc Dong Minh Hoi). Pro-Japanese political party formed by Prince Cuong De at the beginning of World War II. The Party, often called the Phuc Quoc for short, was composed of anti-French nationalist groups living in exile in South China, and was probably a successor of Phan Boi Chau's League for the Restoration of Vietnam (Viet Nam Quang Phuc Hoi), formed in 1912. It first saw action during the brief Japanese invasion on the Sino-Vietnamese border in September 1940. During World War II it joined with such other groups as the Cao Dai in a broad alliance under Japanese sponsorship and based in Vietnam. The organization collapsed when Japan surrendered in August 1945. (See Cao Dai; Cuong De)

LEFEBVRE, MONSIGNOR DOMINIQUE. French missionary and ecclesiastical official in Vietnam. A vigorous advocate of an activist missionary policy in Vietnam, Lefebvre was seized by Vietnamese authorities and sentenced to death in 1847. He was subsequently released by order of Emperor Thieu Tri, but a belligerent French naval commander used the incident as a pretext to shell the Vietnamese port city of Da Nang. (See Thieu Tri)

LI-FOURNIER TREATY (See Treaty of Tientsin).

LIEN VIET FRONT (National United Vietnamese Front) (Hoi Lien Hiep Quoc Dan Viet Nam). Front organization set up by the Indochinese Communist Party (ICP) in May 1946. The Front was created as a means of broadening the popular base of support for the Party and the Democratic Republic of Vietnam. It included several political parties and mass organizations not previously linked with the ICP's existing front organization, the Vietminh. The president of the new front was the veteran nationalist Huynh Thuc Khang. The vice-president was Ton Duc Thang, a party member and later President of the DRV.

In 1951, the Lien Viet was merged with the Vietminh Front, and in 1955 it was replaced by the Fatherland Front, which became the legal front organization in the Democratic Republic of Vietnam. (See League for the Independence of Vietnam)

LIN-YI (Lam Ap). Chinese name for an early state in Vietnam. The kingdom of Lin-yi (in Vietnamese, Lam Ap) was apparently founded in A.D. 192 by rebellious officials in the province of Nhu Nam, the southernmost region of Vietnam, then under Chinese rule. At first it remained linked with the Chinese political and cultural world of East Asia. By the fourth century, however, it was increasingly influenced by Indian elements moving north along the coast of the China Sea. For several centuries it controlled an area from the Hoanh Son Spur to the present-day city of Da Nang and was in perpetual conflict with its neighbors. Eventually it was transformed into the kingdom of Champa, which was a rival of Vietnam until its destruction in the seventeenth century. (See Champa)

LINH NAM TRICH QUAI (Fantasies selected from the South of the Pass). Anonymous historical work written during the Tran Dynasty. It recounted many of the legends concerning the origins and early years of the Vietnamese people. It was later used by the fifteenth-century historian Ngo Si Lien in writing his comprehensive history of Vietnam, Dai Viet Su Ky Toan Thu (See Ngo Si Lien)

LITERATURE. During the traditional era, Vietnamese literature was essentially divided into two basic forms--a classical form based on the Chinese model and a vernacular form based on indigenous themes and genres. Classical literature was written in literary Chinese and utilized genres popular in China, such as poetry, history, and essays. Vernacular literature, written in chu nom, the written form of spoken Vietnamese, may have originally been expressed in the form of poetry and essays but by the seventeenth and eighteenth centuries began to take the form of verse or prose novels, often involving caustic commentary on the frailties of Vietnamese society.

Vietnamese literature was changed irrevocably by the imposition of colonial rule. By the 1920s the classical style was on the decline and increasingly replaced by a new literature based on the Western model. Drama, poetry, and the novel, often imitating trends in the West, were written in quoc ngu, the new romanticized transliteration of spoken Vietnamese.

The Westernization of Vietnamese literature continued to evolve in the Republic of Vietnam, formed in the South after the Geneva Conference of 1954. In the North, the Democratic Republic of Vietnam (DRV) brought about the emergence of a new form of literature based on the Marxist-Leninst concept of socialist realism, emphasizing the transformation of the human personality, the sacred task of completing the Vietnamese revolution, and the building of an advanced socialist society. Socialist realism remains the sole accepted form of literary expression in the Socialist Republic of Vietnam today.

LOCAL GOVERNMENT. The administrative division of Vietnam below the central level has varied considerably over the two thousand years of recorded history. In general, however, local administration in Vietnam has usually taken place at three levels: 1) province (tinh, lo, tran), 2) district (huyen, quan, chau), and 3) commune, or canton (xa, tong). On occasion, two other levels were also used, the prefecture, or phu (an intermediate echelon between the province and the district) and the region (bo), between the central government and the province.

In the Socialist Republic of Vietnam, administration is at four levels: 1) central, 2) province (tinh), 3) district (huyen), and 4) village, or commune (xa). The village itself is often divided into smaller "natural villages" (lang, or thon) and hamlets (ap, or xom). The SRV is currently divided into 37 provinces and three municipalities (Hanoi, Haiphong, and Ho Chi Minh City) directly subordinated to the central government. The government has not published a complete list of districts. Unofficial sources indicate there are currently 445 districts throughout the country.

LODGE, HENRY CABOT. U.S. ambassador to the Republic of Vietnam from August 1963 until June 1964, and from August 1965 until early 1967. Lodge, a veteran Republican politician from the state of Massachusetts, was named ambassador by President John F. Kennedy just as the latter was losing patience with Vietnamese President Ngo Dinh Diem, and some observers believed he had been appointed specifically to handle the task of hastening Diem's overthrow. Replaced by General Maxwell Taylor in the summer of 1964, he returned for a short second tour one year later. (See Ngo Dinh Diem; Taylor, Maxwell)

LONG, MAURICE (1866-1923). Governor-general of French Indochina from 1920 to 1923. A lawyer and a parliamentarian representing the Radical Socialist Party, Maurice Long increased the number of Vietnamese members in consultative assemblies in Annan and Tonkin and the local administration in Cochin China.

LUC BO (Six Boards). Ministries of State in precolonial Vietnam. Based on the Chinese System adopted originally by the T'ang Dynasty in China, the six boards consisted of the Boards of Appointments (Lai Bo), Finance (Ho Bo), Justice (Hinh Bo). Public works (Long Bo), War (Binh Bo), and Rites (Le Bo). Operating as part of the central bureaucracy, they supervised the primary functions of the imperial government. Each was headed by a president (thuong thu), with two vice-presidents and two counsellors. Each ministry was divided into several panels, and a corps of inspection for the provinces. It was created by Emperor Gia Long, founder of the Nguyen Dynasty (1802-1945).

LUTTE, LA (The Struggle). French-language weekly newspaper published in colonial Vietnam. Published by returned students from France, its first issue appeared in 1933. Most of the founding members, such as Ta Thu Thau, Tran Van Thach and Ho Huu Tuong, were Trotskyites, although several members of the Indochinese Communist Party (ICP), such as Nguyen Van Tao and Duong Bach Mai, also took part in the editing or contributed articles until prohibited from doing so by the Soviet Union in 1937.

Adopting relatively moderate political views, La Lutte was

tolerated by the French colonial regime until it was closed in 1939. (See Journalism; Ta Thu Thau; Trotskyites)

LUU VINH PHUC (See Black Flags).

LY ANH TONG (Reigned 1137-1175). Emperor during Ly Dynasty in twelfth-century Vietnam. Ly Anh Tong was still an infant when he ascended the throne on the death of his father, Ly Than Tong. Until reaching his maturity, power was in the hands of his mother and her lover, the court figure Don Anh Vu. His reign was generally peaceful, although rebellion broke out among minority tribesmen in the mountain areas surrounding the Red River Delta. It was also marked by growing trade relations with such neighboring countries in the area as China, Siam, Angkor and the trading states in Malaya and the Indonesian archipelago.

In 1175, Ly Anh Tong became ill and turned power over to a regent, the respected general To Hien Thanh. He died the following year, at the age of 37.

LY BI. (Ly Bon). Leader of a major revolt against Chinese occupation in sixth-century Vietnam. Ly Bi was an ethnic Chinese whose ancestors had fled to Vietnam at the time of the Wang Mang rebellion. Born in a family with a military background, Ly Bi served as an official in the bureaucracy of the Liang Dynasty in Vietnam. Disappointed in his ambitions, he launched a rebellion against Chinese rule in A.D. 542 and despite conflict with the state of Champa to the south, was successful in overthrowing the unpopular local Chinese administration and in 544 established the independent state of Van Xuan (10,000 Springs). Ly Bi styled himself the emperor of Nam Viet, thus invoking the memory of the short-lived dynasty of Trieu Da with the same name. The capital was probably located at Gia Ninh, near his family home at the foot of Mount Tam Dao, northwest of Hanoi at the edge of the Red River Delta.

At first, Ly Bi's successes paralleled his ambition, and he was able to unite much of the traditional Vietnamese heartland, along with the northern sections of the state of Champa, under his rule. But in 545 the Liang Dynasty organized a military force under the capable command of the experienced general Ch'en Pa-hsien. Ch'en captured Ly Bi's capital, then engaged and defeated the latter's forces a few miles to the south. Ly Bi escaped but was soon killed by mountain tribesmen and his kingdom of Van Xuan collapsed, although resistance to Chinese rule continued among some of his followers for several years.

LY BON (See Ly Bi).

LY CAO TONG (reigned 1176-1210). Emperor of Vietnam in the late twelfth and early thirteenth centuries. Ly Cao Tong ascended the throne in 1176 at the age of three. During the regency of General To Hien Thanh, his mother wished to replace him on the

throne with his older brother, but General To's wife refused
to be bribed.

Ly Cao Tong's reign was marked by social unrest and frequent rebellion. According to the fifteenth-century Vietnamese
historian Ngu Si Lien, Ly Cao Tong was oppressive and corrupt,
and his rule marked a major stage in the decline of the Ly Dynasty. In 1208, a rebellion led by Pham Du forced him to flee
the capital. He was eventually restored to power with the aid
of the powerful Tran family, but died two years later, at the
age of 37. (See Ly Anh Tong; Ly Dynasty; Ly Hue Tong)

LY CHIEU HOANG (Reigned 1224-1225). Last ruler of Ly Dynasty
in thirteenth-century Vietnam. Ly Chieu Hoang (proper name
Phat Kim), was a daughter of Emperor Ly Hue Tong (1210-1224).
In 1224 the emperor, sickly and probably demented, decided to
abdicate the throne. Lacking sons, he turned over the throne
to his daughter Phat Kim, who was named Empress Ly Chieu Hoang,
with Tran Tu Khanh, a member of the influential Tran family,
serving as regent. She was then married to Tran Canh, eight-
year old nephew of Tran Thu Do, a cousin of ex-queen Tran
Thi and a dominant figure at court. In 1225, Tran Canh was
declared Emperor Tran Thai Tong of a new Tran Dynasty (1225-
1400).

Ly Chieu Hoang reigned as queen for twelve years but did
not produce an heir and in 1236 she was divorced by the king
in place of her older sister. (See Ly Hue Tong; Tran Thai Tong;
Tran Thu Do)

LY CONG UAN (See Ly Thai To).

LY DYNASTY (Nha Ly) (1009-1225). First major dynasty after the
restoration of Vietnamese independence in the tenth century
A.D. During the first several decades after the overthrow of
Chinese rule, three successive dynasties struggled unsuccessfully to consolidate the new Vietnamese state and guarantee its
separate existence. It was the Ly Dynasty which developed the
political and social institutions that would provide stability for
the Vietnamese Empire, known after 1054 as Dai Viet, and
place it on a firm footing for the next several hundred years.

The successes of the Ly were achieved primarily by a series
of gifted rulers with relatively long reigns during the first
hundred years of the dynasty. Later monarchs were often in-
competent or morally depraved, a characteristic that contributed
to the fall of the dynasty in the thirteenth century. (See Ly
Thai To)

LY HUE TONG (reigned 1210-1224). Next-to-last emperor of the Ly
Dynasty in thirteenth-century Vietnam. Ly Hue Tong ascended
the throne on the death of his father, Ly Cao Tong, in 1210.
During his reign, he was under the domination of the powerful
Tran family, which had helped to restore his father to the throne

after the Pham Du rebellion in 1208. Ly Hue Tong, then the crown prince, had fled the capital with his father during the revolt and sought refuge with a member of the Tran family in Nam Dinh, south of the present-day capital of Hanoi. There he met Tran Thi, one of the daughters of his host, and on becoming emperor in 1210, took her as his queen. During the next few years, the Tran family, and particularly Tran Thu Do, a cousin of the queen, became increasingly dominant at court.

During his reign, Le Hue Tong was frequently ill and suffered from periodic bouts of insanity. In 1224 he abdicated in favor of his daughter Ly Chieu Hoang, who was still a child. Ly Hue Tong retired to a monastery, but was eventually forced to commit suicide by Tran Thu Do, who eliminated the entire Ly family to ensure the security of the new Tran Dynasty (1225-1400) (See Ly Cao Tong; Ly Chieu Hoang; Ly Dynasty; Tran Dynasty; Tran Thu Do)

LY NHAN TONG (reigned 1072-1127). Fourth emperor of the Ly Dynasty in eleventh-century Vietnam. In 1072, at the age of seven, he ascended the throne on the death of his father Ly Thanh Tong. During the period of regency under the mandarin Ly Dao Thanh, two events of major significance to the future of the Vietnamese Empire took place. In the capital of Thang Long (on the site of the modern city of Hanoi), the first competitive civil service examinations for entrance into the bureaucracy were held. The examinations took place at the Temple of Literature (Van Mieu), established by Emperor Ly Thanh Tong only two years before his death. To train candidates of noble extraction for the examinations and provide a refresher course for existing members of the mandarinate, a national training institute (Quoc Tu Giam, literally, Institute for Sons of the State) was established in 1076 on the grounds of the Temple of Literature.

The second major event of Ly Nhan Tong's early years on the throne was renewed war with China. Anticipating an attack, General Ly Thuong Kiet in 1075 launched a two-pronged attack on China by land and by sea. The Sung Dynasty struck back quickly, and launched an invasion of the Red River Delta. But Ly Thuong Kiet was able to stabilize his defense line north of the capital of Thang Long, and China agreed to peace. Intermittent war also continued with Champa, Vietnam's perennial rival to the south.

In some respects, the reign of Ly Nhan Tong continued the pattern that had been laid down by his immediate predecessors. The power of the Buddhist church remained strong, with monks prominent at court and temples possessing great landholdings like manor lords. The power of the landed aristocracy, based on the system of feifdoms granted by the state, continued to increase.

After a long and relatively prosperous reign of 56 years, Ly Nhan Tong died in 1127. (See Civil Service Examination System; Confucianism; Ly Dynasty; Ly Thanh Tong; Temple of Literature)

LY PHAT TU. Relative of Vietnamese rebel Ly Bi who formed a
shortlived "kingdom of the south" in sixth-century Vietnam. His
first capital was at O-Dien, west of Hanoi. Later it was moved
to Co Loa, the ancient capital in the pre-Chinese period. Ly
Phat Tu was a patron of Buddhism, thus his sobriquet "Son of
the Buddha" (Phat Tu). In the early seventh century, Ly Phat
Tu's kingdom was attacked and defeated by an army sent by
the rising Sui Dynasty. Phat Tu surrendered and was sent to
exile in the Sui capital at Ch'ang An. The Chinese Army then
marched South and sacked the Champa capital near the modern
city of Da Nang. (See Buddhism; Ly Bi)

LY THAI TO (Ly Cong Uan) (reigned 1010-1028). Founder of the
Ly Dynasty, one of the greatest dynasties of independent Vietnam. Ly Thai To (original name Ly Cong Uan), was born in
974. Little is known about his family background. An orphan,
he was reportedly raised in a Buddhist temple in what is today
Bac Ninh province, and became a member of the palace guard at
Hoa Lu, the capital of the Le Dynasty.
    After the death of emperor Le Long Dinh in 1010, Ly Cong
Uan seized the throne through court intrigue and declared the
foundation of the Ly Dynasty (1010-1225). One of the first
actions of the new emperor, who styled himself Ly Thai To,
was to move the imperial capital from Hoa Lu to Dai La, site
of the administrative center of the protectorate of annam under
Chinese rule and the location of the modern day capital of Hanoi.
The new capital was given the name Thang Long (soaring dragon),
in honor of the mystical dragon which the new emperor had reportedly seen rising above the city into the clouds as he first
approached the city. The reasons for the move may have been
both economic and political. The old capital had been located
south of the Red River Delta in a relatively unpopulated region
surrounded by mountains, suitable for defensive purposes but not
for an administrative center of a growing society. Thang Long,
on the other hand, was centrally located in the heart of the
Red River Delta and the most densely populated region of the
country. Above all, the shift represented a vote of confidence
in the future of an independent Vietnam.
    During the reign of eighteen years, Ly Thai To initiated a
number of actions that would significantly affect the development
of the new state. In the first place, he reorganized the administration, dividing the nation into a new series of provinces, prefectures, and districts, above the historic communes at the village level. As a rule, leading administrators were chosen from
members of the royal family, who were called Vuong (king) and
assigned major responsibility for maintaining security and raising
revenue through taxation in the areas under their control. To
provide an ideological base for Vietnamese society, the emperor
ardently supported Buddhism, building a number of new temples
to train monks, not only for religious purposes, but also to provide a literate elite to staff the growing bureaucracy. In the

realm of economics, he built new dikes and irrigation canals to promote an increase in grain production, and initiated new taxes to establish a stable revenue base for the state.

Le Thai To's reign provided a firm foundation for the Ly Dynasty, and set it on a path that would maintain it in power for over two centuries, one of the longest in Vietnamese history. Unfortunately, he did not resolve one of the chronic problems of the time, that of guaranteeing the succession. On his death at the age of 55, his son and designated successor Ly Phat Ma (who would later assume the reign title of Ly Thai Tong) had to fight the armed forces of three of his brothers before managing to seize firm control over the throne. (See Le Hoan; Ly Dynasty; Thang Long)

LY THAI TONG (Ly Phat Ma) (reigned 1028-1054). Second emperor of the Ly Dynasty (1010-1225). Ly Phat Ma, crown prince under founding emperor Ly Thai To, rose to the throne on the death of his father in 1028. Taking the royal title Ly Thai Tong, he continued many of the practices of his father, attempting to strengthen the state and lay the foundation for a stable and prosperous society. Having ascended the throne only after a bitter struggle with three of his brothers, Ly Thai To was determined to build a strong army to guarantee the continuity of the dynasty He set up a system of national military conscription and created an elite guard called the Thien Tu Binh (Army of the Son of Heaven) to protect the royal palace and the capital city from attacks. In an effort to reduce the immense power possessed by princes of the blood, he attempted to transfer authority at the provincial and prefectural level from members of the royal family to a class of professional officials selected from the landed aristocracy. To guarantee their loyalty, such administrators were granted substantial amounts of state land for exploitation and tax revenue. Although these lands remained theoretically under the ownership of the crown, in practice they were often passed on within the family. Ly Thai To also attempted to strengthen the infrastructure of the state, building roads and a postal system to speed up communications. Like his father, Ly Thai To was an ardent Buddhist. He joined the aristocratic Vo Ngon Thong sect, a branch of the Ch'an (in Japanese, Zen) sect that was founded in Vietnam in the ninth century, and relied on monks as his confidential advisers at court. Yet he apparently also promoted Confucianism as a means of training officials and providing an ideological basis for strengthening the centralized state.

Like most of his predecessors, Ly Thai Tong was frequently preoccupied with foreign policy problems. The state was almost constantly at war with the state of Champa along the coast to the south. Lands conquered from the Cham were often turned over as fiefs to high military or civilian officials, or to the Buddhist church. On several occasions Vietnamese armies were sent into the mountains north of the Red River Delta to quell rebellions launched by the Nung tribes peoples near the Chinese border.

Ly Thai Tong died in 1054 at the age of 55 and was succeeded peacefully by his son Ly Thanh Tong. (See Buddhism; Confucianism; Ly Dynasty)

LY THAN TONG (reigned 1127-1137). Fifth emperor for the Ly Dynasty in twelfth-century Vietnam. When Emperor Ly Nhan Tong died childless in 1127, his adopted son Sung Hien Hau was chosen to succeed him as Emperor Ly Than Tong while still an adolescent. His short reign of ten years of relatively uneventful, although intermittent conflict took place with Vietnam's neighbors to the south and west, Champa and the Angkor Empire. A new policy was adopted in the armed forces, permitting conscripts to spend six months of every year working the fields of their native village.

Ly Than Tong died in 1137 at the age of 23. (See Ly Anh Tong; Ly Dynasty; Ly Nhan Tong)

LY THANH TONG (reigned 1054-1072). Son of Ly Thai Tong and third emperor of Ly Dynasty in eleventh-century Vietnam. Ly Thanh Tong succeeded to the throne on the death of his father in 1054, at the age of 32. Although changing the name of the Empire from Dai Co Viet to Dai Viet, in general the new ruler followed the policies of his predecessors in strengthening the centralized power of the state while staunchly defending its National Security from potential internal and foreign threats. Chinese power along the northern border was held at bay, and attacks from Champa beyond the southern frontier led the emperor to launch a major offensive in 1068. The campaign was a spectacular success. The capital of Champa was occupied and the king seized. To obtain his release the latter ceded three provinces along the central coast (comprising the contemporary provinces of Quang Binh and Quang Tri) to the Vietnamese Empire.

In domestic affairs, Ly Thanh Tong favored the growth of Confucianism as a foundation for the state. In 1070, he ordered the construction of the Temple of Literature (Van Mieu) for the study of Confucian philosophy and the training of officials in the capital city of Thang Long. Ly Thanh Tong died on 1072 and was succeeded by his eldest son, the seven year old Ly Nhan Tong. (See Ly Dynasty; Ly Thai Tong; Van Mieu)

LY THUONG KIET (1030-1105). Mandarin and military commander during the Ly Dynasty in eleventh-century Vietnam. Born in 1030 of an aristocratic family in the capital of Thang Long, Ly Thuong Kiet served Emperor Ly Thanh Tong (1054-1072) as a military officer and commanded a successful invasion of Champa in 1069 that resulted in major territorial concessions to the Vietnamese and the temporary cessation of the threat from the South.

In the 1070s, Ly Thuong Kiet commanded Vietnamese armed

forces in a war with the Sung Dynasty in China. In 1075, anticipating a projected Chinese invasion of the Red River Delta, he launched a preemptive attack on South China. The offensive, launched on two fronts, by land and by sea, was briefly successful, resulting in the destruction of Chinese defensive positions in the frontier region. But China, allied with Champa and the Angkor Empire, launched a counterattack in late 1076. Ly Thuong Kiet fortified the Cau river north of Hanoi and was able to prevent an enemy occupation of the capital. In later years, Ly Thuong Kiet served as a provincial governor, and died in 1105 at the advanced age of 75.

Ly Thuong Kiet is viewed by Vietnamese historians as one of the major figures in Vietnam's historic struggle to defend itself against Chinese domination. He is also considered to be a military strategist of considerable repute, and is identified with the concept of a preemptive strike ("attacking in self-defense") against an enemy in order to avoid having to fight a war simultaneously on two fronts. Military strategists in contemporary Vietnam such as General Vo Nguyen Giap acknowledge their debt to his genius. (See Ly Nhan Tong; Ly Thanh Tong)

- M -

MA YUAN (Ma Vien). Chinese military commander who suppressed the Trung Sisters rebellion in A.D. 39-43 and restored Vietnam to Chinese occupation. When the rebellion broke out, General Ma Yuan, who had recently put down a rebellion in Anhui province in central China, was appointed commander of a force of 20,000 soldiers to suppress the revolt in Vietnam and restore Chinese rule.

Advancing south along the coast, Ma Yuan defeated the Vietnamese army and had the Trung Sisters put to death. He then set out to remove the potential sources of discontent by destroying the local landed nobility (the "Lac Lords") and replacing it with a bureaucracy staffed by officials sent from China. The administrative structure was reformed to conform with the model of the Han Dynasty in China. Vietnamese Territory was divided into three prefectures (Giao Chi, Cuu Chan, and Nhat Nam). These prefectures (quan) were in turn divided into 56 districts (huyen).

Although the role of the Ma Yuan in Vietnamese history was to destroy Vietnamese independence and bind the country even closer to China, he apparently earned the respect of many of the people under his charge. In later generations many legends grew up around his memory and the prodigious feats with which he was identified. (See Trung Sisters)

MAC DANG DUNG (reigned 1527-1530). Founder of the Mac Dynasty in sixteenth-century Vietnam. Mac Dang Dung was the son of a fisherman in present-day Haiphong, and claimed to be a descendant of Mac Dinh Chi, a scholar-official during the Tran Dynasty.

After becoming a military officer, Mac Dang Dung came to the attention of Le Uy Muc, known as the "devil king," and was soon an influential figure at court.

In 1516, a major rebellion lead by the Tran pretender Tran Lao broke out and led to the seizure of the capital and the murder of the reigning emperor, Le Tuong Duc. With the help of Mac Dang Dung, the Le were able to return to power, but in a weakened condition, and in 1527 Mac Dang Dung usurped the throne and proclaimed himself emperor.

Many leading figures in the court and the bureaucracy remained loyal to the Ly Dynasty, but Mac Dang Dung was able to consolidate his power in the capital of Thang Long and even obtained legitimation from the Ming Emperor in Beijing. In 1530 he turned the throne over to his son, while maintaining an influential role as royal adviser (Thai Thuong Hoang). Members of the Le family continued to struggle for a restoration of the Le Dynasty, however, and in 1533 with the help of the loyalist mandarin Nguyen Kim, Le Trang Tong, a son of Emperor Le Chien Tong (1516-1524) was declared the legitimate ruler, although for several years he was forced to live in exile in Laos. Mac Dang Dung died in 1540. (See Le Dynasty; Le Uy Muc; Mac Dynasty)

MAC DYNASTY (Nha Mac) (1527-1592). Royal dynasty established by Mac Dang Dung in 1527. Mac Dang Dung, a military officer and influential figure at the Le court in the early sixteenth century, seized power during a time of political instability and declared himself founding emperor of a new Mac Dynasty. The dynasty was unable to consolidate its power, however, as it was not accepted by many influential elements in Vietnam.

In 1533, a member of the Le Dynasty, Le Trong Tang, declared himself the legitimate ruler of Vietnam, although he was forced to maintain his court in exile in Laos. By the early 1540s, with the help of the mandarin Nguyen Kim, the Le controlled considerable territory in Central Vietnam and established their court at Tong Do (Western Capital) in modern-day Thanh Hoa Province. For the next several decades, Vietnam was divided in two between North and South.

In 1591, forces loyal to the Le seized the capital of Thang Long and captured the Mac Emperor, Mac Mao Hop. Remnants of the Mac family managed to retain power at Cao Bang, near the border with China, until 1667. (See Ly Dynasty; Mac Dang Dung; Nguyen Kim)

MAI THUC LOAN. Rebel leader who led revolt against Chinese rule in early eighth-century Vietnam. A native of the central coast near the present-day city of Ha Thinh, Mai Thuc Loan led a rebellion of alienated peasants, mountain tribesmen, and vagabonds against oppresive Chinese occupation in A.D. 722. The revolt was briefly successful, and after seizing most of the protectorate of Annam, Thuc Loan declared himself the "Black Emperor"

(Mai Hac De). The T'ang Dynasty struck back quickly and a Chinese army under General Yang Ssu-Hsu put down the rebellion. Mai Thuc Loan was killed and thousands of his followers were executed. Unrest against Chinese rule continued, however, for several years.

MARCH TO THE SOUTH (Nam Tien). Vietnam's historic expansion southward from the Red River Delta to the Gulf of Thailand. The process began after the restoration of Vietnamese independence in the tenth century A.D. For the next several centuries the Vietnamese Empire and its neighbor to the South, the kingdom of Champa, clashed periodically in a struggle for control over territories along the central coast. By the fifteenth century, the power of Champa was on the decline, and Vietnamese troops occupied the Cham capital of Indrapura and forced the king of Champa to move further to the south. After a series of further defeats, Cham resistance collapsed and the kingdom was placed in a tributary relationship with Vietnam.

After the absorption of the kingdom of Champa, Vietnam continued its expansion southward into areas of the Mekong River Delta controlled by the virtually moribund Angkor Empire. After achieving the military conquest of a particular area, the Vietnamese established colonial settlements (don dien) composed of soldiers or peasants resettled from the North and usually under military command. Once the security of the area had been achieved, the settlements would be turned over to civilian leadership. By the end of the seventeenth century, the entire Delta area down to the Ca Mau Peninsula was under Vietnamese rule. (See Champa; Don Dien; Indrapura; Vijaya)

MEKONG RIVER (Song Cuu Long, or "River of Nine Dragons"). Eleventh longest river in the world and largest and longest in Southeast Asia. Originating in the mountains of Tibet, the Mekong travels 2,700 miles 4,184 kilometers) to its final exit into the South China Sea south of Ho Chi Minh City (previously known as Saigon). After entering mainland Southeast Asia from the north, it forms the border for several hundred miles between Thailand and Laos. At the Cambodian capital of Phnom Penh it receives additional water from the Tonle Sap and splits into two main branches, the Makong (northern branch, or Tien Giang) and the Bassac (southern branch, or Hau Giang). After entering South Vietnam, the northern branch then splits into several additional branches before entering the South China Sea.

The Mekong River is navigable up to a series of rapids at the Laotian border. Its main importance to Vietnam, however, lies in the rich sediment that the river leaves as it empties into the sea. The entire Mekong River Delta has been built up over the centures by sedimentary soil brought down from the highlands of south China. (See Mekong River Delta)

MEKONG RIVER DELTA. The delta region of the mighty Mekong

River in South Vietnam. Built up by alluvial soils brought by the river from its source in South China, the Mekong Delta consists of a total of approximately 26,000 square miles (67,000 kilometers), from the Ca Mau Peninsula in the south to a point south of present-day Ho Chi Minh City (previously Saigon).

Although the Mekong River Delta is composed of rich sedimentary soil, until modern times it did not support a high density of population. Prior to 1700, when the area was controlled by the Angkor Empire, human settlement was relatively sparse. Much of the land was covered with reeds, and the coastal areas were affected by tides which led to flooding by highly saline seawater. During the seventeenth century, the Delta was conquered by the Vietnamese as part of their historic "March to the South." Vietnamese settlers began arriving in the area, and canals were dug to improve irrigation. Later, the French drained much of the Delta and built a series of canals and dikes, making it suitable for cultivation. During the early twentieth century, the area increased rapidly in population, as many peasants migrated to the area to work as tenant farmers on large rice fields owned by absentee landlords. There are an estimated 300,000 Khmer (known as Khmer Krom) living in the area, descendants of subjects of the Angkor Empire who had lived there prior to the Vietnamese conquest.

Today the Mekong River Delta is the great rice basket of Vietnam. With over sixty percent of the total land area under cultivation, the Delta produces over five million metric tons of padi rice each year, representing between thirty and forty percent of total grain production. (See Don Dien; March to the South; Mekong River)

MERLIN, MARTIAL. Governor-general of French Indochina from 1923 to 1925. A previous governor in French West Africa, he was relatively conservative in his views on colonial rule and initiated a number of changes in the educational system in Vietnam, strengthening elementary instruction at the expanse of higher education and specifying that instruction at the basic level in the Franco-Vietnamese system would be in Vietnamese rather than in French. The end result was to render it more difficult for young Vietnamese to advance to higher education in France. Martial Merlin was replaced by Alexander Varenne in the summer of 1925.

MID-AUTUMN FESTIVAL (Tet Trung Thu) (See Festivals).

MILITARY REVOLUTIONARY COUNCIL. Ruling body set up after the military coup that overthrew the South Vietnamese regime of Ngo Dinh Diem in November 1963. The Chairman of the Council was General Duong Van Minh ("Big Minh"), and the top cabinet officers were leading military officers who had taken part in the coup. The Council was initially popular among critics of the previous regime, but it made little headway in the struggle

against the internal insurgency and was overthrown by a second
coup led by Colonel Nguyen Khanh in January 1964. (See Duong
Van Minh; Ngo Dinh Diem; Nguyen Khanh; Tran Van Don)

MINH HUONG (Ming incense). Vietnamese term for residents of Chinese
descent living in Vietnam. Most ethnic Chinese living in traditional Vietnam were descendants of Ming loyalists who had fled
China at the conquest of the Ming Dynasty by the Manchus.
Many moved into separate villages in relatively unpopulated areas
of South Vietnam, but later intermarried with native Vietnamese.
Under the Vietnamese empire, they were viewed as distinct from
both native Vietnamese and the so-called overseas Chinese, and
gradually assimilated into the surrounding environment, although
some remained in commerce and retained their Chinese customs.
Often they were used by the Vietnamese court in dealings with
China. (See Overseas Chinese)

MINH MANG (reigned 1820-1841). Second emperor of the Nguyen
Dynasty in nineteenth-century Vietnam. Minh Mang, second son
of Emperor Gia Long, ascended to the throne on the latter's
death in 1820. Gia Long's first son, Prince Canh, had died in
1801. Gia Long rejected Prince Canh's son and chose the oldest
son of his concubine as his successor, reportedly because of his
strong character and distrust of the West.
    Minh Mang's performance as ruler confirmed his father's esti-
mate. Suspicious of the ultimate motives of Western missionaries,
he reduced their presence in Vietnam and prohibited the practice
of Christianity in the empire. He was more receptive to Western
commerce, so long as it remained under strict governmental supervision.
    In his internal policies, Minh Mang was a vigorous administra-
tor, setting up a number of new administrative offices on the
Chinese model, and reorganizing the empire into 31 provinces
(tinh) under governors (tong doc) or governors-general (tuan
phu) directly subordinated to the central government. He
attempted to improve the economy by improving the irrigation
and road network, putting new land under cultivation, and
attempting to limit large landed holdings. In this he had only
moderate success and rural unrest, provoked by poor economic
conditions, was a regular feature of his reign. In foreign affairs,
Minh Mang extended Vietnamese control over much of Cambodia,
causing strained relations with Siam (Thailand).
    Minh Mang died in 1841 at the age of 50 and was succeeded
by his son Thieu Tri. (See Christianity; Co Mat Vien; Luc
Bo; Nguyen Dynasty; Noi Cac)

MODERNIZATION SOCIETY (Duy Tan Hoi). Anti-colonial organization in French-occupied Vietnam. It was established by the
Vietnamese patriot Phan Boi Chau in 1903 in order to promote
an insurrection against French Rule. Its goal was to evict the
French and establish a constitutional monarchy under Prince

Cuong De, a descendant of Prince Canh, a son of the founding emperor of the Nguyen Dynasty (1802-1945). The organization was replaced by a new one entitled the Vietnamese Restoration Society (Viet Nam Quang Phuc Hoi) in 1912. (See Cuong De; Gia Long; Phan Boi Chau; Restoration Society)

MODUS VIVENDI. Temporary agreement reached between Ho Chi Minh, President of the Democratic Republic of Vietnam (DRV) and the French government in September 1946. (See Fontainebleau Conference)

MONGOL INVASIONS. A series of massive attacks launched against Vietnam by the Mongol (Yuan) Empire in China during the last half of the thirteenth century. The first took place in 1258. The last two occurred during the 1280s. All were defeated because of the brilliant strategy adopted by Vietnamese military leaders and the national resistance by the Vietnamese people. The Mongol Emperor, Kublai Khan, was preparing another invasion of Vietnam when he died in 1294. His successor accepted the Vietnamese offer of a tributary relationship and peace was restored between the two countries until the fall of the Yuan Empire in 1368. (See Tran Hung Dao; Tran Nhan Tong)

MONTAGNARDS. Generic French term for the minority mountain peoples living in French Indochina. (See Tribal Minorities)

MOUNT DO (Nui Do). Prehistoric archeological site located in Thanh Hoa province, North Vietnam. The site was discovered by Vietnamese archeologists in November 1960. Located on a slight elevation about fifty feet above surrounding rice fields, the Mount Do find was the first clear indication of a paleolithic culture in mainland Southeast Asia, thus indicating that prehistoric man inhabited this area as early as 500,000 years ago. Artifacts found at the site included chipped cutters and scrapers and hand axes from the Chellean period. (See Archeology; Hoa Binh Culture; Son Vi Culture)

MUONG. A minority ethnic group in Vietnam. Numbering approximately 700,000 in population, the Muong live primarily in the hilly province of Ha Son Binh, south of Hanoi, although smaller numbers inhabit the neighboring provinces of Son La Vinh Phu, and Thanh Hoa.

In terms of ethnic background and language, the Muong are closely related to the Vietnamese, and some historians speculate that the original separation of the two peoples took place in the first millenium A.D. when some Viet-Muong peoples migrated into the Red River Delta and became the ancestors of the modern Vietnamese.

Like the neighboring Tay peoples, the Muong lived until recently under a feudal socio-political structure, with a single noble family possessing jurisdiction over several villages (the

term "Muong" is a Tay word for several villages under a single
noble administration). The Muong were integrated into the
majority Vietnamese population during the nineteenth century.
(See Tay; Tribal Minorities)

- N -

NAM BO (South Vietnam, also known as Nam Ky). Term used by
the Vietnamese to refer to the southern provinces of Vietnam.
During the period of French colonial rule it was often applied
specifically to the Colony of Cochin China. The other regions of
Vietnam are Trung Bo (Central Vietnam) and Bac Bo (North
Vietnam).

NAM KY UPRISING (Uprising in South Vietnam). Abortive revolt
launched by Cochin Chinese branch of the Indochinese Communist
Party (ICP) in 1940. Taking advantage of political unrest caused
by troop call-ups, peasant discontent in the Mekong delta provinces, and the growing international crisis in the Pacific, the
ICP's regional committee for South Vietnam (Uy Ban Nam Bo)
planned an insurrection in the Mekong region in the fall of 1940.
The Party Central Committee, holding its Seventh Plenum in
Tonkin, advised a postponement, but emissaries sent to the South
were captured by the French, and the revolt broke out on schedule in late November.
Although the rebels were briefly successful in a few areas,
the French counterattack was successful and the revolt was
quickly suppressed. In the process, the local ICP apparatus
was virtually destroyed.

NAM PHONG (Wind from the South). Literary journal published by the
journalist Pham Quynh in early twentieth-century Vietnam. The
journal, established in North Vietnam in 1917, was sponsored
by the French colonial regime to channel Vietnamese literary
nationalism into the relatively innocuous arena of cultural reform.
The journal published articles in three languages (French,
Vietnamese, and Chinese) on various literary subjects, but was
best known for its popularization of quoc ngu (the roman transliteration of the spoken Vietnamese language) as the dominant
form of literary expression in modern Vietnam. It survived over
two hundred issues and finally closed its doors in December 1934.
(See Journalism; Literature; Pham Quynh; Quoc Ngu)

NAM TIEN (See March to the South).

NAM VIET (Nan Yueh). Early kingdom in Vietnam, created in the
late third century B.C. by the Chinese adventurer Trieu Da.
Trieu Da (in Chinese, Chao T'o), was a military commander charged
by the Qin (Ch'in) Empire to occupy newly-conquered areas in
South China. When the Qin Emperor Shih Huang Ti died in 206

B.C., his empire disintegrated and Trieu Da declared himself
ruler of the new state of Nam Viet ("Southern Viet," in
Chinese Nan Yuch), with his capital at Canton (Modern-day
Quangzhou). For several years, Trieu Da received tribute from
the state of Au Lac, located to the south in the Red River Valley,
while he attempted to secure his independence from the newly-
created Han Dynasty in North China. Eventually, however, his
relations with the Han court improved, and Trieu Da attacked
and defeated Au Lac and incorporated its territory into the
kingdom of Nam Viet.

Like his predecessors, Trieu Da ruled through the indigenous
landed aristocracy (the Lac Lords) and maintained local traditions.
In 111 B.C., however, the state of Nam Viet was conquered by
the Han Dynasty, which incorporated the entire territory into
the Chinese Empire. After the restoration of Vietnamese independence in the tenth century A.D., Ngo Quyen, founder of the
short-lived Ngo dynasty, again adopted the term as the formal
title of his new state until 968, when the name was changed to
Dai Co Viet. In 1803, Emperor Gia Long of the newly-established
Nguyen Dynasty briefly considered reviving the term. The idea
was vetoed by the Manchu emperor, however, apparently because
of its anti-Chinese connotations, and the name ultimately adopted
was Viet Nam. (See Nguyen Dynasty; Viet Nam)

NATIONAL ASSEMBLY (Quoc Hoi). Supreme legislative body of the
Socialist Republic of Vietnam. Originally established by decree
in November 1945 and confirmed in the Constitution of 1946, it
has been retained by the later constitutions promulgated in 1959
and 1980. It is a unicameral assembly whose members are elected
by universal suffrage on the basis of one deputy for every
10,000 voters in urban areas and one per 30,000 in the countryside.
In theory, the National Assembly is the sovereign power in the
state. In actuality, it plays a role similar to legislative assemblies in other Marxist-Leninist societies, serving as a rubber
stamp to ratify decisions already taken by the Vietnamese Communist Party leadership and the executive branch. There are
currently 496 seats in the Assembly, with candidates for office
chosen by the Fatherland Front. (See Constitutions of Vietnam;
Democratic Republic of Vietnam; Socialist Republic of Vietnam)

NATIONAL COUNCIL OF RECONCILIATION AND CONCORD (See
Paris Agreement).

NATIONAL FRONT FOR THE LIBERATION OF SOUTH VIETNAM, NLF
(Mat Tran Dan Toc Giai Phong Mien Nam). Revolutionary Front
organization established in South Vietnam in 1960. Usually referred
to as the National Liberation Front, or NLF, the National
Front for the Liberation of South Vietnam was created in December 1960 at a secret location near the Cambodian border in the
Republic of Vietnam. Composed of South Vietnamese citizens from
a wide variety of backgrounds, it was organized under the

sponsorship of the Democratic Republic of Vietnam (DRV) in the North as a broad front organization to mobilize popular sentiment against the regime of Ngo Dinh Diem in Saigon. Like its predecessor, the League for the Independence of Vietnam, or Vietminh, the program of the Front stressed relatively uncontroversial objectives such as democratic freedoms, peace, and land reform in order to appear to moderate sentiment in the South. There was no reference to communism or to the Front's links with the DRV, and references to national reunification with the North were vague, indicating that the process would be peaceful and take place over a number of years.

Structurally, the National Liberation Front was directed by an elected central committee and a presidium. At the grass roots level, it functioned through a series of mass associations for peasants, workers, writers and artists, women, students, Buddhists, and so forth. In the mid-1960s, membership in the Front and its mass organizations was estimated in the millions. It continued to function until the end of the Vietnam War in 1975, but was practically superseded by the Provisional Revolutionary Government of South Vietnam (PRG), created in 1969. After national reunification in 1975, the NLF was merged into the Fatherland Front (Mat Tran To Quoc), its counterpart in the North. (See Fatherland Front; Provisional Revolutionary Government)

NATIONAL SALVATION ASSOCIATIONS (cuu quoc hoi). Mass organizations set up by the Indochinese Communist Party (ICP) as a component of its struggle against the French and the Japanese during World War II. Associations were established representing various ethnic, functional, and religious groups in Vietnam under the overall umbrella of the League for the Independence of Vietnam, or Vietminh. After 1954, the so-called cuu quoc were simply called mass associations. (See League for the Independence of Vietnam)

NATIONALIZATION OF INDUSTRY AND COMMERCE. In accordance with Marxist-Leninist doctrine, it is the intention of Vietnamese Communist Party leaders to put all industry and commerce in Vietnam under state or community control as part of a broad program to build a socialist and ultimately a communist society. During the late 1950s, heavy industry and most natural resources were placed under state control in the Democratic Republic of Vietnam (DRV), although a small private commercial and manufacturing center, mainly composed of overseas Chinese, was tolerated in large cities like Hanoi and Haiphong.

After reunification in 1975, Party leaders nationalized major industries and utilities in the South, but permitted a small private sector until March 1978, when a government decree announced the nationalization of all industry and commerce above the family level throughout the country. The measure, probably undertaken to undercut the growing economic power and influence of the

Chinese community in Ho Chi Minh City (previously known as Saigon), aroused widespread resentment and led to the flight abroad of thousands of urban residents during the next few years.

During the 1980s, official policy has attempted to achieve a balance between the desire to complete socialist transformation in the South and the realistic acceptance of the need to tolerate the existence of a small capitalist sector to promote industrial growth and the production of consumer goods. Current policy permits the operation of private enterprises in certain areas of the urban economy while at the same time seeking to improve the managerial capacity of the state to assume a larger role for the state-owned sector in the future. (See Industry)

NAVARRE, HENRI. Commander-in-chief of French expeditionary forces in Indochina from May 1953 until July 1954. General Navarre was appointed to the post as a replacement for General Raoul Salan as a means of placating the Eisenhower Administration in the United States, which was demanding a more forceful prosecution of the war on the part of the French. General Navarre produced an ambitious three-stage plan to clean out pockets of Vietminh control in Central and South Vietnam and then launch a major military offensive in the spring and summer of 1954 to destroy Vietminh positions in the North.

The Eisenhower administration gave its approval to the so-called "Navarre Plan" and increased U.S. aid to the French to assist in the war effort. But the French government, under growing pressure from public opinion to bring the unpopular war to an end, did not send sufficient reinforcements or equipment to Indochina, and the Navarre Plan was never fully put into effect. After their disastrous defeat at Dien Bien Phu in the spring of 1954, the French accepted a compromise settlement at the Geneva Conference in July. (See Dien Dien Phu, Battle of; Geneva Accords)

NAVARRE PLAN (See Navarre, Henri).

NEOLITHIC ERA. The final stage of the Stone Age characterized by the development of sophisticated stone tools and domestication of agriculture. It is the general view of archeologists that in Vietnam the Neolithic era commenced with the development of agriculture during the Hoabinhian period about 11,000 years ago, and thus somewhat earlier than the arrival of the New Stone Age civilization elsewhere in Asia and in the West. By the third millenium B.C., the use of stone tools coexisted with the appearance of bronze technology. The Neolithic era gave way to the Bronze Age with the rise of the advanced Dong Son culture after the seventh century B.C. (See Bronze Age; Hoa Binh Culture)

NEW ECONOMIC ZONES. Agricultural settlements established by the Socialist Republic of Vietnam (SRV) to relieve the refugee problem

in the cities after the Vietnam War. The concept had originated
in North Vietnam in the 1960s when economic planners promoted
the construction of urban centers at the district level to combine
both agricultural and manufacturing activities. Although hampered by war requirements and the reluctance of many Vietnamese
to leave their native villages, nearly one million peasants had been
resettled from the crowded Red River Delta to underpopulated
areas in the mountains by the end of the war.

In 1975, the Hanoi regime revived the concept in an effort to
resettle the three million refugees who had fled the southern
countryside to settle in refugee camps in the major cities during
the last years of the war. So-called "new economic zones" were
hurriedly set up in the Central Highlands and other sparsely
populated regions in the South. Recruits were provided with
seeds, farm tools, building materials, and food for several months.
Most of the land was held in common, but each family received a
private plot to cultivate vegetables or fruit for its own use.

The aim of the program was to settle nearly two million people
in the new settlements as part of a major resettlement program
that would result in the transfer of ten million Vietnamese from
crowded regions into less-populated areas. Between 1976 and
1980, over one million people were sent to the New Economic
Zones. Recruitment was intended to be voluntary, but there
were persistent reports of coercion, and the zones soon earned
a bad reputation for poor preparation and unattractive conditions.
The program continues, however, and official sources report the
resettlement is taking place at a rate of over 300,000 annually.

NEW SOCIETY GROUP (Tan Xa Hoi Doan). Informal legislative group
that functioned in the Republic of Vietnam in the late 1960s and
early 1970s. Loosely identified with General Duong Van (Big)
Minh, and the Buddhist movement in South Vietnam, the group
served as a potential opposition to the government of President
Nguyen Van Thieu, but never evolved into a major political party.
(See Duong Van Minh; Nguyen Van Thieu; Republic of Vietnam)

NEW VIETNAMESE REVOLUTIONARY PARTY (See Tan Viet Cach Menh
Dang).

NGHE TINH REVOLT. Major uprising against French Colonial rule
in Central Vietnam in 1930-1931. The unrest began in early 1930
with factory strikes and riots throughout the country on rubber
plantations in Cochin China. By late spring, peasants in the
central provinces of Nghe An and Ha Tinh began to demonstrate
against high taxes and mandarin corruption. The unrest was encouraged by activists of the newly-formed Indochinese Communist
Party (known until October as the Vietnamese Communist Party),
but was provoked to a considerable degree by poor economic and
social conditions, exacerbated by the Great Depression.

During the summer and fall of 1930, angry peasants in the
central provinces seized power in the villages and set up local

peasant associations (known as "Soviets") which reduced rents and in some instances confiscated land and punished unpopular landlords. Communist Party leaders, caught by surprise by the violence of the revolt, supported the rebels but attempted to limit the damage to their own apparatus.

The French reacted swiftly, and by spring 1931 the revolt--which had never spread effectively beyond the central provinces of Nghe An and Ha Tinh (thus the name Nghe-Tinh)--had been suppressed. In the process, several communist leaders were captured, and the party's local organization was virtually destroyed. The revolt had thus been disastrous for the Communist Party, but had indicated the potential power of the rural masses, a lesson that would be learned and applied after World War II. (See Indochinese Communist Party)

NGHE-TINH SOVIETS (See Nghe-Tinh Revolt).

NGO DINH DIEM (1901-1963). Prime Minister and President of the Republic of Vietnam from 1954 until 1963. Born in a family of mandarins with court connections in the imperial capital of Hue in 1901, Ngo Dinh Diem attended the prestigious National Academy (Quoc Hoc) and then took a law degree at the University of Hanoi. He entered imperial service under Emperor Khai Dinh and was eventually appointed Minister of the Interior under the government of Emperor Bao Dai in 1933, but resigned shortly thereafter in protest against French interference in Vietnam's internal affairs.

For several years, Diem was inactive in politics. In late 1945 he refused an offer by Ho Chi Minh to collaborate with the Vietminh. A fervent Catholic, he was as opposed to communism as he was to French colonialism, and was further angered by the Vietminh assassination of his brother Ngo Dinh Khoi, governor of Quang Ngai province. A few years later he refused an offer from ex-Emperor Bao Dai to serve as prime minister in the proposed government of the Associated State of Vietnam.

In the early 1950s Diem came to the attention of U.S. officials as a potential leader of a free Vietnam. As a Catholic and an anti-French patriot, his credentials were appealing to Washington and in the summer of 1954, under pressure from the Eisenhower Administration, Bao Dai appointed him prime minister of Vietnam just as the Geneva Conference was coming to a close. After Geneva, Diem moved rapidly to consolidate his power in South Vietnam, eliminating the Binh Xuyen, cowing the religious sects, and removing supporters of Chief of State Bao Dai from positions of influence in his government. In 1955 he rigged a referendum which led to the resignation of Bao Dai and the election of Ngo Dinh Diem, the following year, as President of a new Republic of Vietnam (RVN).

Diem eventually won full support from the United States, which hoped to use him to transform South Vietnam into a viable, anti-communist, democratic society. But Diem had several weaknesses.

He had authoritarian instincts and alienated key groups in South
Vietnamese society. He was beholden to his primary supporters,
the Catholic community and the wealthy landed classes, and failed
to carry through on a promised land reform program. By 1959,
social and political unrest, backed by the communist regime in
North Vietnam, was on the rise.

In 1961, President John F. Kennedy reaffirmed U.S. support
for South Vietnam, but pressured Diem to introduce reforms in
the hope of reducing internal discontent. Diem agreed, but in
subsequent months ignored U.S. advice, cracking down on
Buddhist critics concerned over his increasing tendency to favor
Catholics. In 1963, Buddhist demonstrations erupted, leading
to police reprisals and an outcry of criticism in the West. When
discontented military officers secretly sought U.S. approval for
a coup to overthrow the Diem regime, the Kennedy Administration approved. On November 1, 1963, coup leaders seized key
installations in the capital of Saigon. Diem was captured with
his brother Ngo Dinh Nhu and assassinated the following day.
While Kennedy was reportedly horrified at the murder, the United
States quickly indicated its approval of the new military government under the leadership of General Duong Van (Big) Minh.

The Diem regime has inspired controversy among scholars
and close observers of the Vietnam War. Some argue that Diem
was the only strong anti-communist leader in South Vietnam, and
that his overthrow guaranteed an eventual communist takeover.
Others counter that Diem was the source of the problem, inciting
the very dissent that led to his own downfall. Whatever the
answer to that debate, it remains true that the Diem era set
South Vietnam on a course which its own leaders, and those of th
United States, would be unable to reverse. (See Bao Dai; Bao
Dai Solution; Duong Van Minh; Ngo Dinh Nhu)

NGO DINH NHU (1910-1963). Brother of Ngo Dinh Diem, President
of South Vietnam from 1956 to 1963, and Minister of the Interior
in the Diem regime. The son of Ngo Dinh Kha, an influential
figure at the imperial court, Nhu was educated in France and
eventually became active as an organizer of Catholic labor union
movement, the Vietnamese Federation of Christian Workers.

After the rise to power of his older brother Diem in 1954,
Nhu became the driving force behind the regime. Although officially serving in the influential post of Minister of the Interior,
it was as an advisor and the organizer of Diem's secret Can Lao
Party that Nhu exercised enormous influence behind the scenes in
Saigon. Widely viewed as manipulative and feared for his tactics
in ridding the regime of its enemies, Nhu (along with his wife,
madame Nhu) came to be seen by U.S. officials as a prime source
of Diem's unpopularity, and in 1963 the Kennedy Administration
privately demanded that he be removed as Diem's chief advisor.
When the latter refused, Washington signalled its approval for
the military coup that overthrew the regime on November 1, 1963.
The next day, Nhu and Diem were executed by supporters of the

group. (See Can Lao Party; Ngo Dinh Diem; Ngo Dinh Nhu, Madame)

NGO DINH NHU, MADAME (Maiden name Tran Le Xuan). Wife of Ngo Dinh Nhu and self-styled "first lady" of the Ngo Dinh Diem regime in South Vietnam. A daughter of Tran Van Chuong, Vietnamese Ambassador to the United States during the 1950s, Madame Nhu was born Tran Le Xuan in 1924. Educated in Hanoi and Saigon, she married Ngo Dinh Nhu, younger brother of the Catholic politician Ngo Dinh Diem, shortly after graduation from the lycée. A woman of immense energy and intensity, she became a figure of considerable importance under the Diem regime. Operating behind the scenes, she was active in promoting Catholic causes, the struggle against communism, and the fortunes of the Diem regime itself, and was the guiding spirit behind the Women's Solidarity Movement, an anticommunist paramilitary organization established in South Vietnam after the Geneva Conference. Known by foreigners as the "dragon lady" for her influence and steely determination, she was considered by critics as an evil force within the Diem regime and a key source of its unpopularity among non-Catholics in the population.

Since the assassination of Ngo Dinh Diem and her husband in 1963, she has lived abroad. (See Ngo Dinh Diem; Ngo Dinh Nhu)

NGO DUC KE (1879-1929). Journalist and scholar in colonial Vietnam. A Confucian scholar and editor of the Hanoi review, Huu Thanh, Ngo Duc Ke in the early 1920s waged a literary war with the Francophile journalist and writer Pham Quyuh over the relative merits of the Tale of Kieu (Truyen Kieu) as a symbol of Vietnamese nationalism. Where Pham Quynh had argued that so long as Truyen Kieu survived, Vietnamese national identity still existed, Ngo Duc Ke countered that the Vietnamese language and the literature would not survive unless the nation survived. (See Literature; Pham Quynh; Tale of Kieu)

NGO DYNASTY (939-965). First independent dynasty in Vietnam after the overthrow of Chinese occupation by Ngo Quyen in 939. Ngo Quyen, member of prominent family and a military commander in the army of Duong Dinh Nghe, seized power in Vietnam from pro-Chinese elements after the assassination of his patron in 937. In 939, Quyen declared himself ruler of Nam Viet (thus restoring the name used for the kingdom of Vietnam prior to the Chinese conquest in the late second century B.C.).

Ngo Quyen's reign was marked by factionalism and instability and he died in 944. He was succeeded by his brother-in-law Duong Tam Kha, a son of Duong Dinh Nghe who seized the throne while serving as regent for Ngo Quyen's sons. The latter, however, quickly deposed Duong Tam Kha and in 950 declared himself the legitimate ruler. The new ruler, calling himself the Nam Tan Vuong (King of Southern China), sought legitimacy by sending

a tribute mission to the emperor of the Southern Han, but his
reign was marked by instability and when he was killed in battle
in 963, the dynasty rapidly colapsed. A period of anarchy
followed (called the period of the twelve warlords or su quan) un
the rise of the Dinh Dynasty in 968. (See Dinh Bo Linh; Ngo
Quyen)

NGO QUYEN. Rebel leader who restored Vietnamese independence
from Chinese rule in A.D. 939. Ngo Quyen, son of a provincial
official and a native of the western Red River Delta near Mount
Tan Vien, became a military commander and a son-in-law of
Duong Dinh Nghe, who had seized control of Vietnam in the
unstable conditions following the collapse of the T'ang Empire
in China. After Dinh Nghe was assassinated in 937, Ngo Quyen
launched an attack on the troops loyal to the assassin and a
Chinese army which supported him. At the mouth of the Bach
Dang River, at the entrance to the Tonkin Gulf, Quyen won a
major victory by sinking wooden poles into the mud at the mouth
of the river. When the tide fell, the Chinese fleet was impaled
on the poles and destroyed.

The After the Battle of Bach Dang River, Ngo Quyen declared himself king of the independent kingdom of Nam Viet, with its new
capital at Co Loa, the ancient capital of Vietnam before the Chinese conquest. He died in 944 at the age of 47, leading to a
period of political stability which ended only with the rise to
power of Dinh Bo Linh.

Although Ngo Quyen had restored Vietnamese independence
after one thousand years of Chinese domination, his rule was
too brief and marked by factionalism to convince later Vietnamese
historians to consider him the true founder of Vietnamese independence. That honor has usually been ascribed to Dinh Bo
Linh, founder of the Dinh Dynasty in 968. (See Dinh Bo Linh;
Duong Dinh Nghe)

NGO SI LIEN. Noted Vietnamese historian during the Le Dynasty
(1428-1788). A member of the Bureau of History, Ngo Si
Lien had participated in an examination of historical records
during the early years of the reign of Emperor Le Thanh Tong
(1460-1497). He later wrote a comprehensive history of the Vietnamese nation from its prehistorical origins to the Le Dynasty,
Dai Viet Su Ky Toan Thu (Complete Book of the Historical Records of Vietnam), published in 1479.

The Dai Viet Su Ky Toan Thu made use of Le Van Huu's
Dai Viet Su Ky, written during the Tran Dynasty, as well as
Phan Phu Tien's Dai Viet Su Ky Tuc Bien (Supplementary Com-
pilation of the Historical Records of Great Viet), which had carrie
Le Van Huu's narrative history from the Tran to the founding
of the Le Dynasty in 1428. The work was unique in that it
utilized both Chinese sources and Vietnamese historical records
contained in Linh Nam Tich Quai, an anonymous work which
collated the folk legends concerning the earliest origins of the

Vietnamese people.

Later, Ngo Si Lien's work was periodically revised and became recognized as the official imperial history of the state of Vietnam. (See Le Thanh Tong; Le Van Huu; Literature)

NGO TAT TO (1894-1954). Realistic novelist of the 1930s whose writings criticized feudal society in colonial Vietnam. He also attempted to make Vietnamese history and traditional literature available to the average Vietnamese by publishing quoc ngu translations of extant historical works dating back to the Ly Dynasty (1009-1025). (See Literature)

NGO THI NHAM (also known as Ngo Thoi Nham) (1746-1803). Scholar and official in late eighteenth-century Vietnam. Born in 1741 in a scholar-gentry family, Ngo Thi Nham was a gifted student, passing his doctoral examination at the relatively young age of 30. Serving in the bureaucracy during the declining years of the Le Dynasty, he later became a supporter to the Tay Son leader Nguyen Hue, whom he served as a diplomat and an official. He was put to death shortly after the rise of the Nguyen Dynasty to power in 1802.

Ngo Thi Nham is well known as a major contributor to the historical work, Hoang Le Nhat Thong Chi (Chronical of the Imperial Le Dynasty).

NGUYEN AI QUOC (Nguyen the Patriot). Pseudonym of Ho Chi Minh, founder of the Vietnamese Communist movement. Ho Chi Minh, born Nguyen Tat Thanh, adopted the name after World War I in Paris, and used it during his early revolutionary career until 1945, when he became known as Ho Chi Minh (he who enlightens). As President he often denied his earlier revolutionary identity and described himself simply as a patriot. (See Ho Chi Minh)

NGUYEN AN NINH (1900-1943). Influential journalist and patriotic activist in early twentieth-century colonial Vietnam. Nguyen An Ninh was born in 1900 near Saigon. His father was a scholar who had participated in the anti-French Can Vuong (Save the King) movement before the turn of the century. Nguyen An Ninh was educated in French schools and then studied law in Paris. He returned to Cochin China in 1922 and immediately became engaged in political activities, publishing a newspaper entitled La Cloche Fêlée and giving speeches criticial of the colonial regime.

Although he repudiated revolutionary violence and admired the teachings of Mahatma Gandhi and Rabindranath Tagore, his fiery speeches galvanized the emotions of many young intellectuals in Cochin China, loosely organized under the name "The Hopes of Youth" (Thanh Nien Cao Vong), and earned the distrust of Governor Cognacq. He was arrested and briefly imprisoned for his outspoken ciriticism of France in March 1926. On his release, Ninh began to agitate among rural villagers in the Mekong Delta and developed a mystical streak. Once again, his organization was dispersed. In the 1930s, he began to collaborate with the Indochinese Communist Party, although he himself never became a member. He was a frequent contributor to the newspaper La Lutte (the Struggle) published by Party members and Trotskyites in Saigon.

In September 1937 Nguyen An Ninh was arrested and sentenced to five years in prison. He died on Poulo Condore Island, allegedly of torture, in 1943. (See Can Vuong; Cloche Fêlée; Hopes of Youth Party; Lutte, La)

NGUYEN ANH (Emperor Gia Long). Founding emperor of the Nguyen Dynasty in early nineteenth-century Vietnam. Born in the princel house of the Nguyen lords in 1761, Nguyen Anh was practically the only member of the family to survive when the Nguyen Capital of Gia Dinh (Saigon) was seized by the Tay Son Rebellion in 1778. Escaping to the marshy Mekong Delta, the young Nguyen Anh proclaimed himself king and was able to restore Nguyen power briefly, but then was driven out again in 1783. Taking refuge on Phu Quoc island in the Gulf of Thailand, he accepted aid from the French Bishop of Adran, Pigneau de Behaine. In 1787 he signed a treaty with France to restore the Nguyen in power in South Vietnam in return for the cession port of Tourane (Da Nang) and the island of Poulo Condore. The promised assistance from the French court did not materialize, but Pigneau de Behaine helped to organize the armed forces which attempted to overthrow the rule of the Tay Son in Vietnam.

In 1802, Nguyen Anh's troops seized the capital of Thang Long and after investiture in 1806 by China, proclaimed himself Emperor Gia Long of a new Nguyen Dynasty (1802-1945). The dynastic name Gia Long, taken from the names of the southern (Gia Dinh) and northern (Thang Long) capitals, symbolized the reunification of the empire after a long period of division. The new capital was placed at Hue (Phu Xuan), near the central coast. (See Gia Long; Nguyen Dynasty; Nguyen Hue; Pigneau de Behaine; Tay Son Rebellion)

NGUYEN BINH KIEM (1491-1585). Scholar and writer in sixteenth-century Vietnam. His father was a mandarin, and he too served as an official in the Mac Dynasty and then, disgusted at the high level of corruption within the bureaucracy and at court, resigned his office in 1542 to become a teacher and a poet. For much of the remainder of his life he lived at his famous retreat, Bach Van Am, (Hermitage of the White Cloud) in Hai Duong Province, where he became renowned for his prophecies and was visited by a number of prominent political figures of his day, including Trinh Kiem and Nguyen Hoang, the respective founders of the Trinh and Nguyen lords.

A noted Confucian like his great predecessor Nguyen Binh Kiem represented the tradition of resigning from office and living a life of seclusion rather than becoming involved in a corrupt society. He wrote over 1,000 poems, many about the beauty of nature and the ironies of life, in both nom and Chinese. (See Literature; Nguyen Hoang; Nguyen Trai; Trinh Kiem)

NGUYEN CAO KY (1930-   ). Flamboyant Vietnamese air force officer and Vice President of the Republic of Vietnam from 1967 to 1971. A native of North Vietnam, Nguyen Cao Ky chose a military career after graduation from high school and rose to the rank of air force colonel under the regime of President Ngo Dinh Diem. In January 1964, Ky participated in the "young Turk" rebellion that put General Nguyen Khanh in power as chairman of the Military Revolutionary Council. Now an Air Vice Marshall, he played an active role in the factional struggles that followed and in June 1965 joined with fellow young Turk Nguyen Van Thieu in overthrowing the weak regime, headed by a so-called National Leadership Committee. The Committee named Ky Prime Minister of a new Executive Council which assumed day-to-day responsibility over national affairs.

In 1967 Nguyen Cao Ky was elected Vice President on a ticket led by Nguyen Van Thieu that took office after the approval of a new constitution. Ky's relations with President Thieu declined, however, and after being disqualified from running for president in the 1971 elections, he retired from politics. After the communist takeover of Saigon he settled in the United States. (See Ngo Dinh Diem; Nguyen Khanh; Nguyen Van Thieu)

NGUYEN CHI THANH (1915-1967). Senior General in the People's Army of Vietnam (PAVN) during the Vietnam War. Nguyen Chi Thanh was born in 1914 or 1915 in a poor peasant family in Central Vietnam. He became active in revolutionary activities in the mid-1930s and a member of the Indochinese Communist Party (ICP) in 1937. Named head of the Party Committee in Thua Thien province, he was arrested in 1938 and spent much of World War II in prison. In August 1945 he attended the Tan Trao Conference and was named to the Party Central Committee.

Placed in charge of Party operations in central Vietnam, Nguyen Chi Thanh rose rapidly in the ranks of the PAVN and was head of its Political Department in 1950. He joined the Politburo in 1957 and General of the Army in 1959. During the Vietnam War he was placed in charge of military operations in South Vietnam, where he recommended an activist policy of big unit warfare against U.S. military forces in South Vietnam. His strategy was criticized by Vo Nguyen Giap for the high casualities incurred, and a more modest approach was adopted. He died either of a heart attack or a U.S. bombing attack in July 1967 while formulating initial plans for the Tet Offensive. (See Tet Offensive; Vo Nguyen Giap)

NGUYEN CO THACH (1925-   ). Foreign minister of the Socialist Republic of Vietnam (SRV). Born in 1925 in a peasant family in North Vietnam, Nguyen Co Thach entered revolutionary activities in the late 1930s, and was jailed by the French. In 1954 he served as a staff officer in the People's Army of Vietnam at Dien Dien Phu.

After Geneva, he entered the Ministry of Foreign Affairs and was named Ambassador to India in 1956. In 1980 he replaced the veteran Nguyen Duy Trinh as Minister of Foreign Affairs and rose to Politburo rank in the Party in 1982, the first career diplomat to do so. In March 1987 he was named Vice Premier on a government shakeup after the Sixth Party Congress. Knowledgeable about the West and considered a moderate in domestic affairs, he is considered a prime candidate for future leadership in the SRV.

NGUYEN CONG HOAN (1903-1977). Well-known realistic novelist in colonial Vietnam. Beginning as a teacher in Hai Duong province, Nguyen Cong Hoan came to public attention in the late 1930s as a novelist dealing with serious social themes concerning the life of poor villagers and the corruption and arrogance of officialdom. Among his most famous works are Master Minh (Co Giao Minh) and Leaves of Jade, Branches of gold (La Ngoc Canh Vang). (See Literature)

NGUYEN CONG TRU (1778-1858). Noted scholar-official in early Nguyen Dynasty Vietnam. Born the son of a mandarin from Ha Tinh province who held a high position under the Le Dynasty, Nguyen Cong Tru encountered difficulties with the civil service examinations and did not enter officialdom until the relatively advanced age of 41. From that point he rose rapidly in the bureaucracy, becoming a provincial governor, governor-general, and eventually Minister of War under the Nguyen Dynasty (1802-1945). Nguyen Cong Tru was equally well known as the author of poems satirizing hypocrisy, social-climbing, and other foibles of human nature, many of which he shared. After retiring from office in 1848, he volunteered to participate in the struggle against the French, but died shortly after. (See Literature)

NGUYEN DINH CHIEU (1822-1888). Scholar and poet in nineteenth-century Vietnam. Blind from childhood, Nguyen Dinh Chieu taught school in his home province of Gia Dinh until the French conquest of Cochin China. He then resigned and moved to Ben Tre, where be began to write poetry in Nom. The primary theme of his writing was that of patriotism and resistance to Foreign rule. One of his most famous works was a funeral ovation for Truong Cong Dinh, the military commander who fought against French troops in South Vietnam. His autobiography, entitled Luc Van Tien, is both a moral essay and a pastiche of life in nineteenth-century Vietnam. (See Literature)

NGUYEN DU (1765-1820). Well-known Vietnamese writer and author of a classic verse novel. Born in a family of scholars and officials in Ha Tinh Province in 1765, he grew up during the turbulent years of the Tay Son Rebellion, which broke out in 1771 and resulted in the formation of a new dynasty in 1789. His family supported the declining Le Dynasty, and Nguyen Du did not enter officialdom until the overthrow of the Tay Son and and rise of the Nguyen Dynasty in 1802. He served as a provincial official and a diplomat on a mission to the Ch'ing court in Peking. He eventually became vice president of the Board of Rites in Hue and died by 1820.

It is as an author and commentator on social conditions in Le Dynasty Vietnam that Nguyen Du's reputation rests. Although he wrote a number of poems in Chinese, he is best known for his famous poem in Nom, Truyen Kieu (the Tale of Kieu), a classic which quickly became a favorite of his countrymen and has been widely praised as the greatest work in Vietnamese literature. (See Literature; Tale of Kieu)

NGUYEN DYNASTY (Nha Nguyen) (1802-1945). Last imperial dynasty in Vietnam, founded by Nguyen Anh (Emperor Gia Long) in 1802. The origins of Nguyen political influence dates back to the sixteenth century when the powerful mandarin Nguyen Kim assisted the Le family to restore its control over the throne from the regime of the Mac. Under the restored Le dynasty the Nguyen family, known as the Nguyen Lords, controlled the South in the name of the Le Dynasty, which was controlled by the Trinh Lords in the North. In the late eighteenth century the Nguyen were driven from power by the Tay Son Rebellion, but a member of the house, Prince Nguyen Anh, defeated the Tay Son and founded the Nguyen Dynasty in 1802.

The Nguyen was a conservative dynasty, ruling in Hue according to Confucian precepts and imitating Ch'ing practice in China. Rule tended to be repressive, and the first several decades were marked by intermittent rural unrest. The dynasty's problems were compounded by French ambitions to establish French political and economic influence in Southeast Asia. The court's efforts to fend off the challenge were ineffective, and in 1884 the empire was transformed into a French protectorate. The South was ceded to France as a colony.

During the next half century, the Nguyen Dynasty emperors were mere puppets of the French colonial regime. The last emperor, Bao Dai ruled at French whim until March 1945 when Japanese occupation forces granted him a spurious independence. When Japan surrendered to the Allies in August, Vietminh forces seized power in Vietnam and persuaded Bao Dai to abdicate, bringing the dynasty to an end. Since 1945, all Vietnamese governments have been republics. (See Bao Dai, Nguyen Anh; Nguyen Lords; Treaty of Protectorate)

NGUYEN GIA THIEU (1741-1798). Renowned poet in late eighteenth-century Vietnam. Born in a mandarin family, he was the author of Cung Oan (Lament of an Edalisque), the story of a beautiful woman forced to live in a royal harem.

NGUYEN HAI THAN (1878- ?). Non-communist nationalist figure
in colonial Vietnam. Born in North Vietnam in 1878, he joined
Phan Boi Chau's movement to overthrow French rule in Vietnam
and later lived for many years in China. During World War II
he cooperated with Nationalist General Chang Fa-k'uei in setting
up the Vietnamese Revolutionary League (Dong Minh Hoi), a non-
communist front organization designed to achieve Chinese objectives in French Indochina. After World War II, Than returned
to Vietnam and served briefly as vice president in Ho Chi Minh's
Democratic Republic of Vietnam. When he realized the extent
of communist domination over the government, he resigned and
returned to China. (See Phan Boi Chau; Vietnamese Revolutionary
League)

NGUYEN HOANG. Influential political figure in sixteenth-century
Vietnam and founder of the Nguyen Lords. Nguyen Hoang was
the son of the noted mandarin Nguyen Kim (1467?-1545). When
Nguyen Kim supported the restoration of the Le Dynasty against
the usurper Mac Dang Dung and his successors, Nguyen Hoang
became a military commander of the Le armed forces and helped
to build a resistance base and capital in Thanh Hoa province,
south of the Red River Delta. But Nguyen Hoang preferred his
powerful brother-in-law Trinh Kiem who, according to rumor,
had been poisoned by Nguyen Hoang's older brother Vong in an
effort to increase his own political influence. In 1558 he sought
and received an appointment as governor of the southern provinces
of Thuan Hoa and Quang Nam.
  In succeeding years Nguyen Hoang consolidated his power in
Central Vietnam while helping Trinh Kiem and his successor Trinh
Tong conquer the Mac regime in the North. After the Mac were
driven out of the capital of Thang Long (present-day Hanoi) in
1592, Nguyen Hoang returned to the South and maintained good
relations with the Trinh family, now dominant over the restored
Le Dynasty in Thang Long, until his death in 1613. (See Le
Dynasty; Mac Dynasty; Nguyen Kim; Nguyen Lords; Trinh Kiem;
Trinh Lords)

NGUYEN HUE (Emperor Quang Trung). Leader of Tay Son Rebellion
and founding emperor of the Tay Son Dynasty in late eighteenth-
century Vietnam. Nguyen Hue was the second eldest of three
brothers from the village of Tay Son in An Khe District, Nghia
Binh Province in Central Vietnam. The family, originally from
Nghe An Province and reportedly descendents of the fifteenth-
century figure Ho Quy Ly, were farmers and small merchants.
In the early 1770s the brothers, led by the eldest Nguyen Nhac,
revolted against the rule of the Nguyen lords, who controlled
the southern provinces of Vietnam in the name of the Later Le
Dynasty. In 1785, the Tay Son seized the Nguyen capital of
Saigon and began to move against the Trinh Lords, who controlled
the North. Marching under the slogan of "Restore the Le, destroy the Trinh," Nguyen Hue seized the imperial capital of Thang

Long in July 1786.

At first, Nguyen Hue kept his campaign slogan and recognized the legitimacy of the aged ruler, Le Hien Tong, who had
reigned as a figurehead under the domination of the Trinh lords
since 1740. In return, the emperor gave his daughter Le Ngoc
Han to Nguyen Hue in marriage, who returned to the South.
When Le Hien Tong died in late 1786, the throne passed to his
grandson Le Chien Tong, who called on Chinese assistance to
restore the power of the Le Dynasty and remove the influence of
the Tay Son. When Chinese troops entered Vietnam in late 1788
and occupied the capital of Thang Long, Nguyen Hue declared
himself emperor Quang Trung and launched an attack on the
North. The invasion succeeded and the Chinese forces retreated
across the border.

After his victory, Emperor Quang Trung set his capital at
Phu Xuan (modern-day Hue) and offered tribute to China. He
also moved vigorously to strengthen the state, reorganizing the
military, promoting land reform, and stimulating trade relations
with the West. To promote a sense of national identity, chu
nom was recognized as the official language at court and in the
civil service examinations. But he died suddenly in 1792 at age
39, and was succeeded by his ten-year old son, Canh Thinh.
The young emperor was unable to prevent the outbreak of internal dissention within the regime, and was overthrown in 1802.
(See Nguyen Anh; Tay Son Rebellion)

NGUYEN HUU THO (1910-   ). Leading figure in the National Liberation Front (NLF) in South Vietnam during the Vietnam War and
a leading official in the Socialist Republic of Vietnam (SRV).
Born the son of an official in Vinh Long province in 1910, Nguyen
Huu Tho studied in France and became a lawyer in Cochin China
in the 1930s.

A member of the French Socialist Party, Nguyen Huu Tho
joined the Vietminh Front in the late 1940s and took part in anti-
U.S. and anti-French activities in Saigon. Arrested for fomen-
ting a demonstration in 1950, he was placed under surveillance near
Lai Chau on the Chinese border. After the Geneva Conference
in 1954, Nguyen Huu Tho became Vice Chairman of the Saigon
Peace Committee. Arrested by the regime of Ngo Dinh Diem,
he served seven years in prison and on his release in 1961, he
became a leading figure in the NLF. After reunification in 1975,
he was named Vice President of the SRV and Acting President on
the death of Ton Duc Thang. He is currently chairman of the
Standing Committee of the National Assembly of the SRV. (See
National Assembly; National Front for the Liberation of South
Vietnam; Ton Duc Thang)

NGUYEN KHAC HIEU (1888-1939) (See Tan Da).

NGUYEN KHANH. South Vietnamese military officer and head of
"young Turks" movement that took power in Saigon in January

1964. Born of a modest background in North Vietnam, Nguyen Khanh became a career military officer and rose rapidly in the ranks after the Geneva Conference in 1954, becoming deputy chief of staff under the regime of President Ngo Dinh Diem. In January 1964 he led a coup organized by younger military officers against the senior officers under General Duong Van Minh that had removed President Ngo Dinh Diem from power.

General Khanh and his "young Turks," middle-ranking military officers such as Nguyen Chanh Thi, Nguyen Van Thieu and Nguyen Cao Ky, were younger than the generation that had overthrown Diem and were inclined to favor the Americans over the French. They lacked political experience, however, and suffered from factionalism in their ranks. Acting under U.S. advice, Khanh established a civilian government, headed by a so-called Supreme National Council which replaced General Duong Van Minh as Chief of State. The factionalism continued, punctuated by growing tension between Catholic and Buddhist elements in Saigon and General Khanh was ousted from power in February 1965. (See Duong Van Minh; Military Revolutionary Council; Nguyen Cao Ky; Nguyen Van Thieu; Tran Van Huong)

NGUYEN KIM (1467-1545). Court official who fought against the Mac Dynasty to restore the later Le Dynasty to power in sixteenth-century Vietnam. A native of Thanh Hoa province, he was related to the Le royal family by marriage and supported their struggle for reinstatement when power was usurped by Mac Dang Dung in 1527. After 1533 he supported Emperor Le Trang Tong, who had declared himself the legitimate ruler of Vietnam while living in exile in Laos. By the early 1540s, supporters of the Le established their court in Thanh Hoa Province, south of the Red River Delta, and continued to fight the Mac, with their capital in Thang Long (present-day Hanoi). In 1545 Nguyen Kim died, allegedly poisoned by the Mac, at the age of 78.

After Nguyen Kim's death, his family continued to support the restoration of the Le Dynasty. A son-in-law, Trinh Kiem, became dominant at the Le court. A son, Nguyen Hoang, feared assassination at the hands of his ambitious brother-in-law and sought appointment as Governor of Thuan Hoa, in the South. The two cooperated to achieve the overthrow of the Mac in 1592, but the split between Trinh Kiem and Nguyen Hoang led in later years to the civil war between the Trinh and Nguyen lords over control of the weak Le Dynasty. (See Later Le Dynasty; Mac Dang Dung; Mac Dynasty; Nguyen Hoang; Trinh Kiem)

NGUYEN LORDS (Chua Nguyen). Powerful aristocratic family and founder of the Nguyen Dynasty (1802-1945) in Vietnam. The family rose to prominence during the decline of the Le Dynasty (1428-1788) in fifteenth-century Vietnam, when an influential mandarin, Nguyen Kim, supported the restoration of the Le against the usurping dynasty established in 1527 by Mac Dang

Dung. After Nguyen Kim's death in 1545, two branches of the family, represented by his son, Nguyen Hoang, and his son-in-law Trinh Kiem, assisted the Le in returning to power in 1952.

During the next two centuries Le Dynasty rulers were dominated by the two powerful families--the Trinh and the Nguyen--who had restored them to the throne. The Trinh lords were dominant in the North, and in the capital of Thang Long (present-day Hanoi), where the imperial family was located. The Nguyen Lords controlled the area of Vietnam south of the Hoanh Son Spur, where Nguyen Hoang had been named governor in 1558. At first the two families cooperated against their common enemy, the Mac. But after the Mac were driven from Thang Long in 1592, the Trinh and the Nguyen themselves became rivals. For two centuries Vietnam was divided, although both accepted the legitimacy of the powerless Le Dynasty.

Under Nguyen rule, the Vietnamese boundary gradually extended toward the south. The rump state of Champa was destroyed, and the lower Mekong Delta seized from the disintegrating Kingdom of Angkor in the late seventeenth century. But rural unrest led to the outbreak of the Tay Son Rebellion in 1771. In 1783, the Nguyen capital at Saigon was conquered by the Tay Son and Nguyen regime overthrown. Nguyen Anh, a prince of the deposed Nguyen family, was able to survive, however, and in 1802 he defeated the Tay Son and proclaimed the establishment of the Nguyen Dynasty (1802-1945). (See Nguyen Anh; Nguyen Hoang; Nguyen Kim; Tay Son Rebellion; Trinh Kiem; Trinh Lords)

NGUYEN PHAN LONG (1889- ?). Reformist political figure in early twentieth-century Vietnam. Born of a South Vietnamese father in Hanoi in 1889, he went to Cochin China and after taking employment as a customs official became a journalist, founding his own newspaper, L'Echo Annamite, in 1920. For several years he cooperated with Bui Quang Chieu in the moderate reformist constitutionalist Party, based in Saigon. In 1925 he presented a famous list of demands for reform (Cahier des Voeux Annamites) to Governor-general Alexander Varenne.

By the 1930s, the two had parted political company as Nguyen Phan Long disagreed with Chieu's close relationship with the French. In 1949, he was named Foreign Minister in the first government of the Associated State of Vietnam under Chief of State Bao Dai. Becoming Prime Minister in January 1950, he was forced out by the French two months later after attempting to obtain direct economic assistance from the United States. (See Bui Quang Chieu; Constitutionalist Party)

NGUYEN THAI HOC (1904-1930). Radical Vietnamese patriot and founder of the Vietnamese Nationalist Party (VNQDD). Born in a peasant family in Vinh Yen Province in the Red River Delta in 1902, he studied Education and Commerce in Hanoi. At first Nguyen Thai Hoc was inclined toward moderate reform, but when his letter to Governor-general Alexander Varenne was ignored, his political persuasions turned more radical. Using a publishing firm as a front, Nguyen Thai Hoc founded a new political party, the Vietnamese Nationalist Party (Viet Nam Quoc Dan Dang, usually known as VNQDD for short) in the fall of 1927. The new party was modelled after Sun Yat-sen's political party of the same name, the Chinese Nationalist Party, (Guomindang), and had as its objective a violent revolution to overthrow French rule and restore Vietnamese independence.

During the next two years the VNQDD organized among radical youth, workers, and soldiers in Central and North Vietnam. In December 1928, Nguyen Thai Hoc was replaced as chairman, while the party suffered badly from French repression. In the summer of 1929 Nguyen Thai Hoc called for an insurrection based on revolts staged at military posts in the Red River Delta in early 1930. The so-called Yen Bay revolt broke out in February 1930 as scheduled, but arrangements were faulty and many of the troops were reluctant to follow the militants. After a few days the uprisings were put down and Nguyen Thai Hoc was himself arrested. He and several top leaders were executed by the French in mid-June. (See VNQDD; Yen Bay Revolt)

NGUYEN THE TRUYEN (1898-1969). Prominent political figure in colonial Vietnam. Born in 1898 in Nam Dinh Province, Nguyen The Truyen went to Paris in 1920 and was soon involved in radical political activities connected with the journal Le Paria (the Pariah) and the Intercolonial Union, (l'Union Intercoloniale), a front organization of the French Communist Party (FCP) composed of radical exiles from French colonies in Asia and Africa. An engineer by profession, he became a member of the FCP's Colonial Section and headed the Intercolonial Union after Ho Chi Minh's departure for Moscow in 1923.

In 1926, he set up a new Vietnamese language journal, the Viet Nam Hon (Soul of Vietnam) and organized a new political party among Vietnamese expatriates in Paris called the Annamite Independence Party (Parti Annamite de l'Indépendance). The party dissolved after his return to Vietnam in the late 1920s.

By the 1940s, Nguyen The Truyen had abandoned radical activies and supported the Bao Dai government in 1949. He died in Saigon in September 1969. (See Annamite Independence Party)

NGUYEN THI MINH KHAI (1910-1941). Prominent woman revolutionary and leading member of the Communist Party in colonial Vietnam. Born the daughter of a railway clerk, in Nghe An Province, Nguyen Thi Minh Khai attended school in the province capital of Vinh and became involved in anticolonial activities. Joining the Tan Viet Revolutionary Party, she became a member of the Indochinese Communist Party in the early 1930s and married Le Hong Phong, a leading member of the Party. Her sister married another colleague, Vo Nguyen Giap.

In the mid-1930s she studied in Moscow and attended the
Seventh Comintern Congress in 1935 with her husband. Returning to Vietnam a few years later, she was named secretary of
the Party's municipal committee for the city of Saigon. She was
captured by French authorities in July 1940 and executed a year
later. She is now considered one of the heroic figures of the
Vietnamese revolution. (See Indochinese Communist Party; Le
Hong Phong; Tan Viet Revolutionary Party; Vo Nguyen Giap)

NGUYEN TRAI. Famous scholar and statesman in early fifteenth-
century Vietnam. Nguyen Trai was the son of Nguyen Phi Khanh,
a scholar and official who had been sent to China after the occupation of China by the Ming. Nguyen Trai passed his doctoral
examination in 1400 at the age of twenty and entered into the
bureaucracy under the new Ho Dynasty founded the same year.
When Chinese forces occupied Vietnam in 1407, Nguyen Trai refused to collaborate with the new regime and was placed under
house arrest in Thang Long, (present-day Hanoi).
    When Le Loi raised the standard of revolt against the Ming
in 1418, Nguyen Trai escaped from confinement and became Le
Loi's closest adviser and the primary strategist of the latter's
victory over the Chinese in 1428. In his numerous writings,
Nguyen Trai stressed the importance of political struggle, of
"winning hearts and minds" ("it is better to conquer hearts than
citadels"), of strategem, of protracted struggle, and of the use
of negotiations to mislead the enemy and of the necessity to
choose the right opportunity to strike for victory. Many of
his works on strategy, such as Quan Trung Tu Menh Tap (writings composed in the army), Binh Ngo Sach (Book on Defeating
the Wu) and Bai Phu Nui Chi Linh (essay on Chi Linh mountain),
have become classics of Vietnamese literature. Binh Ngo Dai Cao
(proclamation on defeating the Wu) written after victory, became
Vietnam's declaration of independence.
    After victory in 1428, Nguyen Trai served the new emperor
as a high official in the bureaucracy. As a staunch Confucianist,
Nguyen Trai emphasized the importance of such Confucian values
as integrity, righteousness, and purity of purpose. Such high
moral standards frequently aroused resentment and jealousy
among his colleagues in the bureaucracy and even aroused the
suspicion of Emperor Le Thai To himself. He retired after the
death of Le Thai To and the accession of the latter's son Le Thai
Tong. But when the emperor died mysteriously in 1442 after a
short visit to Nguyen Trai's retirement home in Hai Hung Province, Nguyen Trai was accused of regicide and executed along
with his entire family. Twenty years later his name was rehab-
ilitated by Emperor Le Thanh Tong.
    Nguyen Trai is viewed in modern Vietnam as one of the truly
great figures in Vietnamese history. His ideas on formulating
a strategy to defeat the Ming were not only respected and admired, they were consciously imitated by leading strategists of
the Communist Party in their own struggle for national unification

against the French and the United States. Although few of his
writings have survived, he is considered one of the foremost
writers in Vietnamese history and a pioneer in the use of chu
nom (the written form of the spoken Vietnamese language).
Above all, his integrity, his sense of loyalty and human-hearted-
ness, representing the best elements of Confucian humanism,
have won him the respect and admiration of generations of Vietnamese. (See Confucianism; Later Le Dynasty; Le Loi)

NGUYEN TRI PHUONG (1799-1873). Vietnamese military commander
under the Nguyen Dynasty. Born in Thua Thien Province in
Central Vietnam, General Nguyen Tri Phuong was commander of
Vietnamese troops in South Vietnam at the time of the French
attack on the area in 1859-1860. Although larger than that of
its adversary, his army was defeated by the French in February
1861 at the Battle of Chi Hoa (Ky Hoa) near Saigon. After their
victory, the French gradually extended their control over the
neighboring provinces of Bien Hoa, Gia Dinh, and Dinh Tuong.
In November 1873, as governor of Hanoi, he received an ultimatum
from the French adventurer Francis Garnier demanding the surrender of the city. When he refused, Garnier attacked the citadel. When the bastion was taken Nguyen Tri Phuong committed
suicide. (See Battle of Ky Hoa; Garnier, Francis)

NGUYEN TRONG THUAT (1883-1940). Vietnamese novelist in the
early twentieth century. Born in 1883 in a scholar-gentry family,
Nguyen Trong Thuat received a Confucian education, and remained all his life an admirer of Confucianism and Buddhism.
A frequent contributor to Pham Quynh's literary journal Nam
Phong, he wrote a novel entitled Qua Dua Do (The Watermelon)
in 1926 that achieved a widespread if brief popularity. Based
loosely on Daniel Defoe's Adventures of Robinson Crusoe, it was
an escapist adventure novel exemplifying the traditional Confucian virtues of loyalty and self-sacrifice and was understandably praised by the colonial regime. In 1932 Nguyen Trong
Thuat replaced Pham Quynh as editor of Nam Phong. (See
Literature; Nam Phong; Pham Quynh)

NGUYEN TRUONG TO (1828-1871). Reformist intellectual in nineteenth
century Vietnam. A native of Nghe An Province, Nguyen Truong
To was born in a scholar-gentry family that had converted to
Catholicism. Prohibited from taking the civil service examinations because of his religion, he studied in France and became
an admirer of Western culture. On his return to Vietnam in 1861,
he served the court in negotiations with the French after the
latter's seizure of the southern provinces.
After the Treaty of Saigon in 1867, Nguyen Truong To submitted several petitions to the court suggesting reforms that
were needed to prevent the collapse of the empire. His sugges-
tions ran the gamut from politics to education and economic reform, and included the separation of powers, educational reform,

the sending of students abroad, and the modernization of agriculture and industry. It was To's belief that Vietnam needed
to conciliate France in order to buy time for self-strengthening.
Arrested on suspicion of treason in 1861, he was released to
join an educational delegation to France. He died of illness in
1871.

NGUYEN VAN LINH (1913-   ) (real name Nguyen Van Cuc).
Leading member of the Vietnamese Communist Party (VCP) and
current General Secretary of the Party. Born in Hanoi in 1913,
Nguyen Van Linh was brought up in South Vietnam, where he
joined the revolutionary movement as an adolescent and was
arrested for political activities in 1930. Released from prison in
1936, he took part in Communist Party operations in Cochin China,
reportedly as a protégé of Le Duan. He was rearrested in 1941
and spent the war years in Poulo Condore prison.

After World War II Nguyen Van Linh served under Le Duan
in the Party apparatus in the South and (under the pseudonymn
Muoi Cuc) was director of the Central Office for South Vietnam
(COSVN) from 1961 until his replacement by General Nguyen Chi
Thanh in 1964. He remained as deputy to Thanh and later to
Thanh's successor Pham Hung until the end of the war.

In 1976 Nguyen Van Linh was raised to Politburo rank and
headed the Party committee for Ho Chi Minh City (the new name
for Saigon). In 1978 he was dismissed, reportedly because of
his failure to carry out the Party's plans for socialist transformation in the South. At the Fifth National Congress of the Party,
held in March 1982, he lost his Politburo seat, but shortly thereafter he returned as Party chief in Ho Chi Minh City and was
quietly reinstated in the Politburo in 1985. At the Sixth National
Party Congress in December 1986, Linh was named General Secretary to replace the aging Truong Chinh. As General Secretary he has pushed reforms to stimulate the stagnant Vietnamese
economy. (See Central Office for South Vietnam; Vietnamese
Communist Party)

NGUYEN VAN SAM (? -1947). Moderate political figure in colonial Vietnam. A journalist and editor of the Vietnamese-language newspaper
Duoc Nha Nam, Nguyen Van Sam became active in politics with
the moderate reformist Constitutionalist Party. In 1936 he took
part in activities to promote an Indochinese Congress movement
to present a list of demands to the Popular Front government in
France.

After World War II, Nguyen Van Sam became active in the
movement to persuade ex-emperor Bao Dai to return to Vietnam
as chief of state in an Associate State in the French Union. He
was assassinated, apparently by the Vietminh, in October 1947.
(See Bao Dai; Bao Dai Solution; Indochinese Congress; Popular
Front)

NGUYEN VAN TAM (1895- ?). Prime minister of the Associated

State of Vietnam from June 1952 until December 1953. A native of Tay Ninh province in South Vietnam, Nguyen Van Tam became a French citizen and served in several official positions within the French colonial administration before and after World War II. As a police official he became noted for his vigorous suppression of the Nam Ky revolt in November 1940, which earned him the sobriquet "the tiger of Cay Lai." After the formation of the Associated State of Vietnam, Tam served under Prime Minister Tran Van Huu as Minister of the Interior and, after November 1951, as Governor of North Vietnam. He succeeded Tran Van Huu as prime minister in the summer of 1952. During his stay in office he attempted to promote land reform and a democratization of the political process, but widespread official corruption undermined such efforts and led to his severe defeat in national elections held in January 1953. Nguyen Van Tam belatedly attempted to win nationalist support by demanding increased autonom within the French Union but won little support from either patrioti elements or the French and was asked to resign from office in December. (See Bao Dai Solution; Nam Ky Revolt; Tran Van Huu)

NGUYEN VAN THIEU (1923-   ). President of the Republic of Vietnam from 1967 until 1975. Born in a family of farmers and fishermen in Ninh Thuan province, Central Vietnam in 1923, Nguyen Van Thieu served briefly with the Vietminh forces after World War II but later left the revolutionary movement and joined the Vietnamese National Army, organized by the French to serve as the official armed forces of the Associated State of Vietnam.

After service as a combat officer during the Franco-Vietminh War, Nguyen Van Thieu was named superintendant of the National Military Academy in 1956 and later assumed command of the Fifth Division of the Army of the Republic of Vietnam (ARVN).

After the overthrow of the regime of President Ngo Dinh Diem in November 1963, Nguyen Van Thieu, now a general, became involved in politics. In June 1965 he was a member of the "young Turk" movement that overthrew the civilian government in Saigon and was named Chairman of the military-dominated National Leadership Committee.

During the next several months, Thieu shared power with General Nguyen Cao Ky, a fellow member of the "young Turk" faction in Saigon. In September 1967 he was elected President of the Republic of Vietnam under a new constitution approved the previous year. Nguyen Cao Ky served as his Vice President. During the next four years he attempted with only moderate success to bring political stability to South Vietnam and progress in the war against revolutionary forces under the leadership of the Hanoi regime in the North. He did issue a land reform decree entitled "land to the tiller" that severely reduced the inequality of landholdings that had characterized agriculture in South Vietnam since the colonial period.

In 1971 Nguyen Van Thieu was re-elected President for a second four-year term. Technically he was unopposed, although

it was widely believed that other potential candidates were
persuaded not to run by the U.S. Mission in Saigon. During
his second term Thieu unsuccessfully resisted the U.S. decision
to sign the Paris Agreement in January 1973. President Nixon
promised to provide adequate military assistance to provide for
the defense of South Vietnam, but when the Democratic Republic
of Vietnam (DRV) launched a major military offensive against
the South in early 1975, Nixon's successor Gerald Ford was unable to persuade the U.S. Congress to increase U.S. to the Saigon
regime. After several serious military reverses, Thieu decided to
abandon the entire northern half of the country to revolutionary
forces. The decision led to panic, and in late April, a few days
before North Vietnamese entered Saigon in triumph, Nguyen Van
Thieu left South Vietnam for exile in Taiwan. He currently
lives in Great Britain. (See Ho Chi Minh Campaign; Ngo Dinh
Diem; Nguyen Cao Ky; Republic of Vietnam)

NGUYEN VAN THINH (1884-1946). Moderate political figure and
president of the abortive "Autonomous Republic of Cochin China"
in 1946. A medical doctor by profession, Nguyen Van Thinh
joined the Constitutionalist Party in 1926 and then founded his
own party, the Dang Dan Chu (Democratic Party), in 1937.
After World War II he supported the French-sponsored movement
for Cochinchinese autonomy and was named the president of
the so-called Autonomous Republic of Cochin China in 1946. Discouraged at his failure to achieve credibility for the new republic, he committed suicide in November 1946. (See Autonomous
Republic of Cochin China)

NGUYEN VAN VINH (1882-1936). Journalist and reformist political
figure in colonial Vietnam. Born in Ha Dong Province in 1882,
Nguyen Van Vinh attended interpreter's school in Hanoi and
entered the colonial administration, where he served in Lao Cay,
Haiphong, Bac Ninh, and Hanoi. Becoming a journalist, he
founded the quoc ngu journal Dong Duong Tap Chi (Indochinese
Review) in 1913. Through the pages of the Review, he attempted
to popularize Western ideas, institutions, and customs. His
political ideas were reformist rather than militant. (See Dong
Duong Tap Chi)

NGUYEN VAN XUAN. Prime minister in the provisional government
established by the French in 1948. Educated in France, Nguyen
Van Xuan became a French citizen and a career officer in the
French Army. After World War II he became involved in the
separatist movement in Cochin China and was named Vice President and Minister of National Defense in the provisional Cochinchinese government under Doctor Nguyen Van Thinh. He became
head of the government, which he renamed the Provisional Government of South Vietnam, in October 1947. In 1948, with French
sponsorship, he was named president of a provisional central
government. But General Xuan's efforts to win nationalist support

foundered on his reputation as a Cochinchinese separatist.
After failing to achieve significant concessions from the French,
he resigned as president after the return of Bao Dai in June of
1949. A new government under Chief of State Bao Dai was
appointed on July 1, with Xuan as Vice President and Minister
of National Defense. After the Geneva Conference of 1954,
Nguyen Van Xuan, with other pro-French politicians, made an
unsuccessful attempt to prevent the ascendance of Ngo Dinh Diem
to power in South Vietnam. (See Autonomous Republic of Cochin
China; Bao Dai Solution; Ngo Dinh Diem; Nguyen Van Thinh)

NGUYEN XUAN ON (1825-1889). Anti-French resistance leader in
late nineteenth-century Vietnam. A poet and a scholar-official
from Nghe An Province, Hoang Xuan On resigned from the
bureaucracy to respond to Emperor Ham Nghi's "Can Vuong"
appeal in July 1885 and commanded guerrilla forces in Central
Vietnam until his capture in 1887. He died in prison in 1889.
(See Can Vuong Movement; Ham Nghi)

NHAT LINH (1906-1963) (Nguyen Tuong Tam). Well-known novelist
and founder of the Self-Reliance Literary Group (Tu Luc Van
Doan) in colonial Vietnam. Born in 1906, Nhat Linh (real name,
Nguyen Tuong Tam) studied painting in Hanoi and science in
Paris. Returning to Vietnam in 1930, with his younger brother
Nguyen Tuong Lang (Hoang Dao) he founded the Self-Reliance
Literary Group, a collection of writers anxious to Westernize
Vietnamese literature.
    During the next few years he wrote a number of celebrated
novels, including Doi Ban (Friends), Doan Tuyet (Rupture),
and Buon Trang (the White Butterfly). Romantic in style, they
reflected an implicit mood of rebellion and individualism against
the accumulated evils in modern Vietnamese society. In the late
1930s Nhat Linh became actively involved in politics, joining the
VNQDD and spending World War II in exile in China. After
World War II he served briefly as minister of foreign affairs in
the Democratic Republic of Vietnam. In the spring of 1946,
however, he left suddenly for China and joined the anti-communist
national United Front set up in Hong Kong. He later withdrew
from the Front to protest against what he considered the pro-
French attitudes of other members of the organization.
    Nhat Linh moved to South Vietnam after the Geneva Conference
in 1954. Arrested by the Diem regime in 1960, he committed
suicide in 1963, reportedly in protest against Diem's policies.
(See Hoang Dao; Literature; Ngo Dinh Diem; Tu Luc Van Doan)

NHAT NAM. Administrative term used to refer to one of several provinces in occupied Vietnam during the period of Chinese rule.
The term referred to an area along the South China Sea coast
south of the Hoanh Son spur and comprising the modern-day
provinces of Nghe An and Ha Tinh. The term is Sino-Vietnamese
and means "South of the Son." Under Chinese rule, the area

was a relatively primitive frontier region and the site of a number of rebellions against the Chinese administration. During the first millenium A.D. it was frequently under the control of Champa, an Indianized state located on the coast of present-day Central Vietnam. After the restoration of Vietnamese independence it reverted to Vietnamese rule.

NOI CAC (Grand Secretariat). Influential administrative body in nineteenth-century Vietnam. Known in English as the Grand Secretariat, the Noi Cac (in Chinese, Nei Ko) was established in 1829 and, like much of the imperial administration under the Nguyen Dynasty, was based on the Chinese model. It functioned as an intermediary between the emperor and the ministers of the Six Boards (Luc Bo), and was composed of four "Grand Secretaries," a number of lesser officials, and six sections comprising Finances, Interior, Justice, Rites, War, and Public Works. It replaced the Van Thu Phong (Records Office), which had been established in 1820. (See Luc Bo)

NORTH VIETNAMESE ARMY (NVA) (See People's Army of Vietnam).

NUNG. An ethnic minority group related to the Tay (Tho) who live in contemporary North Vietnam. According to Vietnamese historians, the original home of the Nung people was somewhere south of the Yangtse River in China. They migrated southward several centuries ago and many settled in the narrow river valleys just south of the Sino-Vietnamese frontier, where they practice slash-and-burn or wet-rice agriculture. For a time, the Nung were able to form a separate kingdom, but they were eventually conquered and absorbed into the Vietnamese Empire.

During the Vietnamese Revolution, many Nung joined the Vietminh movement, and several became leading members of the Communist Party. Today there are approximately 600,000 Nung living in the Socialist Republic of Vietnam (SRV). (See Tay; Tribal Minorities)

- O -

OC EO. An ancient seaport on the western coast of the Ca Mau peninsula in Kien Giang Province in South Vietnam. Oc Eo was a major port city of the ancient Khmer State of Funan, predecessor of the Angkor Empire in what is today known as Kampuchea. During the early Christian period it was located on the trade route between East Asia and the Indian Ocean which crossed southern Indochina to the Isthmus of Kra. Archeologists have found Indian and Roman coins at the site. The port eventually declined when a new route developed further to the south through the straits of Malacca.

ONE-PILLAR PAGODA (Chua Môt Cot). A famous pagoda set on a

single pillar in the city of Hanoi. Built in the eleventh century by Emperor Ly Thai Tong (reigned 1028-1054), it was originally part of a larger Buddhist complex called the Dien Hau (Prolonging Life) Temple. According to popular belief, Ly Thai Tong dreamt of a Bodhisattva seated on a lotus flower who invited him to join him in conversation. To commemorate the dream, the emperor built the pagoda on a model of a lotus flower. Until its destruction, the temple was used by the Ly rulers to worship the Buddha. The Pagoda itself was destroyed by the French in 1954, and has been rebuilt by the current government. (See Ly Thai Tong)

OPERATION ATTLEBORO (See Zone C).

OPERATION CEDAR FALLS. Military operation by U.S. ground forces in the Vietnam War. (See Iron Triangle)

OVERSEAS CHINESE (Hoa). Ethnic Chinese residing in Vietnam. Known as hoa (a local name for China) to the Vietnamese, the overseas Chinese are descendants of migrants who settled in Vietnam during the eighteenth and nineteenth centuries. Most overseas Chinese went into trade or manufacturing, although some became miners, longshoremen, or fishermen.

During the traditional period, overseas Chinese were viewed as a distinct group in Vietnamese society, maintaining their own language and customs. The Nguyen Dynasty (1802-1945) dealt with them as a separate social unit, placing them in so-called "congregations" (bang), with their own leaders, schools, and other social institutions. This practice was retained under French colonial rule.

After independence in 1954, the governments of both North and South Vietnam attempted to integrate the overseas Chinese into the broader community. In the DRV, they were permitted to retain their own customs, schools, and nationality, but by agreement with the People's Republic of China, were encouraged voluntarily to seek Vietnamese citizenship. In South Vietnam, they were similarly permitted to remain legally distinct, but the regime of Ngo Dinh Diem (1954-1963) pressured them to become Vietnamese citizens. In both societies, most were in commerce and manufacturing. Overseas Chinese interests reportedly controlled nearly ninety percent of the banking and import-export trade in the South Vietnamese capital of Saigon.

After 1975, the Socialist Republic of Vietnam viewed the overseas Chinese with some suspicion because of their cultural and political ties with China and their capitalist habits. In 1978, when the Hanoi regime announced the nationalization of all property above the family level, thousands of ethnic Chinese fled by foot or on boats to other countries in the region, fearing that the government was attempting to eliminate them. For those remaining in Vietnam (approximately one million), the problem of assimilation into Vietnamese society remains unresolved. (See Minh Huong)

- P -

PALLU, FRANCOIS. Apostolic delegate appointed by Vatican City
    to direct Catholic missionary activities in seventeenth-century
    Vietnam. Appointed as head of the Vietnamese office of the
    Society of Foreign Missions in 1658, Pallu solicited the support
    of French commercial interests in the missionary effort to promote
    a French presence in mainland Southeast Asia. Because of oppo-
    sition to Christian activities by Vietnamese officials, the Asian
    headquarters of the Society was established in Thailand, where
    the society was also active in the missionary effort. Later Pallu
    was active in the Philippines, where he was arrested by the
    Spanish. Released from prison in 1677, he returned to Siam
    and died in China in 1684. (See Christianity; Rhodes, Alex-
    ander of; Society of Foreign Missions)

PARACEL ISLANDS (Quan Dao Hoang Xa). A cluster of small islands
    in the South China Sea. Located about 190 miles (300 kilometers)
    east of the central Vietnamese coast, the islands were only
    sporadically occupied by traders and pirates from several neigh-
    boring nations during the traditional period. During the colonial
    era the French claimed the islands and a small enterprise to ex-
    tract guano (used in the manufacture of phosphate fertilizer)
    was established there. In 1951, several of the islands were seized
    by the People's Republic of China, which claimed that the islands
    had been historically Chinese. In the 1960s, a few of the islands
    were occupied by the South Vietnamese, but they were driven out
    by Chinese forces in 1974. Spokesmen for the Democratic Re-
    public of Vietnam protested the action, claiming that the islands
    had been Vietnamese since traditional times. The dispute is one
    of several territorial issues currently dividing China and Vietnam.
    The islands themselves have relatively little intrinsic importance,
    but the owner of the islands can state a claim to control of the
    surrounding territorial seas, reported to hold extensive oil re-
    serves. (See Spratly Islands)

PARIA, LE (The Pariah). Newspaper founded by Ho Chi Minh in
    Paris in early 1920s. The newspaper was designed to focus on
    the evils of the French colonial system in Asia and Africa and
    to promote interest in social revolution. The first issue appeared
    in April 1922. For several months, Ho Chi Minh (then known as
    Nguyen Ai Quoc, or Nguyen the Patriot) not only served as
    editor, he also wrote many of the articles and distributed the
    newspaper on the streets. After Ho's depature for Moscow in
    1923, Le Paria declined in popularity but survived through 37
    issues until 1926. (See Ho Chi Minh)

PARIS AGREEMENT. Treaty signed by the Democratic Republic of
    Vietnam (DRV), the Republic of Vietnam (RVN), the Provisional
    Revolutionary Government of South Vietnam (PRG) and the United
    States on January 27, 1973. The agreement, reached after four

years of negotiations which began in late 1968, brought the
Vietnam War temporarily to an end. It called for the removal of
U.S. troops from South Vietnam and a cease-fire in place by the
armed forces of the Republic of Vietnam and the PRG. It made
no reference to the presence in South Vietnam of over nearly
200,000 troops of the People's Army of Vietnam (PAVN).

The Paris Agreement also made provisions for a political settlement of the war. The PRG and the RVN were instructed to
set up a so-called National Council of Reconciliation and Concord
(NCRC) to organize "free and democratic general elections" to
elect a new government in South Vietnam. In the meantime, the
existing government of President Nguyen Van Thieu remained in
office in Saigon.

The Paris Agreement did not end the Vietnam War, although
it brought direct U.S. involvement to an end. Arrangements
for the formation of the NCRC broke down, and clashes between
forces of the Saigon regime and the PRG took place throughout
the country. In early 1975, North Vietnamese forces launched a
major offensive on the South, leading to the seizure of Saigon
by PAVN units on April 30, 1975.

PASQUIER, PIERRE (1877-1934). Governor-general of French Indochina from 1928 to 1934. A graduate of the Colonial School in
Paris, he was appointed governor-general of Indochina in 1928
after extended service in the area. While knowledgeable about
Vietnamese affairs and author of a popular history of Vietnam
in French, Pasquier's efforts to improve conditions in Indochina
were hindered both by resistance from French commercial interests
and by Vietnamese radicals, whose activities culminated in the
Yen Bay Mutiny and the Nghe-Tinh Revolt in 1930. Even his
efforts to transfer some authority to the Young Emperor Bao Dai
were marked by acrimony. He died in a plane crash in January
1934. (See Bao Dai; Nghe-Tinh Revolt; Yen Bay Revolt)

PAU CONVENTIONS. A series of agreements dealing with French
relations with the Associated States of Vietnam, Laos, and Cambodia
and signed at Pau, France on November 27, 1950. The Elysée
Accords of March 8, 1949 had stipulated the holding of interstate conferences to work out arrangements governing communications, foreign trade and customs, immigration control, economic
planning, and finances. As a result of the conventions, a series
of interstate agencies consisting of representatives of all four
countries was set up to handle the "common services" formerly
handled by the High Commissariat of the Indochinese Union. Included in the convention was an agreement on a monetary and
customs union for all the countries concerned. (See Bao Dai
Solution; Elysée Accords)

PEOPLE'S ARMY OF VIETNAM (PAVN) (Quan Doi Nhan Dan Viet Nam).
Army of the Socialist Republic of Vietnam (SRV). The army was
created at a conference of the Indochinese Communist Party in

Bac Thai province on May 15, 1945. It was formed from a Union of the National Salvation Army (Cuu Quoc Quan) the Armed Propaganda Brigades (founded December 1944) and other revolutionary forces preparing for an insurrection against French and Japanese occupation forces at the end of World War II. Originally known as the Vietnamese Liberation Army (Viet Nam Giai Phong Quan), the PAVN bore the brunt of the fighting against the French during the Franco-Vietminh War (1945-51). Later it played an active role in promoting the revolutionary war in South Vietnam and was the dominant force in the final "Ho Chi Minh Campaign" which conquered the Saigon regime on April 1975. Beginning as an ill-equipped armed force relying predominantly on guerrilla tactics against stronger adversaries, it was eventually transformed through experience and Soviet military assistance into one of the most powerful and modern armies in the world.

After 1975, the PAVN played a role in peacetime reconstruction and the occupation of South Vietnam until 1978, when it played a dominant part in the Vietnamese invasion of neighboring Democratic Kampuchea. Two months later it bolstered local forces in defending the northern border against a Chinese invasion. Today there are approximately 150,000 PAVN troops serving as an occupation force in Kampuchea while other units defend against a possible second invasion of North Vietnam.

Today the PAVN is estimated at slightly over 1.2 million men, making it the fourth largest in the world. Of this number, about 15,000 are in the Air Force, 12,000 in the Navy, and 60,000 in air defense units. There are an additional 3 million in the reserve, and over one million in the local militia. The army is under strict party rule through the Central Military Committee under the party Central Committee and so-called "Military Councils" at various echelons of the army. But such military leaders as Nguyen Chi Thanh, Van Tien Dung, and Vo Nguyen Giap have often played an influential role in the Communist Party and the PAVN is usually represented by two or three members in the party's ruling body, the Politburo. (See Armed Propaganda Brigades; Ho Chi Minh Campaign; Vietnamese Liberation Army)

PEOPLE'S COMMITTEES (Uy Ban Nhan Dan). Executive bodies at the local level in the Socialist Republic of Vietnam. (See People's Councils)

PEOPLE'S COUNCILS (Hoi Dong Nhan Dan). Legislative body at lower echelons in the Socialist Republic of Vietnam (SRV). Originally created in the Democratic Republic of Vietnam as a result of the Constitution of 1946, People's Councils exist at all levels below the central level as the supreme legislative organ of authority. They are elected by all adult residents at each echelon and are responsible for local adminstration. A People's Committee (Uy Ban Nhan Dan) is elected by the People's Council at each level to handle executive duties in the interim between meetings of the Council.

In some respects, the functions of People's Councils resemble those of local administrative bodies in Western democracies. Constitutional provisions protect the right of Councils to question decisions taken by other governmental organs at each level, and government regulations severely limit Communist Party membership in the Councils. In practice, however, the People's Councils (as in other Marxist-Leninist systems) serve essentially as an instrument of the state in the effort to build an advanced socialist society. (See Constitutions of Vietnam; Socialist Republic of Vietnam; Vietnamese Communist Party)

PEOPLE'S LIBERATION ARMED FORCES (Nhan Dan Giai Phong Quan). Formal name for the armed forces of the revolutionary movement in South Vietnam during the Vietnam War. Commonly known in the West as the "Viet Cong" (a pejorative term first applied by the regime of Ngo Dinh Diem), the People's Liberation Armed Forces (PLAF) came into existence at a secret military conference held near Saigon in February 1961. The new PLAF merged armed units formerly operating independently in the lower Mekong Delta and the Central Highlands and was placed under the operation of the Central Office of South Vietnam (COSVN), the southern branch office of the Central Committee of the Vietnamese Workers' Party in Hanoi.

The PLAF was organized on the three-tiered basis used earlier in the Franco-Vietminh War, with fully armed regular units under the command of COSVN or regional military command. Below that level were full-time guerrillas organized in companies and operating under provincial or district command, and the village militia, part-time troops used in combat villages for local defense.

At first, the PLAF was comprised almost entirely of troops recruited within South Vietnam, and supplemented by a small number of trained officers and advisers infiltrated from the North. Until 1965, the PLAF carried the primary burden of fighting against the troops of the Saigon regime. But beginning in the mid-1960s, units of the People's Army of Vietnam (PAVN) infiltrated from North Vietnam played a larger role in the war, and the PLAF occupied a more subsidiary role. During the Tet Offensive in 1968, however, the PLAF bore the brunt of the fighting and suffered heavy casualties. It had not fully recovered as an effective fighting organization as the war came to an end. (See Central Office for South Vietnam; People's Army of Vietnam)

PEOPLE'S REVOLUTIONARY PARTY OF VIETNAM (Dang Nhan Dan Cach Mang Viet Nam). Southern branch organization of the Vietnamese Workers' Party (VWP) set up in South Vietnam in 1962. Described by official sources in the Democratic Republic of Vietnam as an independent party representing revolutionary elements in South Vietnam, the People's Revolutionary Party (PRP) was directly subordinate to the VWP in the North, through the Central Office of South Vietnam (COSVN). Described as "a revolutionary party of the working class in South Vietnam," it was Marxist-Leninist in orientation, and was merged with the parent VWP in the North in 1976 under the new name Vietnamese Communist Party (Dang Cong San Viet Nam). (See Central Office for South Vietnam; Vietnamese Communist Party; Vietnamese Workers' Party)

PERSONALISM (Thuyet Nhan Vi). Philosophical creed adopted by Ngo Dinh Diem, President of the Republic of Vietnam from 1954 to 1963. A blend of the Western concept of individual freedom and the Confucian emphasis on community responsibility, the philosophy of Personalism represented an attempt by President Diem to create a living philosophy for the Vietnamese people that would avoid the extremes of Marxist collectivism and Western materialistic hedonism. The European source of Diem's ideas was the Catholic Existentialism of Jacques Maritain and Emmanuel Mounier, which promoted a spirit of personal dignity without the egotism characteristic of much of Western capitalist society.

To many South Vietnamese, it was a confusing ideology which displayed little departure from traditional Confucian morality and obedience to authority. It achieved little popularity within Vietnamese society at large and its influence was limited to the inner circle of the regime within the Can Lao (Personalist Labor) Party. (See Can Lao Party; Ngo Dinh Diem; Ngo Dinh Nhu)

PHAM CONG TAC (-1955). Pope of the Cao Dai religion in South Vietnam from 1935 until 1955. He joined the Cao Dai movement while serving as a customs official in Saigon in the 1920s. On the death of the first "Temporal Pope" Le Van Trung, Pham Cong Tac succeeded him as head of the Church in 1935. Under his leadership the church became more directly involved in political and social causes. The movement grew rapidly in both urban and rural areas in Cochin China, leading to an unsuccessful French attempt to suppress it in the early 1940s. Pham Cong Tac himself was exiled to the Comoros Islands in 1941.

He returned from exile in August 1946 and resumed direct authority over the Cao Dai movement. At first he supported the French against the Vietminh, but eventually adopted a neutralist position during the ensuing Franco-Vietminh War, while supporting the return of Bao Dai as Chief of State of a new Vietnamese government. After the Geneva Conference he opposed the rise to power of Ngo Dinh Diem. In October 1955 Diem's troops occupied the Cao Dai capital at Tay Ninh and deposed him. Tac fled to Cambodia and died shortly after.

PHAM HONG THAI (1893-1924). Radical political figure in early twentieth-century Vietnam. The son of an educational administrator who had once supported the anti-French Can Vuong movement, Pham Hong Thai was born in 1893 in the province of Nghe An. Pham Hong Thai left school at a relatively early age to work in a factory where he first took part in radical activities. In 1923 he joined with such other radicals as Le Hong Phong and Ho Tung Mao in forming a radical political party in Canton, China with the name of Tam Tam Xa (Association of Like Minds). The aim of the group was to promote a general uprising against French rule.

In June 1924, Pham Hong Thai made an attempt to assassinate French governor-general Martial Merlin while the latter was attending an official banquet in Shamian, the international settlement in Canton. The attempt was unsuccessful, and Pham Hong Thai drowned while trying to escape.

Pham Hong Thai's gesture was commemorated by Phan Boi Chau in a pamphlet entitled Truyen Pham Hong Thai (the story of Pham Hong Thai), published late in 1924. Many members of the Tam Tam Xa, including Le Hong Phong and Ho Tung Mao, later became founding members of the Indochinese Communist Party. (See Association of Like Minds; Le Hong Phong; Ho Chi Minh; Ho Tung Mao; Merlin, Martial; Phan Boi Chau)

PHAM HUNG (1912-1988). Veteran member of the Vietnamese Communist Party. Born in a scholar-gentry family in Vinh Long in Cochin China, Pham Hung became a founding member of the Indochinese Communist Party (ICP) in 1930.

Arrested in 1931, he was imprisoned in Poulo Condore until the end of World War II. During the Franco-Vietminh conflict he served as deputy to Le Duan in the Party's branch office in South Vietnam. In 1955 he was summoned to Hanoi and raised to Politburo rank two years later.

In 1967 Pham Hung returned to South Vietnam as a replacement for General Nguyen Chi Thanh as chief of the Central Office for South Vietnam (COSVN) and the Party's branch organization in the South, the People's Revolutionary Party. After the end of the war Pham Hung returned to Hanoi and became the fourth ranking member of the Politburo and was named Minister of the Interior in 1979. He was replaced as Minister by Le Duc Tho's brother Mai Chi Tho in early 1987, but in June he was elected Prime Minister to replace the Veteran Pham Van Dong, who had retired. He died in March 1988. (See Central Office for South Vietnam; People's Revolutionary Party; Vietnamese Communist Party)

PHAM NGOC THACH. Vietminh sympathizer and progressive figure in colonial Vietnam. A doctor by profession, Thach formed the so-called Vanguard Youth (Thanh Nien Tien Phong) movement in Cochin China near the end of World War II. Although the movement was formed under Japanese sponsorship, Thach was a secret Vietminh sympathizer and used the movement to mobilize support for the popular uprising which seized power in Saigon in late August 1945. He became a member of the Committee of the South (Uy Ban Nam Bo) under the presidency of Tran Van Giau, and later was appointed Minister of Health in the new Democratic Republic of Vietnam (DRV) established in Hanoi. (See August Revolution; Vanguard Youth Movement)

PHAM QUYNH (1892-1945). Leading literary figure and Francophile
in early twentieth-century Vietnam. Born in 1892 the son of a
village scholar in Hai Duong Province, Pham Quynh was educated
at the School of Interpreters, where he learned French and Chinese, and the Ecole Française d'Extreme Orient (French School
of the Far East), a French-run research institute in Hanoi.
    Pham Quynh entered journalism in 1913 as a writer with Nguyen
Van Vinh's Dong Duong Tap Chi (Indochinese Review). In 1917
he founded a new journal entitled Nam Phong (Wind from the
South) with official encouragement from the colonial regime. The
new journal published articles on various literary subjects in
three languages (French, Chinese, and Vietnamese), but Pham
Quynh's primary objective was to popularize the use of quoc ngu,
the written form of spoken Vietnamese based on the roman alphabet, as the national literary language.
    Pham Quynh's political views made him a controversial figure
on the colonial scene. Traditionalist and pro-French in his political
preferences, he favored a careful synthesis of Western and Confucian values based on a continued French presence in Vietnam.
By the 1930s he was increasingly active in politics, serving as
Minister of Education and then Director of the Cabinet in Hue
under Emperor Bao Dai.
    Dismissed from power after the Japanese coup d'etat in March
1945, he was assassinated in August, presumably on orders of
the Vietminh. (See Bao Dai; Nam Phong; Quoc Ngu)

PHAM VAN DONG (1906-   ). Leading member of the Vietnamese Communist Party and Prime Minister of the Socialist Republic of Vietnam (SRV) until June 1987. Born in 1906 in a mandarin family
in Quang Ngai, Central Vietnam, Pham Van Dong was educated at
the National Academy (Quoc Hoc) in Hue. He went to Canton in
1926 and joined the Revolutionary Youth League. After attending
the Whampoa Academy he returned to Vietnam and served as a
member of the League's regional committee in the South. In 1931
he was arrested and imprisoned in Poulo Condore until granted
an amnesty in 1937.
    During the next several years he was involved in Party work
in South China under the alias Lam Ba Kiet (Lin Pai-chieh) and
became one of Ho Chi Minh's top lieutenants during World War
II. Named Minister of Finance of the Democratic Republic of
Vietnam in 1946, he became Minister of Foreign Affairs in 1954
and Prime Minister the following year. He was elected to the
Party Politburo in 1951.
    As Prime Minister for over thirty years, Pham Van Dong
gained a reputation as an effective administrator and a conciliatory
figure who could reconcile divergent opinions within the Party
and government leadership. He was generally considered to be
a moderate in internal affairs and neutral in the Sino-Soviet dispute. Troubled with eye problems, Pham Van Dong was rumored
to be replaced during the 1980s and finally resigned from the
Politburo because of "advanced age and ill health" at the Sixth

Party Congress in December 1986. He was replaced as Prime
Minister by Pham Hung in June 1987. (See Democratic Republic
of Vietnam; Indochinese Communist Party; Vietnamese Communist
Party)

PHAN BOI CHAU (1867-1940). Leading figure in the anti-colonial
movement in early twentieth-century Vietnam. Born in a scholar-
gentry family in Nghe An Province, Phan Boi Chau showed a
quick mind as a youth and earned a second class degree (Pho
bang) in the metropolitan examinations in 1900. He appeared
destined to pursue a career in officialdom, but Chau's patriotic
instincts led him in a different direction. In 1903 he formed a
revolutionary organization called the Restoration Society (Duy
Tan Hoi) under the titular leadership in Prince Cuong De, a
member of the Nguyen ruling house. Two years later he established his headquarters in Japan, where he wrote patriotic tracts
designed to stir anti-French sentiments among the general population and encourage young Vietnamese to flee abroad and join
his exile organization.

In 1908, Phan Boi Chau was ordered to leave Japan, forcing
him to turn to China, where Sun Yat-sen's Revolutionary Alliance
(T'ung-meng-hui) was attempting to overthrow the tottering
Ch'ing Dynasty. In 1912 he transformed the Modernization Society
into a new organization, the Vietnamese Restoration Society (Viet
Nam Quang Phuc Hoi), modelled after Sun Yat-sen's own republican
party. The new organization had little more success than its
predecessor, and several attempted uprisings in Vietnam failed.
Phan Boi Chau himself was briefly imprisoned in China. On his
release in 1917, he appeared temporarily discouraged at the pros-
pects of victory, writing a pamphlet entitled "France-Vietnamese
Harmony" (Phap-Viet De Hue) which suggested the possibility
of reconciliation with the colonial regime.

In 1925 Phan Boi Chau was seized by French agents while
passing through the International Settlement in Shanghai. Brought
under guard to Hanoi, he was tried and convicted of treason.
He spent the remainder of his life in house arrest in Hue and
died in 1940, one of the most respected patriots in modern
Vietnam. (See Modernization Society; Vietnamese Restoration Society)

PHAN CHU TRINH (1872-1926). Leading reformist figure in early
twentieth-century Vietnam. Phan Chu Trinh was born in Quang
Nam Province in Central Vietnam, the son of a military officer.
He received a traditional Confucian education and achieved the
degree of Pho Bang in 1901. His father, a supporter of the
Can Vuong (Save the King) movement, was assassinated by one
of his colleagues on suspicion of treason.

Phan Chu Trinh accepted a minor job with the imperial
Ministry of Rites, but was soon involved in political activities,
sending a famous public letter to French Governor-general
Paul Beau in 1906 in which he appealed to Beau to live up to

the French civilizing mission in Vietnam by reforming Vietnamese Society along Western lines. He also became involved in the so-called Tonkin Free School (Dong Kinh Nghia Thuc), a private institution financed by patriotic elements to introduce Western ideas into Vietnamese society. It was Phan Chu Trinh's conviction that Vietnam's primary enemy was not the French, but its own antiquated feudal system.

In 1908, Phan Chu Trinh was imprisoned for his part in supporting a peasant demonstration (popularly known as the "Revolt of the Long Hairs") in Central Vietnam. After spending time on Poulo Condore, he was sent to live in exile in France, where he supported himself as a photo-retoucher and contributed occasionally to the patriotic cause with writings on contemporary issues. In 1925 he was permitted to return to Vietnam and he died in Saigon the following year. His funeral became the occasion of a fervent expression of patriotic fervor in Vietnam.

Phan Chu Trinh is often contrasted with Phan Boi Chau as representing the non-violent reformist wing of the patriotic movement in early twentieth-century Vietnam, while Chau represented the path of revolutionary violence. (See Beau, Paul; Dong Kinh Nghia Thuc; Phan Boi Chau)

PHAN DINH PHUNG (1847-1895). Anti-French resistance leader in late nineteenth-century Vietnam. Raised in a scholar-official family from Ha Tinh Province, Phan Dinh Phung himself showed talent at an early age and received a doctorate (tien si) in the civil service examinations given in 1877. He served in the Imperial Censorate (Do Sat Vien), where he was noted for his integrity and was briefly imprisoned in 1883 for refusing to sanction a successor to the deceased emperor Tu Duc not designated by the emperor himself.

When Emperor Ham Nghi issued his famous "Can Vuong" (Save the King) appeal in July 1885, Phan Dinh Phung responded and launched a revolt in his native province of Ha Tinh. The movement quickly spread to neighboring provinces and lasted several years, despite numerous appeals to Phan Dinh Phung from colleagues who had chosen to collaborate with the French, and despite the desecration of his ancestral plot by the colonial regime. The movement was a nuisance to the French, but the rebels lacked weapons and central direction from the puppet court in Hue, and shortly after Phan Dinh Phung died of dysentery in December 1895 it collapsed.

Today Phan Dinh Phung is viewed as one of the great patriots in the struggle for Vietnamese independence. (See Can Vuong movement; Ham Nghi; Tu Duc)

PHAN KHAC SUU. Political figure and Chief of State of the Republic of Vietnam from September 1964 until June 1965. An agricultural engineer by profession and a nominal member of the Cao Dai sect, Phan Chac Suu was chosen Chief of State in a civilian government placed in office by General Nguyen Khanh in the fall of 1964. Suu's government was unable to gain a grip on the nation's complicated problems and was overthrown by a military coup led by Nguyen Cao Ky and Nguyen Van Thieu in June 1965. (See Nguyen Cao Ky; Nguyen Khanh)

PHAN KHOI (1887-1960). Progressive scholar and intellectual in twentieth-century Vietnam. Educated in the traditional Confucian system, Phan Khoi, in a long career devoted to scholarship and journalism, became a renowned critic and commentator on the cultural scene. Through his etymological analyses he contributed significantly to the development of quoc ngu as a serviceable Vietnamese national language. In 1930, he became involved in a highly publicized polemic with the Confucian scholar Tran Trong Kim over the latter's effort to synthesize traditional Confucian values with those of the modern West. In Phan Khoi's view, the key to forming a new national culture was value, not whether it conformed to "national essence." Phan Khoi remained in North Vietnam after the Geneva Conference and was publicly critical of the Hanoi regime over the lack of freedom and Democracy in the Democratic Republic of Vietnam. He died in 1960. (See Tran Trong Kim)

PHAN XICH LONG REBELLION. Revolt against the French colonial regime in early twentieth-century Vietnam. The leader, Phan Xich Long (real name Phan Phat Sanh), was the son of a Saigon merchant who became involved in Messianistic activities near the Cambodian border. In March 1913, taking advantage of widespread unrest caused by high taxes and corvée labor in the Mekong Delta area, Pham Xich Long planned an uprising to seize power in Saigon, but was arrested by the French and the revolt proved abortive. Three years later, supporters of Phan Xich Long launched a new insurrection aimed at freeing him from prison, and a number of disturbances broke out in Saigon metropolitan area. The French repressed the uprising with severity and the ringleaders were executed.

PHAN THANH GIAN (1796-1867). Vietnamese official who signed the Treaty of Saigon with the French in June 1962. Born the son of a minor government official in Ben Tre Province in 1796, Phan Thanh Gian earned a doctorate in the civil service examinations in 1826 and entered the imperial bureaucracy. He served as a military commander in Quang Nam, deputy chief of a diplomatic mission to China, and later was named province chief in Quang Nam and Binh Dinh provinces.

In 1862 Phan Thanh Gian was appointed plenipotentiary to negotiate a peace treaty with France following the disastrous defeat by French forces at Ky Hoa. In the Treaty of Saigon signed in June, Phan Thanh Gian accepted the loss of three provinces in the South and the opening of the remainder of Vietnam to French commercial and missionary activity. A year later he was sent to Paris on an unsuccessful mission to persuade the French to return their newly-acquired territory.

In 1865, Phan Thanh Gian was appointed viceroy of the remaining three provinces of Cochin China. When the local French
commander attacked and seized the provinces in June 1867, Phan
Thanh Gian assumed personal responsibility for the humiliation
and committed suicide. (See Grandière, Admiral de la; Treaty of
Saigon; Tu Duc)

PHILASTRE, PAUL. French diplomat and naval officer who negotiated
the Treaty of 1874 between France and Vietnam. (See Dupré,
Admiral Jules-Marie; Garnier, Francis; Treaty of 1874)

PHO BANG. Second highest degree granted in the civil service
examination in traditional Vietnam. The degree, meaning "subordinate list," was awarded to candidates who had passed the
metropolitan exam (thi hoi) but whose performance did not merit
permission to compete for the highest degree (tien si) in the
palace examination (thi dinh). Pho bang graduates were eligible
for employment as officials, normally at the provincial or prefectural level. (See Civil Service Examinations; Tien Si)

PHU NU TAN VAN (Women's News). Weekly periodical devoted to
women's concerns published in Saigon under the French colonial
regime. First published in May 1929, it reflected a rising concern for women's rights among the Western-educated middle class
in the major cities. At its peak it reached a weekly circulation
of 8,500 copies and became a formidable rival for Nam Phong,
the literary journal published by the conservative journalist Pham
Quynh. Written in a fluid and precise modern style, it helped
to advance the cause of quoc ngu as the national language of
Vietnam. Politically, it reflected the vacillating attitude of its
primary leadership--the Vietnamese bourgeoisie--craving independence but fearing social revolution. In the end, it was suppressed
by the colonial regime in December 1934.

PHUC QUOC (Viet Nam Phuc Quoc Dong Minh Hoi) (See League for
the National Restoration of Vietnam).

PHUNG HUNG. Vietnamese military leader who briefly ruled Vietnam
in the eighth century. Son of a leading local figure of the western edge of the Red River Delta, Phung Hung became commander
of a military garrison to guard the protectorate of Annam from
rebel attacks by tribal groups in the mountains to the west.
When the local Chinese administration, reflecting instability within
the T'ang Dynasty in China, virtually disintegrated, Hung's influence rapidly increased. In the early 780s, Phung Hung seized
the capital of La Thanh (on the site of present-day Hanoi) and
ruled the protectorate until his death in 789. The so-called
Phung Hung period is remembered as one of peace and prosperity,
marked by growing commercial contacts with other countries in
the region. In later centuries Phung Hung's prodigious physical

strength and allegedly superhuman capacities made him a folk hero in Vietnam.

PHUNG NGUYEN CULTURE (<u>Van Hoa Phung Nguyen</u>). A Neolithic culture in prehistoric Vietnam. Named from a site in the mountains north of the Red River Delta uncovered in 1958, Phung Nguyen culture flourished at the end of the third millenium B.C. and was characterized by the use of polished stone implements and decorated pottery. The economy was based on slash-and-burn agriculture and animal husbandry and dwellings were constructed of wood and bamboo and placed on stilts. Phung Nguyen culture is often considered the beginning of the bronze age in Vietnam. (See Bronze Age; Dong Son Culture)

PIGNEAU DE BEHAINE (1744-1798) (Bishop of Adran). French Bishop and adventurer who assisted in the formation of the Nguyen Dynasty in early nineteenth-century Vietnam. In 1766, the young Pigneau de Behaine was sent to Asia as a missionary by the French Society of Foreign Missions. For over two years he served as head of a Catholic seminary in Ha Tien Province on the Gulf of Thailand in South Vietnam. Forced to flee by official persecution, he went to Malacca and was eventually sent to India as Bishop of Adran.

In 1775 Pigneau returned to Ha Tien, where he met Nguyen Anh, last surviving member of the Nguyen house which had just been driven from Gia Dinh (Saigon) by the Tay Son Rebellion. From that point, Pigneau dedicated himself to restoring Nguyen Anh to the throne as the rightful ruler of Vietnam. In 1787 he arranged a visit to Paris, where a treaty was signed between Nguyen Anh and the French court, providing for French assistance against the Tay Son in return for French occupation of the port of Tourane and the island of Poulo Condore. France did not live up to the terms of the treaty, but Pigneau helped build up Nguyen Anh's armed forces on his own initiative, undoubtedly hoping that after his restoration to power, the latter would grant commercial and missionary privileges to the French.

In 1807, Nguyen Anh completed his defeat of the Tay Son and established a new Nguyen Dynasty in Hue. Pigneau did not live to see the triumph of his protégé, however. He died of dysentery at the seige of Qui Nhon in 1799. (See Nguyen Anh; Nguyen Dynasty; Nguyen Hue; Nguyen Lords; Tay Son Rebellion)

PIGNON, LEON (1908-). French High Commissioner in Indochina from October 1948 until December 1950. A career official in the colonial civil service, Pignon was Commissioner of Cambodia at the time of his appointment. Earlier, he had served as Counselor to High Commissioner Thierry d'Argenlieu shortly after the end of World War II, and shared the latter's anti-communist sentiments and dedication to the preservation of a French colonial presence in Indochina.

As High Commissioner, Pignon followed the path traced out

by his predecessor, Emile Bollaert, and presided over the completion of arrangements for the establishment of an Associated State of Vietnam under Chief of State (and ex-Emperor) Bao Dai. The new state was intended to provide the Vietnamese with an alternative to Ho Chi Minh's Democratic Republic of Vietnam (DRV), now fighting a protracted struggle against French forces in Indochina. He was replaced as High Commissioner by General de Lattre de Tassigny in December 1950. (See Bao Dai; Bao Dai Solution; de Lattre de Tassigny, Jean; Elysée Agreements; Ha Long Bay Agreement)

POPULAR FRONT. Period of relative liberalization in pre-World War II colonial Indochina. The period was opened with the formation of a coalition government led by the Socialist Party under premier Léon Blum in May 1936. The new government promised to appoint a governmental commission to look into conditions in the French colonies and to recommend necessary reforms. In Indochina, the colonial regime introduced a number of measures to improve conditions, including a more liberal attitude toward the freedom of speech and organization, and a new labor code, but rising popular agitation made local authorities nervous, and eventually the projected visit of an inspection commission to Indochina was cancelled. The Popular Front government came to an end in 1939. (See Brevié, Jules; Indochinese Communist Party; Indochinese Congress)

POPULATION. Rapid population growth is a fact of life in most rice-growing societies, and Vietnam is no exception. In 1986, the population of the Socialist Republic of Vietnam (SRV) was estimated at approximately 62 million, an increase of over thirteen million since the end of the Vietnam War in 1975. Demographers estimate that the population is increasing at an annual rate of about one million a year, and could reach 90 million by the year 2000.

Until recently, Party leaders in the SRV had expressed little public concern over the potential implications of rapid population growth. As early as 1963 the Hanoi regime had set up a Committee for Family Planning, but little was achieved during the war. By the early 1980s, however, the program was promoted with an increased sense of urgency. At the Fifth National Congress of the Vietnamese Communist Party in 1982, the Party announced its intention of reducing the growth rate from the existing 2.4 percent to 1.7 percent by 1985.

Progress has been slow, hindered by popular resistance and lackadaisical enforcement by cadres. Unofficial estimates suggest, however, that the annual rate of increase has declined in the mid-1980s to about 2.2 percent.

POPULATION RESETTLEMENT (See New Economic Zones).

POULO CONDORE (Con Son Island). A small island in the South

China Sea about 50 miles off the coast of South Vietnam. Essentially uninhabited in precolonial times, it was transformed into a penitentiary for Vietnamese political prisoners during the French colonial regime. Many members of anticolonial parties, including the Indochinese Communist Party (ICP), spent time there, transforming the prison (in the words of communist leaders) into "schools of Bolshevism," as prisoners were hardened by their brutal treatment and many left convinced supporters of the ICP.

After the Geneva Conference of 1954, the island continued to be used as a prison by the Republic of Vietnam, leading to charges by critics in Vietnam and abroad that the regime was mistreating its prisoners in so-called "tiger cages" unfit for human habitation. Under the current government of the Socialist Republic of Vietnam, the island has become a national park. (See Con Dao; Indochinese Communist Party; Ngo Dinh Diem)

PRODUCTION COLLECTIVES (Tap The San Xuat). Low-level collective organization used by the Socialist Republic of Vietnam (SRV) as a transitional stage to full collectivization. Production collectives are small cooperative organizations in which the basic means of production are collectively owned, and the peasants within the collective are divided into teams to produce according to plan. The production collective is normally smaller than the usual collective (formally known as an agricultural producers' cooperative) and consists of 60 to 70 farm families working on a cultivated area of 30 to 35 hectares.

Production collectives, along with the more primitive "production solidarity teams," were first adopted in the southern provinces in the late 1970s as a means of introducing private farmers to the collective concept. Currently about 85 percent of the farm population in South Vietnam is enrolled in approximately 40,000 production collectives. (See Agricultural Producers' Cooperatives; Collectivization of Agriculture; Production Solidarity Teams)

PRODUCTION SOLIDARITY TEAMS. Primitive form of collective organization used by the Socialist Republic of Vietnam (SRV) as a transitional stage to full collectivization. The production solidarity team (also known as a "work exchange team") is a first stage in the collective process. Private farmers at the hamlet level establish contractual relations with the authorities on production goals, but the means of production (land, machinery, and draft animals) are not collectively owned. Teams are usually composed of 50 to 60 farm families on a cultivated area of 30 to 40 hectares.

The SRV adopted the concept in the southern provinces as a means of achieving full collectivization of the land by the end of the Second Five-year Plan in 1980. It was used in conjunction with the more prevalent "production collective" and was utilized in areas where private farmers were likely to be particularly resistant to collectivization. (See Agricultural Producers' Cooperative; Collectivization of Agriculture; Production Collectives)

PROVISIONAL REVOLUTIONARY GOVERNMENT OF SOUTH VIETNAM (PRG). Alternative administration set up in May 1969 by revolutionary forces operating in South Vietnam. Formally known as the Provisional Revolutionary Government of the Republic of South Vietnam, it was intended to provide a legitimate alternative to the Republic of Vietnam (RVN), with its capital in Saigon. Leading figures in the PRG were Huynh Tan Phat and Nguyen Huu Tho, both active in the National Liberation Front, Hanoi's front organization which had been established in December 1960. The PRG was recognized by the Democratic Republic of Vietnam (DRV) and several other socialist countries as the legitimate government of South Vietnam, and was represented as a legal entity in the Paris peace talks. After the fall of Saigon in 1975, the PRG was abolished with the reunification of North and South Vietnam into a single Socialist Republic of Vietnam (SRV). (See Huynh Tan Phat; National Front for the Liberation of South Vietnam; Nguyen Huu Tho)

- Q -

QUAN. Administrative term for prefecture in ancient Vietnam. The term, adopted from the Chinese quan, was used during the period of Chinese occupation. (See Ma Yuan)

QUANG TRUNG (Nguyen Hue). Founding emperor of the Tay Son Dynasty in late eighteenth-century Vietnam. (See Nguyen Hue)

QUOC NGU (National Language). Romanized written form of Vietnamese language currently in use in the Socialist Republic of Vietnam. Quoc ngu was invented by Christian missionaries in the seventeenth century as a tool for teaching scripture to Vietnamese converts. At that time, the official language of the Vietnamese court was Chinese, while a separate script based on Chinese characters, known as Chu Nom (southern characters), was used as the written form of the Vietnamese language.

In the late nineteenth century, quoc ngu was popularized by French authorities in the colony of Cochin China. At first the innovation was resisted by intellectuals in the protectorates of Annam and Tonkin, but in the early twentieth century reformist figures like Phan Chu Trinh began to see its value as a replacement for the cumbersome writing system inherited from the Chinese. Eventually the convenience and simplicity of quoc ngu overcame the alleged aesthetic qualities of Chinese characters and gained wide acceptance throughout Vietnam. In 1924, quoc ngu was established as a primary tool of instruction at the elementary level throughout Vietnam. After the division of the country in 1954, the governments in both the North and the South adopted quoc ngu as their national script.

- R -

RED RIVER (Hong Ha, or Song Cai). Second major river in Vietnam.
Originating in Yunnan province in South China, the Red River
flows over seven hundred miles in a southeasterly direction into
the Tonkin Gulf. Of that distance, 316 miles lie within the territory of Vietnam. Its primary tributaries are the Black River
(Da Giang) and the Lo river (Lo Giang).

RED RIVER DELTA. Delta of the Red River in North Vietnam. The
Delta region was built up over centuries by the deposit of alluvial
soils brought down the Red River from its source in South China.
Surrounded by mountains to the north and west, the Red
River Delta consists of a total area of 5,792 square miles (14,994
square kilometers) and has exerted a formative influence on the
history of the Vietnamese people. It was on the fringes of the
Delta that the Vietnamese first emerged as a distinct people in
Southeast Asia. It was here that the first Vietnamese state
emerged in the first millenium B.C., and it was here too, that
the Vietnamese Empire placed its capital after the restoration of
independence from China in the tenth century A.D. Even after
the southward expansion of the Vietnamese state to the Gulf of
Thailand, the Red River Delta has generally been considered the
heartland of Vietnamese civilization and is the location of its
present-day capital of Hanoi.
The importance of the Delta in Vietnamese history is essentially
economic. Here, on the rich sedimentary soils left by the river
on its passage to the sea, the early Vietnamese mastered the
cultivation of wet rice, the staple food of the Vietnamese diet.
But the Red River was not only a boon to the peasants living
near its banks. It was also a constant threat, as the sediment
left by the river gradually built up the bed underneath and led
to disastrous floods which destroyed crops and often caused widespread starvation. To protect their rice fields from flooding,
Vietnamese peasants built dikes along the banks that often reached
heights of over twenty feet, while the river bed itself is often
several feet above the surrounding riceland. During the Vietnam
War, some U.S. strategists proposed the bombing of the dikes
as a means of destroying the North Vietnamese economy and
forcing the Hanoi regime to abandon its effort to bring about
national reunification. (See Red River)

RE-EDUCATION CAMPS. Detainment centers established by the Hanoi
regime in South Vietnam after the Vietnam War. After the seizure
of Saigon by North Vietnamese forces in April 1975, a new revolutionary administration was established in the South. All individual
suspected of possible hostility to the new regime were instructed
to report to re-education camps for ideological indoctrination and
possible reassignment. According to official sources, over one
million South Vietnamese required re-education in some form.
The majority received a short period of indoctrination and then

were released. The remainder were sent to work camps for longer periods of time. According to critics of the regime, several hundred thousand South Vietnamese were housed in these camps, often under intolerable conditions. Official sources in Hanoi insist that most have been released, and knowledgeable observers estimate that there are currently about 10,000 prisoners still in the camps.

REFUGEES (See Boat People).

RELIGION (See Buddhism; Cao Dai; Christianity; Confucianism; Hoa Hao; Taoism).

REPUBLIC OF COCHIN CHINA. (See Autonomous Republic of Cochin China).

REPUBLIC OF VIETNAM (Viet Nam Cong Hoa). Formal name for the government established in South Vietnam after the Geneva Accords established two separate administrative entities in North and South in 1954. The Republic of Vietnam (RVN) was administratively the successor of the Associated State of Vietnam established within the French Union in 1949. Its first chief of state, ex-emperor Bao Dai, had served in the same capacity in the Associated State prior to 1954, but Bao Dai was defeated in a referendum arranged by Prime Minister Ngo Dinh Diem, who then became president under a new constituion approved in 1956. The political structure established by the 1956 Constitution combined the parliamentary and the presidential systems, with a strong president presiding over a unicameral National Assembly.

After the overthrow of Ngo Dinh Diem by a military coup in 1963, South Vietnam came under military rule until 1967, when a new constitution was approved by the then-Chief of State, General Nguyen Van Thieu. The form of government was essentially retained, although in practice there were a number of dissimilarities.

The Republic of Vietnam consisted of a territory comprising 173,809 square kilometers (6,608 square miles) and was divided into 43 provinces (tinh) stretching from the demilitarized zone at the seventeenth parallel to the southern tip of the Ca Mau peninsula. The total population rose from about 13 million in 1954 to nearly 25 million in the mid-1970s. The Republic of Vietnam was abolished on April 30, 1975 with the inauguration of a new provisional regime in Saigon. The following July, South and North Vietnam were united into a single Socialist Republic of Vietnam (SRV). (See Associated State of Vietnam; Constitutions of Vietnam; Ngo Dinh Diem; Socialist Republic of Vietnam)

REVOLT OF THE SHORT HAIRS. Peasant tax revolt in early twentieth-century Vietnam, so called because many participants cut their hair short as a symbol of protest against the system.

It began in Quang Nam Province in Central Vietnam in March 1908, and eventually spread southward to Quang Ngai and Binh Dinh, with some unrest among students in the imperial capital at Hue. The French repressed the revolt with severity and one of the leaders, Tran Quy Cap, was executed. (See Phan Chu Trinh)

REVOLUTIONARY YOUTH LEAGUE OF VIETNAM (Viet Nam Thanh Nien Cach Minh Dong Chi Hoi, or Thanh Nien). Early Vietnamese revolutionary organization founded by Ho Chi Minh in South China in 1925. The League was the first avowedly Marxist-Leninist political organization in Vietnam and was apparently established on the instructions of the Communist International (Comintern) in Moscow. Ho Chi Minh, a Comintern agent, did not feel that the level of political sophistication and ideological awareness within the Vietnamese radical movement justified a formal communist party. He did set up a core organization of six dedicated members within the League, called the Thanh Nien Cong San Doan (Communist Youth Group), to serve as the nucleus of a future communist party. The headquarters of the League was set up in Canton in order to avoid French repression.

The League's objectives were broadly focussed on national independence and social revolution, but the former issue received more emphasis in order to win the support of anticolonial elements throughout Vietnam. This concentration on nationalism earned the League considerable popularity, and by the late 1920s it had recruited more than 1,000 members, many of whom had gone through training in Marxism-Leninism in Canton. But the muted emphasis on social revolution led to a split in the League after Ho Chi Minh' departure for Europe in 1927, and at the First National Congress of the League, held in Hong Kong in May 1929, radical elements stalked out of the conference to found their own Indochinese Communist Party (Dong Duong Cong San Dang). Remaining members of the League then changed the name of the organization to Annamese Communist Party (An Nam Cong San Dang).

In February 1930, at the behest of Comintern, Ho Chi Minh united the two factions, along with remnants of the Tan Viet Cach Menh Dang (New Vietnamese Revolutionary Party) into a new Vietnamese Communist Party (Dang Dong San Viet Nam). In October, the name was changed to Indochinese Communist Party (Dang Cong San Dong Duong). (See Annamese Communist Party; Ho Chi Minh; Indochinese Communist Party; Tan Viet Cach Menh Dang; Vietnamese Communist Party)

RHADE (Also known as Ede). Tribal minority people living in the Central Highlands of South Vietnam. They number slightly under 150,000 people in the 1980s, and inhabit an area stretching from eastern Cambodia to western Phu Khanh province near the coast of the South China Sea. Most live in the province of Dac Lac.

The Rhade are a Malayo-Polynesian people who probably

migrated into Southeast Asia well before the Christian era. Their language is related to Cham, and most practice spirit worship, although some became Christian in the twentieth century. Society is matrilinear, and most practice slash-and-burn agriculture.

Like several other tribal groups in the Highlands, the Rhade have traditionally resisted assimilation into Vietnamese society and many were active in the United Front for the Liberation of Oppressed Peoples (FULRO) that opposed the integrationist policies followed by both the Republic of Vietnam and the present-day government based in Hanoi. (See United Front for the Liberation of Oppressed Peoples; Jarai; Tribal Minorities)

RHODES, ALEXANDER OF (1591-1660). French missionary involved in the propagation of Christianity in seventeenth-century Vietnam. A native of the Papal city of Avignon in southern France, he arrived in Hanoi as a Jesuit missionary in 1627. At first he had considerable success in converting mandarins and aristocrats at the Trinh court to Roman Catholicism. Eventually, his activities aroused suspicion among Confucian elements convinced of the radical character of the Western doctrine and he was expelled from Vietnam in 1630.

For the remainder of his life, Alexander of Rhodes worked indefatigably to promote the missionary effort in Vietnam. He wrote a Portuguese-Latin-Vietnamese dictionary and helped to devise a roman alphabet transliteration of the Vietnamese spoken language (thereafter known as quoc ngu, or national language) in order to facilitate the training of local priests in Christian teachings. Between 1640 and 1645 he was based in the Portuguese colony of Macao, from which he undertook a number of short trips to Vietnam to promote missionary work there. Eventually he became exasperated at the failure of the Vatican bureaucracy to increase Church activities in Vietnam and prevailed upon the church hierarchy in France to form a Society of Foreign Missions to undertake the operation. He died on a mission to Persia in 1660. (See Christianity; Quoc Ngu; Society of Foreign Missions; Vietnamese Language)

RICE CULTURE. Since prehistoric times, rice has been the primary crop in Vietnam. During the traditional period, up to ninety percent of the population was engaged in the cultivation of wet rice, with the bulk of production centered in the rice bowls of the Red River and the Mekong River deltas.

Until recently, historians had assumed that the cultivation of rice was brought to Vietnam from China, where irrigated agriculture was introduced in the Yellow River Valley several thousand years ago. During the past few years, however, archeologists have uncovered evidence of the domestication of wild rice on sloped terraces in the mountain valleys northwest of the Red River Delta as early as 4,000 B.C., and perhaps earlier. While the precise date of its first appearance has not yet been established, it is probably safe to say that the peoples of the Red

River region were among the first in Asia to cultivate rice.

After the Vietnamese people began to settle in the Delta about 4,000 years ago, they began to cultivate rice in the plains. At first, irrigation took place by tidal action, and dikes were built solely to prevent flooding. Later dikes and canals became part of an extensive irrigation system throughout the region.

Since then, rice culture has developed into the primary economic activity of the Vietnamese people, spreading along the central coast and into the rich delta of the Mekong River to the south. The basic social units of the Vietnamese state--the village (xa, or thon) and the family (gia)--developed around the requirements of the harvest cycle. Rice culture has also strongly influenced the mores and political attitudes and institutions of the Vietnamese, placing supreme importance on the virtues of cooperation, hard work, and sacrifice of individual needs to those of the broader community. (See Agriculture)

RIVIERE, CAPTAIN HENRI. French military officer prominent in the seizure of North Vietnam in the 1880s. A captain in the French Army, Rivière in early 1882 was ordered by Le Myre de Vilers, the French governor of Cochin China, to undertake a military operation designed to increase French political influence in North Vietnam. On his own initiative, Rivière stormed the Hanoi citadel and assumed authority in the city. In May 1883, he was killed in a skirmish with Vietnamese troops and Black Flag Units under the command of Luu Vinh Phuc. (See Le Myre de Vilers)

RUBBER. One of the primary export crops in Vietnam. The tree heveas brasiliensis, from which natural rubber has traditionally been produced, is not native to Southeast Asia, but to the Amazon River basin in Brazil. But in the late nineteenth century, French naturalists brought seedlings to French Indochina and by the end of the century, extensive rubber plantations had been founded in the so-called "terre rouge" (redlands) area of Cochin China and eastern Cambodia. Most of the plantations were owned by French interests and farmed by Vietnamese laborers recruited for the task. Living conditions were frequently atrocious, and strikes by plantation workers were a common occurrence before World War II. But rubber became a major export earner in French Indochina, with exports rising to 60,000 tons in 1938.

Today the Vietnamese government is trying to revive the export of rubber as a major source of foreign currency. In the mid-1980s, the amount of land devoted to rubber had increased to 100,000 hectares (as compared with 140,000 before World War II) and rubber production totalled 51,000 tons in 1985. The goal is to increase acreage to nearly one million hectares by the end of the century.

- S-

SABBATIER, GENERAL GABRIEL (1892-?). Military commander of

French forces in Tonkin during World War II. After the Japanese occupation authorities abolished the French colonial regime in March 1945, General Sabbatier led two thousand French troops through the mountains to safety in South China.

SAIGON (Sai gon) (now known as Ho Chi Minh City). Major commercial and industrial center in South Vietnam and before 1975 capital of the Republic of Vietnam. At the time of the Vietnamese conquest of the Mekong River Delta, Saigon was a small trading post on what is known today as the Saigon River. During the next two centuries, the area was settled by Vietnamese farmers and Chinese traders and the Nguyen lords built a citadel on the site of modern Saigon, calling it Gia Dinh (the term Saigon was originally used for the area of present-day Cholon).

After the French conquest of the southern provinces in 1860, Saigon became the capital and commercial center of the colony of Cochin China. Surrounded by the relatively rich lands of the South, the city became the residence of an affluent class of Westernized Vietnamese bourgeoisie. After World War II, Saigon and its surrounding area was occupied by the French while the northern provinces were controlled by Ho Chi Minh's Democratic Republic of Vietnam. In 1949 Saigon became the administrative seat of the Associated State of Vietnam (usually referred to as the "Bao Dai" government). After the Geneva Conference it became the Capital of the Republic of Vietnam (RVN).

During the next twenty years, Saigon was exposed to a heavy dose of U.S. cultural and economic influence. Flagrant wealth coexisted with grinding poverty, and the city as whole vibrated with a pervasive sense of permanent political instability. In February 1968, the local apparatus of the National Liberation Front (NLF) attempted to provoke a general uprising in Saigon as a counterpoint to the Tet offensive in the countryside, but as a whole the local population did not respond, although the occupation by suicide squads of key installations, including the ground floor of the U.S. Embassy, had a significant impact on U.S. public opinion.

With the capture of Saigon on April 30, 1975 by North Vietnamese forces, Saigon joined the Vietnamese revolution and was purged of the "poisonous weeds" of bourgeois capitalism. As a symbol of the dawning new era, the city was renamed the City of Ho Chi Minh (Ho Chi Minh Thanh). (See Associated State of Vietnam; August Revolution; Cochin China; Ho Chi Minh City)

SAINTENY, JEAN (1907-1978). French representative in Indochina at the close of World War II. A son-in-law of ex-Governor-general Albert Sarraut and an international banker with experience in Indochina, Jean Sainteny supported General Charles de Gaulle's Free French movement during World War II and was sent to South China in 1944 to represent Free French interests in the area as the war came to an end. In August 1945 he went to Hanoi as French Commissioner for the protectorates of Annam and Tonkin and negotiated with Ho Chi Minh, president of the Democratic Republic of Vietnam (DRV) to resolve mutual differences over postwar Indochina. In March, 1946, the two signed a preliminary agreement recognizing the DRV as a "free state" in the French Union. The agreement broke down, leading to war in December 1946. (See Ho-Sainteny Agreement; Sarraut, Albert)

SARRAUT, ALBERT (1872-1962). Prominent French official and two-time governor-general in early twentieth-century Indochina. Born in 1872, Sarraut became a journalist and a Radical Socialist deputy in the French National Assembly. In 1911 he was named Governor-general of Indochina. A firm believer in the French civilizing mission in Indochina, on his arrival Sarraut promised a new era of Franco-Vietnamese harmony. Returning to France in 1914 on the grounds of ill health, he was reappointed for a second term in 1917. During his two terms in office, he inaugurated a number of reforms in the political and social arena, setting up a new system of education based on a two-track system and setting up provincial assemblies in Annam and Tonkin.

He returned to France in 1919 and served as Minister of Colonies from 1920 to 1924. He served as Prime Minister of the French government on two occasions during the 1930s.

SCHOLAR GENTRY. English-language term for the ruling class in traditional Vietnam. Membership, at least in theory, was not based on the right of birth, but on merit, through success in the civil service examination, the route to entrance into the prestigious imperial bureaucracy. In fact, there was usually a relatively direct relationship between education, official status, and wealth. For the most part, only the affluent landed-class possessed the resources to provide a classical Confucian education to its children. In turn, officialdom provided an opportunity to accumulate wealth through the purchase of land, the primary source of wealth in traditional Vietnam.

Not all who passed the examinations became members of the bureaucracy, and not all officials became landlords. But the identification between education, official position, and land was the general mark of success in traditional Vietnam. (See Civil Service Examination; Confucianism)

SINO-VIETNAMESE CULTURE. Form of civilization that developed in Vietnam under Chinese rule from the first century to the tenth century A.D. Although the country had been conquered by the Chinese in the late second century B.C., until A.D. 43 the Han Dynasty ruling in China had been satisfied to rule indirectly through the indigenous landed aristocracy, known as the "Lac lords." After the famous Trung Sisters rebellion in A.D. 39, however, China attempted to integrate the conquered Vietnamese provinces directly into the Chinese empire. Chinese political and social institutions were introduced, the Chinese language became the official means of communication in administration, and the bureaucracy was staffed by officials from China.

On the surface, the strategy was a success. During the next several hundred years, Vietnamese society in many respects took on the pattern of the Chinese model. Confucian institutions and values permeated the political system and other areas of society. Vietnamese literature, art, and architecture reflected Chinese motifs. Even the Vietnamese spoken language was given a written form based on Chinese characters.

In one key respect, however, the system failed. Despite the massive effort to assimilate Vietnam politically and culturally into the Chinese empire, the Vietnamese sense of national consciousness was not broken. Even within the bureaucracy, a sense of local tradition prevailed. Officials sent from China intermarried with the local population and began to identify with local aspirations and concerns. In the tenth century A.D., Vietnamese leaders took advantage of the disintegration of the T'ang Dynasty in China and restored Vietnamese independence.

Even after independence, however, Chinese influence permeated Vietnamese society and culture. Vietnamese rulers found Chinese political institutions useful in forging a strong centralized state. Scholars, intellectuals, and artists viewed Chinese civilization as the most advanced known to man and parroted Chinese models. Paradoxically, it was the last Vietnamese ruling house, the Nguyen (1802-1945), which made the greatest effort to pattern Vietnamese Institutions and values after those of its larger neighbor. In education, politics, literature, and law, Nguyen rulers attempted to suppress indigenous customs and institutions in favor of classical patterns from China.

Ironically, it was the French conquest that finally freed the Vietnamese people from the legacy of the past. Under the impact of modern Western culture, the Sino-Vietnamese tradition rapidly disintegrated, and when Vietnamese independence was restored after World War II, the nation's cultural and political leaders sought to build a new nation based on other models. (See Confucianism; Education; Literature; Nguyen Dynasty)

SOCIALIST REPUBLIC OF VIETNAM (Cong Hoa Xa Hoi Viet Nam). Successor to the Democratic Republic of Vietnam (DRV) and current name of the State of Vietnam. The Socialist Republic of Vietnam (SRV) came into existence on July 2, 1976, approximately fourteen months after the seizure of Saigon by revolutionary forces and the fall of the government of South Vietnam. The new republic united the two separate states--the DRV in the North and the Republic of Vietnam in the South--which had existed in Vietnam since the Geneva Conference of 1954. Like its predecessor, the DRV, the Socialist Republic of Vietnam is a Marxist-Leninist state, ruled by the Vietnamese Communist Party (the new name for the Vietnamese Workers' Party, adopted in December 1976). It inherited the political and administrative system already in existence in the North and now extended to the entire country. The capital remained in Hanoi, and a new one-house National Assembly, consisting of 492 members elected from both North and South, was elected in April 1976. A new constitution promulgated in 1980 introduced a number of minor changes in the political system, notably the establishment of a collective presidency, known as the Council of State (Hoi Dong Nha Nuoc).

The total land area of the SRV is 127,259 square miles (331,888 square kilometers). It consists of 37 provinces (including the Vung Tao-Con Dao Special Zone) and three municipalities directly subordinate to the central government (Hanoi, Ho Chi Minh City, and Haiphong). The population was estimated as approximately 62 million in 1986. (See Constitutions of Vietnam; Democratic Republic of Vietnam).

SOCIETY OF FOREIGN MISSIONS (Société des Missions Etrangères). French-run organization for the promotion of Roman Catholicism in Asia set up in the seventeenth century. The society was primarily the result of the efforts of the French Jesuit Alexander of Rhodes who was an active force in the spread of Christianity to Vietnam beginning in 1627. When the Vatican was reluctant to promote missionary efforts in Vietnam against the opposition of Portugal, Alexander turned to the French Church and was able to find financial support for a new organization established in France. The Society was formally established in Paris in 1664 and represented both missionary and commercial interests ambitous to find a new outlet for French activities in Asia.

During the next few years, the Society was actively involved in missionary efforts in Southeast Asia, but encountered opposition from other forces within the Church and was eventually limited to its activities in Vietnam, where official antagonism made the Society's operations increasingly difficult. Despite such opposition, the Society was relatively successful in promoting Christianity among the Vietnamese population, and there were an estimated 450,000 Christian converts in Vietnam by the mid-nineteenth century (See Christianity; Pigueau de Bahaine; Rhodes, Alexander of)

SON VI CULTURE (Van Hoa Son Vi). Prehistoric culture dating from the late Paleolithic period located in the hilly region of Vinh Phu province, North Vietnam. Son Vi culture, discovered by Vietnamese archeologists in 1968, is generally considered to predate the more advanced Hoe Binh culture into which it may have evolved. Chipped pebbles found at Son Vi sites are technologically less advanced than the tools found at sites dating from the Hoe Binh era. Carbon-14 methods date the Son Vi sites at approximately 12,000 years ago, placing Son Vi culture in the Pleistocene, or late Paleolithic era. (See Hoa Binh Culture; Mount Do)

SOVIET-VIETNAMESE TREATY OF FRIENDSHIP AND COOPERATION. Treaty between the Socialist Republic of Vietnam (SRV) and the Soviet Union signed on November 3, 1978. It was scheduled to run for 25 years and calls for mutual consultations in case of a military attack on either party.

The treaty was apparently requested by Vietnam in order to deter China from taking action in response to a planned Vietnamese invasion of Democratic Kampuchea. In an unpublished annex, the SRV reportedly agreed to provide the USSR with the use of port and air base facilities in Vietnam.

SPRATLY ISLANDS (Quan Dao Truong Xa). Scattered small islands in the South China Sea. Consisting of hundreds of tiny sand spits and coral reefs stretching over several hundred square miles between southern China, the Philippine Islands, the island of Borneo, and mainland Southeast Asia, the Spratlys were rarely occupied before the present century. France laid claim to the islands in 1933 and put a small meteorological station on one of the largest. After Japanese occupation during World War II, several of the islands have been claimed or occupied by most of the nations in the vicinity, including the Philippines, the Republic of China, the People's Republic of China (PRC), Malaysia, the Republic of Vietnam, and recently, the Socialist Republic of Vietnam (SRV). Hanoi, like the PRC, has presented historical evidence to support its claim to ownership over the islands, but has recently expressed a willingness in negotiations with the Philippines to share ownership with its neighbors.

As with the Parcel Islands to the north, the primary importance of the Spratlys is not the islands themselves, but the surrounding seas, which reportedly contain substantial oil reserves. (See Paracel Islands)

STRATEGIC HAMLETS (ap chien luoc). Program adopted by the Saigon regime during the Vietnam War to improve security in the countryside. The program began in 1963 at the suggestion of the Kennedy Administration, which hoped that the concept, successfully put in operation by the British in Malaya, could be reproduced in South Vietnam. Smaller than the so-called Agrovilles (khu tru mat), which had been created by the regime of Ngo Dinh Diem in 1959, the strategic hamlet was to be built, where possible, on the basis of existing villages and hamlets in rural areas. The new hamlets were to be provided with funds to help build schools, wells, and clinics, and were expected to provide for their own security.

U.S. officials suggested that the program initially be adopted only in secure areas to enhance confidence and popular support for the concept. But the Diem regime opted to promote the program with a greater sense of urgency, and organized many hamlets in contested areas, where revolutionary activity was high. The results were mixed. Although the hamlets created severe problems for People's Liberation Armed Forces (PLAF, popularly known as the Viet Cong), persistent efforts resulted in the destruction or takeover of many of them. Moreover, the usual problems of corruption and mismanagement plagued the program, and led to its widespread unpopularity. By the mid-1960s, the program was virtually moribund. (See Agrovilles; Ngo Dinh Diem; People's Liberation Armed Forces)

- T -

TA THU THAU. Prominent member of the Trotskyite faction in colonial Vietnam. The son of a poor carpenter, Ta Thu Thau was a follower of Nguyen An Ninh in Saigon during the early 1920s. While studying in Paris he joined Nguyen The Truyen's Annamese Independence Party, and then embraced Trotskyism. Evicted from France in 1930 for his political activities, he returned to Vietnam and joined the Trotskyite journal in Saigon, La Lutte, (The Struggle). For the next several years he was an active force in the Trotskyite movement, and on the journalistic scene. He was assassinated by the Vietminh in late 1945. (See Annamese Independence Party; Lutte, La; Nguyen An Ninh; Trotskyites)

TALE OF KIEU (Truyen Kieu) (Also known as Kim Van Kieu). Classic poem written by Vietnamese author Nguyen Du (1765-1820) in the early nineteenth century. Generally considered to be the greatest literary work written in the Vietnamese language, the Tale of Kieu is based on a Chinese love story and relates the story of a beautiful and intelligent young woman who sells herself as a concubine while remaining true to her real lover. Underlying the narrative plot is a powerful criticism of the greed, hypocrisy, and viciousness of contemporary Confucian society in Vietnam. The dramatic plot, as well as the beauty and the delicacy of the language, have made this 3,254-line poem the favorite literary work of millions of Vietnamese.

In the 1920s, the Tale of Kieu became the centerpiece of a literary controversy between supporters and opponents of French rule in colonial Vietnam. (See Literature; Ngo Duc Ke; Nguyen Du; Pham Quynh)

TAM TAM XA (See Association of Like Minds).

TAN DA (1888-1939). Pen-name of Nguyen Khac Kieu, a popular Vietnamese poet during the early twentieth century. Born in Son Tay province, Tan Da received a classical education and unsuccessfully took the regional civil service examination in 1912. Becoming a journalist, he worked for Nguyen Van Vinh's Dong Duong Tap Chi (Indochinese Review) and then established his own journal, An-Nam.

During his active life Tan Da became famous as a poet, writing in the modern idiom of quoc ngu but evoking traditional Confucian themes that still appeal to conservative elements within the population. He also wrote moral primers designed to preserve traditional virtues in a rapidly changing society. Yet Tan Da also states publicly that the Vietnamese needed the French to assist

them in adjusting to the challenges of the modern world.
    After his journal ceased publication in 1933, Tan Da retired
to his native village. He died in 1939. (See Literature)

TAN TRAO CONFERENCE (August 1945). National Congress held by
    the League for the Independence of Vietnam (Vietminh) in August
    1945 which launched the August Revolution. The conference,
    composed of delegates from localities throughout the country,
    was held on August 13-15, 1945. Prior to the opening of the
    Conference, a plenary session of the Central Committee of the
    Indochinese Communist Party (ICP), convened to prepare a re-
    sponse to the imminent surrender of Japan. On hearing of the
    Japanese surrender on August 14th, the Central Committee in-
    structed the Vietminh conference to declare a nationwide uprising
    to liberate Vietnam and create an independent republic.
    Tan Trao (new movement) is a small village in a deeply
    forested area of Tuyen Quang province, and had become the
    capital of the liberated zone of the Viet Bac in 1944.

TAN VIEN MOUNTAIN. A sacred mountain in North Vietnam, located
    near the point where the Red River leaves the mountains and
    enters the Delta, about twenty miles northwest of Hanoi. Accord-
    ing to legend, it was the home of the mountain spirit, a son of
    Lac Long Quan, who protected the city of Thang Long (present-
    day Hanoi). (See Lac Long Quan; Thang Long)

TAN VIET CACH MENH DANG (New Vietnamese Revolutionary Party).
    Radical political party founded by anti-colonial Vietnamese in 1920s.
    Originally known as the Phuc Viet (Revive Vietnam) party, it was
    composed of Hanoi intellectuals and released prisoners, along with
    some workers and students. Prominent members included Le Hoan,
    Dao Duy Anh, Ton Quang Phiet, and Dang Thai Mai. The party
    went through a number of name changes, settling on Tan Viet
    Cach Menh Dang in 1928, with its headquarters at Vinh, in Nghe
    An Province.
    The overall aim of the party was to restore Vietnamese inde-
    pendence, but party leaders disagreed over whether to use the
    tactics of reformation or violence. It cooperated as well as com-
    peted with Ho Chi Minh's Revolutionary Youth League (Viet Nam
    Thanh Nien Cach Menh Dong Chi Hoi) for followers, but even-
    tually the latter became dominant, and several members of the
    Tan Viet party like Tran Phu joined Ho Chi Minh's League. In
    early 1930 the Tan Viet merged with the League into a new Viet-
    namese Communist Party, which would soon change its own name
    to Indochinese Communist Party (Dang Cong San Dong Duong) in
    October. (See Ho Chi Minh; Indochinese Communist Party; Rev-
    olutionary Youth League; Tran Phu)

TAOISM (Dao Giao). One of the major religions in traditional Viet-
    nam. Taoism originally entered Vietnam from China during the
    beginning of the Christian era. It was probably brought in by

Chinese immigrants and, as in China, briefly flourished as a
philosophical alternative to the dominant Confucian ideology,
stressing inaction (wu wei) and harmony with nature as opposed
to the activist approach adopted by Confucianism. Eventually,
however, Taoism degenerated into a popular religion, incorporat-
ing elements of spirit worship, the search for immortality, and
the deification of famous personalities.

During the Ly and Tran Dynasties, Taoism ranked with Confucianism and Buddhism as one of the "Three Religions" (Tam
Giao) to be mastered by candidates for public office taking the
civil service examination. Under the Le, Taoism, like Buddhism,
was subordinated to the Dominant Confucian ideology and was
frequently used by rebel leaders as a means of sorcery to rally
popular support. (See Buddhism; Confucianism)

TAY (Tho). An ethnic minority in North Vietnam. The Tay are
numerically the largest mountain minority group in Vietnam, with
a total population of nearly 900,000. Related to the Thai in ethnic
background and language, their original habitat may have been
south of the Yangtse River in present-day China. Today they live
in the mountain provinces north of the Red River Delta.

Like most tribal peoples in Vietnam, the Tay reside primarily
in rural villages (ban) where they practice slash-and-burn agriculture or rice farming. Political authority traditionally rested
in a hereditary nobility, headed by a noble called the chau muong,
who typically ruled several villages and had the right to allocate
lands to his kin. Most Tay are spirit worshipers, although some
became Buddhists or Confucianists as the result of contact with
the lowland Vietnamese.

During the Vietnamese Revolution, the Tay were actively
enlisted into the Vietminh Front, led by Ho Chi Minh, and many
Tay reached high positions in the Communist Party. In recent
years, however, active proselytizing by China has reportedly led
to some official distrust of their loyalty. (See Thai; Tribal Minorities; Viet Bac)

TAY BAC AUTONOMOUS REGION (Khu Tay Bac Tu Tri). Autonomous
zone created by the Democratic Republic of Vietnam in the northwest part of North Vietnam. Originally established as the Tay-
Meo Autonomous Region in 1955 to provide local self-government
to tribal groups in the area, it was renamed the Tay Bac Autonomous Region in 1961. It included the provinces of Lai Chau,
Son La and Nghia Lo. A second autonomous zone, called the Viet
Bac Autonomous Region, was created northeast of the Red River
Delta. The Tay Bac Autonomous Region contained a total of
2.5 million people, and had 60 representatives in the National
Assembly.

The region was abolished after the end of the Vietnam War
and replaced by the provinces of Lai Chau, Son La, and Hoang
Lien Son. (See Thai; Tribal Minorities)

TAY SON BROTHERS (See Tay Son Dynasty; Tay Son Rebellion; Nguyen Hue).

TAY SON DYNASTY (Nha Tay Son) (1788-1802). Short-lived dynasty formed after the Tay Son Rebellion in eighteenth-century Vietnam. The dynasty was founded in 1788 by Nguyen Hue, second oldest of the three so-called Tay Son Brothers who launched the revolt in 1771 that eventually defeated the Nguyen and Trinh Lords, who had ruled southern and northern Vietnam in the name of the effete Le Dynasty since the sixteenth century. After the seizure of the capital Thang Long (Hanoi) in 1786, Nguyen Hue at first recognized the legitimacy of the reigning Le ruler. But when the Le called on Chinese aid to drive out Tay Son influence, Nguyen Hue defeated the Chinese, forced the Le emperor to flee to Peking, and declared himself Emperor Quang Trung of a new Tay Son Dynasty in 1788.

Quang Trung proved to be a very vigorous and effective ruler, but he died suddenly in 1792. His son and successor, Quang Toan (dynastic name of Canh Thinh), was young and inexperienced, and the dynasty soon fell prey to internal dissension. In 1802 it was overthrown by Nguyen Anh, last surviving member of the Nguyen house in the South. On seizing power, the latter had Canh Tinh and all remaining members of the Tay Son Dynasty executed. (See Nguyen Dynasty; Nguyen Hue)

TAY SON REBELLION. Peasant revolt lead by the so-called "Tay Son brothers" in eighteenth-century Vietnam. The rebellion originated in rural unrest which affected wide areas of South Vietnam under the rule of the so-called "Nguyen Lords" in the 1760s and early 1770s. In 1771, three brothers from the village of Tay Son (western mountain) in modern day Nghia Binh Province raised the standard of revolt against the corruption and misrule of the latest Nguyen court and called for the distribution of land to the poor. The rebellion won broad support from peasants, townspeople, local members of the scholar-gentry, and tribal minorities and achieved the overthrow of the Nguyen regime in 1785. Shortly thereafter, Tay Son armies attacked and defeated the Trinh lords in the North. In 1788, the last ruler of the Le Dynasty was deposed and the leading Tay Son brother, Nguyen Hue, ascended to the throne as Emperor Quang Trung. The new dynasty began to decline after the death of Quang Trung in 1797, and was replaced by the Nguyen Dynasty in 1802. (See Le Dynasty; Nguyen Dynasty; Nguyen Hue; Nguyen Lords; Tay Son Brothers; Tay Son Dynasty; Trinh Lords)

TAY VU. Administrative and territorial term for an ancient district in Vietnam. Located in the lower Red River Delta around the city of Co Loa, not far from present-day Hanoi, Tay Vu became an administrative district under the Au Lac and Nam Viet dynasties. The area was one of considerable political importance and had been the site of heavy fighting in early struggles against Chinese occupation. After the Trung Sisters rebellion in 39-43 A.D., General Ma Yuan divided Tay Vu into two separate administrative units. (See Co Loa; Ma Yuan)

TAYLOR, MAXWELL. U.S. Ambassador to the Republic of Vietnam from August 1964 until August 1965. In 1961 he was sent to Saigon by the incoming Kennedy Administration to assess the situation in South Vietnam and provide advice on future U.S. policy. His suggestion to send two divisions of U.S. combat troops to stiffen Vietnamese resolve, however, was rejected. After serving as chairman of the Joint Chiefs of Staff under Kennedy, he was appointed Ambassador to Saigon in August 1964 in the hope of improving the performance of the military junta in power. He was replaced by Henry Cabot Lodge the following summer. (See Lodge, Henry Cabot)

TEA. The origins of tea cultivation in Vietnam are unknown. Tea was grown in small quantities during the traditional period and, as in China, tea drinking served as a sign of hospitality.

Tea cultivation began to expand during the period of French rule. The first tea plantation was founded in Vinh Phu province in 1924, and soon other plantations appeared in the Central Highlands, where the climate and the red basaltic soil were particularly favorable for the plants. Tea exports reached 2,446 tons in 1940.

Today tea is produced on state farms in the Socialist Republic of Vietnam, mainly in the provinces of Vinh Phu, Hoang Lien Son, and Son La. Total tea production in the early 1980s was about 20,000 tons, with approximately half exported.

TEMPLE OF LITERATURE (Van Mieu). Historical site in Hanoi and location of the national academy used to train officials in Confucian scholarship during the traditional era in Vietnam. The Temple was first opened during the reign of Emperor Ly Thanh Tong (1054-1072) of the Ly Dynasty. It was the site of the metropolitan level of the civil service examinations during much of the traditional era and stone tablets were erected at the temple to honor the successful candidates. It also housed the National Academy (Quoc Tu Giam), used to train potential candidates and imperial officials in Confucian doctrine.

The Temple and other buildings on the temple grounds were periodically repaired and the site is one of the most important tourist attractions in the city of Hanoi. (See Civil Service Examinations; Confucianism; Education; Ly Thanh Tong)

TET (Tet Nguyen Dan). The New Year's Holiday in Vietnam, based on the lunar calendar. (See Festivals)

TET OFFENSIVE. Major military offensive and general uprising launched by the revolutionary forces in South Vietnam during the traditional New Year Holiday in early 1968. The offensive was planned by Hanoi military strategists in an effort to shake the stability of the Saigon regime and undermine public support for the war effort in the United States. It began during the Tet holidays on January 31st with a series of major attacks on the capital of Saigon and other cities and towns throughout South Vietnam. It concluded with smaller thrusts (often called "Mini-Tet") on urban areas later in the year.

Most of the troops involved in the offensive were members of the People's Liberation Armed Forces (PLAF), although regular forces of the People's Army of Vietnam (PAVN) took part in an extended attack on the old imperial capital of Hue, which they occupied for two weeks. The offensive resulted in heavy casualties for the revolutionary forces and did not achieve its maximum objective of provoking general uprisings in the big cities leading to the collapse of the Saigon regime. But televised reports of the offensive--notably the seizure of the ground floor of the U.S. Embassy in Saigon by a PLAF sapper team--seriously undermined public confidence in the war effort in the United States and led eventually to the reduction of American force levels in South Vietnam. (See People's Army of Vietnam; People's Liberation Armed Forces)

THAI (Tai). Tribal people living in modern-day North Vietnam. The Thai are numerically the third largest tribal minority in Vietnam with an estimated population of over 600,000 people in 1979. The vast majority of Thai live in the mountainous provinces of the far Northwest. Related to the Tay (Tho) peoples north of the Red River Delta, as well as a number of other mountain peoples scattered across the northern tier of mainland Southeast Asia, the Thai migrated into North Vietnam from the southern provinces of China during the twelfth and thirteenth centuries.

Located primarily in areas relatively remote from the lowlands of the Red River Delta, the Thai people (who are themselves divided into separate tribal groups according to the color of the blouses worn by the women) were given extensive autonomy during the colonial era, and many of their leaders cooperated with the French during the Franco-Vietminh War. After the Geneva Conference in 1954, the government of the Democratic Republic of Vietnam (DRV) attempted to win their allegiance by turning several provinces inhabited by the Thai into an autonomous region. Known as the Tay-Bac Autonomous Region, it has recently been divided into the provinces of Lai Chau, Son La and Hoang Lien Son. (See Tay; Tay Bac Autonomous Region)

THAI NGUYEN UPRISING. Rebellion against French rule in North Vietnam launched during World War I. The revolt was led by Luong Ngoc Quyen, son of Luong Van Can, the founder of the Dong Kinh Nghia Thuc (Tonkin Free School), and broke out at a military garrison in the Thai Nguyen provincial capital in August 1917. The French counterattacked, but many of the rebels were able to retreat into the mountains, where they were captured in September. (See Dong Kinh Nghia Thuc)

THAI THUONG HOANG (King's father). Royal title adopted during
the Tran Dynasty (1225-1400) to designate a position established
to guarantee an orderly succession on the imperial throne. Under
the preceding Ly Dynasty, court intrigues over the transition to
a new emperor had frequently led to political instability.

The system was first adopted by the founding Tran ruler,
Tran Thai Tong. It called for the existing emperor to retire
from office while still politically active, in order to serve as a
royal adviser (Thai Thuong Hoang) to the crown prince, who
now ascended to the throne. (See Tran Thai Tong; Tran Nghe
Tong)

THANG LONG (Rising Dragon). A historical name for the city of
Hanoi. Located at the confluence of the Red River, the Duong
River, and the To Lich River, the city possessed a central
location, a good defensive position, and was surrounded by fertile land. The area had been inhabited since the Bronze Age,
when it was named Long Do (Dragon's navel). It became a major
administrative center in the seventh century, during the period
of Chinese rule. A defensive citadel, called Dai La (Great Nest),
was built there, and provided the contemporary name for the
city.

In 1010, a half century after the restoration of independence,
Ly Thai To, founding emperor of the Ly Dynasty (1009-1225),
moved his capital there from the town of Hoa Lu, to the south.
According to legend, the emperor saw a golden dragon rising
through the clouds as he arrived at the city. In honor of that
vision, he named the city Thang Long (Rising Dragon).

The city remained the capital of Vietnam for most of the next
nine centuries. Like its model in Peking, it was divided in two
parts, with an imperial city (Hoang Thanh) surrounded by the
remainder of the city (Kinh Thanh). Inside the imperial city
was the royal palace, the Forbidden City (Can Thanh), surrounded by a high wall and a moat.

During the next several centuries the name of the city was
occasionally changed, from Dong Do (Eastern Capital) under the
Ho Dynasty (1400-1407) to Dong Kinh (Eastern Capital) under
Emperor Le Loi (1428-1433), and to Thang Thinh under Nguyen
Hue, founder of the Tay Son Dynasty. For most of the period,
however, it remained Thang Long. But when the Nguyen Dynasty
(1802-1945) moved the capital to Hue, the city was renamed Hanoi
(within the rivers), the name it retains today. (See Dai La;
Hanoi; Hoa Lu)

THANH NIEN (Youth). Weekly newspaper published by Ho Chi Minh's
Revolutionary Youth league in the 1920s. Published in Canton,
South China, it was smuggled to Vietnam for distribution and
first appeared in June 1925. The articles, many of which were
written anonymously by Ho Chi Minh until his departure from
China in 1927, promoted both national independence and the need
for a social revolution led by a communist party. Thanh Nien

ceased publication in May 1930 after publishing 208 issues. (See
Ho Chi Minh; Revolutionary Youth League of Vietnam)

THANH THAI (reigned 1889-1907) Emperor of Vietnam under the
French Protectorate. A son of Emperor Duc Duc, who reigned
briefly in 1883, Thanh Thai was born in 1879 and succeeded
Emperor Dong Khanh on the latter's death in 1889. Sensitive
and intelligent, he resented French domination over his country
and was deposed on suspicion of conspiracy in 1907. Exiled to
the island of Reunion, he was later permitted to return to
Vietnam and received a state pension until his death in 1958.
(See Dong Khanh; Treaty of Protectorate)

THIEU TRI (reigned 1841-1847). Third Emperor of the Nguyen
Dynasty in nineteenth-century Vietnam. Thieu Tri reigned at
a time when the French challenge to Vietnamese independence
was growing increasingly insistent. Like his father Minh Mang,
Thieu Tri was poetic and intellectually curious and cautiously
attempted to learn from the West, but was often hindered by a
cumbersome and xenophobic bureaucracy. He attempted to resolve the continuing dispute over the presence of French missionaries in Vietnam, but his efforts were sabotaged by a brutal
French bombardment of Da Nang in 1847. He died shortly after
at the age of 37. (See Minh Mang; Nguyen Dynasty)

TIEN SI. Highest degree in the civil service examination system
in traditional Vietnam. It corresponded to the degree of Chin-shih
(advanced scholar), the equivalent of a doctorate, in the Chinese
system. The degree was offered to those candidates who had
managed to pass both stages--the metropolitan exam (thi hoi) and
the palace exam (thi dinh)--of the triennial examinations given
at the imperial capital. Only students who had already passed
the regional examination (thi huong) were eligible to compete in
the metropolitan exam. Graduates benefitted from high prestige
and were eligible for top positions in the bureaucracy. (See
Civil Service Examinations)

TO HIEN THANH. Military leader and court figure during the Ly
Dynasty (1010-1225). To Hien Thanh, a respected military com-
mander and strategist, served as regent during the infancy of
Emperor Ly Cao Tong (1178-1210). He died in 1179. (See Ly
Anh Tong, Ly Cao Tong)

TO HUU (1920-?). Revolutionary poet and prominent political figure
in the Socialist Republic of Vietnam (SRV). Born in 1920 near
Hue, To Huu became active in revolutionary work in the 1930s
and gained a reputation as the most prominent poet of the Vietnamese revolution.
    After World War II To Huu served in a variety of posts in the
Democratic Republic of Vietnam (DRV) and became a member of
the Central Committee of the Vietnamese Worker's Party (VWP)

in 1951. In 1976 he rose to alternate rank in the Politburo and
became a full member in 1980. Named vice premier the same
year, he was active in ideological and economic work and was
identified with the conservative faction under Truong Chinh that
promoted rapid socialist transformation in the South. His reputation suffered because of the failure to achieve a stable currency and he was dropped from the Politburo at the Sixth Party
Congress in December 1986.

TON DUC THANG (1888-1980). Veteran member of the Vietnamese
Communist Party and President of the Democratic Republic of
Vietnam (DRV) after the death of Ho Chi Minh. Born in 1888 in
a poor peasant family in Long Xuyen province in South Vietnam,
Ton Duc Thang became a mechanic in Saigon and later joined
the French navy. He participated in a 1918 uprising by French
sailors in the Black Sea and in 1920 returned to Saigon, where
he formed the first workers' organization in French Indochina.
Joining Ho Chi Minh's Revolutionary Youth League, he was arrested for revolutionary activities in 1919, and imprisoned in
Poulo Condore until 1945.

After World War II Ton Duc Thang was named Inspector General for Political and Administrative Affairs and President of
the Standing Committee of the National Assembly. In 1960 he
was named Vice President of the DRV. He succeeded Ho Chi
Minh as President after the latter's death in 1969 and died in
March 1980. (See Democratic Republic of Vietnam)

TON THAT THUYET. Anti-French resistance leader in nineteenth-
century Vietnam. After the Treaty of Protectorate in 1884
established French control over the Vietnamese Empire, Ton That
Thuyet, an influential court official, fled with the young Emperor
Ham Nghi in the hope of launching a nationwide revolt against
French rule. Seeking refuge in the mountains north of Hue,
Ton That Thuyet and Ham Nghi issued an appeal entitled "Save
the King" (Can Vuong) to the Vietnamese people for support.
In 1886 Ton That Thuyet went to China to seek arms and support
from the Ch'ing Dynasty. Ham Nghi was captured in 1888 and
the movement gradually declined. (See Can Vuong movement;
Ham Nghi)

TON THO THUONG (1822-1877). Reformist and supporter of collaboration with the French in nineteenth-century Vietnam. Descended from a family of scholar-officials, Ton Tho Tuong failed
in his examination, but became influential while serving as an
intermediary between the French and the Court in 1862. He was
named a prefect by the French and served in the colonial administration until his death in 1877.

TONKIN. One of three regions of Vietnam under French colonial
rule. In 1884, by a treaty signed between France and the Nguyen
Dynasty, France declared a protectorate over the Vietnamese

Empire. France divided Vietnam into two regions, Annam (Central Vietnam) and Tonkin (the Red River Delta, from the Chinese border to the province of Thanh Hoa). The southern provinces of Vietnam had already been transformed into the French colony of Cochin China by treaty in 1874.

The name Tonkin is adapted from the Chinese term Tong Ching (Eastern capital), a name for Hanoi under Chinese rule. It was often referred to by the Vietnamese as Bac Bo (Northern region). Annam was left under imperial rule, while Tonkin was placed under French administration, although the emperor was permitted to maintain a viceroy (kinh luoc) in the regional capital of Hanoi. In 1886 the French abolished the position of viceroy and transferred his authority to the resident superieur, the highest French official in Tonkin, who governed in the name of the emperor, although frequently without consulting him.

Tonkin was included with Annam and Cochin China in the Associated State of Vietnam created by the Elysée Accords in 1949. (See Annam; Cochin China; Elysée Accords; Treaty of Protectorate)

TONKIN GULF. Body of water off the coast of North Vietnam. A part of the South China Sea, the Tonkin Gulf is bounded on the east of Hainan Island, on the north by China's Guangdong province, and on the west by the coast of Vietnam. Traditionally considered part of the open sea, in recent years the Tonkin Gulf has been the scene of a growing rivalry between China and Vietnam as both attempt to validate their claim to the mineral resources lying under the sea bed in the area. In 1964 it was the site of a well-publicized clash between naval forces of the Democratic Republic of Vietnam and the United States. (See Tonkin Gulf Incidents)

TONKIN GULF INCIDENTS. Two alleged clashes between naval craft of the Democratic Republic of Vietnam and the United States in August 1964. The Administration of Lyndon Johnson contended that Vietnamese ships fired on two U.S. destroyers, the Maddox and the C. Turner Joy, without provocation and in the open sea. According to the United States, a second incident took place a few days later. The Johnson Administration retaliated by launching air strikes against North Vietnamese cities and seeking a resolution from Congress authorizing the White House to take appropriate military measures to protect U.S. security interests in the area.

Further investigation revealed that the two U.S. warships operating near the North Vietnamese coast were monitoring Vietnamese radar capabilities in the area. The Hanoi regime may have identified the presence of the U.S. ships with South Vietnamese guerrilla operations on the nearby coast. The second incident probably never occurred. (See Tonkin Gulf Resolution)

TONKIN GULF RESOLUTION. A resolution passed by the U.S.

Congress authorizing President Lyndon Johnson to take necessary measures to protect U.S. security interests in the area of mainland Southeast Asia. Approved by a near-unanimous vote, it later became controversial as many Americans criticized the broad powers it granted the President to make war without consulting Congress. The resolution was passed after two alleged incidents involving U.S. and North Vietnamese warships in the Tonkin Gulf (See Tonkin Gulf Incidents)

TRAN ANH TONG (reigned 1293-1314). Fourth emperor of the Tran Dynasty in Vietnam. Tran Anh Tong succeeded his father Tran Nham Tong as emperor in 1293 when the latter retired from office to serve the new ruler as adviser. In contrast to that of his predecessor, the reign of Tran Anh Tong was a generally peaceful one. The Mongol invasions had come to an end with the death of Emperor Kublai Khan in 1294, and the intermittent wars with Champa had been succeeded by a period of peace marked by the marriage in 1306 of the Emperor's daughter Huyen Tranh to the king of Champa in return for the transfer of two districts in northern Champa to the Vietnamese. This uneasy relationship was interrupted, however, when Tran Anh Tong refused to permit his daughter to be buried with the Cham king on the latter's death, in accordance with local custom. War broke out and, as had so often been the case under the Tran, Champa was defeated.
Tran Anh Tong abdicated in 1314 in favor of his son, the Crown Prince Tran Minh Trong, and served as royal adviser until his death in 1320.

TRAN CAO. A rebel against the Le Dynasty who claimed to be a descendant of the Tran royal family. (See Le Uy Muc; Mac Dang Dung)

TRAN DU TONG (reigned 1341-1369). Seventh emperor of the Tran Dynasty in fourteenth-century Vietnam. Son of Emperor Tran Minh Tong (1314-1329), Tran Du Tong succeeded his older brother Tran Hien Tong as emperor on the latter's death at the age of 22 in 1341. Tran Du Tong's reign was marked by financial extravagance and official corruption in a time of climatic disaster and pestilence. Yet when one of his officials, the Confucian scholar Chu Van An, appealed to the emperor for an end to official malfeasance, the appeal was ignored.
Internal difficulties resulted in a more perilous situation in foreign affairs. China, in the throes of the collapse of the Yuan (Mongol) Dynasty, was pacified by tribute, by Champa took advantage of Vietnamese weaknesses and launched repeated attacks on the southern frontier.
Tran Du Tong died without issue in 1369. After a court intrigue, he was succeeded by his brother, the inept Tran Nghe Tong, who allowed the mandarin Le Quy Ly (later known as Ho Quy Ly) to become dominant at court. (See Chu Van An; Ho Quy Ly; Tran Minh Tong)

TRAN DUE TONG (reigned 1372-1377). Ninth emperor of the Tran
Dynasty in fourteenth-century China. Tran Due Tong succeeded
Tran Nghe Tong on the abdication of the latter in 1372. But
Tran Nghe Tong retained substantial influence through his pos-
ition as royal adviser. Tran Due Tong was killed in battle in 1377
during a war with Champa. (See Tran Nghe Tong)

TRAN DYNASTY (Nha Tran) (1225-1400). Second major dynasty
after the restoration of Vietnamese independence in A.D. 939.
The Tran family, who were originally fishermen, rose to a position of power at court during the declining years of the preceding Ly Dynasty (1009-1225). In 1225, the powerful court
figure Tran Thu Do took advantage of the collapse of the Ly
to place a member of his own family on the throne as the first
emperor of the new Tran Dynasty.

The Tran are best known for their staunch defense of Viet-
namese independence against attack by the Yuan (Mongol)
Dynasty in the thirteenth century. Through the outstanding
leadership of Tran Hung Dao and other Vietnamese leaders, the
Tran were able to defeat the most powerful military force in Asia
on three separate occasions, while simultaneously extending
Vietnamese territory to the south at the expense of neighboring
Champa.

But two centuries of Tran rule also had a significant impact
on the internal development of the Vietnamese Empire. The Tran
continued the process of extending the centralized power of the
state through a series of administrative reforms that strengthened
the bureaucracy and resolved the problem of imperial succession
through the adoption of the position of royal adviser. They were
assisted in some measure by the adoption of Confucian institutions
and values which became increasingly influential, although the
Tran emperors themselves remained influenced primarily by Buddhist teachings. Economic growth was promoted through the expansion of trade and manufacturing and the extension of land
under cultivation through territorial expansion and the expansion
of the irrigation networks.

Like the Ly Dynasty, however, the Tran fell victim to a
series of weak rulers that led in the fourteenth century to the
decline and ultimately the overthrow of the dynasty. They
contributed to their own downfall by their failure to resolve
the land problem. Under the Tran, landholding was increasingly
concentrated in the hands of nobles and powerful mandarins, who
received land from the court and often seized private lands belonging to individual peasants or rural villages. Some of the
fiefdoms consisted of thousands of peasants, most of whom were
serfs or slaves. Growing landlessness (created by land seizures
and a growing population) and high taxes led to a rising incidence
of peasant rebellion during the mid-fourteenth century.

In the long run, the Tran Dynasty was unable to avoid the
fate of its predecessor. After a series of competent if not brilliant rulers, the dynasty gradually lost its momentum during the

fourteenth century and did not survive into the next. (See Buddhism; Confucianism; Mongol Invasions; Tran Thu Do)

TRAN HIEN DE (Tran Phe De) (reigned 1377-1388). Tenth emperor of the Tran Dynasty in fourteenth-century Vietnam. Tran Hien De ascended to the throne on the death of his predecessor, Tran Due Tong, in battle. His was a troubled reign. Externally, Vietnam was involved in war with Champa and a strained relationship with the rising power of the Ming Dynasty in China. Internally, the court was rife with intrigue, one faction supporting Ex-Emperor Tran Nghe Tong, now serving as royal adviser (Thai Thuong Hoang) since his abdication in 1372, and another Le Quy Ly (later known as Ho Quy Ly), a high-ranking mandarin and a cousin by marriage of Tran Nghe Tong. As a result of scheming at court, Le Quy Ly persuaded Tran Nghe Tong to replace Tran Phe De as emperor with the former's own son, Tran Thuan Tong (reigned 1388-1398). Le Quy Ly then had the ex-emperor assassinated. He has thus come to be known in history as Tran Phe De (the deposed Tran) rather than by his royal name of Tran Hien De. (See Ho Quy Ly, Tran Nghe Tong)

TRAN HIEN TONG (reigned 1329-1341). Sixth emperor of the Tran Dynasty in fourteenth-century Vietnam. Tran Hien Tong succeeded his father, Tran Minh Tong, as emperor in 1329, but the latter remained dominant at court through his position as royal adviser (Thai Thuong Hoang). Tran Hien Tong died in 1341 at the age of 23. (See Tran Minh Tong)

TRAN HUNG DAO (Tran Quoc Tuan). Famous general who defeated two Mongol invasions in late thirteenth-century Vietnam. A prince in the Tran royal family, in 1287 he was appointed commander-in-chief of the Vietnamese armed forces in the face of the growing threat of a Mongol invasion. Asked by Emperor Tran Nhan Tong whether the Vietnamese Empire should appease the Mongols rather than fight, Tran Hung Dao had replied with a famous declaration in which he appealed to his sovereign and to the population at large, for a policy of national resistance.

When the Mongol army invaded in 1283, Tran Hung Dao carried out a brilliant defense that resulted in a massive victory over the Mongol forces. After initially giving ground and allowing the numerically larger enemy troops to occupy the Red River Delta, Tran Hung Dao inaugurated a policy of guerrilla warfare and scorched-earth tactics, and then launched a major counter-offensive that liberated the capital city of Thang Long, won a major battle at Tay Ket, and drove the Mongol forces back into China.

In 1287, the Mongols resumed their attack. Tran Hung Dao continued the same tactics, avoiding a pitched battle until the enemy had occupied the capital and then launching a series of attacks which culminated at the mouth of the Bach Dang River,

where Tran Hung Dao repeated the feat of Ngo Quyen over
three hundred years earlier, sinking metal-tipped stakes into the
river which impaled the ships of the Mongol fleet as they sailed
into the river at high tide. The defeat led to the evacuation of
the enemy armed forces and the end of the last Mongol threat
to Vietnamese independence. Tran Hung Dao died in 1300, at
the age of 87. A temple, which still exists, was built at Kiep
Bac, his final home in what is today Hai Hung Province.

Tran Hung Dao is viewed today as one of the truly great
military strategists in Vietnamese history. His use of guerrilla
warfare to harass a more powerful enemy became a model for
revolutionary military planners of the twentieth century as they
sought to devise a strategy to defeat the powerful armed forces
of France and the United States. His emphasis on the importance
of national unity, with the entire nation fighting as one, was
citied by communist leaders as they attempted to mobilize the
population of North Vietnam in the struggle to reunify the North
with the South. His peroration of resistance to the invaders and
his book on military strategy, entitled Essentials of Military Art
(Binh Thu Yeu Luoc) have become classics of Vietnamese literature. (See Mongol invasions; Tran Dynasty; Tran Nhan Tong)

TRAN MINH TONG (reigned 1314-1329). Fifth emperor of the Tran
Dynasty in fourteenth-century Vietnam. He succeeded to the
throne in 1314, when his father Tran Anh Tong, in accordance
with local custom, retired from office to play the role of imperial
adviser. His reign was a relatively peaceful one, marked only
by a brief war with Champa in 1318, resulting in the seizure of
Cham capital.

According to Vietnamese historians, Tran Minh Tong was somewhat of an innovator. He issued a decree prohibiting the traditional practice of tattooing in the Vietnamese armed forces; a
practice that had been made famous in the previous century when
Vietnamese soldiers fighting under Tran Hung Dao had tattooed
themselves with the phrase "death to the Mongols" (sat That).
After his retirement in 1329, he played an active role as adviser
to the throne during the reign of two of his sons, Tran Hien
Tong (1329-1341) and Tran Du Tong (1341-1369), until his death
in 1358.

TRAN NGHE TONG (reigned 1370-1372). Eighth emperor of the Tran
Dynasty in fourteenth-century Vietnam. Although his reign was
a short one, he remained an influential figure at court while
serving as royal adviser for nearly thirty years. During that
time he frequently conspired to affect policy and once intervened
to place his own son, Tran Thuan Tong, on the throne. (See
Ho Quy Ly; Tran Hien De)

TRAN NHAN TONG (reigned 1278-1293). Third emperor of the Tran
Dynasty in late thirteenth-century Vietnam. Tran Nhan Tung
(proper name Tran Cam) was born in 1257 and succeeded his

father, Tran Thanh Tung, as emperor in 1278. His reign of fourteen years was marked, above all, by war with the Mongol Dynasty in China. His predecessor had attempted to placate the Mongols by adopting a conciliatory attitude toward their demands and accepting tribute status with the Emperor in Peking. By the late 1270s, the Mongols had seized all of southern China from the remnants of the Sung Dynasty and continued their southward expansion with an attack on the kingdom of Champa, south of Vietnam on the central coast. When the Cham government took to the hills to continue guerrilla warfare against the invaders, Kublai Khan demanded the right of passage for Mongol troops through the Tran State of Dai Viet. When the Vietnamese refused the Mongol Dynasty launched an invasion which resulted in the seizure of most of the Red River Delta and the occupation of the capital of Thang Long (modern-day Hanoi). Supported by the outstanding generalship of Tran Hung Dao, Emperor Tran Nhan Tong rallied the population behind a defensive effort which defeated the Mongols and forced the withdrawal of their forces from China.

China resumed its attack in 1287 and once again occupied the Vietnamese capital but the Mongol fleet was destroyed on the Bach Dang River (in a manner and in a place reminiscent of the first Battle of Bach Dang won by Ngo Quyen in A.D. 939) and its army was once again forced to withdraw. Tran Nhan Tong sought negotiations and offered to recognize Chinese suzerainty, but Kublai Khan was reportedly planning a new invasion of Vietnam when he died.

Tran Nhan Tong's staunch defense of Vietnamese independence galvanized the Vietnamese nation and made General Tran Hung Dao one of the heroic figures in Vietnamese history. The price of survival was high, however, for the Vietnamese countryside wa devastated by the two wars and many suffered from hunger. Tra Nhan Tong abdicated in 1293 and served as an adviser to his son and successor Tran Anh Tong (1293-1314) until his death in 1308. (See Mongol invasions; Tran Dynasty; Tran Hung Dao)

TRAN PHU (1904-1931). Founding member of Indochinese Communist Party in 1930. Born in Quang Ngai Province, the son of a district official, Tran Phu attended the National Academy in Hue and after graduation became a teacher in Vinh. In the mid-1920s he became a member of the New Vietnamese Revolutionary Party. Sent to Canton in 1926 to discuss a merger with Ho Chi Minh's Revolutionary Youth League, he defected to the latter.

As a promising member of the League, Tran Phu was sent to Moscow in 1927 to study at the Stalin School (Communist Universit for Toilers of the East). In early 1930 he returned to Vietnam and was chosen as General Secretary of the newly-formed Vietnamese Communist Party (renamed in October the Indochinese Communist Party, or ICP) and, at a Central Committee meeting held in Hong Kong in October, a member of the three-man presidium.

Tran Phu was arrested by French police in March 1931 while attending the party's second plenum in Saigon. He died in prison in September of torture or tuberculosis. (See Indochinese Communist Party; Tan Viet Cach Menh Dang)

TRAN QUANG KHAI. Military leader who fought against Mongol invasion in late thirteenth-century Vietnam. Tran Quang Khai, a son of Emperor Tran Thai Tong (1225-1258), commanded Vietnamese military forces in the south, near the border of Champa. In 1285 Mongol troops, fresh from a successful military campaign against the Cham, launched an attack on the Vietnamese Empire through the area known today as Nghe Tinh Province. General Tran Quang Khai was unable to prevent the Mongol advance and retreated northward, but eventually his force joined with those of Tran Hung Dao to defeat the Mongol armies and drive them out of Vietnam. (See Mongol Invasion; Tran Hung Dao)

TRAN QUOC PAGODA (Chua Tran Quoc). A famous pagoda in Hanoi. Originally called the Khai Quoc Pagoda, it was first built in the fifth century A.D. on the banks of the Red River near the present-day city of Hanoi. Later it was moved to a peninsula on the West Lake on the northern edge of the city, and renamed the Tran Quoc Pagoda. During the Ly Dynasty (1009-1225), it housed a Buddhist Monastery.

TRAN QUOC TUAN (See Tran Hung Dao).

TRAN THAI TONG (reigned 1225-1258). First emperor of the Tran Dynasty in thirteenth-century Vietnam. Tran Thai Tong (proper name Tran Canh) ascended the throne at age seven in 1225, through the influence of the powerful Tran family which had been dominant at court during the final years of the Ly Dynasty (1010-1225). The throne was solidified by marrying the young emperor to Empress Ly Chien Hoang, the last Ly ruler.

During his youth, the dynasty was under the influence of his scheming uncle Tran Thu Do. In 1236, Thu Do forced the young emperor to abandon his wife, who was childless, in favor of her older sister, who was already married to another member of the Tran family and already pregnant. In protest Tran Thai Tong, a fervent Buddhist fled the capital and sought refuge at a Thien Buddhist monastery on nearby Mount Yen Tu. Tran Thu Do cajoled the Emperor to return to the palace and he reigned for twenty more years.

The reign of Tran Thai Tong was marked by the further centralization and regularization of the Vietnamese state. Through the influence of Tran Thu Do, who remained a dominant figure at court until his death in 1264, a number of administrative reforms were introduced. The civil service examination system, (based on the "Three doctrines," Buddhism, Confucianism, and Taoism) was extended, a national system of taxation and several new bureaucratic institutions were established, and a penal code

was promulgated. Tran Thai Tong also attempted to resolve the
continuing problem of imperial succession by introducing a new
system whereby the emperor retired from the throne while still
active inorder to serve the new emperor as an adviser.

Tran Thai Tong's three decades on the throne was also a
period of active Vietnamese involvement in regional affairs. In
the early 1250s, the empire fought a new war with the state of
Champa to the south. While that campaign was a striking success, a new and more ominous threat now appeared on the hori-
zon in the form of the rise of the Mongol Empire in China. In
1257 Kublai Khan demanded that Dai Viet grant passage to Mongol troops through Vietnamese territory to attack the Southern
Sung. Tran Thai Tong refused. A mongol army invaded the
Red River Delta and briefly occupied the capital at Thang Long
(modern-day Hanoi), but disease, the weather, and Vietnamese
attacks forced them to retreat.

In 1258, Tran Thai Tong abdicated the throne in favor of his
son, who became Emperor Tran Thanh Tong (1258-1278). He
served his son as adviser for nineteen more years and died at
age 60 in 1277. (See Civil Service Examination Systems; Ly
Chieu Hoang; Tran Dynasty; Tran Thu Do)

TRAN THANH TONG (reigned 1258-1278). Second emperor of the
Tran Dynasty in thirteenth-century Vietnam. Tran Thanh Tong
rose to the throne in 1258 when his father, Tran Thai Tong,
abdicated to become a royal adviser. Unlike the previous period,
which had been marked by war with Champa and a Mongol invasion of the Red River Delta in 1257, the reign of Tran Thanh
Tong was a relatively peaceful one. Although pressure on the
northern border from the Yuan (Mongol) Dynasty continued,
Emperor Than Thanh Tong followed a policy of conciliation,
accepting the role of tribute status with the Mongol Emperor,
and was able to avoid war with China. In preparation for a
possible attack from the North, however, he strengthened the
armed forces and enforced national conscription to create a
peacetime army of over 100,000 men.

In domestic affairs, Tran Thanh Tong essentially continued
the policy of his father, promoting the centralization of government and the rationalization of administration. A massive program
to open virgin lands to cultivation through the contruction of
dikes was put in operation. The new lands were then turned
into estates (in Vietnamese, trang dien) owned by great noble
and mandarin families and farmed by peasants whose social and
legal position resembled those of serfs in feudal Europe. While
the land policy may have had economic benefits for the state,
it led to the creation of powerful autonomous fiefdoms that would
later undermine the power of the monarchy and a rising level of
social unrest in the countryside.

In 1278, Tran Thanh Tong followed the model of his father and
retired from the throne in place of his son, who became Emperor
Tran Nhan Tong (1279-1293). He remained influential as royal

adviser (<u>Thai Thuong Hoang</u>) until his death in 1291 at the age
of 51. (See Tran Dynasty; Tran Nhan Tong; Tran Thai Tong)

TRAN THI. Wife of Ly Hue Tong, emperor of Ly Dynasty (1210–
1224). (See Ly Hue Tong; Tran Thu Do)

TRAN THUAN TONG (reigned 1388–1398). Eleventh emperor of the
Tran Dynasty in late fourteenth-century Vietnam. A son of the
retired emperor Tran Nghe Tong (1370–1372), Tran Thuan Tong
was elevated to the throne by his father, then serving as royal
adviser at court, as a replacement for his cousin, Tran Hien
De (Tran Phe De). He was later removed from power and assassinated at the order of Ho Quy Ly. (See Tran Nghe Tong;
Ho Quy Ly)

TRAN THU DO. Powerful political figure in thirteenth-century Vietnam and founder of the Tran Dynasty (1225–1400). Tran Thu
Do was a cousin of Tran Thi, wife of Emperor Ly Hue Tong (1210–
1224) and an influential member of the Tran family, which had
restored Emperor Ly Cao Tong to power after a rebellion in 1208.
In 1225 Ly Hue Tong abdicated in favor of his daughter, Ly
Chien Hoang. Thu Do, now a lover of ex-queen Tran Thi, arranged a marriage between Empress Ly Chien Hoang with his
nephew, the seven-year old Tran Canh, who became founding
Emperor Tran Thai Tong of the new Tran Dynasty in 1221. Tran
Thu Do then arranged for the death of remaining members of the
Ly family, including the retired ex-emperor Ly Hue Tong.
    During the next several decades, Tran Thu Do remained a
dominant figure at the Tran court. When Ly Chien Hoang failed
to produce an heir, he arranged for her to be replaced as wife
of Emperor Tran Thai Tong by her older sister. Thu Do's
scheming caused widespread outrage and led to rebellion by other
influential figures at court, whom he pacified by providing them
with state land or official titles.
    Tran Thu Do also used his influence to achieve administrative
reforms to strengthen the Tran Dynasty, promulgating a new
penal code and setting forth new regulations on hiring and
promotions within the bureaucracy. He died in 1264. (See Ly
Chieu Hoang; Ly Hue Tong; Tran Dynasty; Tran Thai Tong)

TRAN TRONG KIM (1883–1953). Conservative historian and politician
in colonial Vietnam. Tran Trong Kim began his professional career by writing elementary school textbooks on Confucian ethics
and philosophy. In the 1920s he published two major volumes on
Asian history and civilization, <u>Nho Giao</u> (The Teachings of Confucius) and <u>Viet Nam Su Luoc</u> (Outline History of Vietnam). Kim's
attempt to preserve and interpret Confucianism for his contem-
poraries provoked a literary war with such critics as Phan
Khoi, who argued that traditional Confucian culture had little
value in twentieth-century Vietnam.
    Tran Trong Kim was briefly prime minister of Vietnam after

the Japanese coup d'état which overthrew the French colonial administration in March 1945. His government resigned with the defeat of Japan in August. (See August Revolution; Bao Dai; Confucianism; Literature; Phan Khoi)

TRAN VAN DON. General in the South Vietnamese Army and participant in the coup that overthrew President Ngo Dinh Diem in 1963. Born and raised in France, Tran Van Don was trained in economics and then joined the French Army at the outbreak of World War II. Respected for his competence and integrity, he rose rapidly in rank and was appointed Chief of Staff of the Army of the Republic of Vietnam by President Ngo Dinh Diem, whom he had supported during the latter's rise to power after the Geneva Conference of 1954. He eventually lost Diem's confidence, however, and was deprived of his command. In 1963 he joined the "coup group" that overthrew the Diem regime, and briefly served as Minister of Defense.

Arrested in early 1964 by General Nguyen Khanh on the suspicion of dealings with neutralist elements in France, General Don retired from active service and eventually settled in the United States. (See Army of the Republic of Vietnam; Ngo Dinh Diem; Nguyen Khanh)

TRAN VAN GIAU (1910–   ). Leading communist militant and prominent historian in Vietnam. Born in a village south of Saigon in 1911, Tran Van Giau received his education in France, where he entered radical activities and in 1933 was recruited to study at the Stalin School in Moscow. After completing a two-year program he was sent back to Vietnam to help reconstruct the ICP after its virtual destruction during the Nghe Tinh Revolt.

For the next several years Tran Van Giau directed the ICP apparatus in Cochin China, where he began to display the independence in thought and action that made him one of the most powerful if undisciplined members of the party. Arrested in 1935 and sent to Poulo Condore, he was apparently released in time to help plan the disastrous uprising in Cochin China in November 1940, (the so-called Nam Ky Uprising) that resulted in the arrests of several of its top operatives.

Immediately after World War II, Tran Van Giau led the Party's activities in the South and was briefly chairman of the Committee for the South (Uy Ban Nam Bo) during the August Revolution. But his harsh methods of operation were considered unsuitable by Party leaders in Hanoi, and he was replaced in 1946 by Nguyen Binh. Tran Van Giau became a historian and has published a number of major works on the history of the Communist Party and the Vietnamese Revolution. (See Nam Ky Uprising)

TRAN VAN HUONG. Political figure in South Vietnam and briefly president of the Republic of Vietnam prior to the communist takeover in 1975. A native of Cochin China, Tran Van Huong was a schoolteacher who had gone into politics and become the

mayor of Saigon under the regime of President Ngo Dinh Diem.
A critic of the Diem regime, he became briefly prominent after
the latter's overthrow when he was named prime minister under
the elderly politician Phan Khac Suu in a civilian government
established by General Nguyen Khanh in the fall of 1964.

In late April 1975, Huong was named president of the Republic
of Vietnam when Nguyen Van Thieu resigned on the eve of the
fall of Saigon. Communist leaders in North Vietnam refused to
deal with Huong, however, and he was replaced a few days later
with General Duong Van (Big) Minh. (See Duong Van Minh;
Ho Chi Minh Campaign; Nguyen Khanh; Nguyen Van Thieu)

TRAN VAN HUU. Prime minister of the Associated State of Vietnam
from May 1950 until June of 1952. A wealthy landlord and a
French citizen, Tran Van Huu was trained as an agricultural
engineer and served as an official in the French Department of
Agrigulture after World War I. Amassing considerable wealth as
a landlord, he became active in the movement to restore Bao
Dai to power in the late 1940s and was rewarded with the gover-
norship of South Vietnam in 1949. In May 1950 he was appointed
to replace Nguyen Phan Long as prime minister. Although as
governor Huu had vigorously defended Cochinchinese separatism,
as prime minister he attempted to broaden Vietnamese autonomy
within the French Union. Like his predecessor Nguyen Phan
Long, he eventually turned to the United States as a means of
applying pressure on the French. His gamble was not successful,
and he was dismissed from office in June 1952.

TRAN VAN TRA (1918-). Veteran communist leader and military
commander in Vietnam. Born in Quang Ngai province in 1918,
Tran Van Tra became involved in anti-colonial activities while
working as a railroad laborer in the 1930s. Arrested in 1939,
he was released from prison in March 1945 and became a leading
figure in the Ba To Uprising launched in Quang Ngai province
that month.

During the Franco-Vietminh War, Tran Van Tra served as
a military commander with Vietminh forces in South Vietnam and
political officer of the Saigon-Cholon zone. After the Geneva
Conference he was reassigned as deputy chief of staff of the
People's Army of Vietnam (PAVN). He returned to the South
at the beginning of the Second Indochina War as a ranking military officer and chairman of the Central Military Commission of
the Central Office for South Vietnam (COSVN).

After the end of the war in 1975, he briefly headed the Military Management Committee in Saigon and became a member of the
Central Committee the following year, and Vice Minister of Defense of the Socialist Republic of Vietnam (SRV). He was dropped
from all his party and government positions in 1982, reportedly
because of policy criticisms which appeared in his memoirs. (See
Central Office for South Vietnam; People's Army of Vietnam)

TRANSPORTATION. Lack of transport facilities is one of the key obstacles to rapid economic growth in contemporary Vietnam. During the traditional period, most goods were transported by oxcart or along Vietnam's many rivers and canals. After the establishment of colonial rule, the French built a railroad from Saigon to Hanoi and a network of metalled roads that were un-rivaled in Southeast Asia. Since the departure of the French, however, little had been done to build on that foundation, while war damage destroyed much of the existing transportation facili-ties in both North and South.

Since 1975, the Socialist Republic of Vietnam (SRV) has attempted with only modest success to modernize the transpor-tation network in order to provide a foundation for economic growth. The North-South railroad has been put back in oper-ation, but the road system is still seriously inadequate. Even on Highway Number One, which runs from the Chinese border to the Mekong River Delta, ruts on the road surface make it difficult to travel more than 25 miles per hour. The truck fleet is ancient, and one source recently estimated that as many as one-third of all transport vehicles in Vietnam were out of operation at any given time for lack of spare parts. The SRV possesses a small state-owned airline, but service is spotty and most of the planes are Soviet-made Ilyushins, in operation since the Viet-nam War.

TREATY OF 1874 (also known as Philastre Treaty). Treaty between France and Vietnam signed on March 15, 1874. After the occupa-tion of North Vietnam by Francis Garnier and the latter's death in battle in December 1873, the French government decided to evacuate French troops from the area and seek a settlement. The agreement was negotiated by Paul Philastre, an opponent of an aggressive French policy in Asia. According to the terms of the agreement, the Vietnamese court, fearful of a new French military action, recognized full French sovereignty over all six provinces of Cochin China. The Red River was opened to international commerce, French consular offices were to be opened in Hanoi, Haiphong, and Qui Nhon. Vietnam promised that its foreign policy would conform with that of France. (See Dupré, Admiral Jules-Marie; Garnier, Francis; Tu Duc)

TREATY OF PROTECTORATE (1884) (also known as Patenotre Treaty) Treaty signed between France and the Vietnamese Empire in June 1884. It replaced a similar Treaty of Protectorate between the two countries negotiated by Francois Harmand in August 1883. Like its predecessor, it granted France extensive rights to represent Vietnam in foreign affairs and oversee the internal policy in the Vietnamese Empire. The emperor remained the legitimate ruler but with sharply reduced power. The new agreement differed from its predecessor in providing France with increased authority in North Vietnam, henceforth to be known as Tonkin. It was negotiated by the Vietnamese court official Nguyen Van Tuong, regent during the minority of Emperor Kien Phuoc, and the French diplomat Jules Patenotre. It was declared abolished on March 12, 1945, when Emperor Bao Dai declared Vietnamese independence. (See Bao Dai; Harmand Treaty)

TREATY OF SAIGON. Peace treaty signed between Vietnam and France in June 1862. The treaty was negotiated after a series of military victories won by French forces in the southern provinces of Vietnam. The Vietnamese court ceded these provinces in the South to France (Bien Hoa, Dinh Tuong, and Gia Dinh), as well as the island of Poulo Condore, and Vietnam was required to pay a large indemnity. Three ports were opened to French commerce, and French missionaries were permitted to propagate their faith on Vietnamese soil. The treaty had been negotiated on behalf of Emperor Tu Duc by the mandarin Phan Than Gian.

A later treaty, signed in March 1874, ceded the remaining southern provinces to the French. (See Ky Hoa, Battle of; Nguyen Tri Phuong; Phan Thanh Gian; Truong Dinh)

TREATY OF TIENTSIN (1885) (also known as Li-Fournier Treaty). Treaty signed between China and France in May 1884. Signed by the Chinese plenipotentiary Li Hung-chang and French representative François Fournier, it provided Chinese recognition of the French protectorate over Vietnam (established by the Harmand Treaty in August 1883). China renounced its suzerainty over Vietnam and agreed to withdraw its troops from Vietnam, which had been sent at the request of Emperor Tu Duc to help resist French attacks in the Red River Delta.

Clashes broke out between the two sides, however, leading to a resumption of war and the signing of a second Treaty of Tientsin in June 1885. (See Harmand Treaty)

TREATY OF VERSAILLES (1787). Treaty signed between France and Nguyen Anh, pretender to the Vietnamese throne in November 1787. Pigneau de Behaine, French Bishop of Adran, had promised to assist Nguyen Anh, a prince of the family of the deposed Nguyen lords in South Vietnam, in return for future French privileges in Vietnam. France agreed to provide Nguyen Anh with naval craft, troops, and financial support for the latter's effort to defeat the Tay Son, now in power in Vietnam. In return, Nguyen Anh promised to grant commercial and missionary rights as well as the city of Da Nang and the island of Paulo Condore to France. In the end, France failed to live up to its commitments. (See Nguyen Anh; Nguyen Lords; Pigneau de Behaine)

TRI QUANG. Buddhist monk and neutralist political figure in South Vietnam during the Vietnam War. A member of the influential An Quang Buddhist Association in Hue, Tri Quang became actively involved in anti-government policies in the early 1960s, opposing both the pro-Catholic policies followed by the regime of President Ngo Dinh Diem and the latter's attempt to eradicate the insurgency movement in South Vietnam. After Diem's overthrow, Tri Quang became a prominent advocate of neutralism in the war, and was forced to seek refuge in the U.S. Embassy in Saigon. Often accused of being influenced by the communists, he was actually distrusted by the Hanoi regime as a "petty bourgeois intellectual. He remained in South Vietnam after the communist takeover and was reportedly arrested in 1982 as part of a government crackdown on dissident Buddhist activities. (See Buddhism; Ngo Dinh Diem)

TRIBAL MINORITIES. Tribal peoples comprise about eight percent of the total population of the Socialist Republic of Vietnam (SRV). The tribal population, currently estimated at slightly over four million, is divided into about fifty ethnic groups and several major linguistic families of which the Thai-Tay, the Mon-Khmer, the H'mong-Dao, the Viet-Muong, the Malayo-Polynesian, and the Tibeto-Burman are the most numerous.

The vast majority of the tribal peoples live in two major geographical areas--the mountainous provinces surrounding the Red River Delta in the North and the Central Highlands. Key groups in the region of the Red River Delta are the Thai, the Tay, the Muong, and the Nung. In the Central Highlands, the most dominant tribal peoples are the Rhade and the Jarai. Most of these people live by slash-and-burn agriculture, although some peoples living in valley areas engage in the cultivation of wet rice.

Throughout most of Vietnamese history, the tribal areas have been governed separately from the remainder of the country. This policy was continued during the colonial era, when the Frenc set up distinct administrative districts in tribal regions in the northwest and the Central Highlands; that policy was continued by the Democratic Republic of Vietnam, which set up separate autonomous districts and provinces whose elected representatives were composed of members of the chief tribal groups in the area. It was not followed in the Republic of Vietnam, which attempted unsuccessfully to assimilate the mountain minorities into the general population.

After the formation of the SRV, the government in Hanoi abolished the autonomous regions in the North and is now seeking to erase the existing cultural differences between the tribal peoples and the majority Vietnamese. According to official statistics, several hundred thousand tribesmen have been induced to abandon their nomadic habits and adopt a settled way of life. (See Jarai; Muong; Nung; Rhade; Tay; Thai)

TRINH KIEM (?-1570). Political figure of the sixteenth century and founder of the Trinh Lords. A native of Thanh Hoa Province of unknown origin, Trinh Kiem married a daughter of Nguyen Kim, a noted mandarin who supported the restoration of the Le Dynasty after the usurpation of power by Mac Dang Dung. After Nguyen Kim's death in 1545, Trinh Kiem became the dominant figure in a

movement to put the Le claimant, Le Trang Tong, back in power
in the capital of Thang Long (present-day Hanoi). His main
potential rival for influence within the Le was his brother-in-law
Nguyen Hoang, whom he appointed governor of Quang Nam and
Thuan Hoa Provinces.

Trinh Kiem commanded the Le armed forces which defeated
the Mac on several occasions and carved out a resistance basin
in Thanh Hoa Province. He reportedly considered seizing power
in his own name but, on being advised against it by the noted
scholar and oracle Nguyen Binh Kiem, satisfied himself with being
the power behind the throne. He died in 1570. (See Mac Dynasty; Le Dynasty; Nguyen Binh Kiem; Nguyen Kim; Nguyen
Hoang; Trinh Lords)

TRINH LORDS. Powerful family that dominated the political scene
during the last half of the Le Dynasty (1428-1788). The Trinh
arose during the mid-sixteenth century, when the Le Dynasty
had been overthrown by Mac Dang Dung, who established a new
Mac Dynasty in the capital of Thang Long (present-day Hanoi).
With the aid of Trinh Kiem, the first of the so-called "Trinh
Lords," the Le drove out the Mac and returned to Thang Long
in 1529.

But the Le Dynasty was now dependent on the successors of
Trinh Kiem, who became the dominant force at court and deposed
emperors at will until the Le dynasty was finally overthrown in
1788. The Trinh, however, never controlled the southern part
of the country, which was dominated by their main rivals, the
"Nguyen Lords," descendants of a brother-in-law of Trinh Kiem
who had become governor of Thuan Hoa and Quang Nam Provinces
in 1588.

Intermittent civil war between the two regions began in the
seventeenth century and continued until the overthrow of both
families, along with the Le Dynasty, by the Tay Son Rebellion
in the 1780s. (See Later Le Dynasty; Nguyen Lords)

TROTSKYITES. Radical wing of the Vietnamese revolutionary movement in colonial Vietnam. The faction originated among Vietnamese
intellectuals studying in France in the late 1920s, some connected
with the shortlived Annamese Independence Party (PAI), organized by Nguyen The Truyen.

On their return to Vietnam in the early 1930s, many Trotskyite
leaders like Ta Thu Thau, Ho Huu Tuong, and Pham Van Hum
played a significant role on the political scene, mainly in the
Cochinchinese capital of Saigon, where the Trotskyites published
a popular newspaper, La Lutte, and ran candidates in several
local elections. Trotskyite activities involved them in competi-
tion with their rivals in the Indochinese Communist Party (ICP),
whom they accused of betraying the interests of revolution by
their united front activities. In 1937, the Soviet Union prohibited
any cooperation between the two groups.

Despite inner splits within the movement, the Trotskyites

remained active in Vietnam until the post-World War II period,
when they were essentially eliminated as a political force by the
Vietminh. (See Lutte, La; Popular Front; Ta Thu Thau)

TRUNG BO (Central Vietnam, also known as Trung Ky). Vietnamese
term for the provinces along the central coast of Vietnam. During the period of French colonial rule it was often applied to the
Protectorate of Annam.

TRUNG SISTERS (Hai Ba Trung). Sisters who led a rebellion against
Chinese rule in Vietnam in the first century of the Christian era.
The revolt was caused by the attempt of Chinese administrators
to raise taxes and consolidate their control over the "Lac lords,"
the indigenous landed aristocracy in occupied Vietnam.
The two sisters, Trung Trac and Trung Nhi, were the daugh-
ters of a Lac Lord from Tay Vu, on the Red River northwest of
the modern capital of Hanoi. Trung Trac, the elder, had married
Thi Sach, a landed aristocrat from nearby Chu Dien. When in
A.D. 39 Thi Sach complained about exactions demanded by the
Chinese prefect Su Ting, he was arrested and apparently put to
death. In revenge, Trung Trac, supported by her younger sister,
raised the flag of rebellion. Revolt quickly swept through all of
Chinese-occupied Vietnam, with participation both by aristocrats
and peasants, and Su Ting fled China. Trung Trac was declared
queen and set up a royal government at Me Linh, seat of the
Vietnamese kingdom during the Au Lac dynasty.
China, however, returned to the attack, sending the veteran
military commander Ma Yuan to pacify the territory and return it
to Chinese rule. In A.D. 41 Trung Trac, now abandoned by
most of her "Lac lord" followers, was defeated, captured, and
with her sister Trung Nhi put to death (popular mythology holds
that they committed suicide or died in battle). Although the Trung
sisters' rebellion ended in failure, the two later became cult figures in the pantheon of heroic patriots struggling to restore
Vietnamese independence. (See Ma Yuan; Sino-Vietnamese culture)

TRUONG CHINH (1907-1988) (real name Dang Xuan Khu). Veteran
member of the Vietnamese Communist Party and chief of state of
the Socialist Republic of Vietnam (SRV) until June 1987. Born
in 1907 in an illustrious scholar-gentry family in Nam Dinh province, Truong Chinh received a baccalaureate at the Lycée Albert
Sarraut in Hanoi. After briefly embarking on a teaching career,
he joined Ho Chi Minh's Revolutionary League and in 1930 its
successor, the Indochinese Communist Party (ICP). Arrested that
same year, he served six years in Son La prison until his release
in 1936. During the Popular Front period he served the Party
in Hanoi as a journalist under the pen name Qua Ninh, and was
named chairman of the North Vietnamese regional committee of the
ICP in 1940.
In 1941 Truong Chinh was elected general secretary of the ICP
and became one of the leading figures in the Party. Considered a

admirer of the Chinese revolution (his revolutionary alias, Truong Chinh, is a Vietnamese version of the Chinese term "long march"), he became a leading ideologist and advocate of the use of Chinese revolutionary strategy in Vietnam. In 1956, however, he was dropped from his position as general secretary because of criticism of the land reform campaign.

Truong Chinh retained his seat on the Politburo, however, and was an influential force in the Party leadership throughout the Vietnam War. Generally considered a hardliner in domestic matters, he reportedly opposed Le Duan's emphasis on winning the war in the South. In 1981 he was named chairman of the new Council of State established as a collective presidency under the 1980 Constitution, and was viewed as the leading figure in the faction that opposed granting capitalist incentives to promote economic growth in the SRV. On the death of Le Duan in July 1986, Truong Chinh replaced him as general secretary of the Party, but resigned at the Sixth Party Congress in December. Truong Chinh was replaced as chairman of the State Council in June 1987, but served as an adviser to the Party Politburo until his accidental death in October 1988. (See Council of State; Indochinese Communist Party; Socialist Republic of Vietnam)

TRUONG DINH (Truong Cong Dinh) (1820-1864). Military commander of Vietnamese forces resisting the French conquest of South Vietnam in the early 1860s. Born in modern-day Quang Nam Province, he was the son of a career military officer, who was appointed commander of royal troops in Gia Dinh Province, near present-day Saigon. After his father's death, he remained in the South to marry a woman from a wealthy southern family. When the threat of French invasion loomed in the late 1850s, he helped organize military settlements (cong dien) and became deputy commander of militia forces in the region.

After taking part in the Battle of Ky Hoa (February 1861), Truong Dinh withdrew his forces south of Saigon, where he launched a prolonged guerrilla resistance against French occupation. Ordered to desist by the imperial court after the Treaty of Saigon (June 1962), he refused and continued the struggle. Wounded in battle in August 1864, he committed suicide. (See Nguyen Tri Phuong; Treaty of Saigon)

TRUONG SON (Annamite Mountains). Mountain chain along the western border of Vietnam. Known in the West as the Annamite Mountains, the Truong Son (central mountains) stretch for over 700 miles (1,200 kilometers) in a north-south direction from slightly below the Red River Delta to the southern slopes of the Central Highlands (Tay Nguyen) north of Ho Chi Minh City. Along much of its length, the range forms the border between Vietnam and its neighbors to the west, Laos and Cambodia. The highest mountains in the Truong Son, located in Gia Lai-Kontum province, rise over 8,000 feet in height.

TRUONG VINH KY (Petrus Ky) (1837-1898). Pro-French Vietnamese official in nineteenth-century Vietnam. Born the son of a Catholic military official, Truong Vinh Ky attended a missionary school in Penang and in 1863 served as an interpreter in the delegation of Phan Thanh Gian in Paris. Convinced of the benefits of French rule, he later became an official in the colonial administration, a teacher at the College des Interprètes in Saigon and editor of the Vietnamese-language newspaper Gia Dinh Bao (Journal of Gia Dinh), the first newspaper to be published in quoc ngu. (See Gia Dinh Bao; Phan Thanh Gian)

TU DUC (Reigned 1847-1883). Fourth emperor of the Nguyen Dynasty (1802-1945). Tu Duc ascended the throne on the death of his father, Thieu Tri, as the result of a court intrigue against his older brother Hong Bao, who later plotted to reclaim his right to the throne and died in prison. It was a difficult time for the Vietnamese Empire and Tu Duc, sickly and pessimistic by nature, was unequal to the task. Internal rebellion in the mid-1850s was followed by an attack by France in 1858. After a brief effort to drive out the invaders, Tu Duc became resigned to French domination of his country which, by a series of stages, eventually became a French protectorate in 1884. At the last, Tu Duc had attempted to resist, calling on the Ch'ing Dynasty for assistance against a French invasion of North Vietnam in 1882, but he died in July 1883 at the age of 56. The court was badly divided between advocates of peace and of resistance, leading to a succession crisis. Tu Duc was succeeded by his nephew Duc Duc, who reigned for only three days and was replaced by his uncle Hiep Hoa, who died shortly thereafter, and then by Kien Phuc, his cousin. In July 1883, Kien Phuoc's younger brother Ham Nghi acceded to the throne. (See Ham Nghi; Nguyen Dynasty; Treaty of 1874)

TU LUC VAN DOAN (Self-reliant Literary Group). Literary organization established by Vietnamese writers in early 1930s. Established by the romantic novelists Nhat Linh (Nguyen Tuong Tam) and Khai Hung (Tran Khanh Du) in 1932, the organizers of Tu Luc Van Doan had as an objective to promote the Westernization of Vietnamese literature and society as a whole. Novels written by members of the group, who also included Nhat Linh's brother Nguyen Tuong Long (pen name Hoang Dao), Ho Trong Hieu, Nguyen Thu Le, and Ngo Gia Tri, were romantic in style and consciously avoided the literary allusions and pretentiousness of earlier Confucian writers. Many expressed a strong concern over social conditions and the legacy of feudal society in colonial Vietnam, but tended to promote an attitude of individual rebellion rather than of organized resistance.

Mouthpiece for the group was the newspaper Phong Hoa (Manners), replaced in 1935 by Ngay Nay (Today), while many of its novels were issued by its own publishing house, Doi Nay. The group gradually lost influence in the late 1930s as the

romantic style of writing gave way to a more realist approach
adopted by a new group of writers influenced by Marxism, and
many members of Tu Luc Van Doan became involved in politics
during World War II. (See Khai Hung; Literature; Nhat Linh)

TU TAI. Lowest degree granted in the civil service examinations
in traditional Vietnam. Based on the Chinese term hsiu-ts'ai
(cultivated talent), the degree was granted to those candidates
who passed local qualifying examinations for the regional civil
service examinations, and was given yearly at the district or prefectural level. Successful candidates could then seek the degree
of cu nhan at the regional examinations. They were not eligible
to enter the bureaucracy, and most candidates who remained at the
tu tai level became teachers. (See Civil Service Examinations)

TU THANH. An early name for the city of Hanoi during the period
of Chinese rule. (See Hanoi, Dai La)

- U -

UNITED FRONT FOR THE LIBERATION OF OPPRESSED PEOPLES
(FULRO). Organization founded by tribal minority leaders to
seek autonomy from South Vietnamese rule during the Vietnam
War. Popularly known as FULRO, the Front first emerged during the early 1960s when tribal groups in the Central Highlands
attempted to resist efforts by the Saigon regime to assimilate
the tribal regions into the central administration. An additional
source of resentment was the occupation of tribal lands by settlers who migrated from the North after the Geneva Conference
in 1954.

After the reunification of the two zones in 1975, the FULRO
organization revived as tribal peoples attempted to prevent the
integration of tribal areas into the Socialist Republic of Vietnam
(SRV). The Hanoi regime now claims that the organization has
been virtually destroyed, although there have been sporadic reports of resistance activities in mountain areas of South Vietnam.
(See Jarai; Rhade)

- V -

VAN LANG. An early Vietnamese kingdom at the dawn of the historical
era. It was founded by the so-called Lac peoples living in the
Red River Delta some time during the first millenium B.C. and
lasted until its eventual destruction in the late third century B.C.
by the military adventurer Thuc Phan, who created a new kingdom in the area named Au Lac.

Until recently, scholars had believed that the kingdom of Van
Lang was a legend invented by Vietnamese historians to explain
and embellish the origins of Vietnamese civilization. Early Vietnamese historical sources referred to a prehistoric kingdom in the

Red River Valley created by the legendary figure Lac Long Quan 4,000 years ago and ruled over by eighteen long-lived monarchs, the so-called Hung Kings. This legend bears clear resemblance to Chinese versions of the prehistoric birth of Chinese civilization and was viewed by modern historians as pure myth.

In recent years, however, archeological discoveries have produced evidence that an advanced Bronze Age civilization, known as Dong Son from the original site excavated by archeologists, had existed in the area during the first millenium B.C. and it is now generally believed that the state of Van Lang existed in fact, and is identified with the archeological finds connected with the Dong Son civilization.

Little is known about the nature of society in Van Lang. The origins of the name itself are obscure, although it has been speculated that it comes from a mythical bird used as a totem by the Hung Kings. The capital was near the present-day city of Viet Tri, northwest of Hanoi in the Red River Delta. It was culturally advanced, based on settled agriculture and the use of implements made of bronze and iron. The political system was feudal in nature, and the throne was hereditary, but the king ruled through a landed aristocracy known as the "Lac Lords" who owned landed estates farmed by peasants organized in rural communes (xa). The economic system was based primarily on the cultivation of rice and other agricultural products, although there is some evidence of regional trade. (See Au Lac; Bronze Age; Dong Son Culture; Hung Kings)

VAN TIEN DUNG (1917-   ). Senior general in the People's Army of Vietnam (PAVN) and leading political figure in the Socialist Republic of Vietnam (SRV). Born in Ha Dong Province in a poor peasant family, Van Tien Dung worked in a French-owned textile factory in the 1930s and joined the Indochinese Communist Party in 1937. Arrested twice, he escaped both times and was named secretary of the Party's regional communist for North Vietnam in 1944.

During the Franco-Vietminh War, Van Tien Dung rose rapidly in the ranks of the PAVN and was elected to the Party Central Committee in 1951. He attained full Politburo rank in 1972. He was sent to the South in 1974 to command North Vietnamese forces during the so-called "Ho Chi Minh Campaign" which resulted in the seizure of Saigon the following spring.

In 1980, Van Tien Dung was appointed Minister of Defense and reportedly played an active role in directing the Vietnamese invasion of Cambodia in 1979. He was reportedly criticized, however, for his autocratic leadership style, and was dropped from the Politiburo and his position at the Ministry of Defense in December 1986. (See Ho Chi Minh Campaign; People's Army of Vietnam)

VAN XUAN (Ten Thousand Springs) (See Ly Bi).

VANGUARD YOUTH MOVEMENT (Thanh Nien Tien Phong). Quasi-

revolutionary youth movement in colonial Vietnam. The movement was established under Japanese sponsorship during World
War II by Doctor Pham Ngoc Thach, a secret supporter of the
communist-dominated Vietminh. Resembling the Boy Scout operation, it recruited followers in schools, factories, and rural villages and by the end of the war had over one million members in
virtually every province in Cochin China.

In August 1945, radical elements within the movement were
organized into paramilitary units which participated in the takeover of Saigon at the moment of Japanese surrender. (See August
Revolution; Pham (Ngoc Thach)

VARENNE, ALEXANDER. Governor-general of French Indochina from
1925 to 1928. A member of the French Socialist Party and a deputy
in the National Assembly, Varenne was appointed governor-general
of Indochina in 1925. Varenne's liberal views led him to undertake a number of reforms to reduce the rising level of discontent
in Vietnam. Shortly after his arrival he granted clemency to Phan
Boi Chau, the revolutionary patriot who had just been sentenced
to death in Hanoi. He followed up that symbolic act by promising
reforms in the areas of education, civil rights, and local administration, and implied that at some future date the French would
grant Vietnam independence.

Varenne's statements aroused a storm of criticism among French
residents in Indochina, and he was forced to back down on a
number of his pledges, although he did achieve several changes
in social and administrative policy, setting up a regional assembly
in Annam and offices to inspect labor conditions and expand rural
credit. He resigned from office in January 1928.

VIET BAC (Northern Vietnam). Vietnamese language term for the
mountainous provinces north of the Red River Delta and south
of the Chinese border. A traditional refuge for bandits and
rebels, the Viet Bac was used by the Vietminh as a liberation base
area during World War II and the Franco-Vietminh conflict that
followed. The region comprises an area of 36,000 square kilometers and includes the present-day provinces of Ha Giang, Cao
Bang, Bac Thai, Lang Son, and Tuyen Quang.

VIET CONG (Vietnamese Communists). Popular name in the West for
the People's Liberation Armed Forces (PLAF) in South Vietnam.
The term was originally applied by the regime of President Ngo
Dinh Diem. (See People's Liberation Armed Forces)

VIET NAM. The formal name of the country of Vietnam since 1803.
The term "Viet" (in Chinese, Yüeh) was originally a Chinese term
for all non-Chinese peoples south of the Yangtse River and is
now used by the Vietnamese to refer to themselves. The term
"Nam" is the Vietnamese language equivalent of the Chinese word
for "south" (Nan). Placed together, the phrase can either mean
"Southern Viet" or "South of Viet." Because Vietnamese is a

monosyllabic language, the Vietnamese separate the two words into "Viet Nam." Through long usage, most Westerners refer to the country in the single word "Vietnam."

The term Viet Nam was first applied to the country by Emperor Gia Long, founder of the Nguyen Dynasty. He had planned to use the term Nam Viet, a name used by two previous Vietnamese dynasties that had struggled against Chinese domination, but when representatives from the new dynasty went to Peking to seek legitimacy from the China court, the latter objected to a term that had rebellious connotations. Gia Long relented and selected "Viet Nam." (See Nam Viet; Nguyen Dynasty)

VIET NAM CACH MENH DONG MINH HOI (Dong Minh Hoi) (See Vietnamese Revolutionary League).

VIET NAM DOC LAP DONG MINH (or Vietminh) (See League for the Independence of Vietnam).

VIET NAM GIAI PHONG DONG MINH (Vietnamese Liberation League) (See Vietnamese Liberation League).

VIET NAM GIAI PHONG QUAN (Vietnamese Liberation Army) (See Vietnamese Liberation Army).

VIET NAM QUANG PHUC HOI (See Vietnamese Restoration Society).

VIET NAM QUOC DAN DANG (VNQDD) (See Vietnamese Nationalist Party).

VIET NAM THANH NIEN CACH MENH DONG CHI HOI (Thanh Nien) (See Revolutionary Youth League of Vietnam).

VIETMINH FRONT (See League for the Independence of Vietnam).

VIETNAMESE COMMUNIST PARTY, or VCP (Dang Cong San Viet Nam). Current name of the Communist Party in the Socialist Republic of Vietnam (SRV). The name was adopted at the Fourth National Congress of the party in December 1976 and replaced the previous name, Vietnamese Workers' Party (Dang Lao Dong Viet Nam). The first name of the party, created in February 1930, was Vietnamese Communist Party. In October 1930, the name was changed to Indochinese Communist Party (Dang Cong San Dong Duong) at the request of the Comintern. Its name was changed to Vietnamese Workers' Party (VWP) in 1951.

The new Vietnamese Communist Party created in 1976 included past members of both the VWP and the so-called People's Revolutionary Party of Vietnam (Dang Nhan Dan Cach Mang Viet Nam), created as a branch office of the VWP in South Vietnam in 1962. It is currently the ruling party in the Socialist Republic of Vietnam. It had a total membership in 1986 of 1.85 million members. The supreme body of the party is the National Congress, which meets approximately every five years. Delegates to the National Congress, elected by party branches at lower echelons, approve major policy decisions and elect a Central Committee which functions in the intervals between the National Congresses. The Central Committee, which holds plenary sessions twice a year to approve key decisions by party leaders, elects a Politburo which serves as the ruling body of the party. The Politburo which normally meets once or twice a month, consisted in July 1988 of thirteen full members. (See Ho Chi Minh; Indochinese Communist Party; People's Revolutionary Party of Vietnam; Vietnamese Workers' Party)

VIETNAMESE DEMOCRATIC PARTY (Dang Dan Chu Viet Nam). One of two small non-Communist political parties in the Socialist Republic of Vietnam (SRV). Created on June 30, 1944 as part of the Vietminh Front, the Democratic Party plays a largely ceremonial role in contemporary Vietnam as a representative of patriotic intellectuals and a symbol of the coalition of classes led by the Vietnamese Communist Party that is leading Vietnam through the so-called "national people's democratic revolution" to socialism. (See League for the Independence of Vietnam; Socialist Republic of Vietnam; Vietnamese Communist Party; Vietnamese Socialist Party)

VIETNAMESE LANGUAGE. Language spoken by the ethnic Vietnamese, the majority population in modern Vietnam. It is sometimes referred to as Viet-Muong, because of the close generic resemblance between Vietnamese and the language spoken by the Muong, a minority people living in modern Vietnam. Scholars believe that Vietnamese is essentially an Austroasiatic language, a family of languages spoken in prehistoric times throughout much of mainland Southeast Asia as far west as the Bay of Bengal. It bears closest resemblance to Mon-Khmer, an Austroasiatic language spoken by the Khmer of present-day Cambodia and the Mon people of Lower Burma. In grammar, vocabulary, and syntax, it also has some similarities with other languages in the area, such as Chinese, Malay or Polynesian (Austronesian) and Thai. (See Muong; Vietnamese people)

VIETNAMESE LIBERATION ARMY (Viet Nam Giai Phong Quan). Revolutionary armed forces under the command of the Indochinese Communist Party (ICP) after World War II. The Vietnamese Liberation Army was created on May 15, 1945 as the result of a decision by the ICP leadership to unite two separate military units under party leadership, the Army for National Salvation (Cuu Quoc Quan) under the command of Chu Van Tan, and the Armed Propaganda Brigade (Doi Viet Nam Tuyen Truyen Gia Phong Quan). The new army was placed under the overall command of Vo Nguyen Giap and would receive its ultimate direction from the ICP through the latter's Military Revolutionary Committee.

After the Geneva Conference and the creation of de facto separate states in North and South Vietnam, the Vietnamese Liberation Army was renamed the People's Army of Vietnam (Quan Doi
Nhan Dan Viet Nam).

(See Armed Propaganda Brigade; Army of National Salvation;
Chu Van Tan; People's Army of Vietnam; Vo Nguyen Giap)

VIETNAMESE LIBERATION LEAGUE (Viet Nam Giai Phong Dong Minh).
Front organization set up by Ho Chi Minh in South China in
1941. Established at Chinghsi near the Sino-Vietnamese border,
it was designed to unite the various anti-French nationalist
organizations under the overall leadership of the Indochinese
Communist Party (ICP). But the ICP's role was to be disguised,
and a non-communist, Ho Ngoc Lam, was named chairman.

For the next few months, the League trained cadres in South
China for the patriotic cause. After Ho Chi Minh's arrest by
Chinese authorities in 1942, however, the League was taken over
by non-communists, who expelled the ICP members, and it virtually disintegrated. In 1942, its remaining members were incorporated into a new front organization under Chinese sponsorship,
the Vietnamese Revolutionary League (Dong Minh Hoi). (See
League for the Independence of Vietnam; Vietnamese Revolutionary
League)

VIETNAMESE NATIONAL ARMY (VNA). Armed forces of the Associated State of Vietnam set up in the fall of 1950. According to
the Elysée Accords of March 1949, the new Associated State was
to have its own national army, which would cooperate with
French expeditionary forces in the spreading conflict with Ho
Chi Minh's Vietminh. The concept had originated in a military
conference held at Cap St. Jacques early in the year, and the
final military agreement was signed on December 8, 1950.

According to arrangements reached between the two countries,
Chief of State Bao Dai was designated Supreme Commander of the
Army, but he was responsible to the French High Command in
Indochina. During the next three years, the Vietnamese National
Army gradually grew into a fighting force of nearly 200,000 men.
Constant bickering marked its growth, however. The French
government, dubious about its fighting capacity and suspicious
that it could provide the Vietnamese with the temptation to turn
against French forces in Indochina, was stingy in providing trained
personnel and modern equipment, and used it primarily for pacification operations. The United States viewed the VNA as an
important vehicle for leading Vietnam toward independence, and
pressured the French to permit U.S. advisers to provide training
to Vietnamese troops. When the Franco-Vietminh War came to
an end in 1954, the army had not lived up to the expectations of
any of its sponsors. After the Geneva Conference, the VNA was
replaced by a new Army of the Republic of Vietnam (ARVN),
created by the Saigon regime. (See Army of the Republic of
Vietnam; Bao Dai Solution; Elysée Accords)

VIETNAMESE NATIONALIST PARTY (Viet Nam Quoc Dan Dang, or VNQDD). Radical political party in colonial Vietnam. The party was organized in the fall of 1927 by a number of radical intellectuals and merchants around the Nam Dong Thu Xa (Southeast Asia Publishing House) in Hanoi. The party was modelled after Sun Yat-sen's Kuomintang (Nationalist Party) in China, then under the control of Chiang Kai-Shek. Its goal was to promote a violent uprising to evict the French regime and establish a democratic republic in Vietnam. The party's social and economic goals were rudimentary, and most members were not sympathetic to Marxism.

In February 1930, the VNQDD launched an insurrection at Yen Bay and several other military posts in Tonkin. But poor coordination and the reluctance of many of the troops to support the uprising led to disaster. Most of the party's leaders were captured and executed. From that time on the VNQDD lived a shadow existence as an exile organization in South China.

After World War II, the VNQDD participated briefly in the government formed in Hanoi by Ho Chi Minh's Vietminh Front. But armed clashes took place with the communists and in the summer and fall of 1946 many members of the VNQDD were arrested or fled into exile. After 1954, the VNQDD became one of several minor political parties in South Vietnam. (See Nguyen Thai Hoc; Yen Bay Mutiny)

VIETNAMESE PEOPLE. Majority population of the modern state of Vietnam. Known as ethnic Vietnamese, they compromise today about ninety percent of the total population of the country.

The ancestors of the present-day Vietnamese are the so-called Lac peoples, who during the first millenium B.C. inhabited the area of the Red River Delta in what is today North Vietnam. Their racial origins are obscure, although it is generally believed that they are an admixture of Australoid-Negroid peoples living in mainland Southeast Asia during the Paleolithic era and Mongoloid peoples who migrated into the area from the North. It is also believed that the ethnic Vietnamese were originally related to other peoples living along the coast of the South China Sea up to the Yangtse River estuary in Central China. Unlike the ethnic Vietnamese, most of these peoples, known to the Chinese as "Yueh," were eventually assimilated into Chinese civilization. Prior to the rise of the Chinese empire in the third century B.C. however, they lived on the borderland of Chinese culture. They did not speak a Sinitic language but, like the ethnic Vietnamese, an Austroasiatic language common to many other peoples in prehistoric mainland Southeast Asia.

Eventually the Vietnamese people expanded south from their original homeland in the Red River Delta and settled along the central coast of modern Vietnam and into the Mekong River Delta. Today the Vietnamese are numerically dominant in all lowland regions of modern Vietnam. (See Lac Peoples; March to the South; Vietnamese Language; Yüeh)

VIETNAMESE RESTORATION SOCIETY (Viet Nam Quang Phuc Hoi)
(also known as Restoration Society). Anti-French political organization established by the patriot Phan Boi Chau in 1912. Unlike
its predecessor, the monarchist Modernization Society (Duy Tan
Hoi), its program called for the establishment of an independent
Vietnamese republic patterned after the plans of Sun Yat-sen's
Nationalist Party (Kuomintang) in China. It is likely that Phan
Boi Chau founded the new party in order to win the sympathy
of Sun Yat-sen and his colleagues in China, where Chau was
living in exile.

The Vietnamese Restoration Society launched several unsuccessful revolts in succeeding years, and gradually declined into
an ineffective nationalist organization in exile during the 1920s
and 1930s. It underwent a brief resurgence before World War
II when it was reorganized under the name of the Viet Nam
Phuc Quoc Dong Minh Hoi (Alliance for the Restoration of Vietnam) led by Prince Cuong De. (See Duy Tan Hoi; Phan Boi
Chau)

VIETNAMESE REVOLUTIONARY LEAGUE (Viet Nam Cach Menh Dong
Minh Hoi, or Dong Minh Hoi). Vietnamese nationalist organization
founded under Chinese sponsorship in August 1942. Founded
at Liuchow, in South China, it included a number of Vietnamese
nationalist parties and factions, including the VNQDD, the so-
called Phuc Quoc, and members of a previous front organization
called the Vietnamese Liberation League (Viet Nam Giai Phong
Dong Minh Hoi), set up in 1941 by Ho Chi Minh. It was the
brainchild of Nationalist General Chang Fa-k'uei, who hoped to
use the Dong Minh Hoi as a vehicle for obtaining intelligence on
Japanese troop movements in Indochina, and perhaps as the basis
for a pro-Chinese political organization following the end of the
war.

Led by Nguyen Hai Than, an ex-follower of Phan Boi Chau,
the Dong Minh Hoi specifically excluded the Indochinese Communist
Party, and it competed with Ho Chi Minh's Vietminh for support
during the remainder of World War II. After the end of the
war in August 1945, members of the Dong Minh Hoi were briefly
included in the government organized by Ho Chi Minh in Hanoi.
They were later expelled, as Ho tightened his control over the
government. (See August Revolution; League for the Independence of Vietnam; Vietnamese Liberation League)

VIETNAMESE REVOLUTIONARY YOUTH LEAGUE (See Revolutionary
Youth League of Vietnam).

VIETNAMESE SOCIALIST PARTY (Dang Xa Hoi Viet Nam). One of the
non-communist political parties in contemporary Vietnam. A
successor of the French Socialist Party, active in pre-World War
II Indochina, was formally created in 1946, shortly after the
establishment of the Democratic Republic of Vietnam. Ideologically linked to social democratic parties elsewhere in the world,

the party plays a negligible political role in a country dominated by the ruling Vietnamese Communist Party and serves, along with the small Vietnamese Democratic Party, to provide a ceremonial basis for the regime's claim to lead a "united front" of progressive classes to the final goal of communism. (See Vietnamese Communist Party; Vietnamese Democratic Party)

VIETNAMIZATION. Strategy adopted by President Richard Nixon in 1969 to seek an end to U.S. involvement in the Vietnam War. Coming into office at a time of rising opposition to the war in the United States, Nixon devised a plan to withdraw U.S. troops from South Vietnam on a gradual basis while simultaneously strengthening the armed forces of the Republic of Vietnam. According to Nixon's schedule, the last U.S. combat forces would be withdrawn in June 1972, just before the 1972 presidential elections.

"Vietnamization" took place roughly on schedule, but the final withdrawal took place as a result of the Paris Agreement, signed in January 1973. (See Army of the Republic of Vietnam; Paris Agreement)

VIJAYA. Capital of the kingdom of Champa in Central Vietnam. Previously the Cham capital had been located further north, at Indrapura in modern-day Quang Nam Province. But Vietnamese attacks forced the Cham to move their capital south to Vijaya, in Binh Dinh Province, in the year 1000. The new capital was itself frequently attacked and conquered by Vietnamese, Mongol, and Khmer armed forces and was finally seized by the Vietnamese in 1471, the date that marks the final collapse of the Cham kingdom. (See Champa; Indrapura; Le Thanh Tong)

VILLAGE (Xa, or Thon). Basic administrative unit in Vietnam. There were actually three levels of basic-level administration in traditional Vietnam, the commune (xa), the natural village (thon), and the hamlet (ap, or xom). The commune was the largest, and possessed the most extensive administrative apparatus. Below the commune was the natural village. Many villages were themselves often divided into smaller hamlets. A typical commune would contain about 5,000 inhabitants and incorporate two or three villages and several hamlets.

In the traditional period, the village (xa) was essentially autonomous and was only indirectly linked to the central government. Village affairs were administered by a Council of Elders (Hoi Dong Ky Muc) composed of leading members of the dominant families in the village. The Council was assisted by a village chief (xa truong) subordinate to its authority who served as village executive officer and liaison with higher government echelons. Today the village remains the basic governmental unit in the Socialist Republic of Vietnam. Local administration is handled by a People's Council (Hoi Dong Nhan Dan) elected by adult residents of the village and a People's Committee (Uy Ban Nhan Dan) that

handles executive functions. (See Council of Elders; Local
Government; People's Committees; People's Councils; Village
Chief)

VILLAGE CHIEF (Xa Truong). Chief administrative officer in the
Vietnamese village. In the traditional period, the village chief
was subordinated to the Council of Elders (Hoi Dong Ky Muc)
and served as an intermediary between the village and the government administration. In the Republic of Vietnam, the position
was raised in importance, and the chief reported directly to
higher levels of administration. In the Socialist Republic of Vietnam, the position has been replaced by an elected People's Council
(Hoi Dong Nhan Dan). (See Council of Elders; People's Council)

VO CHI CONG (1912-   ). Leading figure in the Vietnamese Communist
Party and currently Chief of State of the Socialist Republic of
Vietnam (SRV). Born near Da Nang in 1912, Vo Chi Cong be-
came active in the Indochinese Communist Party in the 1930s.
After imprisonment in World War II, he served in a number of
Party and government posts, rising to Politburo ranking in
1961, and was a leading member of the Party's apparatus in the
South during the Vietnam War.

In 1976 he was named Minister of Agriculture in 1977. He
was replaced as Minister by Nguyen Ngoc Triu in 1979 and became
active in Party affairs. Known as an ally of General Secretary
Le Duan, he rose to the number three ranking in the Politburo
and in July 1987 was named Chief of State to replace Truong
Chinh, who retired. In recent years, Vo Chi Cong has reportedly
supported reformist efforts to provide incentives in order to promote economic growth in the SRV.

VO NGUYEN GIAP (1910?-   ). Senior General in the People's Army
of Vietnam (PAVN) and leading figure in the Socialist Republic
of Vietnam (SRV). Born in a peasant family with reported scholar-
gentry connections in Quang Binh province, Vo Nguyen Giap
attended the National Academy (Quoc Hoc) in the imperial capital
of Hue. In the mid-1920s he joined the Tan Viet (New Vietnamese Revolutionary Party) and participated in demonstrations
following the death of the Vietnamese patriot Phan Chu Trinh,
leading to his expulsion from school. In 1930 he joined the new
Indochinese Communist Party (ICP) and was immediately arrested.
Released in 1932, he graduated from the University of Hanoi in
Law and taught history at the Thang Long school in Hanoi, where
he married Nguyen Thi Minh Giang, a daughter of the progressive
intellectual Dang Thai Mai and sister of ICP member Nguyen Thi
Minh Khai.

During the Popular Front period, Vo Nguyen Giap worked as
a journalist in Hue and co-authored a short pamphlet entitled
"The Peasant Question" with fellow ICP member Truong Chinh.
During World War II he became a chief lieutenant of Ho Chi
Minh in the Vietminh movement and in 1944 was named commander

of the Armed Propaganda Brigade, the predecessor of the Vietnamese Liberation Army. After World War II he became the
chief military strategist in the Party and advocate of the concept of "people's war" which borrowed loosely from Maoist
techniques in China.

During the Vietnam War, Vo Nguyen Giap was a leading member of the Party Politburo and attained the highest ranking of
Senior General in the PAVN. Although serving as Minister of
Defense in the Democratic Republic of Vietnam and widely viewed
in the West as the prime architect of Vietnamese revolutionary
strategy in South Vietnam, he was actually replaced as chief
strategist by his colleague and reported rival, General Nguyen
Chi Thanh, of whose aggressive tactics Giap did not fully approve.
After the end of the war in 1975, he was reduced to the role
of elder statesman, losing his position as Minister of Defense and
dropped from the Politburo at the Fifth Party Congress in March
1982. The reasons for his decline have been widely rumored but
never clarified. In recent years he has become active in promoting science and technology in the SRV. (See Armed Propaganda
Brigade; Indochinese Communist Party; People's Army of Vietnam;
Tan Viet Cach Menh Dang)

VO VAN KIET (1922-   ). Leading reformist figure in the Socialist
Republic of Vietnam (SRV). Born in an educated family in Can
Tho, Cochin China in 1922, Vo Van Kiet entered revolutionary
activities in Saigon in the early 1940s. After World War II he
was a leading member of the Party apparatus in South Vietnam,
and secretary of the Saigon Municipal Party Committee in the
last years of the Vietnam War.

After the seizure of Saigon in 1975 he was appointed chairman
of the city's People's Committee. When Nguyen Van Linh was
called to Hanoi in 1976 to take charge of the trade union movement,
Vo Van Kiet succeeded him as chairman of the Ho Chi Minh City
Party Committee. He remained in that position until 1982 and
gained a reputation as a moderate who emphasized economic
growth over ideological purity. In 1982 he was elected a full
member of the Politburo and was appointed Vice Chairman of the
Council of Ministers in Hanoi. In March 1988 he was appointed
acting prime minister on the death of Pham Hung, but was defeated in an election to fill that post at the National Assembly
meeting in June. He is considered a leading member of the reformist faction in the Party leadership. (See Ho Chi Minh City;
Nguyen Van Linh)

VUA. Vietnamese language term for ruler, or king. While the Vietnamese have often used the Chinese term vuong (in Chinese,
Wang), the native term vua, which implies a more intimate and
paternalistic form of authority than the Chinese (the written
form, expressed in chu nom, combines the Chinese character for
king with the nom character for father), began to be used with
increasing frequency after the restoration of Vietnamese independence in the tenth century. (See Vuong)

VUONG. Vietnamese word for king, derived from the Chinese (Wang). In early times, Vietnamese rulers used the term to describe themselves. After the restoration of independence in the tenth century A.D., Vietnamese monarchs, following the pattern of their powerful counterparts in China, sometimes referred to themselves as Vua (a Vietnamese term of ruler) or Hoang De (a Vietnamese adaptation of the Chinese term for emperor, Huang Ti), a reflection of the rising power and influence of the Vietnamese state.

- W -

WESTMORELAND, WILLIAM C. General in the U.S. Army and commander of the U.S. Military Assistance Command in Vietnam (MAC/V) from 1964 until 1968. Under General Westmoreland's command the U.S. troop presence in South Vietnam increased from about 22,000 on his arrival to 525,000 in mid-1968, and from an advisory role to the full combat role in the Vietnam War. During that period U.S. troops played a major role in combat operations in Vietnam, carrying out search and destroy operations against North Vietnamese regular forces while South Vietnamese units concentrated on the pacification effort in the countryside. Westmoreland was replaced by General Creighton Abrams in July 1968.

WOMEN. As in most Asian societies, women played a relatively subordinate role in traditional Vietnam. While there is some evidence that in early Vietnamese society women played a strong part in family and local affairs, after the imposition of Chinese rule, traditional Confucian attitudes took precedence. At least in terms of official policy, as entry into the imperial bureaucracy was restricted to males, the place of women was assumed to be in the home. A residue of pre-Chinese practice survived, however, in the Hong Duc Code passed in the fifteenth century, which gave women greater legal rights than those possessed by their counterparts in Confucian China.

Behind such official restrictions, women nonetheless often played an active part in Vietnamese society, led by such role models as the poet Ho Xuan Huong who used irony and sarcasm to criticize the failings of male-dominated society in eighteenth-century Vietnam.

Under French colonial rule, Vietnamese women began to press for an extension of their rights. Beacon of this effort was the Saigon-based periodical Phu Nu Tan Van (Women's News, published by middle-class women intellectuals during the late 1920s and early 1930s. The Democratic Republic of Vietnam (DRV), established in September 1945, promised sexual equality, a guarantee that has been incorporated into the Constitution promulgated in 1980. In fact, women played an active role in many areas of Vietnamese society under the DRV, including the struggle for national liberation, where women formed a so-called "long haired

army" to carry provisions to the men at the front. Women in
the Socialist Republic of Vietnam (SRV) today are active in many
areas of Vietnamese life, and several have served in the government at the cabinet level. Their position in the ruling Communist
Party remains a subordinate one, however, and none has served
on the Politburo. Official sources concede that male-chauvinist
attitudes continue to prevail in many areas of Vietnamese society.
(See Hong Duc Code; Phu Nu Tan Van)

- Y -

YEN BAY MUTINY (Khoi Nghia Yen Bay). Insurrection launched by
the Vietnamese Nationalist Party (VNQDD) against French rule in
February 1930. The revolt, planned by VNQDD leader Nguyen
Thai Hoc, erupted at Yen Bay and several other military posts
in North Vietnam. But poor coordination and lack of support by
local troops doomed the uprising and it was crushed within a
few days. Nguyen Thai Hoc and several other party leaders were
caught by the French and executed. (See Nguyen Thai Hoc;
Vietnamese Nationalist Party)

YOUTH PARTY (Dang Thanh Nien). Short-lived political party
formed by Saigon intellectuals around Tran Huy Lieu in late
1925. It was established at a time of rising effervescence but
limited political experience within the nascent nationalist movement in Cochin China. The party had no specific platform or
strategy beyond a vague desire to promote the establishment of
a constitution in Cochin China and was dispersed by the colonial
regime within a few months. Tran Huy Lieu would later become
a member of the Indochinese Communist Party. (See Nguyen An
Ninh)

YUEH (Viet). Generic name used by early Chinese to describe proto-
Chinese peoples living in coastal regions south of the Yangtse
River in South China. The first recorded use of the term was the
Kingdom of Yueh which arose in China during the so-called War-
ring States (480-222 B.C.) period in the coastal region south
of the Yangtse River Delta. In the late fourth century B.C.
the state of Yueh broke up into a number of smaller states sometimes called the Bai Yueh (Bach Viet or "hundred Yueh"). Eventually, the term was applied to other non-Chinese peoples living
in South China and mainland Southeast Asia, including the Lac
peoples of the Red River Delta, the ancestors of the present-day
Vietnamese. In the third century B.C., the Lac Kingdom was
conquered and absorbed into a larger state called Nan Yueh
(Nam Viet or "southern Yueh"), with its capital in the present-
day city of Guangzhou (Canton).
     After the conquest of the Red River region by the Han dy-
nasty, Chinese sources began to refer to the peoples of the area
as the Lac Yueh (Lac Viet, or "Yueh people of Lac"). Eventually
the Lac peoples began to use the Vietnamese equivalent of the

term (Viet) to describe themselves, and after the restoration of independence in the tenth century, Vietnamese monarchs used the term as the formal title for their country, as in Dai Co Viet (939-1054), Dai Viet (1054-1802) and Viet Nam (1802-1884). (See An Duong Vuong; Lac Viet; Nam Viet; Vietnamese people)

- Z -

ZONE C. Base area used by revolutionary forces in South Vietnam during the Vietnam War. Located in Tay Ninh province adjacent to the Cambodian border, Zone C was used by the People's Liberation Armed Forces (PLAF) as a staging area for operations near Saigon and was the site of the movement's headquarters, the Central Office for South Vietnam (COSVN), after 1961. The area was ideal because of its heavy jungle cover and its location adjacent to the sanctuary of eastern Cambodia.

In April 1966 U.S. forces launched "Operation Attleboro" into the area in an effort to wipe out PLAF fortifications and seize COSVN. The operation probably inflicted severe damage on the revolutionary infrastructure in South Vietnam but did not seize COSVN, which retreated across the border into Cambodia. (See Central Office of South Vietnam; People's Liberation Armed Forces

ZONE D. (See Iron Triangle)

BIBLIOGRAPHY

INTRODUCTORY ESSAY

Until fairly recently, books in English about Vietnam were quite rare. Virtually all scholarship on Vietnamese culture and history produced in the West was written in the French language. As in the case of commerce, scholarship followed the flag as French scholars, benefiting from their nation's control over all of Indochina during the late nineteenth and early twentieth centuries, were the first to introduce Vietnam to the Western world.

The French monopoly ended with the Vietnam War. During the past three decades, interest in Vietnam on the part of English-speaking scholars has increased dramatically. Much of the recent literature in English, of course, has been directly related to the war and to its impact on international politics and American society. But the war also spawned a rising level of interest about other aspects of Vietnamese civilization--about its archeology and ancient history, its customs and folklore, its art, literature, and music.

The bibliography that appears below reflects the evolution of Western knowledge about and interest in Vietnamese history and society. Most of the classical works written about the traditional era in Vietnam were written by French scholars during the colonial period. The first comprehensive history of precolonial Vietnam written in English was Joseph Buttinger's The Smaller Dragon (New York: Praeger, 1958). Although it is now somewhat out of date, it still serves as a useful introduction to the history of Vietnam. In recent years, two new narrative histories of Vietnam have appeared, Thomas Hodgkin's Vietnam: The Revolutionary Path (New York: St. Martin's, 1981) and Stanley Karnow's Vietnam: A History (New York: Penguin, 1984), the latter written as a companion volume to the PBS documentary on the Vietnam War. Although both concentrate on the modern period, they contain useful information on traditional Vietnam.

Unfortunately, there are still relatively few book-length studies of the precolonial period. Two of the best are Keith W. Taylor's The Birth of Vietnam (Berkeley: University of California Press, 1983), which carries history up to the tenth century, and Alexander B. Woodside's Vietnam and the Chinese Model (Cambridge: Harvard

University Press, 1971), an exhaustive study of the political and social institutions of nineteenth-century Vietnam. For other aspects of the traditional period, the reader is compelled for the most part to turn to the periodical literature.

Books on the French colonial era are available in much greater abundance. Many of the standard works are in French, but a new generation of English-speaking scholars is beginning to add significantly to our knowledge of the period. There is as yet no comprehensive history of the French colonial regime in English. The best general treatment remains Joseph Buttinger's massive Vietnam: The Dragon Embattled (New York: Praeger, 1967), in two volumes. For a critical view of the effects of colonial policy on the Vietnamese economy, see Martin Murray's The Development of Capitalism in Colonial Indochina (1870-1940) (Berkeley: University of California Press, 1980). A French interpretation, more sympathetic to the French enterprise in Indochina, is Charles Robequain's The Economic Development of French Indochina (London: Oxford University Press, 1944). Another provocative study, which focusses on changes taking place at the village level, is Samuel L. Popkin's The Rational Peasant (Berkeley: University of California Press, 1979). A rival view on the same issue is James C. Scott's The Moral Economy of the Peasant (New Haven: Yale University Press, 1976).

Much of the recent scholarly literature on French colonialism has understandably focussed on the origins of the Vietnamese resistance movement. The first and in many ways still the best account is David G. Marr's Vietnamese Anticolonialism, 1885-1925 (Berkeley: University of California Press, 1971). Other useful studies are Huynh Kim Khanh's Vietnamese Communism, 1925-1945 (Ithaca: Cornell University Press, 1982), John T. McAlister's Vietnam: The Origins of Revolution (New York: Harper & Row, 1970), and William J. Duiker's The Rise of Nationalism in Vietnam, 1900-1941 (Ithaca: Cornell University Press, 1976). For the effects of colonial rule on Vietnamese culture, see David G. Marr's Vietnamese Tradition on Trial (Berkeley: University of California Press, 1985). Another useful work, which focusses on the Vietnamese sense of community, is Alexander B. Woodside's Community and Revolution in Vietnam (Boston: Houghton Mifflin, 1976).

The period of the Franco-Vietminh War (1945-1954) has been subjected to considerable attention by both French and English-speaking specialists. A personal account of the origins of the war is Archimedes Patti's Why Vietnam: Prelude to America's Albatross (Berkeley: University of California Press, 1980). For a useful general survey, see Ellen J. Hammer's The Struggle for Indochina, 1940-1945 (Stanford University Press, 1955), or Donald Lancaster's The Emancipation of French Indochina (London: Oxford University Press, 1961). The best overall account in French is still Philippe Devillers' Histoire du Vietnam de 1940 à 1952 (Paris: Editions du Seuil, 1952).

The Franco-Vietminh war itself is chronicled in Edgar O'Ballance, The Indo-China War, 1945-1954 (London: Faber & Faber, 1964) and Bernard B. Fall's dramatic accounts, Street Without Joy: Indochina at War, 1946-1954 (Harrisburg: Stackpole Press, 1961) and Hell in a Very Small Place (New York: Lippincott, 1967). This period, of course, marked the beginning of Great Power involvement in the Indochina conflict. The origins of the U.S. role in Vietnam are beginning to attract scholarly attention because of the release of public documents relating to the period. Three recent studies are Robert M. Blum, Drawing the Line: The Origins of the American Containment Policy in Asia (New York: Norton, 1982); George McT. Kahin's Intervention: How America Became Involved in Vietnam (New York: Knopf, 1986); and Ronald H. Spector's Advice and Support: The Early Years (Washington, D.C.: Center for Military History, 1983). On the Chinese side, see King C. Chen's Vietnam and China, 1938-1954 (Princeton: Princeton University Press, 1969) and François Joyaux's fascinating La Chine et le Règlement du Premier Conflit d'Indochine (Paris: Sorbonne, 1979).

On the Geneva Conference of 1954, three classic studies are Robert F. Randle's Geneva 1954: The Settlement of the Indochina War (Princeton: Princeton University Press, 1969); Melvin Gurtov's The First Vietnam Crisis (New York: Columbia University Press, 1967); and Jean Lacouture's La Fin d'une Guerre: Indochine 1954 (Paris: Editions du Seuil, 1960). A recent study, providing a British perspective, is James Cable's The Geneva Conference of 1954 on Indochina (New York: St. Martin's, 1986). Documentation on the U.S. role at Geneva is provided in Foreign Relations of the United States (1952-1954), Volume XVI (Washington, D.C.: Government Printing Office, 1981).

Books about the Vietnam War and its immediate antecedents make up the vast bulk of the books and materials on Vietnam in most American libraries. Little indeed about the war has escaped close scrutiny. Comprehensive narrative histories of the war are still relatively rare, although Stanley Karnow's Vietnam: A History (mentioned above) is a valuable journalistic account. An ambitious attempt to place the war in critical perspective is Gabriel Kolko's Anatomy of a War: Vietnam, the United States, and the Modern Historical Experience (New York: Pantheon, 1985). For a short, balanced account of the war, see William S. Turley's The Second Indochina War: A Short Political and Military History (Boulder: Westview, 1986).

Most that has been written about the war in the English language deals with the American role in the conflict. George Herring's America's Longest War: The United States in Vietnam, 1950-1975 (New York: Wiley, 1979) provides a useful general survey. A more thematic account is Paul M. Kattenburg's The Vietnam Trauma in American Foreign Policy, 1945-1975 (New York: Transaction Books, 1980). John W. Lewis and George McT. Kahin, The United States in Vietnam (New York: Delta, 1967), is also a useful account, although its assumptions about the independence of the revolutionary movement in the South are now somewhat dated. A recent attempt to place the American role in the broader perspective of the postwar period is Guenther Lewy's America in Vietnam (New York: Oxford University Press, 1978).

There are a number of specialized studies on particular incidents or issues connected with the war, many of them written by participants in the decision-making process. Among the most useful are Roger Hilsman's To Move a Nation (New York: Doubleday, 1969); Townsend Hoopes, The Limits of Intervention (New York: David McKay, 1969); Chester Cooper, The Lost Crusade (New York: Dodd, Mead, 1970); and Leslie Gelb and Richard Betts, The Irony of Vietnam: The System Worked (Brookings, 1979). For the attempt to "win hearts and minds," see Robert Komer, Bureaucracy at War (Boulder: Westview, 1985) and Edward G. Lansdale, In the Midst of Wars (New York: Harper and Row, 1972).

There are a number of good journalistic accounts of the war. The first to attract major public attention were Malcolm Browne's The New Face of War (Indianapolis: Bobbs, Merrill, 1965) and David Halberstam's The Making of a Quagmire (New York: Random House, 1965). Halberstam followed up with his best-selling The Best and the Brightest (New York: Random House, 1969), a devastating critique of the failure of leading figures in the Kennedy and the Johnson administrations to come to grips with the realities of the war. Equally well known was Frances Fitzgerald's Fire in the Lake (New York: Vintage, 1972). Awarded the Pulitzer Prize, Fire in the Lake summed up the feelings of many Americans who had now become convinced that the war could not be won at an acceptable price.

There have been several scholarly studies of U.S. policy at the height of the war. Two of the better ones are Herbert Schandler's The Unmaking of a President: Lyndon Johnson and Vietnam (Princeton: Princeton University Press, 1977) and Wallace J. Thies, When Governments Collide (Berkeley: University of California Press, 1980). The primary documentary source on the U.S. role in the war is still The Pentagon Papers, currently available in several versions. The most accessible is the so-called Senator Gravel edition, published by Beacon Press in 1971. A second version, published in twelve volumes by the U.S. Government Printing Office, is less well organized and quite difficult to use. The Office of the Historian in the Department of State has issued three of the post-1954 volumes in the series entitled Foreign Relations of the United States. See Volume I (Vietnam) (1955-1957) and Volume I (Vietnam) (1958-1960), and Volume I (Vietnam) (1961-1963). Additional useful information on Vietnam is available in the microfilm records of the National Security Council, as well as State Department Central Files and CIA Research Reports, all published by University Publications of America.

The Vietnamese side of the war has not been as exhaustively researched, but a number of useful sources exist. On the Diem regime, see Robert Scigliano's South Vietnam: Nation under Stress (Boston: Houghton Mifflin, 1963) and Wesley Fishel's Problems of Freedom: South Vietnam Since Independence (New York: Free Press of Glencoe, 1961), as well as Bernard B. Fall, The Two Vietnams (New York: Praeger, 1967). A number of senior figures in the South Vietnamese regime have recorded their accounts of the war. Most notable are Nguyen Cao Ky's Twenty Years and Twenty Days (New York: Stein and Day, 1976), Bui Diem's In the Jaws of History (Boston: Houghton Mifflin, 1987), and Tran Van Don's Our Endless War (San Rafael: Presidio, 1978). A fascinating inside acount of the National Liberation Movement in South Vietnam is Truong Nhu Tang's A Viet Cong Memoir (San Diego: Harcourt Brace Jovanovich, 1985).

The communist side has been dealt with in a number of recent studies, including James P. Harrison, The Endless War: Fifty Years of Struggle in Vietnam (New York: Free Press of Glencoe, 1982) and William J. Duiker, The Communist Road to Power in Vietnam (Boulder: Westview Press, 1981). The classic study on the revolutionary movement in the South is Douglas Pike, The Viet Cong (Cambridge: MIT Press, 1966), followed up by his War, Peace, and the Viet Cong (Cambridge: MIT Press, 1969).

Hanoi's spokesmen have themselves written extensively about the war. Several of Vo Nguyen Giap's strategical writings are available in English, including People's War, People's Army (New York: Praeger, 1962) and Banner of People's War: The Party's Military Line (New York: Praeger, 1970). Truong Chinh's own early strategical writings are compiled in Primer for Revolt (New York: Praeger, 1963). Other key figures who wrote about the war were General Van Tien Dung, whose account of the final campaign in 1975 is translated in Our Great Spring Victory (New York: Monthly Review Press, 1977) and Tran Van Tra's Vietnam: History of the B2-Bulwark Theater, Volume V. The latter source is particularly interesting as it contains information critical of Hanoi's strategy. Not surprisingly, Tra has been relieved of his official posts, and his book is no longer available in Vietnam. For an official DRV account of the war, see Anti-U.S. Resistance War for National Salvation, 1954-1975: Military Events, translated by Joint Publications Research Service, 80,968 (June 3, 1982).

Hanoi's relations with its allies have been the subject of some scholarship in the West. The Vietnamese role in the Sino-Soviet dispute was analyzed in Donald Zagoria, The Vietnam Triangle (New York: Pegasus, 1972) and William R. Smyser, The Independent Vietnamese (Athens: Ohio University Center for International Studies, 1980). For a highly critical view of Hanoi, see P.J. Honey, Communism in North Vietnam: Its Role in the Sino-Soviet Dispute (Cambridge: MIT Press, 1963).

Documentary sources on the war published in North Vietnam are relatively rare, and scholars have been forced to rely to a considerable degree on captured documents, many of them available in microfilm in the United States. Among the most useful are the so-called Race Documents, a collection of material deposited by Jeffrey Race with the Center for Research Libraries in Chicago, two collections of Viet Cong documents compiled by Douglas Pike, and a selection entitled "Communist Vietnamese Publications" issued by the Library of Congress in Washington, D.C. A massive collection of captured documents compiled by the U.S. Air Force has recently been placed in the National Archives, but search facilities for the material are cumbersome and it may be some time before the material can be exhaustively researched.

The end of the war was dramatically portrayed in a number of accounts, notably Frank Snepp's Decent Interval (New York: Random House, 1977) and Tiziano Terzani's Giai-Phong: The Fall and Liberation of Saigon (New York: St. Martin's, 1976). Also see Alan Dawson's 55 Days: The Fall of South Vietnam (Englewood Cliffs, N.J Prentice-Hall, 1977) and Stephen T. Hosmer et.al. (eds.) The Fall of South Vietnam: Statements by Military and Civilian Leaders (New York: Crane, Russak, 1980). The latter source chronicles the charge by South Vietnamese figures that the fall of Saigon lies at least partly at the feet of the United States for failing to provide adequate support to its ally at the supreme moment of crisis.

Retrospective accounts of the war are beginning to appear with increasing regularity. Richard Nixon recorded his views in No More Vietnams (New York: Arbor House, 1985). Justification for the U.S. effort is provided by Norman Podhoretz in Why We Were in Vietnam (New York: Simon & Schuster, 1982). A more analytical account is Timothy J. Lomperis, The War Everyone Lost--and Won (Baton Rouge: Louisiana State University Press, 1984). For a critical assessment of the military strategy adopted by the United States in Vietnam, see Harry G. Summers, On Strategy: A Critical Analysis of the Vietnam War (Novato, Cal.: Presidio, 1982).

Interest in Vietnam since the end of the war has understandably declined, but a number of books have appeared in recent years which have chronicled Hanoi's difficulties in coping with the postwar situation. Three general studies dealing with the internal situation are William J. Duiker, Vietnam Since the Fall of Saigon (Athens: Ohio University Monographs in International Studies, 1985); Nguyen Van Canh, Vietnam Under Communism, 1975-1982 (Stanford: Hoover Institution Press, 1983); and Robert Shaplen, Bitter Victory (New York: Harper & Row, 1986). On Hanoi's foreign policy entanglements see David W.P. Elliott (ed.), The Third Indochina Conflict (Boulder: Westview, 1981) and Nayan Chanda, Brother Enemy: The War After the War (New York: Harcourt Brace Jovanovich, 1986). Moscow's role in Indochina is analyzed in Douglas Pike, Vietnam and the Soviet Union: Anatomy of an Alliance (Boulder: Westview Press, 1987). Current information on the Socialist Republic of Vietnam is available in English translation in Joint Publications Research Service (South-

east Asia Report) and Foreign Broadcast Information Service, Volume
IV (Asia and the Pacific).

I. HISTORY

A. GENERAL WORKS

Bastin, John S. The Emergence of Modern Southeast Asia. Englewood Cliffs: Prentice-Hall, 1967.

Buttinger, Joseph. The Smaller Dragon. New York: Praeger,
1958.

_____. Vietnam: The Dragon Embattled. Two Volumes. New
York: Praeger, 1967.

_____. Vietnam: A Political History. New York: Praeger, 1968.

Buttwell, Richard. Southeast Asia Today and Tomorrow. New York:
Praeger, 1961.

Cady, John F. Southeast Asia: Its Historical Development. Ithaca:
Cornell University Press, 1958.

Chesneaux, Jean. Vietnam: Contribution a l'Histoire de la Nation
Vietnamienne. Paris: Plon, 1955.

Duiker, William J. Vietnam: Nation in Revolution. Boulder: Westview, 1983.

Hall, D.B.E. A History of Southeast Asia. New York: St. Martin's,
1968.

Hammer, Ellen J. Vietnam Yesterday and Today. New York: Holt,
Rinehart, & Winston, 1966.

Harrison, Brian. Southeast Asia: A Short History. New York: St.
Martin's, 1954.

Hodgkin, Thomas. Vietnam: The Revolutionary Path. New York:
St. Martin's, 1981.

Karnow, Stanley. Vietnam: A History. New York: Penguin, 1984.

Le Thanh Khoi. Le Viet-Nam: Histoire et Civilization. Paris:
Editions du Minuit, 1955.

Masson, André. Histoire du Vietnam. Paris: Presses Universitaires
de France, 1960.

Nguyen Phut Tan. A Modern History of Vietnam, 1802-1954. Saigon: Khai Tri, 1964.

Smith, Ralph B. Vietnam and the West. London: Heinemann, 1968.

Steinberg, David (ed.). In Search of Southeast Asia. New York: Praeger, 1971.

Vella, Walter (ed.). Aspects of Vietnamese History. Honolulu: University of Hawaii Press, 1973.

B. TRADITIONAL PERIOD

Cadiere, Leo and Pelliott, P. "Premieres études sur les sources annamites de l'Histoire d'Annam," in Bulletin de l'Ecole Française de l'Extreme Orient. Number 4 (1904), pp. 617-671.

Coedes, Georges. The Indianized States of Southeast Asia (translated by Susan B. Cowing). Honolulu: East-West Center Press, 1968.

_____. The Making of Southeast Asia (translated by H.M. Wright). Berkeley: University of California Press, 1966.

Cotter, Michael G. "Towards a Social History of the Vietnamese Southward Movement," in Journal of Southeast Asian History. Volume IX, Number 1 (March 1968).

Crawfurd, J. Journal of an Embassy for the Governor-General of India to the Courts of Siam and Cochinchina. Two Volumes. London: 1928.

Deveria, G. Histoire des Relations de la Chine avec l'Annam: Vietnam du XVI au XIX Siecle. Paris: Ernest Leroux, 1980.

Hinton, Harold. China's Relations with Burma and Vietnam. New York: Institute of Pacific Relations, 1958.

Holmgren, Jennifer. Chinese Colonization of Northern Vietnam: Administrative Geography and Political Development in the Tong King Delta. Canberra, 1980.

Lamb, Alistair. The Mandarin Road to Old Hue. London: Chatto and Windus, 1970.

Lamb, Helen. Vietnam's Will to Live: Resistance to Foreign Aggression for Early Times through the Nineteenth Century. New York: Monthly Review Press, 1972.

Maybon, Charles B. Histoire Moderne du Pays d'Annam. Paris, 1920.

Miyakawa, Hisayuki. "The Confucianization of South China," in
Arthur F. Wright (ed.), The Confucian Persuasion. Stanford:
Stanford University Press, 1960.

Nguyen Khac Vien. Traditional Vietnam: Some Historical Stages.
Vietnam Studies Number 21. Hanoi: Foreign Language Press,
no date.

Pasquier, Pierre. L'Annam d'Autrefois. Paris, 1907.

Schreiner, A. Les Institutions Annamites en Basse-Cochinchine
avant la Conquete Française. Three Volumes. Saigon 1900-1902
(reprint 1969).

Taylor, Keith W. The Birth of Vietnam. Berkeley: University of
California Press, 1983.

_____. "An Evaluation of the Chinese Period in Vietnamese History,"
in Journal of Asian Studies (Korea University), Number 23 (January 1980), pp. 139-164.

_____. "Looking Behind the Vietnamese Annals: Ly Phat Ma
(1028-1054) and Ly Nhat Ton (1054-1072) in the Viet Su Luoc
and the Toan Thu," in Vietnam Forum, Number 7 (Winter-Spring
1986).

_____. The Rise of Dai Viet and the Establishment of Thang Long,"
in Hall, K.R. and Whitmore, John K. (eds). Explorations in Early
Southeast Asian History: The Origins of Southeast Asian State-
craft. Ann Arbor: Michigan Papers on South and Southeast
Asia, Number 11 (1976).

Tran Trong Kim. Viet Nam Su Luoc. Saigon: Tan Viet, 1964.

Vietnamese Studies, Number 56. The Confucian Scholar in Vietnamese
History. Hanoi: Foreign Languages Press, 1979.

_____, Number 48. Hanoi: From the Origins to the 19th Century.
Volume One. Hanoi: Foreign Languages Press, 1977.

Wales, H.G. Quaritch. The Making of Greater India. London, 1951.

Whitmore, John K. The Development of Le Government in 15th Century Vietnam. Ph.D. Dissertation. Cornell University, 1968.

_____. Vietnam, Ho Quy Ly, and the Ming. New Haven: Yale
University Southeast Asian Studies, 1985.

Wiens, Herold J. Han Chinese Expansion in South China. Hamden,
Conn.: Shoe String, 1970.

Wolters, O.W. "Historians and Emperors in Vietnam and China: Comments Arising Out of Le Van Huu's History, Presented to the Tran Court in 1272," in Anthony Reid and David G. Marr (eds.), Perceptions of the Past in Southeast Asia. Singapore, 1979.

Woodside, Alexander B. "Early Ming Expansionism (1406-1427): China's Abortive Conquest of Vietnam," in Harvard Papers on China, Number 17 (1963).

_____. Vietnam and the Chinese Model. Cambridge: Harvard University Press, 1971.

C. COLONIAL PERIOD

Adams, Nina S. The Meaning of Pacification: Thanh Hoa under French Rule, 1865-1908. Ph.D. Dissertation. Yale University, 1978.

Azeau, Henri. Ho Chi Minh, Dernière Chance: La Conférence Franco-Vietnamienne de Fontainebleau, 1946. Paris: Flammarion, 1968.

Betts, R.F. Assimilation and Association in French Colonial Theory, 1890-1914. New York: Columbia University Press, 1961.

Bodard, Lucien. The Quicksand War: Prelude to Vietnam (Tr. Patrick O'Brien). Boston: Little, Brown, 1967.

Cable, James. The Geneva Conference of 1954 on Indochina. New York: St. Martin's, 1986.

Cady, John T. The Roots of French Imperialism in Eastern Asia. Ithaca: Cornell University Press, 1954.

Catroux, Georges. Deux Actes du Drame Indochinois. Paris: Plon, 1959.

Chen, King C. Vietnam and China, 1938-1954. Princeton: Princeton University Press, 1969.

Chesneaux, Jean (ed.). Tradition et Revolution au Vietnam. Paris: Anthropos, 1971.

Cole, Allan B. (ed.). Conflict in Indochina and International Repercussions: A Documentary History. Ithaca: Cornell University Press, 1956.

Decoux, Jean. A la Barre de l'Indochine: Histoire de mon Gouvernement-général, 1940-1945. Paris, 1952.

Demariaux, Jean-Claude. Les Secrets des Iles Poulo-Condore:

le Grand Bagne Indochinois. Paris: J. Peyronnet, 1956.

Devillers, Philippe. Histoire du Vietnam de 1940 à 1952. Paris: Editions du Seuil, 1952.

Dorgelès, Roland. Sur la Route Mandarine. Paris, 1929.

Dorsenne, Jean. Faudra t'il Evacuer l'Indochine? Paris: Nouvelles Sociétés d'Editions, 1932.

Doyon, Jacques. Les Soldats Blancs de Ho Chi Minh. Paris, 1973.

Duiker, William J. The Rise of Nationalism in Vietnam, 1900-1941. Ithaca: Cornell University Press, 1976.

Elsbree, Willard E. Japan's Role in Southeast Asian Nationalist Movements. Cambridge: Harvard University Press, 1953.

Ely, Paul. L'Indochine dans la Tourmente. Paris: Plon, 1964.

Ennis, Thomas E. French Policy and Developments in Indochina. Chicago: University of Chicago Press, 1936.

Fall, Bernard B. Hell in a Very Small Place: The Siege of Dien-Bien-Phu. New York: Lippincott, 1967.

_____. Street Without Joy: Indochina at War, 1946-1954. Harrisburg: Stackpole Press, 1961.

Garros, Georges. Forceries Humaines. Paris: André Delpeuch, 1926.

Gurtov, Melvin. The First Vietnam Crisis. New York: Columbia University Press, 1967.

Hammer, Ellen J. The Struggle for Indochina, 1940-1955. Stanford: Stanford University Press, 1955.

Hémery, Daniel. Révolutionnaires Vietnamiens et Pouvoir Colonial en Indochine. Paris: Maspero, 1975.

Huynh Kim Khanh. "The August Revolution Reinterpreted," in Journal of Asian Studies, Volume XXX, Number 4 (August 1971).

Irving, R. The First Indochina War: French and American Policy, 1945-1954. London, 1975.

Isoart, Paul. Le Phénomène Nationale Vietnamien. Paris, 1961.

Joyaux, François. La Chine et le Règlement du Premier Conflit d'Indochine: Genève, 1954. Paris: Sorbonne, 1979.

Lacouture, Jean and Devillers, Philippe. La Fin d'une Guerre: Indochine 1954. Paris: Editions du Seuil, 1960.

Lancaster, Donald. The Emancipation of French Indochina. London: Oxford University Press, 1961.

Langlois, Walter G. André Malraux: The Indochina Adventure. New York: Praeger, 1965.

Laniel, Joseph. Le Drame Indochinois: de Dien-Bien-Phu au Pari de Genéve. Paris: Plon, 1957.

Marr, David G. Vietnamese Anticolonialism, 1885-1925. Berkeley: University of California Press, 1971.

_____. Vietnamese Tradition on Trial. Berkeley: University of California Press, 1985.

McAleavy, Henry. Black Flags in Vietnam. London, 1968.

McAlister, John T. Jr. Vietnam: The Origins of Revolution. New York: Harper & Row, 1970.

_____ and Mus, Paul. The Vietnamese and Their Revolution. New York: Harper & Row, 1970.

Mkhitarian, Suron A. Rabochii klass i Natsional'no-Osvoboditel'noe Dvizhenie vo Vietname. Moscow, 1967.

Mus, Paul. Viet-Nam: Sociologie d'une Guerre. Paris: Editions du Seuil, 1952.

Navarre, Henri. Agonie de l'Indochine (1953-1954). Paris: Plon, 1956.

Ngo Vinh Long. Before the Revolution. Cambridge: MIT Press, 1973.

_____. Peasant Revolutionary Struggles in Vietnam in the 1930s. Ph.D. Dissertation. Harvard University, 1978.

Nguyen Duy Thanh. My Four Years with the Viet Minh. Bombay: Democratic Research Service, 1950.

O'Ballance, Edgar. The Indo-China War, 1945-1954: A Study in Guerrilla Warfare. London: Faber & Faber, 1964.

Ognetov, I.A. "Komintern i revoliutsionnoe dvizhenie vo Vietname," in Komintern i Vostok (Comintern and the East). Moscow, 1969.

Osborne, Milton. The French Presence in Cochinchina and Cambodia. Ithaca: Cornell University Press, 1969.

Patti, Archimedes. Why Vietnam: Prelude to America's Albatross. Berkeley: University of California Press, 1980.

Phan Thien Chau. Transitional Nationalism in Vietnam, 1903-1931. Ph.D. Dissertation. Denver University, 1965.

Porter, Gareth. "Proletariat and Peasantry in Early Vietnamese Communism," in Asian Thought and Society, Volume One, Number 3 (December 1976).

Randle, Robert F. Geneva 1954: The Settlement of the Indochina War. Princeton: Princeton University Press, 1969.

Roy, Jules. The Battle of Dien Bien Phu. (Tr. Robert Baldrich). New York: Harper & Row, 1965.

Sainteny, Jean. Histoire d'une Paix Manquée: Indochine 1945-1947. Paris: Dumont, 1953.

Starobin, Joseph R. Eyewitness in Indochina. New York: Cameron & Kahn, 1954.

Taboulet, Georges. La Geste Française en Indochine. Two volumes. Paris: 1955-1956.

Tanham, George K. Communist Revolutionary Warfare: The Vietminh in Indochina. New York: Praeger, 1961.

Thompson, Virginia. French Indochina. New York: Octagon, 1968.

Tran Huy Lieu. Les Soviets du Nghe-Tinh de 1930-1931 au Viet-Nam. Hanoi: Foreign Languages Press, 1960.

Truong Buu Lam. Patterns of Vietnamese Response to Foreign Intervention, 1858-1900. New Haven: Yale University Southeast Asian Series, Number 11. 1967.

Viollis, André. Indochine S.O.S. Paris: Gallimard, 1935.

D. THE REPUBLIC OF VIETNAM

Brown, Weldon A. Prelude to Disaster. Port Washington, N.Y.: National University Publications, 1975.

Carver, George. "The Real Revolution in South Vietnam," in Foreign Affairs, Number 43 (April 1965).

Fall, Bernard B. Last Reflections on a War. New York: Doubleday, 1967.

_____. The Two Vietnams. New York: Praeger, 1967.

_____. Vietnam Witness, 1953-1966. New York: Praeger, 1966.

Fishel, Wesley R. (ed.). Problems of Freedom: South Vietnam Since Independence. New York: Free Press of Glencoe, 1961.

Greene, Graham. The Quiet American. New York: Viking, 1956.

Halberstam, David. The Making of a Quagmire. New York: Random House, 1965.

Joiner, Charles A. The Politics of Massacre. Philadelphia: Temple University Press, 1974.

Jumper, Roy. "The Communist Challenge to South Vietnam," in Far Eastern Survey." Volume XXV, Number 11 (November 1956).

Lacouture, Jean. Vietnam: Between Two Truces (Tr. Konrad Kellen and Joel Carmichael). New York: Random House, 1966.

Lindholm, Richard W. (ed.). Viet-Nam: The First Five Years. East Lansing: Michigan State University, 1957.

Maneli, Mieczyslaw. War of the Vanguished. New York: Harper & Row, 1971.

Mechlin, John. Mission in Torment. New York: Doubleday, 1965.

Nguyen Tien Hung and Jerrold L. Schecter. The Palace File. New York: Harper & Row, 1986.

Nighswonger, William A. Rural Pacification in Vietnam. New York: Praeger, 1966.

Osborne, Milton E. Strategic Hamlets in South Vietnam. Ithaca: Cornell University Southeast Asian Program, 1965.

Race, Jeffrey. War Comes to Long An. Berkeley: University of California Press, 1972.

Scigliano, Robert. South Vietnam: Nation under Stress. Boston: Houghton Mifflin, 1963.

Smith, Harvey H. et al. Area Handbook for South Vietnam. Washington, D.C.: Government Printing Office, 1967.

E. THE DEMOCRATIC REPUBLIC OF VIETNAM

Burchett, Wilfred G. Vietnam North: A First-Hand Report. New York: International Publishers, 1967.

_____. North of the 17th Parallel.

Fall, Bernard B. "North Vietnam: a Profile," in Problems of Communism (July-August 1965).

_____. The Two Vietnams. New York: Praeger, 1967.

_____. The Vietminh Regime. Ithaca: Cornell University Press, 1954.

Hoang Van Chi. From Colonialism to Communism. New York: Praeger, 1964.

Honey, P.J. Communism in North Vietnam: Its Role in the Sino-Soviet Dispute. Cambridge: MIT Press, 1963.

_____. (ed.). North Vietnam Today: Profile of a Communist Satellite. New York: Praeger, 1962.

Nhu Phong. "Intellectuals, Writers, and Artists," in China Quarterly, Number 9 (January-March 1962)

Porter, Gareth. The Myth of the Bloodbath: North Vietnam's Land Reform Reconsidered . Ithaca: Cornell University Southeast Asian Series, 1972.

Salisbury, Harrison E. Behind the Lines--Hanoi. New York: Harper & Row, 1967.

Smith, Ralph B. "The Work of the Provisional Government of Vietnam, August-December 1945," in Modern Asian Studies. Volume XII, Number 4 (1978).

Thai Quang Trung. Collective Leadership and Factionalism: An Essay on Ho Chi Minh's Legacy. Singapore: Institute of Southeast Asian Studies, 1985.

Turley, William S. (ed.). Vietnamese Communism in Comparative Perspective. Boulder: Westview Press, 1980.

U.S. Department of State. Who's Who in North Vietnam. Washington, D.C.: Government Printing Office, 1972.

Weiss, Peter. Notes on the Cultural Life of the D.R.V. New York: Dell, 1970.

Zagoria, Donald. Vietnam Triangle. New York: Pegasus, 1972.

F. THE VIETNAM WAR

1. General

Bain, Chester A. The Roots of Conflict. Englewood Cliffs, N.J.: Prentice-Hall, 1967.

Browne, Malcolm W. The New Face of War. Indianapolis: Bobbs, Merrill, 1965.

Cao Van Vien and Dong Van Khuyen. Reflections on the Vietnam War. Washington, D.C.: Center for Military History, 1980.

Critchfield, Richard. The Long Charade: Political Subversion in the Vietnam War. New York: Harcourt, Brace, & World, 1968.

Emerson, Gloria. Winners and Losers. New York: Random, 1976.

Herr, Michael. Dispatches. New York: Knopf, 1977.

Isaacs, Arnold R. Without Honor: Defeat in Vietnam and Cambodia. Baltimore: Johns Hopkins University Press, 1983.

Just, Ward. To What End: Report from Vietnam. Boston: Houghton Mifflin, 1968.

Larteguy, Jean. Un Million de Dollars le Viet. Paris, 1965.

Lomperis, Timothy J. The War Everyone Lost--and Won. Baton Rouge: Louisiana State University Press, 1984.

Luce, Donald, and Summer, John. Viet Nam: The Unheard Voices. Ithaca: Cornell University Press, 1969.

Ly Qui Chung (ed.). Between Two Fires: The Unheard Voices of Vietnam. New York: Praeger, 1970.

Millet, Allan (ed.). A Short History of the Vietnam War. Bloomington: Indiana University Press, 1978.

Oberdorfer, Don. Tet! New York: Doubleday, 1971.

Podhoretz, Norman. Why We Were in Vietnam. New York: Simon & Schuster, 1982.

Schell, Johathan. The Military Half: An Account of Destruction in Quang Ngai and Quang Tin. New York: Random House, 1968.

_____. The Village of Ben Suc. New York: Random House, 1967.

Sheehan, Susan. Ten Vietnamese. New York: Knopf, 1967.

Sully, Francois (ed.). Voices from Vietnam. N.Y.: Praeger, 1971.

Thompson, Robert. Defeating Communist Insurgency: Experiences from Malaya. London, 1967.

_____. No Exit from Vietnam. New York: David McKay, 1969.

Thomson, James C. "How Could Vietnam Happen: An Autopsy," in Atlantic Monthly (April 1968).

Tran Van Don. Our Endless War. San Rafael: Presidio, 1978.

Trulliger, James W. Village at War. New York, Longman's, 1981.

Turley, William S. The Second Indochina War: A Short Political and Military History. Boulder: Westview, 1986.

2. The Communist Side

Andrews, W. Vietnam: Anti-U.S. Resistance War for National Salvation, 1954-1975; Military Events. Hanoi: People's Army Publishing House, 1980.

_____. The Village War: Vietnamese Communist Revolutionary Activities in Dinh Tuong Province, 1960-1964. Columbia: University of Missouri Press, 1973.

Berman, Paul. Revolutionary Organization. Lexington: D.C. Heath, 1974.

Burchett, Wilfred. Vietnam: Inside Story of the Guerrilla War. New York: International Publishers, 1965.

_____. Vietnam Will Win. New York: International Publishers, 1969.

Duiker, William J. The Communist Road to Power in Vietnam. Boulder: Westview, 1981.

Elliott, David W.P. NLF-DRV Strategy in the 1972 Spring Offensive. Ithaca: Cornell University IREA Project, 1974.

Fall, Bernard B. "Ho Chi Minh, Like It or Not," in Esquire (November 1967).

Fitzgerald, Frances. Fire in the Lake. New York: Vintage, 1972.

Harrison, James P. The Endless War: Fifty years of struggle in Vietnam. New York: Free Press of Glencoe, 1982.

Hoang Quoc Viet. A Heroic People: Memoirs from the Revolution. Hanoi: Foreign Languages Press, 1965.

_____. Récits de la Resistance Vietnamienne. Hanoi: Foreign Languages Press, 1966.

Langer, Paul, and Zasloff, Joseph J. North Vietnam and the Pathet Lao: Partners in the Struggle for Laos. Cambridge: Harvard University Press, 1970 .

Lansdale, Edward G. "Vietnam: Do We Understand Revolution?" in Foreign Affairs, Number 43 (October 1964).

Leites, Nathan. "The Viet Cong Style of Politics," RAND Corporation Report, Number RM-5487. Santa Monica.

Nguyen Khac Vien. Tradition and Revolution in Vietnam. Berkeley and Washington, D.C.: Indochina Resources Center, 1974.

Nguyen Thi Dinh. No Other Road to Take. Ithaca: Cornell University Southeast Asia Project, 1976.

Pike, Douglas. The Viet Cong. Cambridge: MIT Press, 1966.

_____. War, Peace, and the Viet Cong. Cambridge: MIT Press, 1969.

RAND Corporation. "Interviews Concerning the National Liberation Front for South Vietnam," RAND Corporation Documents Series FD & G. Santa Monica.

Rousset, Pierre. Communisme et Nationalisme Vietnamien. Paris: Editions Galilée, 1978.

Thayer, Carlyle A. The Origins of the National Front for the Liberation of South Viet-Nam. Ph.D. Dissertation. Australian National University, 1977.

Truong Nhu Tang. A Vietcong Memoir: An Inside Account of the Vietnam War and Its Aftermath. San Diego: Harcourt Brace Jovanovich, 1985.

Truong Son. "The Failure of Special War (1961-1965)." Vietnamese Studies, Number 11. Hanoi: Foreign Languages Press, 1967.

Warner, Denis. Certain Victory: How Hanoi Won the War. Kansas City: Sheed Andres and McMeed, 1977.

Woodside, Alexander B. Community and Revolution in Vietnam. Boston: Houghton Mifflin, 1976.

Zasloff, Joseph J. Origins of the Insurgency in South Vietnam, 1954-1960: The Role of the Southern Vietminh Cadres. RAND Corporation Collection, RM 5163/Z ISA/ ARPA. May 1968.

3. U.S. Involvement

Ball, George W. The Past Has Another Pattern. New York: W.W. Norton, 1982.

Bator, Victor. Vietnam: A Diplomatic Tragedy. New York: Faber & Faber, 1967.

Berman, Larry. Planning a Tragedy. New York: Norton, 1972.

Blum, Robert M. Drawing the Line. The Origins of the American Containment Policy in Asia. New York: Norton, 1982.

Braestrup, Peter. Big Story. New Haven: Yale University Press, 1977.

Brown, Weldon A. The Last Chopper: The Denouement of the American Role in Vietnam, 1963-1975. Port Washington, N.Y., 1976.

Chomsky, Noam. At War with Asia. New York: Random House, 1970.

Cooper, Chester. The Lost Crusade. New York: Dodd, Mead, 1970.

Galluci, Robert. Neither Peace nor Honor: The Politics of American Military Policy in Vietnam. Baltimore: Johns Hopkins University Press, 1975.

Gelb, Laslie, and Betts, Richard. The Irony of Vietnam: The System Worked. Washington, D.C.: Brookings Institution, 1979.

Gibbons, William C. The U.S. Government and the Vietnam War. Two Volumes. Princeton: Princeton University Press, 1986.

Goulden, Joseph. Truth is the First Casualty: The Gulf of Tonkin Affair. Chicago: Rand McNally, 1969.

Halberstam, David. The Best and the Brightest. New York: Random House, 1969.

Hayes, S.P. (ed.). The Beginning of American Aid to Southeast Asia: The Griffin Mission of 1950. Lexington: Prentice-Hall, 1971.

Herring, George. America's Longest War: The United States in Vietnam, 1950-1975. New York: Wiley, 1979.

Hilsman, Roger. To Move a Nation. New York: Doubleday, 1969.

Hoopes, Townsend. The Limits of Intervention. New York: David McKay, 1969.

Kahin, George McT. Intervention: How America Became Involved in Vietnam. New York: Knopf, 1986.

_____, and Lewis, John W. The United States in Vietnam. New York: Delta, 1967.

Kattenburg, Paul M. The Vietnam Trauma in American Foreign Policy, 1945-1975. New Brunswick: Transaction Books, 1980.

Kenny, Henry J. The American Role in Vietnam and East Asia. New York: Praeger, 1984.

Kolko, Gabriel. Anatomy of a War: Vietnam, the United States, and the Modern Historical Experience. New York: Pantheon, 1985.

Komer, Rober. Bureaucracy at War. Boulder: Westview, 1985.

Lansdale, Edward G. In the Midst of Wars: An American's Mission to Southeast Asia. New York, 1972.

Lederer, William J. Our Own Worst Enemy. New York: Norton, 1968.

Lewy, Guenter. America in Vietnam. New York: Oxford University Press, 1978.

Lodge, Henry Cabot. The Storm Has Many Eyes. New York: W.W. Norton, 1973.

Montgomery, John D. The Politics of Foreign Aid: American Experience in Southeast Asia. New York: Praeger, 1962.

Nixon, Richard. No More Vietnams. New York: Arbor House, 1985.

Pfeffer, Richard M. (ed.). No More Vietnams? The War and the Future of American Foreign Policy. New York: Harper & Row, 1968.

Podhoretz, Norman. Why We Were in Vietnam. New York: Simon and Schuster, 1982.

Poole, Peter. Eight Presidents and Indochina. New York: Krieger, 1978.

Schandler, Herbert Y. The Unmaking of a President: Lyndon Johnson and Vietnam. Princeton: Princeton University Press, 1977.

Scheer, Robert. How the United States Got Involved in Vietnam.
Santa Barbara: Center for the Study of Democratic Institutions,
1965.

Schlesinger, Arthur M. Jr. The Bitter Heritage: Vietnam and
American Democracy, 1941-1966. Boston: Houghton Mifflin, 1967.

Shaplen, Robert. The Lost Revolution: The U.S. in Vietnam, 1946-
1966. New York: Harper & Row, 1966.

_____. The Road From War, 1965-1970. New York: Harper &
Row, 1970.

Shawcross, William. Sideshow: Kissinger, Nixon, and the Destruction of Cambodia. New York: Simon & Schuster, 1979.

Snepp, Frank. Decent Interval. New York: Random House, 1977.

Thies, Wallace J. When Governments Collide. Berkeley: University
of California Press, 1980.

Westmoreland, William C. A Soldier Reports. New York: Doubleday,
1976.

Windchy, Eugene. Tonkin Gulf. Garden City, N.Y., 1971.

Zinn, Howard. The Logic of Withdrawal. Boston: Beacon, 1967.

4. Involvement by Other Countries

Bloomfield, L.P. The United Nations and Vietnam. New York, 1968.

Gurtov, Melvin. China and Southeast Asia: The Politics of Survival.
Baltimore: Johns Hopkins University Press, 1971.

King, Peter (ed.). Australia's Vietnam: Australia in the Second
Indochina War. Winchester: Allen & Unwin, 1983.

McLane, Charles B. Soviet Strategies in Southeast Asia. Princeton:
Princeton University Press, 1966.

McVey, Ruth T. The Calcutta Conference and the Southeast Asian
Uprisings. Ithaca: Cornell University Press, 1958.

Ministry of Foreign Affairs. Socialist Republic of Vietnam. The Truth
About Vietnamo-Chinese Relations over the Past Thirty Years.
Hanoi, 1979.

Sar Desai, D.R. Indian Foreign Policy in Cambodia, Laos, and Vietnam,
1947-1964. Berkeley: University of California Press, 1968.

Smyser, William R. The Independent Vietnamese. Athens: Ohio University Center for International Studies, 1980.

Taylor, Jay. China and Southeast Asia. New York: Praeger, 1976.

Zasloff, Joseph J. The Role of the Sanctuary: Communist China's Support to the Vietminh, 1945-1954. RAND Corporation: Santa Monica, 1967.

5. The Negotiations Process

Goodman, Allan. The Lost Peace. Stanford: Hoover Institution Press, 1978.

Herring, George C. (ed.). The Secret Diplomacy of the Vietnam War The Negotiating Volumes of the Pentagon Papers. Austin: University of Texas Press, 1983.

Huntington, Samuel. "The Bases of Accommodation," in Foreign Affairs, Number 46 (July 1968).

Kissinger, Henry. "Viet Nam Negotiations," in Foreign Affairs, Volume 47, Number 2 (January 1969).

Porter, Gareth. A Peace Denied. Bloomington: Indiana University Press, 1975.

6. The End of the War

Cao Van Vien. The Final Collapse. Washington, D.C.: Government Printing Office, 1983.

Dawson, Alan. 55 Days: The Fall of South Vietnam. Englewood Cliffs, N.J.: Prentice-Hall, 1977.

Hosmer, Stephen T., Kellen, Konrad, and Jenkins, Brian M. The Fall of South Vietnam: Statements by Military and Civilian Leaders New York: Crane, Russak, 1980.

Snepp, Frank. Decent Interval. New York: Random House, 1977.

Terzani, Tiziano. Giai Phong: The Fall and Liberation of Saigon. New York: St. Martin's, 1976.

Van Tien Dung. Our Great Spring Victory. New York: Monthly Review Press, 1977.

Warner, Denis. Not With Guns Alone. London: Hutchinson, 1977.

7. The Military War

Air War Study Group. The Air War in Indochina. Boston: Beacon, 1972.

Hoang Ngoc Luong. The General Offensive of 1968-1969. Washington, D.C.: Center for Military History, 1981.

Kinnard, Douglas. The War Managers. Hanover: University Press of New England, 1977.

Littauer, R. and Uphoff, W. N. (eds.). The Air War in Indochina. Boston: Beacon, 1972.

Pisor, Robert. The End of the Line: The Siege of Khe Sanh. New York: Norton, 1982.

Rogers, Bernard. Cedar Falls, Junction City: A Turning Point. Washington, D.C., 1974.

Serong, Brigadier, F.B. "The 1972 Easter Offensive" in Southeast Asian Perspectives, Number 10 (Summer 1974).

Sharp, Ulysses S. Grant. Strategy for Defeat: Vietnam in Retrospect. San Rafael: Presidio, 1978.

Spector, Ronald H. Advice and Support: The Early Years: The U.S. Army in Vietnam. Washington, D.C.: Center for Military History, 1983.

Summers, Harry G. On Strategy: A Critical Analysis of the Vietnam War. Novato: Presidio, 1982.

Taylor, Maxwell D. Swords and Plowshares. New York: Norton, 1972.

Truong Son. Five Lessons of a Great Victory (Winter 1966-Spring 1977). Hanoi: Foreign Languages Press, 1967.

Walt, Lewis W. Strange War, Strange Strategy: A General's Report on Vietnam. New York: Funk & Wagnall's, 1970.

Westmoreland. A Soldier Reports. Garden City, N.Y.: Doubleday, 1976.

8. Collections of Articles or Documents

Boettiger, John (ed.). Vietnam and American Foreign Policy. Boston: D.C. Heath, 1968.

Cameron, Allan W. Viet-Nam Crisis: A Documentary History. Ithaca: Cornell University Press, 1971.

Communist Vietnamese Publications. A microfilm series issued by the Library of Congress, Washington, D.C.

Fishel, Wesley (ed.). Vietnam: Anatomy of a Conflict. Itasca, Ill: Peacock, 1968.

Gettleman, Marvin E. (ed.). Vietnam: History, Documents, and Opinions. New York: Fawcett, 1965.

Lake, Anthony (ed.). The Legacy of Vietnam. New York: NYU, 1976.

McGarvey, Patrick (ed.). Visions of Victory: Selected Communist Military Writings, 1964-1968. Stanford: Hoover Institution Press, 1969.

Pike, Douglas. Catalog of Viet Cong Documents. Series 2. Cornell University Library (February 1969).

_____. Documents of the NLFSVN. Series microfilmed at MIT (1967).

Porter, Gareth (ed.). Vietnam: The Definitive Documentation of Human Decisions. Two Volumes. New York: New American Library, 1981.

Race Documents. A collection of materials deposited by Jeffrey Race with the Center for Research Libraries, Chicago, Illinois.

Raskin, Marcus G. and Fall, Bernard B. The Viet-Nam Reader: Articles and Documents on American Foreign Policy and the Viet-Nam Crisis. New York: Vintage, 1965.

Schlight, John (ed.). The Second Indochina War Symposium: Papers and Commentary. Washington, D.C.: Center for Military History, 1986.

G. THE SOCIALIST REPUBLIC OF VIETNAM

Doan Van Toai and Chanoff, David. The Vietnamese Gulag. New York: Simon & Schuster, 1985.

Duiker, William J. Vietnam Since the Fall of Saigon. Athens: Ohio University Monographs in International Studies, 1985.

Grant, Bruce. The Boat People: An "Age" Investigation. Harmondsworth: Penguin, 1979.

Lacouture, Jean and Simonne. Vietnam: Voyage à Travers une Victoir Paris: Editions du Seuil, 1976.

Mai Thu Van. Vietnam: Un Peuple, des Voix. Paris: Pierre Horay,
    1983.

Marr, David G. and Thayer, Carlyle A. Vietnam Since 1975: Two
    Views from Australia. Brisbane: School of Modern Asian Studies,
    Griffith University, 1980.

Nguyen Long (with Harry Kendall). After Saigon Fell: Daily Life
    Under the Vietnamese Communists. Berkeley: University of Cali-
    fornia Institute of East Asian Studies, 1981.

Nguyen Ngoc Huy. Vietnam Under Communist Rule. Washington,
    D.C.: George Mason University, 1982.

Nguyen Van Canh. Vietnam Under Communism, 1975-1982. Stanford:
    Hoover Institution Press, 1983.

Sagan, Ginetta and Denny, Stephen. Violations of Human Rights in
    the Socialist Republic of Vietnam. Atherton, Cal.: Aurora
    Foundation, 1983.

Shaplen, Robert. Bitter Victory. New York: Harper & Row, 1986.

Turley, William S. "Hanoi's Domestic Dilemmas," in Problems of
    Communism (July-August 1980).

II. POLITICS AND GOVERNMENT

A. GOVERNMENT AND INSTITUTIONS

Boudarel, Georges et al. (eds.). La Bureaucratie au Vietnam. Paris:
    l'Harmattan, 1983.

Donnell, John C. Politics in South Vietnam: Doctrines, Authority in
    Conflict. Ph.D. Dissertation, University of California, 1964.

_____, and Joiner, Charles A. Electoral Politics in South Vietnam.
    Lexington: D.C. Heath, 1974.

Dorsey, John T. "Bureaucracy and Political Development in Vietnam,"
    in Joseph LaPolombara (ed.), Bureaucracy and Political Development.
    Princeton: Princeton University Press, 1963.

Duncanson, Dennis. Government and Revolution in Vietnam. London:
    Oxford University Press, 1968.

Elliott, David W.P. "Institutionalizing the Revolution: Vietnam's
    Search for a Model of Development," in William S. Turley (ed.),

Vietnamese Communism in Comparative Perspective. Boulder: Westview, 1980.

_____. Revolutionary Reintegration: A Comparison of the Foundations of Post-Liberation Political Systems in North Vietnam and China. Ph.D. Dissertation, Cornell University Press, 1976.

Goodman, Allan E. Politics in War: The Bases of Political Community in South Vietnam. Cambridge: Harvard University Press, 1973.

Jumper, Roy. "Mandarin Bureaucracy and Politics in South Vietnam," in Pacific Affairs, Number 30 (March 1957).

Kahin, George McT. Government and Politics of Southeast Asia. Ithaca: Cornell University Press, 1964.

Mus, Paul. "The Role of the Village in Vietnamese Politics," in Pacific Affairs, Number 23 (September 1949).

Nghiem Dang. Vietnam: Politics and Public Administration. Honolulu: East-West Center Press, 1966.

Nguyen Thai. The Government of Men in the Republic of Vietnam. Ph.D. Dissertation, Michigan State University, 1962.

Osborne, Milton E. "The Vietnamese Perception of the Identity of the State," in Australian Outlook, Number 23 (April 1969).

Pham The Hung. Village Government in Vietnam, 968-1954. Ph.D. Dissertation, Southern Illinois University, 1972.

Sacks, I. Milton. "Restructuring the Government in South Vietnam," in Asian Survey, Volumes VII (August 1967).

Wurfel, David. "The Saigon Political Elite: Focus on Four Cabinets," in Asian Survey, Volume VII (August 1967).

B. CONSTITUTION AND LAW

Carley, Francis J. "The President in the Constitution of the Republic of Vietnam," in Pacific Affairs, Volume XXXIV (Summer 1961).

Devereux, Robert. "South Vietnam's New Constitutional Structure," in Asian Survey, Volume VIII (August 1968).

Falk, Richard A. The Vietnam War and International Law. Four Volumes. Princeton: Princeton University Press, 1967-1976.

_____, Kolko, Gabriel, and Lifton, Robert Jay (eds.). Crimes of War: After Songmy. New York: Random House, 1971.

Fall, Bernard B. "North Viet-Nam's New Constitution and Government," in Pacific Affairs, Volume 33 (September 1960).

Fforde, Adam. "Law and Socialist Agricultural Development in Vietnam: the Statute for APCs," in Review of Socialist Law, Volume X (1984).

Grant, J.A.C. "The Vietnamese Constitution of 1956," in American Political Science Review, Volume 52 (June 1958).

Ta Van Tai. "Protection of Women's Civil Rights in Traditional Vietnam: A Comparison of the Code of the Ly Dynasty (1428-1788) with Chinese Codes," Brian McKnight (ed.), in Law and the State in Traditional East Asia: Six Studies on the Sources of East Asian Law. Honolulu: University of Hawaii Press.

Yu Insun. Law and Family in Seventeenth and Eighteenth Century Vietnam. Ph.D. Dissertation, University of Michigan, 1978.

C. POLITICAL PARTIES

Anh Van and Roussel, Jacqueline. An Outline History of the Vietnam Workers' Party. Hanoi: Foreign Languages Press, 1970.

_____. Mouvements Nationaux et Lutte des Classes du Vietnam. Paris: Réamur, no date.

Cook, Megan. The Constitutionalist Party in Cochin China: The Years of Decline, 1930-1942. Clayton, Victoria: Monash University Center of Southeast Asian Studies, 1977.

Dabezies, Pierre. Forces Politiques au Vietnam. Thesis: University of Bordeaux, 1955.

Duiker, William J. The Comintern and Vietnamese Communism. Athens: Ohio University Southeast Asia Program, 1975.

_____. "The Revolutionary Youth League: Cradle of Communism in Vietnam," in China Quarterly, Number 53 (July-September 1972).

Hoang Van Dao. Viet Nam Quoc Dan Dang. Saigon: Khai Tri, 1970.

Huynh Kim Khanh. Vietnamese Communism, 1925-1945. Ithaca: Cornell University Press, 1982.

Nguyen Ngoc Huy. Political Parties in Vietnam. Vietnamese Council on Foreign Relations. Saigon, 1971.

Pike, Douglas. A History of Vietnamese Communism, 1925-1978. Stanford: Hoover Institution Press, 1978.

Rousset, Pierre. Le Parti Communiste Vietnamien. Paris: Maspero, 1975.

Sacks, I. Milton. Communism and Nationalism in Vietnam, 1918-1946. Ph.D. Dissertation, Yale University, 1960.

_____. "Marxism in Vietnam," in Frank Trager (ed.), Marxism in Southeast Asia. Stanford: Stanford University Press, 1959.

Scigliano, Robert G. "Political Parties in South Vietnam Under the Republic," in Pacific Affairs, Volume XXXIII (December 1960).

Smith, Ralph B. "Bui Quang Chieu and the Constitutionalist Party in French Cochin China," in Modern Asian Studies, Volume III (April 1969).

Thompson, Virginia and Adloff, Richard. The Left Wing in Southeast Asia. New York: William Sloane, 1950.

Tran Huy Lieu. Dang Thanh Nien. Hanoi: Su Hoc, 1961.

Turner, Robert F. Vietnamese Communism: Its Origins and Development. Stanford: Hoover Institution Press, 1975.

D. THE ARMED FORCES

Collins, Lawton. The Development and Training of the South Vietnamese Army, 1950-1972. Washington, D.C., 1975.

Pike, Douglas. PAVN: The People's Army of Vietnam. Novato: Presidio, 1986.

_____. "The People's Army of Vietnam," in Edward A. Olsen and Stephen Jurika (eds.), The Armed Forces in Contemporary Asian Societies. Boulder: Westview, 1986.

Tran Van Dinh. "The Vietnamese People's Army," in Indochina Chronology, Number 31 (February 28, 1974).

Turley, William S. Army, Party, and Society in the Democratic Republic of Vietnam. Ph.D. Dissertation, University of Washington, 1972.

E. BIOGRAPHIES AND MEMOIRS

Bao Dai. Le Dragon d'Annam. Paris: Plon, 1980.

Boudarel, Georges (tr.). Phan Boi Chau: Memoirs, in France-Asie, Number 22 (3rd-4th Trimestre, 1968).

Bouscaren, Anthony T. The Last of the Mandarins: Diem of Vietnam.
    Pittsburgh: Duquesne University Press, 1965.

Chack, Paul. Hoang Tham: Pirate. Paris: Editions de France,
    1933.

Chu Van Tan. Reminiscences on the Army for National Salvation
    (tr. Mai Elliott). Ithaca: Cornell University Data Paper, 1974.

Cuong De. Cuoc Doi Cach Mang Cuong De. Saigon, 1957.

Das, S.R. Mohan. Ho Chi Minh: Nationalist or Soviet Agent? Bombay:
    Democratic Research Service, 1951.

Fenn, Charles. Ho Chi Minh: A Biographical Introduction. London:
    Studio Vista, 1973.

Figueres, Leo, and Fourniau, Charles. Ho Chi Minh: Notre Camarade.
    Paris: Editions Sociales, 1970.

Fischer, Ruth. "Ho Chi Minh: Disciplined Communist," in Foreign
    Affairs, (October 1954).

Halberstam, David. Ho. New York: Random House, 1971.

Hoai Thanh et al. Uncle Ho. Hanoi: Foreign Languages Press, 1962.

Lacouture, Jean. Ho Chi Minh: A Political Biography. (Tr. Peter
    Wiles) New York: Random House, 1968.

Neumann-Hoditz, Reinhold. Portrait of Ho Chi Minh. New York:
    Herder, 1972.

Nguyen Cao Ky. Twenty Years and Twenty Days. New York:
    Stein & Day, 1976.

Nguyen Khac Huyen. Vision Accomplished? New York: Collier, 1971.

Nguyen Khanh Toan et al. Avec l'Oncle Ho. Hanoi: Foreign Langu-
    ages Press, 1972.

O'Neill, Robert. General Giap: Politician and Strategist. New York:
    Praeger, 1969.

Pham Van Dong et al. President Ho Chi Minh. Hanoi: Foreign
    Languages Press, 1960.

Rageau, Christiane P. Ho Chi Minh. Paris: Editions Universitaires,
    1970.

Sainteny, Jean. Face à Ho Chi Minh. Paris, 1970.

Sihanouk, Norodom. <u>My War with the CIA</u>. Baltimore, 1973.

Tran Dan Tien. <u>Glimpses of the Life of Ho Chi Minh</u>. Hanoi: Foreign Languages Press, 1958.

Truong Chinh. <u>President Ho Chi Minh</u>. Hanoi: Foreign Languages Press, 1966.

Warner, Denis. <u>The Last Confucian</u>. New York: Macmillan, 1963.

F. INTERNATIONAL POLITICS AND FOREIGN POLICY

Burchett, Wilfred. <u>The China Cambodia Vietnam Triangle</u>. New York: Vanguard, 1979.

Chanda, Nayan. <u>Brother Enemy: The War After the War</u>. New York Harcourt Brace Jovanovich, 1986.

Chang Pao-min. <u>The Sino-Vietnamese Territorial Dispute</u>. New York: Praeger, 1985.

Duiker, William J. <u>China and Vietnam: The Roots of Conflict</u>. Berkeley: University of California Institute of East Asian Studies, 1986.

Elliott, David W.P. (ed.). <u>The Third Indochina Conflict</u>. Boulder: Westview, 1981.

Evans, Grant and Rowley, Kelvin. <u>Red Brotherhood at War</u>. London: Verso, 1984.

Fifield, Russell. <u>The Diplomacy of Southeast Asia, 1945-1958</u>. New York: Harper & Row, 1958.

Lawson, Eugene K. <u>The Sino-Vietnamese Conflict</u>. New York: Praeger, 1984.

Pike, Douglas. <u>Vietnam and the Soviet Union: Anatomy of an Alliance</u>. Boulder: Westview, 1987.

Poole, Peter A. "Vietnam: Focus of Regional Conflict," in <u>Internationa Security Review</u>, Volume VII, Number 2 (Summer 1982).

Porter, Gareth. "Hanoi's Strategic Perspective and the Sino-Vietnamese Conflict," in <u>Pacific Affairs</u>, Volume LVII (Spring 1984).

Turley, William S. (ed.). <u>Confrontation or Coexistence: The Future of ASEAN-Vietnam Relations</u>. Bangkok: Institute of Security and International Studies, 1985.

_____ and Race, Jeffrey. "The Third Indochina War," in Foreign Policy, Number 38 (Spring 1980).

Van der Kroef, Justus. "The South China Sea: Competing Claims and Strategic Conflict," in International Security Review, Volume VII, Number 3 (Fall 1982).

G. COLLECTED WRITINGS

Fall, Bernard B. Ho Chi Minh on Revolution. New York: Praeger, 1960.

Ho Chi Minh. Prison Diary. Hanoi: Foreign Languages Press, 1966.

_____. Selected Works. Four Volumes. Hanoi: Foreign Languages Press, 1961-1962.

_____. Selected Writings. Hanoi: Foreign Languages Press, 1977.

_____. Ho Chi Minh Toan Tap (Complete Works of Ho Chi Minh). Eight Volumes. Hanoi: Su That, 1981- .

Le Duan. On the Right of Collective Mastery. Hanoi: Foreign Languages Press, 1980.

_____. Some Questions Concerning the International Tasks of Our Party. Peking: Foreign Languages Press, 1964.

_____. The Vietnamese Revolution: Fundamental Problems, Essential Tasks. New York: International Publishers, 1971.

Marr, David G. Reflections from Captivity: Phan Boi Chau and Ho Chi Minh. Athens: Ohio University Southeast Asia Translation Series, 1978.

Pham Van Dong. Some Cultural Problems. Hanoi: Foreign Languages Press, 1981.

Stettler, Russell (ed.). The Military Art of People's War. New York: Monthly Review Press, 1970.

Tran Van Dinh (ed.). This Nation and Socialism Are One: Selected Writings of Le Duan, 1976.

Truong Chinh. The August Revolution. Hanoi: Foreign Languages Press, 1958.

_____. Prime for Revolt. New York: Praeger, 1963.

_____. The Resistance Will Win. Hanoi: Foreign Languages Press, 1960.

_____. Selected Writings. Hanoi: Foreign Languages Press, 1977

_____ and Vo Nguyen Giap. The Peasant Question (1937-1938). (Tr. by Christine Pelzer White). Ithaca: Cornell University Southeast Asian Program Data Paper (January 1974).

Vo Nguyen Giap. Banner of People's War: The Party's Military Line. New York 1970.

_____. Big Victory, Great Task. New York: Praeger, 1968.

_____. Dien Bien Phu. Hanoi: Foreign Languages Press, 1974.

_____. People's War, People's Army. New York: Praeger, 1962.

III.   SOCIETY

A. ANTHROPOLOGY AND ETHNOGRAPHY

Cadière, Leopold M. "Vietnamese Ethnographic Papers," in Human Relations Area Files. New Haven, 1953.

Embree, John F. Ethnic Groups of Northern Southeast Asia. New Haven: Yale University Press, 1950.

Gourou, Pierre. The Peasant in the Tonkin Delta: A Study of Huma Geography. Human Relations Area Files. New Haven, no date.

Gregorson, Marilyn, J. "The Ethnic Minorities of Vietnam," in Southeast Asia: An International Quarterly, Volume II (Winter 1972).

Hickey, Gerald C. Free in the Forest. New Haven: Yale University Press, 1982.

_____. The Highland People of South Vietnam: Social and Economi Development. Santa Monica: RAND Corporation, 1967.

_____. Sons of the Mountains. New Haven: Yale University Press, 1982.

Janse, Olov R.T. The Peoples of French Indochina. Washington, D.C Smithsonian Institution, June 1944.

Kahin, George McT. "Minorities in the Democratic Republic of Vietnam," in Asian Survey, Volume XII (July 1972).

Kunstadter, Peter (ed.). Southeast Asian Tribes, Minorities, and Nations. Two Volumes. Princeton: Princeton University Press, 1967.

Le Bar, Frank M. et al. Ethnic Groups of Mainland Southeast Asia. Human Relations Area Files. New Haven, 1964.

Mole, Robert L. The Montagnards of South Vietnam. Tokyo: Tuttle, 1970.

Nguyen Khac Viet (ed.). Ethnographic Data. Vietnamese Studies, Number 32. Hanoi: Foreign Languages Press, 1972.

_____. Mountain Regions and National Minorities in the Democratic Republic of Vietnam. Vietnamese Studies, Number 15. Hanoi: Foreign Languages Press, 1968.

Provencher, Ronald. Mainland Southeast Asia: An Anthropological Perspective. Pacific Palasades: Goodyear, 1975.

Purcell, Victor W. The Chinese in Southeast Asia. London: Oxford University Press, 1951.

Schrock, Joan L. et al. (eds.). Minority Groups in the Republic of Vietnam. Washington, D.C.: Government Printing Office, 1967.

Stern, Lewis M. "The Overseas Chinese in the Socialist Republic of Vietnam," in Asian Survey, Volume 25 (May 1985).

B. ARCHEOLOGY

Davidson, Jeremy H.C.S. "Archeology in Northern Vietnam since 1954," in Ralph B. Smith and William Watson (eds.), Early Southeast Asia: Essays in Archeology, History, and Historical Geography. New York, 1979.

Janse, Olov R. Archeological Research in Indo-China. Cambridge: Harvard University Press, 1947.

Vietnamese Studies, Number 46. Archeological Data. Hanoi, no date.

C. EDUCATION

Anonymous. The Struggle Against Illiteracy in Vietnam. Hanoi: Foreign Languages Press, 1959.

Kelly, Gail P. "Colonial Schools in Vietnam: Policy and Practice." in Phillip G. Altbach and Gail P. Kelly (eds.), Education and Colonialism. New York: Longman's, 1978.

_____. Franco-Vietnamese Schools, 1918-1938. Ph.D. Dissertation, University of Wisconsin, 1975.

Pike, Edgar. "Problems of Education in Vietnam," in Wesley Fishel (ed.), Problems of Freedom: South Vietnam Since Independence. New York: Free Press of Glencoe, 1961.

Tongas, Gerard. "Indoctrination Replaces Education," in China Quarterly, Number 9 (January-March 1962).

Vietnamese Studies, Number 5. Education in the DRV. Hanoi: Foreign Languages Press, 1965.

_____, Number 30. General Education in the DRV. Hanoi: Foreign Language Press, 1971.

Vu Tam Ich. A Historical Survey of Educational Developments in Vietnam. Lexington, Ky., 1959.

Woodside, Alexander B. "Problems of Education in the Vietnamese and Chinese Revolutions," in Public Affairs (Winter 1976-1977).

D. RELIGION

Cadière, Leopold M. Croyances et Pratiques Religieueses des Viet-namiens. Saigon, 1958.

Dumoutier, Gustave. Annamese Religions (Translation of Les Cultes Annamities). Human Relations Area Files. New Haven, 1955.

Fall, Bernard B. "The Political-Religious Sects of Viet-Nam," in Pacific Affairs, Volume XXVIII (September 1955).

Gheddo, Pierre. The Cross and the Bo Tree: Catholics and Buddhi in Vietnam. New York: Twin Circle, 1970.

Gobron, Gabriel. History and Philosophy of Caodaism. (Tr. Pham Xuan Thai). Saigon: Tu Hai, 1950.

Hue-Tam Ho Tai. Millenarianism and Peasant Politics in Vietnam. Cambridge: Harvard University Press, 1983.

Landon, Kenneth. Southeast Asia: Crossroads of Religion. Chicago University of Chicago Press, 1949.

Marr, David G. "Church and State in Vietnam," in Indochina Issues, Number 47 (April 1987).

McLane, John R. "Archaic Movements and Revolution in Southern Vietnam." Norman Miller and Roderick Aya (eds.), National Liberation: Revolution in the Third World. New York: Free Press, 1971.

Oliver, Victor L. Cao Dai Spiritism: A Study of Religion in Vietnamese Society. Leiden: E.J. Brill, 1976.

Schecter, Jerrold. The New Face of Buddha: Buddhism and Policital
Power in Southeast Asia. New York: Coward, 1967.

Thich Nhat Hanh. Vietnam: Lotus in a Sea of Fire. New York:
Hill and Wang, 1967.

Tran Van Giap, "Le Bouddhisme en Annam des Origins au XIIIe
Siecle," in Bulletin de l'Ecole Française d'Extreme Orient, Volume
XXXII (1932).

Werner, Jayne. Cao Dai: The Politics of a Vietnamese Syncretic
Religious Movement. Ph.D. Dissertation. Cornell University, 1976.

_____. "Vietnamese Communism and Religious Sectarianism," in
William S. Turley (ed.), Vietnamese Communism in Comparative
Perspective. Boulder: Westview, 1980.

E. SOCIOLOGY

Cong Huyen Ton Nu Thi Nha Trang. The Traditional Roles of
Women as Reflected in Oral and Written Vietnamese Literature.
Ph.D. Dissertation, University of California, 1973.

Coulet, Georges. Les Sociétés Secrètes en Terre d'Annam. Paris:
Ardin, 1926.

Demarest, André. La Formation des Classes Sociales en Pays Annamite.
Lyon: Ferreol, 1935.

Desbarats, Jacqueline. "Population Relocation Programs in Socialist
Vietnam: Economic Rationale or Class Struggle," in Indochina
Reports (Singapore), April-June 1987.

Eisen-Bergman, Eileen. Women of Vietnam. San Francisco, 1975.

Goodman, Allan E. and Franks, Lawrence M. "The Dynamics of
Migration to Saigon, 1964-1972," in Pacific Affairs, Volume XLVIII
(Summer 1975).

Gourou, Pierre. Les Paysans du Delta Tonkinois: Etude de Géogra-
phie Humaine. Paris: Editions d'Art et d'Histoire, 1936.

Haines, David W. "Vietnamese Kinship, Gender Roles, and Societal
Diversity: Some Lessons from Research on Refugees," in Vietnam
Forum, Number 8 (Summer-Fall 1896).

Hendry, James B. The Small World of Khanh Hau. Chicago: Aldine,
1964.

Hickey, Gerald C. _Social Systems of Northern Vietnam_. Chicago: Chicago University Press, 1958.

_____. _Village in Vietnam_. New Haven: Yale University Press, 1964.

Hoskins, Marilyn W. and Shepherd, Eleanor. _Life in a Vietnamese Urban Quarter_. Carbondale: Southern Illinois University Press, 1971.

Jamieson, Neil. "The Traditional Family in Vietnam" and "The Traditional Village in Vietnam" in _Vietnam Forum_, Number 7 (Summer-Fall 1986) and Number 8 (Winter-Spring 1986)

Mai Thi Tu and Le Thi Nham Tuyet. _Women in Viet Nam_. Hanoi: Foreign Languages Press, 1978.

Ngo Vinh Long and Nguyen Hoi Chan. _Vietnamese Women in Society and Revolution_. Cambridge: Vietnamese Resource Center, 1974.

Popkin, Samuel. _The Rational Peasant: The Political Economy of Rural Society in Vietnam_. Berkeley: University of California Press, 1979.

Scott, James C. _The Moral Economy of the Peasant_. New Haven: Yale University Press, 1976.

Thrift, Nigel and Forbes, Dean. _The Price of War: Urbanization in Vietnam, 1954-1985_. London: Allen & Unwin, 1986.

IV. THE ECONOMY

A. AGRICULTURE

Bredo, William et al. "Vietnam: Politics, Land Reform and Development in the Countryside." _A Symposium in Asian Survey_, Volume X (August 1970).

_____. _Land Reform in Vietnam_. Menlo Park: Stanford Research Institute, 1968.

Chaliand, Gerard. _The Peasants of North Vietnam_. Middlesex: Penguin, 1969.

Fforde, Adam. "The Historical Background to Agricultural Collectivization in North Vietnam: The Changing Role of Corporate Economic Power." Discussion Paper Number 148 (November 1981). Birbeck College, London.

_____. Problems of Agricultural Development in North Vietnam. Ph.D. Dissertation, Cambridge University, 1982.

_____. "Specific Aspects of the Collectivization of Wet-rice Cultivation: Reflections on Vietnamese Experience." Discussion Paper Number 159 (July 1984). Birbeck College, London.

Gittinger, J. Price. "Communist Land Policy in North Vietnam," in Far Eastern Survey, Volume 28, No. 8 (August 1959).

_____. "Agrarian Reform," in Richard W. Lindholm (ed.), Viet-Nam: The First Five Years. East Lansing: Michigan State University, 1959.

Gosselin, Charles. L'Utilization du Sol en Indochine Française. Paris: P. Hartman, 1940.

Henry, Yves. Economie Agricole de l'Indochine. Hanoi, 1972.

Ladejinsky, Wolf, "Agrarian Reform in Vietnam," in Wesley Fishel (ed.), Problems of Freedom: South Vietnam Since Independence. New York: Free Press of Glencoe, 1961.

Moise, Edwin. Land Reform in China and Vietnam. Chapel Hill: University of North Carolina Press, 1983.

Nguyen Tien Hung. "The Red River, Its Dikes and North Viet-Nam's Economy," in Vietnam Bulletin, Volume 7 (September 1972).

Quang Truong. Agricultural Collectivization and Rural Development in Vietnam: A North/South Study (1955-1985). Amsterdam: Vrije Universiteit te Amsterdam, 1987.

Sanson, Robert L. The Economics of Insurgency in the Mekong Delta of Vietnam. Cambridge: MIT Press, 1970.

U.S. Department of Agriculture. Agricultural Economy of North Vietnam. Washington, D.C.: Government Printing Office, 1965.

Vickerman, Andrew. "The Fate of the Peasantry: Premature 'Transition to Socialism' in the Democratic Republic of Vietnam." New Haven: Yale University Southeast Asian Series, 1980.

Vietnamese Studies, Number 75 (New Series Number 5). The Mekong Delta: Social and Economic Conditions. Hanoi: Foreign Languages Press, 1984.

Wurfel, David. "Agrarian Reform in the Republic of Vietnam," in Far Eastern Survey, Volume XXVI, No 6 (June 1957).

Zasloff, Joseph J. "Rural Resettlement in South Vietnam," in Pacific Affairs, Volume XXXV (Winter 1962).

B. ECONOMIC DEVELOPMENT

Boarman, Patrick M. (ed.). The Economy of South Vietnam: A Beginning. Los Angeles: Center for International Business, 1973

_____. "Viet-Nam's Postwar Development: A Symposium," in Asian Survey, Volume XI (april 1971).

Bernard, Paul. Le Problème Economique Indochinois. Paris, 1934.

Dacy, Douglas C. Foreign Aid, War, and Economic Development: South Vietnam, 1955-1975. London: Cambridge University Press, 1986.

Kaye, William. "A Bowl of Rice Divided: The Economy of North Vietnam," in China Quarterly, Number 9 (January-March 1962).

Kimura, Tetsusabura. "Vietnam: Ten Years of Economic Struggle," in Asian Survey, Volume 26 (October 1986.

_____. Vietnam: International Relations and Economic Developmen Tokyo: Institute of Developing Economies, 1986.

Le Thanh Khoi. Socialisme et Développement au Vietnam. Paris, 1978

Lilienthal, David. "Postwar Development in Vietnam," in Foreign Affairs, Volume LXVII (January 1968).

Lindhold, Richard W. Economic Development Policy: With Emphasis on Vietnam. Eugene: University of Oregon Press, 1964.

Murray, Martin. The Development of Capitalism in Colonial Indochina (1870-1940). Berkeley: University of California Press, 1980.

Nguyen Anh Tuan. South Vietnamese Trial and Experience: A Challenge for Development. Athens: Ohio University Southeast Asian Monograph Series, 1980.

Nguyen Tien Hung. Economic Development of Socialist Vietnam, 1955-1980. New York: Praeger, 1977.

Robequain, Charles. The Economic Development of French Indochina. London: Oxford University Press, 1944.

Scigliano, Robert and Fox, Guy H. Technical Assistance to Vietnam: The Michigan State University Experience. New York: Praeger, 1965.

Shabad, Theodore. "Economic Development in North Vietnam," in Pacific Affairs Volume XXXI (March 1958).

Taylor, Milton C. "South Vietnam: Lavish Aid, Limited Progress," in Pacific Affairs, Volume XXXIV (Fall 1961).

Vo Nhan Tri. Croissance Economique de la République du Vietnam. Hanoi, 1967.

————. Socialist Vietnam's Economy, 1975-1985. Tokyo: Institute of Developing Economies, 1987.

Vu Van Thai. "Vietnam's Concept of Development," in Wesley Fishel (ed.), Problems of Freedom: South Vietnam Since Independence. New York: Free Press of Glencoe, 1961.

C. FINANCE

Dacy, Douglas C. The Fiscal System of Wartime Vietnam. Arlington, Va.: Institute for Defense Analysis, 1969.

Elliott, Vance L. "The Agricultural Marketing/Finance System of Vietnam," in Manuscript. Arlington, Va.: Institute for Defense Analysis, no date.

Emery, Robert F. The Financial Institutions of Southeast Asia. New York: Praeger, 1970.

Nguyen Tien Hung. An Analysis of Money and Credit in Vietnam, 1884-1962. Ph.D. Dissertation, University of Virginia, 1965.

Taylor, Milton C. The Taxation of Income in Viet-Nam. Saigon: Michigan State Advisory Group, 1959.

D. INDUSTRY

Moody, Dale L. The Manufacturing Sector in the Republic of Viet-Nam. Ph.D. Dissertation, University of Florida, 1975.

Morrison, Lawrence. "Industrial Development Efforts," in Richard Lindolm (ed.), Viet-Nam: The First Five Years. East Lansing: Michigan State University Press, 1959.

Trued, M.N. "South Vietnam's Industrial Development Center," in Pacific Affairs, Volume XXXIII (September 1960).

E. FOREIGN AID

Dacy, Douglas. Foreign Aid, War, and Economic Development: South Vietnam, 1955-1975. London: Cambridge University Press, 1986.

Fforde, Adam. "Economic Aspects of the Soviet Vietnamese Relationship: Their Role and Importance." Discussion Paper, Number 156 (April 1984). Birkbeck College, London.

V. CULTURE

A. ARCHITECTURE

Nguyen Nang Dac and Nguyen Quang Dac. Vietnamese Architecture. Vietnamese Information Service, Number 34. Washington, D.C.: Embassy of the Republic of Vietnam, 1970.

B. ART

Groslier, Bernard P. The Art of Indochina (Tr. George Lawrence). New York: Crown, 1962.

Hajzlar, J. The Art of Vietnam. Prague, 1973.

Rawson, Philip. The Art of Southeast Asia. New York: Praeger, 1967.

C. LANGUAGE AND LITERATURE

Dang Thai Mai. Van Tho Cach Mang Viet Nam: Dau The Ky XX. Hanoi: Van Hoc, 1964.

De Francis John. Colonialism and Language Policy in Vietnam. The Hague, 1977.

Durand, Maurice and Nguyen Tran Huan. Introduction a' la Litterature Vietnamienne. Paris: Maisonneuve et Larose, 1969.

Hoang Ngoc Thanh. The Social and Political Development of Vietnam as Seen Through the Modern Novel. Ph.D. Dissertation, University of Hawaii, 1969.

Huynh Sanh Thong. "Fishes and Fisherman: Females and Males in Vietnamese Folklore," in Vietnam Forum, Number 8 (Spring-Fall 1986).

_____. (ed.). The Heritage of Vietnamese Poetry. New Haven: Yale University Press, 1979.

Nguyen Khac Vien, et al. Anthologie de la Litterature Vietnamienne. Three Volumes. Hanoi: Foreign Languages Press, 1972-1975.

Nha Trang and Cong-Nguyen Ton-Nhi. Vietnamese Folklore: An
Introduction and Annotated Bibliography. Berkeley, 1970.

Shorto, H.L. "The Linguistic Protohistory of Mainland South East
Asia," in Ralph B. Smith and William Watson (eds.), Early South
East Asia: Essays in Archeology, History, and Historical Geo-
graphy. New York, 1979.

Vietnamese Studies. Glimpses of Vietnamese Classical Literature.
Hanoi: Foreign Languages Press, 1972.

Vo Phien. "Writers in South Vietnam, 1954-1975," in Vietnam Forum,
Number 7 (Winter-Spring 1986).

Vuong Loc. "Glimpses of the Evolution of the Vietnamese Language,"
in Vietnamese Studies, Number 40. Hanoi: Foreign Languages
Press, 1975.

Wolters, O.W., "A Stranger in His Own Land: Nguyen Trai's Sino-
Vietnamese Poems, Written during the Ming Occupation," in Vietnam Forum, Number 8 (Spring-Fall 1986).

D. MUSIC

Addiss, Stephen. "Theater Music of Vietnam," in Southeast Asia:
An International Quarterly, Volume I (Winter-Spring 1971).

_____. "Hat A Dao, the Sung Poetry of North Vietnam," in
Journal of the American Oriental Society, Volume 93 (January-
March 1973).

Dao Trong Tu, et al. Essays on Vietnamese Music. Hanoi: Red
River Publishing House, 1984.

Thai Van Kiem. "Panorama de la Musique Classique Vietnamienne des
Origines a nos Jours," in Bulletin de l'Ecole Française d'Extreme
Orient, Volume XXXIX (First Trimester, 1964).

Tran Van Khe. La Musique Vietnamienne Traditionalle. Paris:
Presses Universitaires de France, 1962.

Whiteside, Dale R. Traditions and Direction in the Music of Vietnam.
Museum of Anthropology, Number 28. Greeley: University of
North Colorado, 1971.

E. CUSTOMS

Crawford, Ann. Customs and Culture of Vietnam. Rutland, Vt.:
Tuttle, 1966.

Huard, Pierre A. and Durand, M. Connaissance du Vietnam. Paris: Ecole Française d'Extrême Orient, 1954.

Huynh Dinh. Vietnamese Cultural Patterns. Ph.D. Dissertation, Columbia University, 1962.

Nguyen Dinh Hoa, (ed.). Some Aspects of Vietnamese Culture. Carbondale: Southern Illinois University, 1972.

Nguyen Khac Kham. Celebrations of Rice Culture in Viet-Nam. Saigon: Vietnamese Council on Foreign Relations, no date.

_____. Introduction to Vietnamese Culture. Saigon: Vietnamese Culture Series, no date.

VI. OFFICIAL DOCUMENTS

A. THE COLONIAL PERIOD

Doumer, Paul. Situation de l'Indochine, 1897-1901. Hanoi: Schneider, 1902.

Government-Generale de l'Indochine. Contribution à l'Histoire des Mouvements Politiques de l'Indochine Française. Five Volumes.

B. THE VIETNAM WAR

Doumer, Paul. Declassified Documents Reference Service. Washington D.C.: Carrollton Press, 1976.

_____. A Party Account of the Situation in the Nam Bo Region of South Vietnam from 1954-1960. Captured document, no date.

_____. Pentagon Papers. (Senator Gravel Edition). Four Volumes. Boston: Beacon Press, 1971.

_____. South Vietnamese National Liberation Front: Documents. South Vietnam: Liberation Publishing House, 1968.

Socialist Republic of Vietnam. Vietnam: The Anti-U.S. Resistance War for National Salvation, 1945-1975. War Experiences Recaptulation Committee of the High Level Military Institute, 1980.

U.S. Department of Defense. United States-Vietnam Relations, 1945-1967. Twelve Volumes. Washington, D.C.: Government Printing Office, 1971.

U.S. Department of State. <u>Aggression from the North: The Record of North Vietnam's Campaign to Conquer South Vietnam</u>. Washington, D.C.: Government Printing Office, 1961.

_____. <u>Foreign Relations of the United States</u>.

_____. <u>A Threat to the Peace: North Viet-Nam's Effort to Conquer South Viet-Nam</u>. Washington, D.C.: Government Printing Office, 1965.

United States Information Service. <u>Viet-Nam Documents and Research Notes</u>. 117 Volumes. Saigon: U.S. Information Service, 1967-1972.

Indochina Archives. <u>The History of the Vietnam War</u>. Berkeley: University of California.

C. THE POSTWAR PERIOD

Democratic Kampuchea. <u>Black Paper: Facts and Evidences of the Acts of Aggression and Annexation of Vietnam against Kampuchea</u>. Ministry of Foreign Affairs, 1978.

People's Republic of Kampuchea. <u>Undeclared War against the People's Republic of Kampuchea</u>. Phnom Penh: Ministry of Foreign Affairs, 1985.

Socialist Republic of Vietnam. <u>The Truth about Vietnamo-Chinese Relations over the Past Thirty Years</u>. Hanoi: Ministry of Foreign Affairs, 1979.

VII. BIBLIOGRAPHIES

Chen, J.H.M. <u>Vietnam: A Comprehensive Bibliography</u>. Metuchen, N.J.: Scarecrow, 1973.

Cotter, Michael. <u>Vietnam: A Guide to Reference Sources</u>. Boston: Hall, 1977.

Embree, John F. and Dotson, B.O. <u>Bibliography of the Peoples and Cultures of Mainland South-East Asia</u>. New Haven: Yale University Press, 1950.

Hobbs, Cecil C., <u>et al</u>. <u>Indochina: A Bibliography of the Land and People</u>. Washington, D.C., Library of Congress, 1950.

Jumper, Roy, and Nguyen Thi Hue. <u>Bibliography of the Political</u>

and Administrative History of Viet-Nam, 1802-1962. Michigan
State University Advisory Group, 1962.

Leitenberg, Milton. The Wars in Vietnam, Cambodia and Laos, 1945-
1982: A Bibliographic Guide. Santa Barbara, ABC-Clio, 1984.

Phan Thien Chau. Vietnamese Communism: A Research Bibliography
Westport, Conn: Greenwood, 1975.

Sugnet, Christopher L., and Hickey, John T. Vietnam War Bibliography. Lexington, Mass.: D.C. Heath, 1983.

Whitfield, Danny J. Historical and Cultural Dictionary of Vietnam.
Metuchen, N.J.: Scarecrow Press, 1976.

VIII.   STATISTICAL COMPLIATIONS

Annuaire Statistique de l'Indochine, Various Years, Hanoi.
Socialist Republic of Vietnam. Basic Data. Hanoi: Foreign
Languages Press, 1978.
Republic of Vietnam. Vietnam Statistical Yearbook, 1971.
Saigon, 1972.

Appendix I

A BRIEF OUTLINE HISTORY OF VIETNAM

I. Prehistory (dates are approximate)

Paleolithic Era (? -10,000 B.C.)
  Mount Do Culture
  Son Vi Culture (? -9,000 B.C.)
Mesolithic Era
  Hoa Binh Culture (9,000-7,000 B.C.)
Neolithic Era
  Bac Son Culture (7,000-3,000 B.C.)
Bronze Age
  Phung Nguyen Culture (2,500 B.C.-1,500 B.C.)
  Dong Son Culture (1,600 B.C.-2nd century B.C.)

II. Ancient History

Kingdom of Van Lang (Hung Kings) (2,000 B.C.-258 B.C.)
  Capital: Phong Chau
Kingdom of Au Lac (258 B.C.-207 B.C.) (Founder: An Duong
  Vuong)
  Capital: Co Loa
Kingdom of Nam Viet (207 B.C.-111 B.C.) (Founder: Trieu Da)
  Capital: Canton (Guangzhou)

III. The Period of Chinese Rule

Western Han and Hsin dynasties (111 B.C.-A.D. 23)
Eastern Han (A.D. 23-39)
Trung Sisters Rebellion (A.D. 39-43)
Eastern Han (A.D. 43-220)
Three Kingdoms (A.D. 221-263)
Western Chin (A.D. 265-316)
Eastern Chin (A.D. 317-419)
Southern Dynasties (A.D. 420-589)
Sui (A.D. 589-618)
T'ang (A.D. 618-544)

Early Ly Dynasty (A.D. 544-545) (Founder: Ly Bi)
   Kingdom: Van Xuan Capital: Gia Ninh
T'ang (A.D. 545-907)
Five Dynasties Period (A.D. 907-939)

IV. The Period of Independence

Ngo Dynasty (A.D. 939-965) (Founder: Ngo Quyen)
   Kingdom: Nam Viet Capital: Co Loa
Period of Twelve Warlords (A.D. 965-968)
Dinh Dynasty (A.D. 968-980) (Founder: Dinh Bo Linh)
   Kingdom: Dai Co Viet Capital: Hoa Lu
Early Le Dynasty (A.D. 980-1009) (Founder: Le Hoan)
   Kingdom: Dai Co Viet Capital: Hoa Lu
Ly Dynasty (A.D. 1009-1225) (Founder: Ly Cong Uan)
   Kingdom: Dai Co Viet (1009-1054); Dai Viet (1054-1225)
      Capital: Thang Long (Hanoi)
Tran Dynasty (A.D. 1225-1400) (Founder: Tran Thu Do)
   Kingdom: Dai Viet Capital: Thang Long (Hanoi)
Ho Dynasty (A.D. 1400-1407) (Founder: Ho Quy Ly)
   Kingdom: Dai Ngu Capital: Tay Do
Period of Chinese Domination (A.D. 1407-1428)
   Name: An Nam Capital: Dong Quan (Hanoi)
Later Le Dynasty (A.D. 1428-1527) (A.D. 1592-1788) (Founder:
Le Loi)
   Kingdom: Dai Viet Capital: Thang Long (Hanoi)
Mac Dynasty (A.D. 1527-1592) (Founder: Mac Dang Dung)
   Kingdom: Dai Viet Capital: Dong Kinh (Hanoi)
Tay Son Dynasty (A.D. 1788-1802) (Founder: Nguyen Hue)
   Kingdom: Dai Viet Capital: Hue and Thang Long (Hanoi)
Nguyen Dynasty (A.D. 1802-1945) (Founder: Nguyen Anh)
   Kingdom: Viet Nam Capital: Hue

V. Period of French Colonial Rule

Indochinese Union (1884-1945)
   Protectorates of Tonkin and Annam; Colony of Cochin China
   Capital: Hanoi
Democratic Republic of Vietnam (1945-1976) (Founder: Ho Chi
Minh)
   Capital: Hanoi
Autonomous Republic of Cochin China (1946-1949) (Founder: None
   Capital: Saigon
Associated State of Vietnam (1949-1954) (Founder: Bao Dai)
   Capital: Saigon
Republic of Vietnam (1955-1975) (Founder: Ngo Dinh Diem)
   Capital: Saigon
Socialist Republic of Vietnam (1976-present) (Founder: None)
   Capital: Hanoi

Appendix II

A BRIEF CHRONOLOGY OF EVENTS
IN VIETNAMESE HISTORY

?-10,000 B.C.	Paleolithic Era
9,000-7,000 B.C.	Hoa Binh Culture
7,000-3,000 B.C.	Bac Son Culture
2,500-1,500 B.C.	Phung Nguyen Culture
2,000-258 B.C.	Kingdom of Van Lang (Hung Kings)
258-207 B.C.	Kingdom of Au Lac
207 B.C.	Foundation of Kingdom of Nam Viet by Trieu Da
111 B.C.	Conquest of Nam Viet by Han Dynasty in China
39 A.D.	Revolt of Trung Sisters against Chinese rule
43	Suppression of Trung Sisters Revolt by Ma Yuan
192	Foundation of Kingdom of Lam Ap, predecessor of the state of Champa, in Central Vietnam
248	Revolt by followers of Lady Trieu (Ba Trieu)
542-545	Ly Bi Rebellion against Chinese rule
722	Mai Thuc Loan Rebellion
939	Restoration of Vietnamese Independence by Ngo Quyen after first battle of Bach Dang
939	Foundation of Ngo Dynasty (939-965)

939	Foundation of Ngo Dynasty (939–965)
965–968	Period of the Twelve Warlords
968	Foundation of the Dinh Dynasty (968–980)
980	Foundation of the Le Dynasty (980–1009) by Le Hoan
982	Vietnamese seizure of Indrapura, capital of Champa moves its capital to Vijaya, further to the south
1009	Foundation of Ly Dynasty (1009–1225) by Ly Thai To
1010	Transfer of capital from Hoa Lu to Dai La (now known as Hanoi)
1070	Construction of the Temple of Literature in Hanoi
1225	Foundation of Tran Dynasty (1225–1400) by Tran Thu Do
1257	First Mongol Attack on Vietnam
1284	Second Mongol Attack on Vietnam
1287	Defeat of Mongols at second battle of Bach Dang
1400	Foundation of Ho Dynasty (1400–1407) by Ho Quy Ly
1407	Conquest of Kingdom of Dai Viet by Ming Dynasty in China
1418	Opening of Le Loi Revolt against Chinese rule
1428	Foundation of Le Dynasty (1428–1788) by Le Loi
1471	Seizure of Vijaya by Vietnamese forces. Kingdom of Champa becomes a Vietnamese protectorate
1527	Usurpation of power by Mac Dynasty (1527–1592)
1592	Restoration of Le Dynasty in Hanoi (then known as Thang Long)

1627	Civil War between the Trinh and the Nguyen (1627-1672)
1627	Arrival of Alexander of Rhodes in Hanoi
1672	Seizure of Gia Dinh (Saigon) by Vietnamese as the latter expand towards Mekong Delta
1692	Champa annexed to Vietnam
1771	Eruption of Tay Son Rebellion
1786	Tay Son armies enter Hanoi
1787	Treaty of Versailles between Nguyen Anh, Nguyen pretender to the Vietnamese throne, and Kingdom of France
1788	Defeat of the Trinh and foundation of Tay Son Dynasty (1788-1802) by Nguyen Hue
1802	Final defeat of the Tay Son and foundation of Nguyen Dynasty (1802-1945) by Nguyen Anh
1807	Establishment of Vietnamese protectorate over Cambodia
1833	Le Van Khoi Revolt in South Vietnam (1833-1835)
1846	Establishment of joint Vietnam-Thai protectorate over Cambodia
1858	French and Spanish fleet attack Vietnam in Da Nang Harbor
1859	French conquest of Mekong Delta territories
1861	Battle of Ky Hoa, near present-day Ho Chi Minh City (Saigon)
1862	Treaty of Saigon, ceding three provinces in South Vietnam to France
1863	Declaration of French protectorate over Cambodia
1867	Conquest of three remaining provinces in South Vietnam by the French

1873	French adventurer Francis Garnier killed near Hanoi by Black Flags
1874	Treaty of 1874 (Philaster Treaty) recognizing French sovereignty over Cochin China
1882	French captain Rivière seizes Hanoi
1883	Harmand Treaty establishing French protectorate over North and Central Vietnam
1884	First Treaty of Tientsin between France and Manchu Empire (May)
1884	Treaty of Protectorate (Patenotre Treaty), confirming French protectorate over Annam (Central Vietnam) and Tonkin (North Vietnam) (June)
1885	Flight of Emperor Ham Nghi from Imperial Court at Hue and opening of Can Vuong Movement (July)
1887	Indochinese Union established over Vietnam and Cambodia
1888	Ham Nghi captured and exiled to Algeria (November)
1896	Dissolution of Can Vuong Movement
1904	Foundation of Modernization Society by Phan Boi Chau
1905	Foundation of Dong Du (Study in the East) Movement
1906	Foundation of Dong Kinh Nghia Thuc (Hanoi Free School) in Hanoi
1912	Foundation of Vietnamese Restoration Society by Phan Boi Chau
1915	Abolition of Civil Service Examinations in Tonkin
1917	Thai Nguyen Rebellion in North Vietnam
1918	Abolition of Civil Service Examinations in Annam

1919	Ho Chi Minh (then known as Nguyen Ai Quoc) presents petition demanding Vietnamese independence to Versailles Peace Conference
1919	Foundation of Cao Dai religion by Ngo Van Chieu
1924	Ho Chi Minh arrives in Canton from Moscow
1925	Formation of Vietnamese Revolutionary Youth League in Canton
	Seizure of Phan Boi Chau by French police in Shanghai (June). Deported to Vietnam, he is placed on trial in November and sent to house arrest in Hue.
1927	Foundation of Vietnamese Nationalist Party (VNQDD) by Nguyen Thai Hoc in Hanoi
1929	National Congress of Revolutionary Youth League in Hong Kong (May)
1930	Unification of radical factions into a single Vietnamese Communist Party (VCP) in Hong Kong (February)
	Yen Bay Revolt, led by VNQDD (February)
	Beginning of Nghe-Tinh Revolt in Central Vietnam (May)
	Meeting of VCP Central Committee adopts new name of Indochinese Communist Party (ICP) (October)
1931	Seizure of ICP leadership by the French (April)
	Ho Chi Minh arrested in Hong Kong
	Suppression of Nghe-Tinh Soviets (July-August)
1932	Emperor Bao Dai returns from schooling in France and assumes limited imperial powers in Annam. (September)
1933	Ho Chi Minh is released from prison in Hong Kong and returns to the Soviet Union
1935	The Indochinese Communist Party holds its first national congress at Macao (March)

1936	Rise of the Popular Front in France
1938	Ho Chi Minh leaves the Soviet Union and travels to China
1939	Foundation of the Hoa Hao religious movement in Cochin China
	Outbreak of war in Europe. Indochinese Communist Party driven underground (September)
1940	Franco-Japanese Treaty granting Japan military facilities in northern Indochina (August)
	Bac Son uprising in northern Tonkin (September-October)
	Nam Bo uprising in Cochin China (November)
1941	Eighth Plenum (Pac Bo Plenum) of the Indochinese Communist Party sets up the League for the Independence of Vietnam (popularly known as the Vietminh) (May)
1942	Ho Chi Minh arrested in South China (August)
	Foundation of Vietnamese Revolutionary League (Dong Minh Hoi) in South China (August)
1943	Ho Chi Minh is released from prison and joins the Dong Minh Hoi (September)
1944	Creation of the first Armed Propaganda Brigades by the Indochinese Communist Party (December)
1945	Japanese coup d'etat abolishes French administration in Indochina and offers emperor Bao Dai independence under Japanese protection. (March 9)
	Vietnamese puppet government formed under Prime Minister Tran Trong Kim (April)
	Armed Propaganda Brigades are merged with National Salvation Army into Vietnamese Liberation Army (May)
	Ho Chi Minh returns from China, sets up Communist Party headquarters at Tan Trao (May)

Indochinese Communist Party conference is
held at Tan Trao and decides on national
insurrection (August 13-15)

Japan surrenders (August 14)

National Congress of the Vietminh appeals
for general uprising throughout Vietnam and
declares Ho Chi Minh president of a provisional republic of Vietnam (August 16)

General uprising in Hanoi (August 19)

Vietminh forces seize imperial capital of Hue
(August 23)

Uprising of communist and nationalist forces
allied in Committee for the South in Saigon
(August 25)

Emperor Bao Dai abdicates and accepts position as supreme political adviser to new
provisional republic (August 30)

Ho Chi Minh declares Vietnamese independence
in Hanoi (September 2)

Chinese occupation forces arrive in Hanoi
as part of Potsdam agreement (September 9)

British occupation forces begin to arrive in
Saigon (September 13)

Committee for the South orders general strike
in Saigon (September 17)

British commander announces martial law in
Saigon (September 21)

French military forces begin to arrive in
South Vietnam (October)

Vietminh forces retreat from Saigon and begin
guerrilla operations against French administration in Cochin China (October 16)

Indochinese Communist Party dissolved and
replaced by an Association of Marxist Studies
(November 11)

Agreement between communist and nationalist

parties on formation of a coalition government in Hanoi. Ho Chi Minh is selected as president of the Democratic Republic of Vietnam (DRV)

1946   Provisional coalition government takes office in Hanoi (January 1)

National elections are held throughout the North for election of a National Assembly (January 6)

Sino-French Agreement on withdrawal of Chinese troops from North Vietnam. (February 28)

Signing of preliminary Ho-Sainteny Agreement creating "free state" of Vietnam and calling for a referendum in Cochin China (March 6)

Dalat Conference between prepresentatives of France and DRV. The conference fails to resolve issues between the two governments (April 18-May 11)

Formation of Republic of Cochin China by pro-French elements in South Vietnam (June 1)

Fontainebleau Conference between representatives of France and the DRV held near Paris (July 6-September 10)

Ho Chi Minh signs modus vivendi in Paris and returns to Hanoi (September 14)

National Assembly of the DRV convenes and reorganizes government without participation of nationalist elements (October 28)

National Assembly approves adoption of first Constitution of the DRV (November 8)

Haiphong incident occurs as French ships bombard native quarter in Haiphong (November 20)

Vietminh attacks on French installations in North Vietnam marks beginning of Franco-Vietminh conflict. Vietminh forces flee to rural areas to reorganize for guerrilla war (December 19)

1947
French scholar Paul Mus meets with Ho Chi Minh, who refuses to accept French terms for an end of the conflict (May)

First Ha Long Bay Agreement reached between ex-Emperor Bao Dai and French High Commissioner Emile Bollaert in Gulf of Tonkin. Later Bao Dai denounces the agreement as providing too little independence for projected new state of Vietnam (December 7)

1948
Second Ha Long Bay Agreement between Bao Dai and French representatives. France recognizes the independence of a provisional central government formed in May, but retains control over foreign affairs and defense. Other functions are to be discussed at a future conference (June 5)

Bao Dai denounces Second Ha Long Bay Agreement as inadequate (July)

1949
Elysée Agreement signed between representatives of France and new Associated State of Vietnam. The new state has many of the attributes of independence, but France retains control of foreign relations and national defense and Vietnam enters the French Union (March 8)

Bao Dai assumes office of Head of State of the new Associated State of Vietnam (June 13)

Official establishment of the Associated State of Vietnam (July 1)

1950
The new People's Republic of China (PRC) grants diplomatic recognition to the DRV (January 18)

The Soviet Union officially recognizes the independence of the DRV (January 25)

The United States officially recognizes the independence of the Associated State of Vietnam. Great Britain follows suit on the 7th (February 4)

France requests U.S. aid in fighting the Vietminh insurgency movement (February 16)

President Harry S Truman approves US$ 15 million in military aid to the French in Indochina (May 1)

U.S. announces intention to set up economic aid mission in the Associated States of Indochina (Vietnam, Laos and Cambodia) (May 25)

Opening of Korean War (June 25)

Opening of Pau negotiations to transfer sovereignty to Vietnam (June 29)

President Truman announces speedup of U.S. military aid to Indochina (July 19)

Vietminh border offensive destroys French outposts along Chinese border (September–November)

1951   Abortive Vietminh general offensive on fringes of Red River Delta (January–May)

Second National Congress of the Communist Party (now renamed the Vietnamese Workers' Party VWP) held in Tuyen Quang province (February 11–19)

1952   Vietminh offensive in the mountains north of Hanoi forces French evacuation of much of the border area (November)

1953   Vietminh offensive in northern Laos (April)

Appointment of General Henri Navarre as commander-in-chief of French forces in Indochina and adoption of the Navarre Plan to win the Franco-Vietminh War (May)

French forces occupy military outpost at Dien Bien Phu to hinder Vietminh movement into Laos (November 20)

In interview with Swedish reporter, Ho Chi Minh offers to negotiate an end to the war (November 29)

1954   Conference among Great Powers held in Berlin agrees to discuss a settlement of the Indochina War at a conference to be convened at Geneva in May (January–February)

Vietminh siege of French outpost of Dien Bien Phu. The post falls to attacking forces on May 6th (March 13-May 6)

Opening of discussions on Indochina at Geneva (May 7)

Ngo Dinh Diem appointed prime minister of the Associated State of Vietnam (July 7)

Geneva Conference concludes with military agreement on a cease-fire and a political protocol calling for national elections in 1956 (July 21)

Creation of Southeast Asia Treaty Organization in Manila (September 8)

Return of Ho Chi Minh's government to Hanoi (October)

President Eisenhower promises aid to South Vietnam (October 1)

1955	Ngo Dinh Diem refuses to hold consultations on elections with representations of the DRV (July)

Ngo Dinh Diem defeats Bao Dai in a referendum in South Vietnam (October 23)

Formation of Republic of Vietnam with its capital in Saigon (October 26)

1955-1956	Land reform program in the Democratic Republic of Vietnam redistributes land holdings throughout the country. Excesses committed against individuals lead to the firing of several government officials and the demotion of Party General Secretary Truong Chinh
1957-1958	Discontent rises among various elements of the population in South Vietnam against the policies of President Ngo Dinh Diem
1958-1960	Adoption by DRV of three-year plan launches collectivization in the North
1959	Central Committee of Vietnamese Workers' Party adopts program to resume revolutionary war in South Vietnam (January)

Adoption of the second constitution of the DRV in Hanoi (December 31)

1960   Third National Congress of the Vietnamese Workers' Party held in Hanoi. The congress decides to escalate the revolutionary struggle in South Vietnam. Le Duan is elected first secretary of the Party (September 5-10)

Abortive coup against President Ngo Dinh Diem in Saigon (November 11)

Formation of the National Front for the Liberation of South Vietnam (NLF) (December 20)

1961   President John F. Kennedy promises continued U.S. aid to the Republic of Vietnam (May 8)

Vice President Lyndon Johnson visits South Vietnam (May)

General Maxwell Taylor visits South Vietnam and reports to the President (October)

1963   Buddhist demonstrations lead to government repression in South Vietnam (May-June)

Dissident military officers contact Kennedy administration with plans to overthrow Diem regime (Summer)

President Diem overthrown and killed in Saigon A Military Revolutionary Council is formed to continue the struggle against the revolutionary movement (November 1)

Central Committee of the VWP decides to escalate the struggle in the South (December)

1964   General Nguyen Khanh seizes power in Saigon (January)

First Tonkin Gulf Incident (August 2)

Congress passes Tonkin Gulf Resolution (August 7)

Deterioration of the political situation in South Vietnam as several governments succeed each other in Saigon. Revolutionary forces take advantage of the situation to extend their control over rural areas (Fall)

1965

Attack by revolutionary forces on U.S. base
at Pleiku provides Johnson Administration with a
pretext to launch bombing campaign on North
Vietnam and begin dispatch of U.S. combat
troops to South Vietnam (February 7)

Young Turks under Nguyen Cao Ky and Nguyen
Van Thieu seize control of government in
Saigon (June)

Battle of Ia Drang Valley pits U.S. troops
against revolutionary forces in the south
for the first time in sustained battle (October)

1966

Honolulu Conference between U.S. and South
Vietnamese representatives on war strategy.
Saigon regime agrees to seek political stability
in the South (February)

Election of a Constituent Assembly in South
Vietnam (September)

1967

U.S. and South Vietnamese forces cooperate
in Operation Cedar Falls to destroy revolutionary emplacements in the Iron Triangle
(January)

New Constitution of the Republic of Vietnam
approved by the National Assembly (April)

In national elections held in South Vietnam,
Nguyen Van Thieu is elected president of the
RVN (September)

1968

Communist-led forces launch Tet Offensive
throughout South Vietnam. Heavy fighting in
Saigon, in Hue, and along the Demilitarized
Zone where the U.S. firebase is under heavy
attack for several weeks (February)

The United States and the DRV agree to hold
peace talks in Paris (May)

1969

Peace talks open in Paris (January)

Formation of the Provisional Government of
the Republic of South Vietnam (PRG) under the
guidance of the DRV (June)

1970

U.S. and South Vietnamese forces invade
Cambodia in an effort to eliminate the

sanctuaries. Demonstrations against the war mount in the United States (April)

1971   President Nguyen Van Thieu re-elected president of South Vietnam (October 3)

1972   North Vietnamese forces launch Easter Offensive in South Vietnam (March-April)

President Nixon approves "Christmas bombing" of North Vietnam (December)

1973   Paris Agreement signed, ending direct U.S. participation in the war (January 27)

1974   As Paris Agreement breaks down, Party leadership in the DRV undertakes policy review and decides to launch a major military offensiv in South Vietnam the following year (Septembe October)

1975   Communist forces launch general offensive designed to liberate South Vietnam from the Saigon regime (January-April)

Nguyen Van Thieu resigns as president of the RVN and is replaced by Tran Van Huong. The latter gives way to Duong Van Minh on th 27th (April 21)

Communist forces occupy Saigon and accept surrender of Duong Van Minh (April 30)

Border clashes (Spring 1975-Fall 1978) take place between Vietnam and Cambodia. The new Indochina government of Democratic Kampuchea charges Hanoi with seeking to dominate Indochina

1976   Elections are held throughout Vietnam to creat a new National Assembly for the entire countr (April)

Announcement of the creation of a new Socialis Republic of Vietnam (SRV), uniting North and South into a single country (July 2)

Fourth National Congress of the Communist Party held in Hanoi. The name of the Party is changed to Vietnamese Communist Party (VCP)(December 4-20)

1978   Government announces the nationalization of
             all private manufacturing and commercial
             enterprises above the family level through-
             out the SRV (March 17)

             Refugees, many of them overseas Chinese,
             begin to flee Vietnam. China accuses the SRV
             of mistreating its Chinese residents and cuts
             off economic aid to Vietnam (May)

             The SRV signs a Treaty of Friendship and
             Cooperation with the Soviet Union (November 3)

             Vietnamese military forces invade neighboring
             Democratic Kampuchea. Phnom Penh is occu-
             pied on January 7, 1979 and a new pro-
             Vietnamese government is established in Kam-
             puchea, entitled the People's Republic of
             Kampuchea (PRK) (December 25)

1979   Military forces of the PRC cross the border
             in a brief but bitter attack on Vietnam. With-
             drawal of Chinese forces begins in mid-March
             (February 17)

             Peace talks between China and Vietnam begin,
             but the two sides are unable to agree on a
             settlement (April)

1980   The SRV promulgates a new constitution, the
             third since the declaration of independence in
             1945. The new charter calls for a rapid
             advance to a fully socialist society (December 18)

1982   Fifth National Congress of the VCP held in
             Hanoi. The Congress approves a compromise
             program calling for a cautious advance to
             socialism (March 27-31)

             Formation by rebel groups of a Coalition
             Government of Democratic Kampuchea to force
             the withdrawal of Vietnamese occupation forces
             from Kampuchea (June)

1986   General Secretary Le Duan dies in Hanoi. He
             is replaced by Politburo member Turong Chinh
             (July 9)

             Sixth National Congress of the VCP held in Hanoi.
             Truong Chinh and other veteran members of the

party are dismissed from the Politburo and Ng
yen Van Linh is elected General Secretary
(December 15-19)

1987   Truong Chinh and Pham Van Dong resign
                       as Chief of State and Prime Minister and
                       are replaced by Vo Chi Cong and Pham Hung
                       (June)

Appendix III

TABLES

A. POPULATION OF VIETNAM (Yearly estimates)

1802 4 million

1840 5 million

1880 7 million

1926 16.3 million (Tonkin 6.6 million; Annam 5.5 million; Cochin China; 4 million)

1936 18.6 million (Tonkin 7.8 million: Annam: 5.6 million; Cochin China 4.6 million)

1945 25 million (North 14 million; South 11 million)

1960 30 million (North 16 million; South 14 million)

1970 38.3 million (North 21.3 million; South 17 million)

1974 44.3 million (North 23.8 million; South 20.5 million) (DRV estimate)
46.7 million (North 24 million; South 22.7 million) (US estimate)

1976 49 million (North 24.6 million; South 24.4 million) (SRV estimate)
49.1 million (North 26 million; South 24.3 million) (US estimate)

1979 52.7 million (North 27.4 million; South 25.3 million) (SRV estimate)
52.5 million (North 26 million; South 26.5 million) (US estimate)

1980 53.9 million (North 28 million; South 25.9 million) (SRV estimate)

53.6 million (North 26.5 million; South 27.1 million)
(US estimate)

1981   54.9 million (North 28.6 million; South 26.3 million)
(SRV estimate)
54.9 million (North 27 million; South 27.9 million) (US
estimate)

1982   56.2 million (North 29.2 million; South 27 million)
(SRV estimate)
56.2 million (North 27.6 million; South 28.6 million)
(US estimate)

1983   57.6 million (North 28.2 million; South 29.4 million)
(US estimate)

1986   62 million (SRV estimate)

Sources: Vietnam Courier (October 1983); U.S. Department of Commerce, Bureau of the Census, The Population of Vietnam, Series
P-95, No. 77 (Issued October 1985)

B. POPULATION DISTRIBUTION ACCORDING TO PROVINCE (October 1, 1979, Census)

Red River Delta provinces	Population	Area (in square kilometer
Hanoi municipality	17,502,748	2,139
Thai Binh province	1,506,235	2,495
Haiphong municipality	1,279,067	1,515
Hai Hung province	2,145,662	2,555
Ha Nam Ninh province	2,781,409	3,763
Vinh Phu province	1,488,348	4,626
Ha Son Binh province	1,537,190	5,978
Thanh Hoa province	2,532,261	11,138

Mekong Delta provinces	Population	Area (in square kilometer
Ho Chi Minh municipality	3,419,978	2,029
Tien Giang province	1,264,498	2,377
Ben Tre province	1,041,838	2,225
An Giang province	1,532,362	3,493
Cuu Long province	1,504,215	3,854
Hau Giang province	2,232,891	6,126
Dong Thap province	1,182,787	3,391
Long An province	957,264	4,355
Minh Hai province	1,219,595	7,697
Kien Giang province	994,673	6,358

Central coastal provinces

Vung Tau-Con Dao special zone	91,610	279
Nghia Binh province	2,095,354	11,900
Dong Nai province	1,304,799	7,578
Nghe Tinh province	3,111,989	22,502
Quang Nam-Da Nang province	1,529,520	11,989
Phu Khanh province	1,188,637	9,804
Binh Tri Thien province	1,901,713	18,340
Thuan Hai province	938,255	11,374

Northern upland and border provinces

Quang Ninh province	750,055	5,938
Bac Thai province	815,105	6,530
Lang Son province	484,657	8,187
Ha Tuyen province	782,453	13,518
Cao Bang province	479,823	8,445
Hoang Lien Son province	778,217	14,852
Son La province	487,793	14,468
Lai Chau province	322,077	17,068

South Central inland provinces

Tay Ninh province	684,006	4,030
Song Be province	659,093	9,859
Lam Dong province	396,657	9,933
Dac Lac province	490,198	19,800
Gai Lai-Kon Tum province	595,906	25,536

Source: U.S. Department of Commerce, Bureau of the Census, The Population of Vietnam, Series P-95, No. 77 (issued October 1985)

C. POPULATION BY ETHNIC BACKGROUND (1979 estimates)

Vietnamese	46,065,000	Dao	317,000
Hoa (Chinese)	935,000	Gia rai (Jarai)	184,000
Tay	901,000	E de (Rhade)	141,000
Thai	767,000	Ba na (Bahnar)	100,000
Khmer	717,000	Cham	77,000
Muong	686,000	San Chay	77,000
Nung	560,000	Xu dang	73,000
Hmong (Meo)	411,000	Co ho	70,000

Source: Statistical Data 1930-1984, published by the SRV Statistics General Department, Statistics Publishing House, Hanoi (translated in Joint Publications Research Service-SEA 86,108)

D. PRODUCTION OF SELECTED PRIMARY INDUSTRIAL PRODUCTS

	Unit	1975	1980	1984
Electricity generated	(millions of kilowatt hours)	2,428	4,184	4,853
Washed coal	(millions of tons)	5.2	6.2	4.9
Steel	(thousands of tons)	36.0	62.3	53.0
Chromium ore	(thousands of tons)	10.4	9.1	5.0
Water pumps	(units)	1,339	1,460	652
Chemical fertilizers	(thousands of tons)	447	313	422
Cement	(thousands of tons)	536.6	641.0	1,296.5
Timber	(thousands of cubic meters)	1,252	1,626	1,425
Paper	(thousands of tons)	41.7	46.8	69.5
Ocean fish	(thousands of tons)	546.1	385.2	567.1
Tea	(thousands of tons)	15.9	15.5	18.0

Source: Statistical Date 1930–1984, published by the SRV Statistics
General Department, Statistics Publishing House, Hanoi (translated
in Joint Publications Research Service - SEA 86,108)

E. AGRICULTURAL PRODUCTION (in millions of metric tons) (estim

1975	11.4
1976	13.5
1977	unknown
1978	12.9
1979	13.9
1980	14.4
1981	15.1
1982	16.6
1983	17.0
1984	17.9
1985	18.4
1986	18.5
1987	17.6

Sources: Indochina Issues; Indochina Chronology; Permanent Missio
to the United Nations; Nghien Cuu Kinh Te (Economic Research)
Vietnam Courier; Far Eastern Economic Review

F. FOREIGN TRADE

Value of Goods Imported into Vietnam (in US$ millions)

1977	1044.00
1978	1465.80
1979	1653.00
1980	1696.50

1981	1817.10
1982	1601.84
1983	1678.92
1986	1700 (estimate)

Value of Goods Exported from Vietnam (in US$ millions)

1977	309.00
1978	406.70
1979	383.10
1980	401.50
1981	384.50
1982	447.50
1983	498.78
1986	800.00 (estimate)

Source: Indochina Chronology Volume III, Number 3 (July–September 1984); Far Eastern Economic Review, July 23, 1987.